FREE SPEECH THEORY

Do free speech rights apply against private actors?

Free Speech Theory challenges contemporary thought on this issue. It champions free speech not for its contribution to epistemic advance or informed democratic participation, but as a product of individuality, located in a system of freedom from state control. This has wide-ranging implications for rights-claims directed against private actors concerning online, workplace, and public-interest based forms of speech.

This innovative, rigorously researched, and comprehensive restatement of free speech principle is both topical and important. It has significance for policy makers, practitioners, and commentators around the world.

Free Speech Theory

A Radical Restatement

Paul Wragg

•HART•

OXFORD • LONDON • NEW YORK • NEW DELHI • SYDNEY

HART PUBLISHING

Bloomsbury Publishing Plc

Kemp House, Chawley Park, Cumnor Hill, Oxford, OX2 9PH, UK

1385 Broadway, New York, NY 10018, USA

Bloomsbury Publishing Ireland Limited, 29 Earlsfort Terrace, Dublin 2, D02 AY28, Ireland

HART PUBLISHING, the Hart/Stag logo, BLOOMSBURY and the Diana logo are trademarks of Bloomsbury Publishing Plc

First published in Great Britain 2025

A catalogue record for this book is available from the British Library.

A catalogue record for this book is available from the Library of Congress.

Library of Congress Control Number: 2025930364

ISBN: HB: 978-1-50995-828-3
ePDF: 978-1-50995-830-6
ePub: 978-1-50995-829-0

Typeset by Compuscript Ltd, Shannon

For product safety related questions contact productsafety@bloomsbury.com

To find out more about our authors and books visit www.hartpublishing.co.uk. Here you will find extracts, author information, details of forthcoming events and the option to sign up for our newsletters.

For Samantha, Daniel and Joey

PREFACE

Free Speech Theory questions the validity of free speech rights-claims in scenarios involving private actors. It does so as a counterpoint to the contemporary view that censorship online, private law actions against public interest speech, and speech-based workplace dismissals are all problems of free speech. By revisiting the theoretical basis of free speech, the book has three broad, interconnected aims. First, by collating its diffuse sources, it seeks to provide an authoritative methodology. Secondly, using this method, it rejects the dominant value-based notions of free speech, relating to democratic participation and epistemic advance. Instead, it champions individual autonomy as the authentic means of delineating the right. Finally, it argues that whereas free speech rights-claims have validity in workplace disputes, they do not in online contexts, at least not as commentators envisage it. Further, it argues that public interest expression is less entitled to protection than the positive law suggests.

The book therefore represents a major departure from current thinking on the topic. It is highly critical of the orthodox methodology by which theory is construed from intuition, political tradition and/or the positive law. It argues that such treatments render theory beholden to practice, and prevent it from guiding the development of law. By tracing the development of free speech theory, the book argues that liberal thought concerning free speech principle has wrongly abandoned its earlier approach. Presently, theory is treated as if it is a socially constructed discourse that must construe the right according to its most favourable societal outcome. This renders free speech as something valuable to society and so places it on the footing of a collective interest or social good, effectively eliminating its status as an individual right. This is a radical departure from previous understandings, especially that given to us by John Stuart Mill, who spoke of its intrinsic worth as the vehicle by which individuality is realised.

By rejecting conventional understandings of free speech, and reframing the right as a product of individual autonomy, *Free Speech Theory* offers a systematic, sustained defence of it that centres on the meaning and nature of freedom. This renewed sense of Mill's radicalism allows for the clearer understanding that the right to free speech is not socially beneficial but socially problematic, for its authentic form is characterised by irrationality. Thus, whereas free speech can aid society in terms of democratic participation and epistemic advance, the law cannot stipulate this, nor use these social goods as the critical lens by which to define the term. This is so because the constitutional arrangements by which individual freedom is secured (ie, democracy) utilises the language of individuality and not community as its base unit.

Accordingly, there can be no grand outcome-based progressive agenda for the greater cultural benefits of tolerating free speech rights in action. There can be no bold claim that free speech is the method by which the perfectly responsive state will thrive and the perfected citizen emerge in her optimised form. The progressive agenda for free speech ends with the radical thought that each is entitled to live autonomously according to her own lights so long as she, in turn, allows others to live freely too. There is always the hope that society will gain from this realisation of perfect autonomy in its constituent parts but no guarantee. This is the social cost of freedom.

ACKNOWLEDGEMENTS

My fascination with free speech began in 2005. It was a momentous year for me. After a brief career as a solicitor, I began my PhD studies, hoping to write a thesis that might address what I saw as the problem of divergent theories of free speech principle. That proved too ambitious, so I scaled back my inquiries to a more technical account concerning free speech under the Human Rights Act 1998. This book is my attempt at revisiting that original idea.

Like most, I'm sure, my PhD was something of an ordeal. Although I had not been in practice for that long, I still found that I had lost most, if not all, of my academic skills. I had to start again. Central to that renewal were three books that had a profound effect upon me. The first of these was *Free Speech: A Philosophical Enquiry* by Frederick Schauer. The ambition of this book is unparalleled in the established literature on the subject. By questioning everything, it begins again, essentially, with the concept of free speech. Although I might disagree with some of the conclusions that Schauer reaches (for reasons that will become apparent), I still can't help but marvel at the technical prowess of what he does in such a slim volume. It is this sense of interrogating everything we know about the subject afresh that I have tried to emulate in what follows.

The second book was *Human Liberty and Freedom of Speech* by C Edwin Baker. This has significance for two reasons. First, it piqued my interest in John Stuart Mill's work. In the preface, Baker says: 'I had found, read, and been totally persuaded by [Mill]'s *On Liberty*' (vii). I found this striking for its incongruence with orthodox thinking which, it seemed to me, was uniformly set *against* Mill's work. Baker's positive treatment of *On Liberty* has had a lasting effect. Relatedly, the second reason is: I admire not only Baker's willingness to progress Millian thought but also defend it from attack, despite it being deeply unfashionable to do so. This is something I have tried to emulate. If it were not for him, I would not have tried. He died in late 2009, days after I had successfully defended my thesis. I regret that I never had chance to meet him, nor Frederick Schauer, who passed away in September 2024.

I am very grateful to RonNell Andersen Jones, Tom Bennett, Pete Coe, András Koltay, David Mangan, Rebecca Moosavian and Gavin Phillipson, each of whom provided valuable comments at various stages. I am especially grateful to Professor Andersen Jones, whose words of wisdom and encouragement kept me going when I was ready to quit. I am grateful also to Roberta Bassi for her constant support and to the team at Hart Publishing, who are without equal. The biggest debt of gratitude is to my family. They have looked after me – and endured me – throughout this period of researching and writing, which started with the end of COVID restrictions in 2021 and ended with the start of my fibromyalgia diagnosis.

Leeds, UK
October 2024

CONTENTS

PART IV
HORIZONTALITY

PART V
CONCLUSION

PART I

Overview

1

Authenticity

I. Introduction

It is common for judges to describe the right to free speech in terms of its ostensible societal worth. In England and Wales, it is said to be 'the lifeblood of democracy', instrumental to 'the self-fulfilment of individuals in society', and enabling truth discovery.[1] The European Court of Human Rights (ECtHR) explains it in much the same terms: 'freedom of expression constitutes one of the essential foundations of a democratic society and one of the basic conditions for its progress and for each individual's self-fulfilment'.[2] We find similar sentiments in the US jurisprudence.[3]

Perhaps we should not take these statements too seriously, and dismiss them instead as mere ornate packaging that contains the right but does not necessarily say much about its nature and meaning. Still, the frequency with which these grand statements of principle appear rather suggests that the judiciary, at least, is committed to an instrumental view in which individual rights-claims must demonstrate a plausible connection to these expected communal benefits before protection can be granted.

Questions arise, at a theoretical level, as to the authenticity of the juridical approach to free speech principle. For instance, we might ask whether the discernible commonality in judicial statements across jurisdictions means that 'free speech' is a universal (or else parochial) term. As we know, the protection afforded to free speech in different jurisdictions differs. In the US, for example, defamation laws are weaker than they are in, say, England and Wales. Does this mean that the English and Welsh free speech right is inferior to the American right? Can we say that the law of England and Wales is wrong as compared to that of its American cousins? If free speech is a universal concept, then this conclusion must follow. If not, then we must accept that talk of free speech principle in some universal sense is misleading unless the jurisdiction is specified.

Alternatively, does universality arise only in the conception of free speech at a theoretical level? If so, we might use theory as the metric by which to measure the health of free speech in different jurisdictions. This is an attractive proposition, but its realisation is complicated by the multitude of theories available to us. Even if we limit our inquiry to established theories, we are still left with four plausible kinds: the argument from

[1] *R v Secretary of State for the Home Department ex parte Simms* [2000] 2 AC 115, 126.
[2] *Bédat v Switzerland* (2016) 63 EHRR 15, [48].
[3] See, eg, *New York Times v Sullivan* 376 US 254, 274–75 (1964).

democratic participation; the argument from self-fulfilment; the argument from truth; and the argument from autonomy. Which of these is the authentic version by which to measure practice?

These are important but neglected questions, both in the academic literature and popular debate; commentators treat free speech as if it were universal but without resolving the mystery of what they mean by this intimation. This problem, if it is a problem, is exacerbated by social and cultural developments by which digital speech, in particular, has assumed greater significance in terms of both epistemic advance and democratic participation. The debate about free speech in this context is coloured by two assumptions – first, the assumption of universality; and, secondly, that the free speech rights-claim attaches to speech itself regardless of context. Thus, both academic and popular commentators decry, regularly, the inadequate protection for free speech online.

This approach to free speech is common to all contexts. Notably, commentators assume that the term 'free speech' is settled or otherwise non-controversial (or, rather, that if it is controversial, it is only at the penumbra and of academic interest in the pejorative sense), such that they can use the term 'free speech' and assume that the audience has an equally clear and settled understanding of its authentic meaning. If there is such a thing as an 'authentic' notion of free speech, then that is surely news to theorists, who agree only to disagree about the meaning and nature of the right. The most that can be said about the term, so far as they are concerned, is that free speech promotes democratic participation, contributes to epistemic advance, benefits self-fulfilment or self-realisation, and is a product of individual autonomy. Beyond that, everything is up for grabs, including the ideal form of the term in practice.

This profound disconnect between what theorists say free speech means and what practitioners, politicians and popular commentators assert is a serious problem in the articulation of authenticity. The academic commentary, of course, is hardly blind to this problem, but sees its resolution in further and better particulars of their respective positions. Thus, surveying the literature, we have something of a pitched battle involving trench warfare in which only marginal gains are available.

If we are to make progress in resolving this problem, then, it seems to me, we must examine again the meaning and nature of the term. This must start with a clear articulation of the methodology by which free speech principle is to be constructed. This is significant, I would suggest, because the literature seems to want for a clear vision of what the ideal methodology is. We find methodological statements in the literature, of course, but they are scattered, and they often disagree. This is vital, I think, to address what is a burgeoning problem in both the literature and in popular debate: the validity of free speech rights-claims on the horizontal plane – that is, as between private actors. This is controversial, of course, because, traditionally, rights-claims belong on the vertical plane when they are constitutional in nature. Where rights with corresponding duties exist horizontally in private law, these tend to be of the kind that are freely entered into (such as contract, property or trusts) or else imposed by the state in circumstances of undue harm (such as tort or criminal law). The intellectualisation of a free speech rights-claim on the horizontal plane is still to be completed.

The notion of authenticity is therefore of central importance to the resolution of these disparate issues, from the universality of the term 'free speech' to its applicability in horizontal contexts, from the relationship of theory to practice, to the question of instrumentality. This book addresses this problem – of what authenticity means – in three distinct stages. First, in part two, it examines the methodology by which free speech theory is derived. The overarching claim of this part is to show that theory's relationship to practice has become inverted, such that theory has become beholden to practice for the formulation of principle. If authenticity is to be determined, then this relationship needs recalibration. It seeks to articulate the ideal methodology by which free speech principle ought to be constructed. Secondly, applying this methodology, it seeks to show that authentic free speech principle is to be found, in Wittgenstein's terms, 'outside the world'[4] – specifically, that normativity – the 'oughtness' of principle – must lie beyond the 'is-ness' of practice. Part three serves this purpose. It argues that authenticity lies in the notion of individual autonomy by which rights-claims are constructed. It follows that epistemology and democratic participation, which are most often associated with free speech, are inauthentic in their exclusive focus upon the collective benefits of a free speech principle. Free speech, it is argued, is individualistic. More than that, it is an individuality rooted in irrationality. Finally, the book seeks to show that the established literature's acquiescence in popular applications of free speech principle to horizontal contexts – that is, circumstances in which private interests are pitted against each other – is misguided and in need of urgent revision. Part four demonstrates this point by scrutinising the applicability of authentic free speech claims in three specific horizontal contexts: as against social media providers (or any other digital speech scenarios), media law disputes involving public interest speech, and employers.

This introductory chapter serves to establish the basic aim concerning the function of free speech theory (section II), and to provide an overview of the book's essential arguments (section III).

II. What is the Point of Theory?

A. Functions

In principle, free speech theory serves two functions. First, it informs juridical practices concerning the content of free speech laws. When policy-makers and judges are asked to protect free speech rights, determine conflicts involving free speech, or else make laws that might affect free speech, positively or negatively, free speech theory serves as the source material, identifying its content and nature from which its parameters are calculated. We can find recognition of this function easily enough in the positive law (albeit we might question the extent of the juridical commitment to it).

[4] L Wittgenstein, *Tractatus Logico-Philosophicus* [1922] (Routledge, 2001) 86 [6.41].

Indeed, the two quotes provided in section I above, demonstrate this. The English and Welsh example, taken from *ex parte Simms*,[5] is suggestive of the judiciary reading from theory to shape practice when read in full:

> Freedom of expression … serves [several] broad objectives. First, it promotes the self-fulfilment of individuals in society. Secondly, in the famous words of Holmes J (echoing John Stuart Mill), 'the best test of truth is the power of the thought to get itself accepted in the competition of the market' … Thirdly, [it] is the lifeblood of democracy. The free flow of information and ideas informs political debate.[6]

We might say the same of the Strasbourg jurisprudence.[7]

The second function is related. Theory also acts as a critical, analytical tool by which to identify flaws in juridical reasoning. It is a metric by which to measure the health of free speech principle in practice. Presumably, these are uncontroversial statements given that, logically, they represent the first function in reverse. If theory determines practice, then practice ought to be judged by theory. However, whether either function is truly realised is questionable. Certainly, this is the question that this chapter (and part two) considers. Does theory authenticate practice as it ought to? And, if not, what are the reasons for this impaired (or non-existent) functionality?

As part two makes clear, theory does not perform these functions. It is disregarded by both practitioners and many academic commentators. This, at least, is the argument to be made in this book. Is this criticism unconvincing? As we have seen, judges do refer to theory and, ostensibly, track the progress of free speech principle against it. In this sense, theory is serving the purpose I have ascribed to it. Even at an academic or popular level, we can easily imagine how theory would perform this role. For example, if a law is passed that outlaws all forms of protest, or prohibits newspapers, or else stops citizens from discussing known miscarriages of justice, then we should have no difficulty in saying that the free speech right has been violated because each of these speech activities are obvious instances of democratic participation in action. Thus, we should say that theory proves these practical developments are (obviously) wrong as a matter of principle.

Let us consider the basis upon which this hypothetical development would be contested. As we shall see in part two, the dominant methodology in construing free speech principle relies upon three distinct sources – the positive law, intuition, and political or historical tradition. The positive law is a (relatively) weak basis upon which to dispute these laws, albeit the American jurist is in a stronger position than the English and Welsh jurist. The difficulty, in both contexts, is the logic by which we should dispute the change in law. All that we can do is point to the inconsistency with precedent. Of course, for the American judge, this is enough – they can strike it down on that basis (unlike the English and Welsh judge).

The logic of strike-down based upon incompatibility is problematic, for it is not a value judgement as such about the new law. It is, in an important sense, valueless – all it is says is that this legislation is a (radical) departure from what existed previously. It

[5] n 1.
[6] ibid, 126.
[7] See discussion in ch 7.

is the fact of difference, then, that signals unconstitutionality. It does not say that the new law is wrong, as a matter of authenticity, for it may be that the old law was right. To know that, however, we must appeal to some other basis that exists beyond the positive law itself.

If that basis is intuition (as it often is in the literature, as we shall also see), then we encounter much the same problem, for all that we acknowledge through this is our inexperience of the new law. What we are really saying is that we are not used to a legal (or political) system that would prevent us from speaking out in this way. However, this is merely a generational objection. Those that live through, say, 50 years of this new law could not appeal to intuition in the same way. For they would say that free speech has *never* included the right to protest or discuss judicial decisions, and they would have no idea what a newspaper was and only an attenuated sense of miscarriages of justice.

Of course, as we know, the juridical tendency is to appeal to our political traditions and shared history to underpin the claim that these new laws are incompatible with free speech. The guiding principle in *New York Times v Sullivan*, that 'debate on public issues should be uninhibited, robust, and wide-open',[8] can be traced to the Madisonian ideals peppered throughout the judgment, including the view that 'the censorial power is in the people over the Government, and not in the Government over the people'.[9]

Of course, the appeal to history requires careful handling, for it depends upon which history we have in mind. For example, it has become fashionable for commentators to champion *Parrhesia*, that ancient world ideal, as the essential meaning of free speech. Timothy Garton Ash is one such commentator. *Parrhesia*, or 'speech that was both free and fearless', ensured those ancients had 'free and equal speech [that] would allow deliberative democracy and that, the ancient Athenians believed, would produce better government'.[10] This sounds wonderful although it does not quite fit with the reality of ancient Athens. Certainly, Socrates would disagree, if he could. He was the very model of *Parrhesia* – and they killed him for it. As we know, the ancient Athenians (and Romans) had structured, hierarchical political systems rooted in patriarchy and slavery. Laws outlawing protests would cause the ancients no conceptual difficulties if it meant sons, daughters and wives could not rail against the patriarch, that slaves could not denounce their non-person status, and that the incumbent system of government itself could not be challenged.

However, our more recent political traditions and shared history is a more promising source by which to denounce these new laws. The European Convention on Human Rights, after all, was a direct response to Nazi atrocities to which these new laws are redolent. Still, who can say that the outlawing of all protest is abhorrent? Not the English, for they were happy to subject women to imprisonment when their protests for voting rights became too noisy. Not the Americans either, for their treatment of Black people during the civil rights movement is hardly a beacon of progressive politics in action. Likewise, McCarthyism is a stain not easily hidden by those that would

[8] n 3, 270.
[9] ibid, 282.
[10] T Garton Ash, *Free Speech: Ten Principles for a Connected World* (Atlantic Books, 2016) 76.

say the American dream tolerates all political creeds. Indeed, the early-twentieth-century decisions on free speech do not easily lend themselves to the promise of robust, uninhibited and wide-open debate on matters of public interest.[11] Even in our own time, the political response to protest about climate change, the treatment of the Black community, and capitalism hardly evinces overwhelming support for the proposition that the outlawing of protest is abhorrent.

To be sure, I am not saying that intuition, political traditions/history and the positive law are worthless in striking down or otherwise condemning authoritarian laws concerning free speech. The point is that they are arbitrary in the final analysis due to their selectivity. The idea of a political commitment to free public debate, especially, is a slippery conceit (certainly, when we compare jurisdictions) that allows some to protest, even outrageously,[12] but not others.[13]

Theory should be capable of addressing the problem of arbitrariness, and yet, as we know, it cannot easily do so because it is insufficiently uniform. The authentication function, therefore, is impaired by what we might call internal disputes, amongst theories and theorists, concerning the ideal. These disputes produce conflicting reports about the compatibility of certain types of speech with the concept. Hate speech, commercial speech and pornography are all topics that speak to this problem. On some analyses, these topics are included categories. On others, they are not. Accordingly, it may be said that disagreements of this kind are so profound to the ambitions of theory as a means of informing practice, that practice must (and does) use different, non-free-speech-based principles to resolve the conflict. To be sure, it is not that theory has no relevance to practice in these scenarios, but that the use of theory appears only in a superficial or trivial sense.

A few decisions help sketch out the point. Consider *RAV v City of St Paul*,[14] a well-known US Supreme Court case concerning the prosecution of a youth for burning a white cross upon the front lawn of a Black family. In striking down the legislation that allowed for that prosecution, the Supreme Court said nothing significant about the speech itself, nor how it facilitated political dialogue in a free society. There is, for example, no impassioned plea for the societal benefits of increased cross-burning. In an important sense, the Court did nothing more than find the legislation to be too wide in its proscriptions.

Similarly, in an ECtHR setting, we find the Court considers less the question of contribution to democratic participation and individual well-being than whether the state's reasons for interfering were sound. In a case on the question of advertising restrictions (specifically, comparative advertising), Article 10 of the European Convention on Human Rights had been violated, the Court said, because the impact of the restrictions was too far-reaching and, therefore, disproportionate to the legitimate aim of preserving

[11] eg, *Schenck v US* 249 US 47 (1919); *Abrams v US* 250 US 616 (1919).

[12] *Snyder v Phelps* 562 US 443 (2011); *National Socialist Party of America v Village of Skokie* 432 US 43 (1977).

[13] *Connolly v DPP* [2007] EWHC 237; *Hammond v DPP* [2004] EWHC 69; *Norwood v DPP* [2003] EWHC 1564.

[14] *RAV v City of St Paul*, 505 US 377 (1992).

reputation and protecting consumer interests.[15] This decision would seem to stand for the proposition that Article 10 protection extends to commercial speech, but there is nothing – or nothing much – on why or how that protection links to democratic participation or individual self-fulfilment.

Finally, consider, an ECtHR decision concerning a collage of pornographic images spliced with images of political figures that made an oblique political comment.[16] The Court acknowledged the importance of open political dialogue, including that which is shocking, disturbing or offensive. Yet it decided the case on entirely pragmatic grounds. Since the picture had been significantly defaced by a protester, such that the offending images were no longer visible, the state's response (compensation and an injunction against further display) was disproportionate to the impact upon reputation in any event. Again, there is nothing, or nothing much, in the decision about the value or significance of obscene imagery to political debate.

Given that theory is sufficiently diverse to explain both possible outcomes (of success and defeat) as compatible with free speech principle, it may be said that theory is failing in its second function: authenticating juridical decision-making. Similarly, theory seems only tangentially involved in the first function, of informing that decision-making. If theory can be described in the broad terms that the English court gave it in *ex parte Simms*, then its critical significance as an analytical tool is surely doubtful. For what is left out in an analysis that describes free speech as inherent in all aspects of life? Applying Frederick Schauer's well-known distinction between coverage and protection,[17] the threshold for coverage seems minimal on this analysis. In this way, practice gives the strong impression that it does not know what to make of theory. It may be that the internal disagreements amongst theorists about the meaning and nature of free speech are so profound that the judiciary considers any preference for one theory over another would be entirely arbitrary and, therefore, as Robert Bork once noted, unprincipled.[18]

In an important sense, this ostensible disillusionment with theory is representative of the wider literature. Although theory is routinely mentioned in free speech commentaries, it is often presented in isolation (usually as an introductory matter) and then ignored or else treated tangentially in the remainder of that work. Theory seems pointless. As part two of this book demonstrates at length, for commentators that take a trivial interest in theory, it is practice, in the form of precedent, intuition and political tradition, rather than theory, that assumes the pivotal role of informing and authenticating future decisions. In this way, theory takes on a performative quality. It is something that orthodoxy recognises should be mentioned, but not in any meaningful sense. Or rather, the underlying presentiment of ennui that this limited treatment projects is not something that the established literature feels it necessary to either defend or resolve. Instead, there is a perceivable sense of hopelessness about theory: that all these

[15] *Krone Verlag GmbH v Austria (No 3)* (2006) 42 EHRR 28. This same reliance upon proportionality in a commercial speech claim can be seen in the English case of *R v British American Tobacco UK Ltd* [2004] EWHC 2493.

[16] *Vereinigung Bildender Kunstler v Austria* (2007) ECDR 7.

[17] F Schauer, *Free Speech: A Philosophical Enquiry* (Cambridge University Press, 1982) 89–92.

[18] R Bork, 'Neutral Principles and Some First Amendment Problems' (1971) 47 *Indiana Law Journal* 1.

different theories of free speech exist, each of which point in different directions, each of which contain fundamental incompatibilities, such that they are irreconcilable with each other, and there is nothing to be done about the apparent deadlock. Moreover, this approach strongly suggests that the connection between theory and practice is unimportant. Certainly, the two functions of theory described above seem doubtful on this analysis.

Of course, I am not suggesting that this approach to theory accounts for the entire literature, for, as part two also makes clear, there remains a rich and, to an extent, vibrant interest in theory. As will be seen, the work of Robert Post, Martin Redish, Seana Valentine Shiffrin and Jack Balkin, to name only a few, retains a strong sense of vitality in identifying, developing and challenging the meaning and nature of free speech in ways that owe much to the heritage received from the earlier works of, say, Jürgen Habermas, Thomas Emerson, Frederick Schauer, C Edwin Baker and Zechariah Chafee, to, again, only name a few.

It is striking that those in the current vanguard reduce theory's purpose to that of advancing a progressive agenda for the right. Thus, the contemporary treatment of theory is notable for its teleological quality. It ascribes to free speech a social purpose that informs not only its political and legal use, but also dictates how individuals should use it. As part two explores more fully, we see expectations for free speech manifest as a prop for democratic institutions, such that certain private actors are co-opted into the realm of fulfilling, or else maintaining, the democratic ideal.

In this way, private institutions, such as the press, must underpin these democratic institutions, regardless of (considerable) private economic interests that pull them away from such noble pursuits. Citizens, too, as audience members, are expected to consume democratically significant information, and so reach informed conclusions concerning matters of public decision-marking, despite the obvious attraction that media-based distractions hold for those seeking escapism from the dispiriting and dull world of politics in action, not to mention the daily grind of life and livelihood. Moreover, the insistence that free speech should be used carefully and proactively by audiences to realise communal goals lacks convincing appeal given widespread disenchantment with the real-world performance of politics and politicians. Such attitudes serve only to further alienate the electorate.

B. Authentication

We might therefore begin to see the problem of authenticity in a different light. If we retrace the steps we took above, we can divide approaches to theory according to this question of authentication that the second function (of theory to practice) holds. Imagine two conceivable groups of commentators, divided according to their regard for theory as an authenticator of juridical decision-making. Thus, when such decisions are made – be that policy decisions resulting in legislation or court matters resulting in judgments – we can say that one of these groups will check the decision against theory to determine its validity.

The other will eschew theory for either precedent (positive law or political/historical tradition) or intuition. This second group needs convincing that theory is superior to precedent or intuition as a means of authenticating decisions (and, more generally, rights-claims). We can explicate the objection to theory, instead, in general terms. The multiplicity of theories offers an obvious reason, as we saw above. Any preference for one theory over another, they will say, is arbitrary. This is a serious problem in free speech theory. Over time, the strong impression has emerged that the division between theorists is insoluble. For we may say, with conviction, that if there were an outstanding candidate, then it would have surfaced long ago, such that remaining disputes between protagonists could be dismissed as trivial skirmishes at the penumbra.

The aversion to theory-as-authenticator, then, is valid. Nevertheless, we might weaken its appeal by recognising that precedent is not immune to this problem. Although precedent must travel in a given direction, it needs an initial heading. We see the variable headings it could have travelled from when we compare jurisdictions. The American, English and European (as in ECtHR) approaches, say, to free speech may appear broadly similar, but there are differences between them, some of which are quite pronounced, in, say, the context of defamation, privacy and contempt of court contexts, as we know (and shall see). These variations mean that when Americans, English and Europeans speak to each other of free speech they may speak, unwittingly, at cross-purposes.

Theory, therefore, acts as a point of externality. This is important as a means of demonstrating that a jurisdiction has it wrong – that precedent is developing in a way that betrays or undermines free speech principle. This externality is significant given what we might call jurisdictional 'emulation'. In the common law tradition, it is quite normal for courts to consider developments elsewhere when novel fact-patterns arise (novel, that is, in a court's jurisdiction). If jurisdictions develop consistently with others, then comparable precedent serves only to reinforce the sense of validity in that specific principle, such that the question of authenticity seems indubitable. Moreover, if commentators also rely upon precedent to establish authenticity, then the problem is compounded. It will be harder to overturn errors, let alone label them as such.

Allied to this is the problem of intuition as an alternative or additional means of verifying precedent. Intuition may be less of a problem in scholarship although, as we shall see, it is used there. However, it is used in popular and political debate, in which assertions of free speech claims are made without much in the way of an inferable basis. Often, issues are labelled as matters of free speech without any explanation or justification. Whether the concept of free speech is especially prone to this treatment is a question for another time. It is notable, though, that politicians and political commentators present themselves as ostensible experts on the meaning and nature of free speech without much in the way of discernible qualification. Accordingly, the most strident, if not stringent, views on free speech endure, especially online, based on no more than the crudest appreciation of the term, as if it means no more than a right to say whatever one wants. Perhaps it can be acknowledged that intuition has some role to play in teasing out the parameters of free speech, but its general (over-)use suggests that the right is in desperate need of rehabilitation as a concept of some intellectual sophistication.

The application of free speech principle to horizontal contexts provides an additional reason for this urgent inquiry. Increasingly, we see it said that platform regulation of digital speech is a free speech problem because platform providers are excluding or otherwise censoring users who (the providers say) are abusing its property. We see it said that strategic lawsuits against public participation (SLAPPs) are a free speech problem because high-profile private individuals seek to suppress speech that sullies their reputation or invades their private life unduly. We see it said that employers are denigrating free speech rights by dismissing employees for things said online. This horizontal application of free speech, to disputes between individuals and private entities, is a radical departure from the traditional vertical application of free speech as a right that citizens have against the state. Thus, as a historical matter – how free speech was once understood and how it is understood now – the difference is stark. Yet, through the process of accrual, the distinction has gone unnoticed. Precedent endorses free speech principle's application to the horizontal plane. Intuition approves of it. If free speech is the freedom to speak without undue interference, then there is no instinctive reason why it should not apply to the digital speech context, as it does civil disputes and employment law.

A key aim of free speech theory, then, is to demonstrate that this horizontal application is more problematic than precedent or intuition would otherwise hold. The book does not assert that horizontal applications are unjustified in all contexts, but that these contexts are more limited than present debate would allow. To do so, then, it seeks to rehabilitate theory as a means of authentication.

C. Community-based Political Agendas

For the other group – those that accept the essential claim that theory does/should authenticate practice – the aims of this book may/will seem unnecessary. They would dispute that this function needs rehabilitation, for they can point to an established practice of using theory in this way. From Alexander Meiklejohn to Robert Post and Jürgen Habermas, from Thomas Emerson to C Edwin Baker and Martin Redish, these authors, and many more, start from the premise that theory validates practice. This is so despite intense disagreement amongst these theorists, and those who follow them, about the value or values that free speech represents.

The distinction to be drawn, in the following discussion, relates to the methodological basis of those accounts. For, as will be shown, there is a sense in each, albeit in varying degrees, that the state's guarantee of free speech is teleological (ie, that it exists for a purpose) and this teleology is to be understood according to the benefit that the guarantee would have for the community at large. In this way, theorists treat theory as a vehicle for pursuing a political agenda, in which a programme for progressive reform is to be articulated. This strategy, as we shall see, also depicts free speech as deontological: that it is valued instrumentally to the extent that a named goal is realised (ie, democratic participation, self-fulfilment, truth-discovery, or autonomy) and that the rights-holder is duty-bound to fulfil those goals (or else is a rights-holder only to the extent that she realises these goals) for the good of her community. In this way, free speech is a community-owned right to all intents and purposes. It is something that the community has a say over precisely because (on this strategy), the community is set to benefit from its use. Accordingly, theorists employing this strategy will appraise ideal laws and legal systems in terms that maximise or optimise the communal goals associated with the underlying nominated free speech value(s). Both speakers and audience members, then, confer and receive duty-bound obligations by which the properties of speech are to be utilised. If the nominated value is democratic participation, then speakers are expected to maximise the properties of democracy-enhancing content in the speech in terms of its verifiability, trustworthiness and accessibility, to take an extreme but not unusual example, and audience members are expected to use this speech to inform their public decisions when asked to vote.[19]

By extension, these qualities allow for the identification of suitable candidates for free speech coverage and protection. In this way, content neutrality is preserved (in principle, at least), if we can say that the speech speaks to the goal of democratic participation, truth-discovery, autonomy or self-fulfilment, regardless of its worth as such. Hence, the two meanings of value play out: whilst the speech's value (subject matter) is relevant, its value (worth) is not. Nevertheless, we sometimes see the two meanings interchanged, if not confused, such that the literature seems to value free speech in terms that render its supposed goals contingent upon individual exercise of the right – and, conversely, access to the right contingent upon satisfaction of the supposed goals by the speech itself.

It is this contingent element that part three of the book tackles chiefly in its overarching argument that the authentic basis of free speech is individualistic and not communal. Specifically, it will be argued that the theory which lies 'outside the world' is one rooted in that perpetual struggle between the individual and the state in which she must constantly resist the overtures of others to dictate her life choices for her. If we did, indeed, live in ancient times, we should find it impossible to resist these overtures and no amount of *parrhesia* could prevent the father or else the state deciding for us whether we were to be soldier, slave or senator. The radical break from those ancient regimes, and by which the *ancien regime*, of feudalism, then monarchical dictatorship, withered away was signified by the inexorable rise of individuality through which organised religion and then Enlightenment gave meaning to the belief that the individual mattered more than the state.

The book's central goals may thus be summarised as follows: first, that theory should be independent of practice and not beholden to it (however practice is defined) if it is to realise its value as a means of authenticating free speech claims. Secondly, that theory should derive authenticity from principles found beyond 'the world' as is. The oughtness of normativity is not to be found in the is-ness of practice. Thirdly, that authenticity is thus to be found in the conditions of freedom that the notion of constitutional rights represents. For radical thought, especially that of John Stuart Mill, this freedom was synonymous with individuality. Yet, and contrary to the community-based political agendas that dominate intellectual thought presently, the protected characteristic of individuality accords with irrationality. It is this irrationality that destroys the community-based goal from the beginning, to the extent that autonomy cannot be denied or otherwise tempered to realise communal objectives. Finally, the radical restatement that this book represents is one which would rehabilitate the value of irrationality as the ultimate basis of free speech principle.

[19] See, eg, O O'Neill, *A Question of Trust* (Cambridge University Press, 2002).

III. Structure

Part two serves to develop some of the themes outlined in this first chapter. It examines those methodological weaknesses within the current approach to free speech theory that obstruct or otherwise obfuscate the search for authentic principle. Chapter two identifies two such reasons, relating, first, to the orthodox approach to defining the term 'free speech' and, secondly, in how its principles are substantiated. Specifically, the first issue is this: the meaning of free speech is derived from the underlying justification for the state's guarantee. Thus, the justificatory argument becomes the critical lens by which instances of free speech are identified. The second issue relates to the problem outlined above – that from this critical lens (ie, the justification), the principles are substantiated by reference to precedent and intuition.

These methods are problematic – but are not recognised as such, as chapter three demonstrates. The argument, in this chapter, is divided into three substantive sections. Through close reading of the established literature, it seeks to show, in the first section, the dominance of this inverted approach (ie, justification leading to definition). It argues that there is little discussion of free speech methodology, and when it does make an appearance, there is no serious recognition that these two approaches are deficient. Instead, there is an apparent consensus that the identification of meaning requires that we ask why the law protects free speech. From the jumble of social values that emerge – autonomy, democratic participation, truth-discovery and self-fulfilment/self-realisation being the most prominent – the principles animating free speech theory are assembled. Accordingly, these social values become the critical lens by which the authenticity of a free speech claim is judged. In the most problematic instances, this logic dictates that the speech-claim which does not serve the nominated value demonstrably (because, say, it does nothing substantial to progress democratic participation) is dismissed as inauthentic.

On this analysis, the authentic rights-claim belongs only to that which furthers autonomy, democratic participation, truth-discovery and/or self-fulfilment in ostensible ways. Speech that does *not* further these values, then, possesses inherent reason to be discounted as a manifestation of the right. Accordingly, we see the familiar arguments that would champion or else deny protection for certain types of speech based upon the fit between taxonomy and nominated value, eg commercial speech denied upon conceptions promoting democratic participation, etc. It is this specification of *how* the right is to be used that represents one of the book's principal concerns. This is a serious problem of intellectual design that, seemingly, goes unnoticed.

Moreover, there is a normative incoherence in this approach to definitional matters. Whereas it might be intuitively appealing, the inclination to include or exclude speech types based upon a value-laden approach fails to explain certain aspects of free speech principle that both the positive law and the literature otherwise take for granted, especially the principle of content neutrality. This technique is defensible only if one accepts it is possible to create a system that excludes certain types of speech but does not prefer manifestations of included (or, even, excluded) speech types. Hence commercial speech could be excluded from the realm of coverage/protection so long as all forms of commercial speech were treated equally. Likewise, political speech, as an included category, would be acceptable so long as some types of political speech were not preferred to others.

This selectivity toward types of speech masks significant structural problems, especially as it relates to horizontality. Specifically, the incremental development of theory has permitted the original context underpinning the granting of rights to citizen by the state (ie, a vertical arrangement) to become so obscured that the apparent shift in concern, from interferences by the state to interferences by private actors, like digital speech providers and employers, is overlooked as if unimportant. Yet this feature *is* important because it is only in the vertical scenario that free speech may have trump status – or, at least, this is what later chapters of the book will argue. The apparent clamour for the free speech rights-claim to have not only application but also trump status in digital speech contexts, especially, speaks to a pronounced methodological failure in orthodox theory to revisit the basis on which trump status is valid. This problem goes unrecognised in the justification-as-definition approach, which leaves us with the clear impression that the free speech rights claim will apply to *any* form of speech that fits the normative model given by the value, no matter the context. Thus, if the democratic process value is selected, then all instances of speech matching that value-laden description will fall within the free speech rights-claim regardless of whether the object of that claim is, say, a corporation seeking to exercise its property rights (as found in moderation policies for digital speech platforms, for example).

The second methodological issue, signalled by chapter two, relates to proof. Chapter four tackles this issue in greater detail. It argues that there is apparent divergence in how the value(s) of free speech, derived from these justificatory arguments, are to be substantiated. As alluded to above, there are two principal methods of proving the argument, which relate to precedent and intuition. Precedent, in this sense, is a broad term. It consists of shared history, political traditions and the positive law. In this way, commentators draw examples from these sources and present them as proof of their interpretation of free speech theory. Free speech *means* X, they will say, because that is how the founding fathers understood it, or because this is what democracy needs, or because this is derivable from decided case law. The literature seems largely silent on the underlying methodology by which these approaches are to be validated. Troublingly, when commentators do eschew the positivism of the world of 'is', they rely instead on something called 'intuition', often without accompanying justification to validate this alternative approach. By rejecting these approaches, chapter four makes the case for a more philosophically informed approach instead.

Specifically, it scrutinises the method by which conventional thought evidences its nominated justification(s) as *the* authentic conception of free speech. In this way, it evaluates the question of normativity as the literature understands it. As we shall see, the preferred method of deriving normativity is to treat theory as a second order principle. Hence, normativity is rooted in the world as it is. This imbues the 'oughtness' of the resultant theory with tremendous fragility. For, through this limited methodology, 'oughtness' cannot withstand the criticism that it is, in reality, 'is' by another name. It lacks the robust independence that we should need if we are to challenge a posited decision for its apparent inauthenticity. This fragility is even more pronounced when intuition is used to inform theory, not least because this method relies upon a series of highly subjective experiences that can (and does) differ as between not only jurisdiction but also, most problematically, people within those jurisdictions.

The problem of deriving authenticity in this way, if it is not obvious, is that theory is constantly indebted to practice. If it is intuition, then the basis of experience is our expectation of the world as it is (or as it seems) and how we expect it to react in certain phenomenological states. If it is the positive law, then the basis of experience is of a specific jurisdiction or jurisdictions. If it is political tradition or shared history, then it is drawn from an event or series of events. Regardless of which basis is chosen, the 'independence' of theory from practice is compromised. If practice establishes sufficient consistency of thought that a constant can be derived – for example, that political speech is an apex form of free speech rights-claim – then it may be thought that theory can achieve independence from practice, such that theory ought to inform practice should practice depart from theory at some later stage. Yet this inference is surely mistaken. If the departure is aberrant, then the basis of the error is precedent, and so remains within the domain of practice. If, though, the departure is norm-setting because, say, it reflects a change in superior law, then it is theory that shall have to change to fit, not practice. Hence, if legislation, say, is introduced to say that scientific speech is now the apex form of free speech claim, or to outlaw political speech altogether, then theory must be modified to find normative coherency within this new position – not practice. Hence, it is practice that retains its supremacy over theory as the ultimate source of authenticity. Thus, when we ask, normatively, what ought to count as an authentic form of free speech, we are constantly dragged back to the world of positivism and the question of what *does* count as such.

Since this would seem to render the value of theory nugatory, the underlying methodology needs rehabilitation. Theory ought to be regarded as superior to practice because it provides the better (the only) safety net by which we can catch substandard juridical decision-making. It is this independence *from* practice that renders it invaluable. Yet, if theory cannot explain its own superiority (as I think it cannot), then a major redesign is needed. For, of the two, it is theory that should determine practice instead of, as we see currently, theory being determined by practice. Theory, then, is failing, currently. It does not inform practice's understanding of what free speech means and where its parameters lie. If this ambition is to be realised, then practice must be dispensed with in the formation of free speech theory.

Nevertheless, whilst this should be our aim, something of our practices must remain within the methodology by which we construct theory. We are, after all, creatures of phenomenal experience and therefore *some* aspect of common experience is inevitable. Whilst we can aim to achieve what Wittgenstein called being 'outside the world',[20] we must still recognise our limitations. Accordingly, any reliance upon the world of experience must be recognised and justified as such. This dilemma animates part three, the largest part of the book. The overall aim of this part is to provide the restatement of theory promised by the title of this book. Across four chapters, it provides the basis on which theory is to be devised (in chapter five), and then explores the possible candidates for this 'authentic' role in chapters six, seven and eight.

[20] n 4.

Chapter five represents something of a bridging chapter which implements the conclusions of part two and anticipates the direction of the remaining chapters. By recognising the ambition (and inherent limitations) of designing theory from 'outside the world' of practice, it begins by restating the choices in intellectual design available to the theorist who seeks to correct the methodological flaws identified in part two. Specifically, I try to locate the right in a conceivable world where the free speech right could exist but is, as yet, unknown. It is only in this world that precedent and intuition can have no bearing on the intellectual design of theory since only in this world are they meaningless. Nevertheless, I am not returning to some hypothetical original position, as Rawls did. Instead, I begin in an intermediate position between the world as is and the world as it ought to be, in which there are established underlying political conditions that the noumenal being[21] finds herself in.

To illustrate this, and the universal quality that free speech possesses, I compare the notions of freedom given to us by Hegel and Mill. Starting with Hegel, the chapter shows the problem of trying to accommodate individuality and collective goals in the same scheme. Dissatisfied with Kant's political writings, in which ethics and law were treated as dichotomous, and the formulation that freedom must be conceived as an 'independence from being constrained by another's choice' so long as 'it can coexist with the freedom of every other',[22] Hegel devised an alternative method. According to it, freedom is not a product of individuality alone but a joint endeavour that fuses individual and collective will. Through this dialectical process, freedom is judged, ultimately, by its conformity to rationality. Thus, only the rational represents the true object of autonomous thought, according to Hegel.

This pattern of thought is entirely at odds with Mill's conception of freedom. Since only the noumenal being can know her own mind, including her wants and needs, and since she has absolute power – and an absolute right – to decide for herself what she thinks and, therefore, what opinions she will hold about herself and the world around her, rationality must be rejected absolutely as the standard by which to judge autonomy in action. For the rational is a community-derived construct. Even if it were not, and even if we could say that rationality is purely objective, the community would act illegitimately if it sought to determine how she should think or behave. Moreover, if rationality is the standard by which freedom is judged, then the community is bound to

[21] As will become apparent, I rely upon the work of Immanuel Kant and GWF Hegel almost as much as I do John Stuart Mill to articulate the free speech principles that the book champions. Kant's work, especially, uses terminology that might be less familiar to lawyers than philosophers, including 'noumena' and 'noumenal', which Kant uses as dichotomous opposites to 'phenomena' and 'phenomenal'. The meaning of noumena/noumenal relates to a world that cannot be experienced, unlike the phenomenal world. In the realm of the noumena belongs the answers to questions about God, the afterlife, etc. These questions cannot be answered because we cannot 'cross over' into that realm, at least not as phenomenal beings existing within the space/time continuum. Yet, within the realm of the unknowable is also the mind of others. Whereas I can know my own mind, I cannot know yours. I can experience the phenomenality of your mind only through speech and action, but I cannot know (as in: with absolute certainty) what you are thinking because I cannot experience it. In effect, then, the noumenal world is that which cannot be experienced. I use the term 'noumenal beings' throughout in a deliberate way to convey that sense of mystery, significance and complexity that the protection of individual rights demands.

[22] I Kant, *The Metaphysics of Morals* (L Denis, ed, M Gregor, trans), rev edn [1797] (Cambridge University Press, 2017) [6:238].

think that any action it disapproves of, collectively, deserves the label 'irrational'. This is incompatible with the notion of autonomy since it disregards the individual's superior knowledge of what she is. Thus, although she can consult, take instruction and even subject herself to the will of others, she cannot be forced to do so. Given this condition, it must be that irrationality, and not rationality, governs the world of freedom as Mill gives it to us.

Nevertheless, because each noumenal being is entitled to determine for themselves how to live, and since irrationality is the ultimate basis upon which to judge autonomy (ie, that it must include both the rational *and* irrational), freedom is a problem that society must accommodate but cannot eradicate (that is, without eradicating the essential premise upon which it is built). This renders the world of Millian freedom to be problematic in ways that the Hegelian world is not, for, in the Hegelian world, society can be constructed according to logic and order. Those that do not conform can be punished for their non-conformity. In Hegel's world, the irrational – the idiosyncratic, the eccentric and the odd – can be removed without damage to the internal logic of the underlying constitutional arrangements by which the people are governed. This is a world in which freedom takes on a fragile quality, for it begins and ends according to what the community will allow. It is, then, an utterly unattractive world to those that value the freedom to resist the oppressive, controlling constraints of legal and moral coercion.

With this ultimate distinction in place, between Millian and Hegelian freedom, between irrationality and rationality, part three proceeds on the basis that the authentic free speech principle conforming most to the political order of our known world depends upon whether individuality or communitarianism rules. In a liberal democracy, of course, the former is the base unit of our constitutional design. We order our world around the immanence of autonomy. Hence, it is argued that only individuality can count as the authentic intermediate value by which to construct free speech theory prospectively: that is, from definition to justification. Moreover, it is the only value that can substantiate theory without descending into, and being beholden to, the experienced world of a free speech norm given to us by precedent and intuition.

Nevertheless, despite making substantial leaps forward into the construction of intellectual design, this claim is not enough to demonstrate that theory must be restated in the radical terms that Mill understood it. In pursuit of this objective, chapters six and seven demonstrate why the two leading candidates for authenticity – epistemic advance (chapter six) and democratic participation (chapter seven) – are invalid.

Starting from the insight that epistemic advance is a common feature of all orthodox theories, chapter six denies epistemology's candidacy for authenticity on the grounds that its base unit must be community. For, although Mill (and also, notably, Justice Holmes in his well-known 'marketplace of ideas' dissent) speaks passionately of the connection between freedom and epistemic advance (both individually and collectively), such that we can say that the free speech guarantee *might* benefit society's epistemological prowess, both would deny that it *must*. Neither can we define free speech according to this metric, for to do so would be to jeopardise the content neutrality principle by which we deny the legitimacy of the state deciding the beneficial value of speech for its populace.

Juridically, it would be disastrous for us to say that epistemology is an analytical tool or lens by which the court should make determinations about the meaning and nature of the term 'free speech'. For whereas both the modern and the Millian system thinks about the scheme of free speech protection in terms of its effect, the two are differentiated by the nature of that effect. The Millian approach is characterised by its preoccupation with harm whilst the modern focuses upon its (beneficial) value. While a political system whose base unit of language is community could construct freedom of speech by this methodology, in a system corresponding to a base unit of individuality, the epistemology metric is meaningless. We cannot use it as a metric since it relies entirely upon a consequentialism that runs contrary to key democratic principles.

Chapter seven asks, alternatively, whether the democratic process value is the authentic method of determining free speech theory. To do so, it explores both Robert Post's and Jürgen Habermas's understanding of the value. For Post, free speech manifests not in terms of its social epistemological benefits, but in its recognition of the speaker as a valued, equal participant in the process of governing. In this way, free speech is not instrumentally valuable, for the good it does, but intrinsically in imbuing the speaker with this status. For Habermas, meanwhile, free speech is valuable both instrumentally and intrinsically for its contribution to government processes in which both the elected and the electorate needs information about the performance of the other. For the electorate, this need represents something of the checking value that Vincent Blasi describes.[23] For the elected, it relates to the economy and voter attitudes toward them. This information is vital so that the terms of their mandate are fulfilled (amongst other things, to correct law and policy if it is not working efficiently) and to enliven their prospects of re-election. The participation value in Habermas, then, is valued instrumentally to the extent that the conduit between elected and electorate is working and, like Post, intrinsically, in its recognition of the electorate as a co-author and co-authority figure in terms of law and policy.

The participation value can be understood in (at least) three different ways. It can be understood as a self-contained principle in which only that of *value* to democratic participation ought to count as a valid free speech rights-claim. By this method, democratic participation is a critical lens by which to filter the authentic from the inauthentic. Thus, according to this method, mis- and disinformation could be eliminated from the Habermasian conduit as inauthentic forms of participation. Given that this approach most obviously contradicts the supremacy of content neutrality, it is eliminated quickly from the inquiry. The two other methods, though, seem more promising. If democratic participation is understood as an organising principle, then we realise the Habermasian–Postian interpretation in its most obvious form. By this method, it is not the value in the speech that counts but the value of the system itself, by which voters are recognised as equal and valued noumenal beings in the governing process. This avoids the obvious difficulties of the first method, but does not entirely remove all its problems. Specifically, this method, it becomes apparent, struggles to replicate the Millian interpretation of freedom succumbing, as it must, to rationality as the ultimate

[23] V Blasi, 'The Checking Value in First Amendment Theory' (1977) 2 *American Bar Foundation Research Journal* 521.

metric. This, in an important sense, is to be expected of the Habermasian model which is clearly influenced by the Hegelian understanding of freedom as a joint enterprise of community norms and individual mores.

The Postian model is better equipped to resist the Hegelian overtures of the Habermasian conduit precisely because it is rooted in an intrinsic understanding of the participation value. Accordingly, in Post's hands, participation is valued not as an organising principle so much as a contingent one. In this third variation, Post can move past the Hegelian hang-ups of Habermas's system. As with Habermas, Post can say that the press can be co-opted to fulfil the conduit role, by providing accurate information, for example, because it, the press, is *not* a participant in the democratic process as such. (To be sure, neither Post nor Habermas say this, although Habermas expresses it as an ethical idea – but they *could*). Yet, what Post can say, that Habermas cannot, is that, with this contingency in place, once the speech is recognised as belonging to the democratic process, it is entitled to the full protection of the free speech guarantee.

However, this contingent interpretation disserves Post's ambitions by putting him on the back foot. Since *only* democratic participation speech counts (meaningfully), then Post's argument needs some sort of structural reinforcement to explain why this contingency applies rather than individuality in its fullest form. We know that this is not something Post is prepared to accept, given his disagreements with, say, Martin Redish over the years that the First Amendment distinguishes political from commercial speech. If this distinction is to have some defensible normative basis, then Post is required to explain why this is so. As chapter seven demonstrates, Post's work struggles to do so. Autonomy is recognised as what we might call a necessary but not sufficient value for free speech. Its necessity manifests in the constitutional arrangements described above – that, without constitutional recognition of individuality as something valuable requiring protection, the voter's entitlement to be treated as an equal co-author of law and policy would fall away. Nevertheless, once this recognition is secured, the autonomy value itself falls away so far as Post is concerned. It has nothing to say to us about free speech beyond this initial guarantee of co-authorship. As we shall see, Post's commitment to intrinsicality is confined only to instances of the participation value at work and not, more generally, in authenticating the free speech rights-claim. Thus, it seems that, for Post, the participation value *is* that qualifying lens by which we separate authentic from inauthentic claims.

This puts Post in the position that he must deny the authenticity of the autonomy value which, as chapter seven demonstrates, is something that his argument does not do convincingly. As will become apparent, the distance between my position and that of Post's is narrower than the analysis so far perhaps suggests. This becomes more apparent in chapter eight in which I seek to defend Millian freedom as the basis upon which authentic principle is designed. My agreement with Post will become clearer to the reader later in the book but, in summary, I agree with him that the free speech claim is best understood as a trump in certain circumstances but not others. Where I disagree is in the label 'public discourse' as the principal means of differentiation since this admits too much and, counterintuitively perhaps, not enough. I shall explain this distinction more at the end of this section.

Chapter eight, then, completes part three by demonstrating the continuing value of *On Liberty* as the basis of free speech theory. In this way, the chapter represents the major plank in the restatement of theory that the book provides. It uses *On Liberty* to reframe the discussion about the meaning and nature of free speech in two ways.

First, it recalibrates our understanding of rights according to the state's role in the dispute. If the speech is directed at the state and the state responds by penalising the speech, then we should describe the scenario as being vertically orientated. If, however, the speech is not so directed and other citizens object, the scenario is to be described as horizontal. In vertical scenarios, the right to free speech is, in Hohfeldian terms, of the right-duty variety. Since the state exists only as a vessel to fulfil the will of the people who have vested power in it for that purpose, then free speech is the product of that pact. Although power is transferred centrally, some power is retained, including the power over oneself. This retained power includes the power to criticise the state, as a vessel of individual will-fulfilment in a collective sense, such that the state has no right (or power) to prevent criticisms of it. Thus, whereas individuals retain their autonomy, the state has no autonomy as such and, therefore, no power or right to resist criticism based on, say, individual autonomy. Since the right to speak is secured by the duty to protect it, in the vertical orientation, the state cannot resist that right. It is an absolute right as it relates (strictly) to criticisms of the state and no others.

On the horizontal plane, though, the 'duty' to tolerate speech cannot be vested in other private actors. The fact of their autonomy ensures this. Whereas the right to free speech can have application to the horizontal plane it is, necessarily, of a more restricted kind. In this context, the rights-claim to speak is met by corresponding rights-claims that are also derived (and derivable) from autonomy, such as rights to privacy, reputation, a fair trial and free enjoyment of property. To resolve these disputes, the parties ask the state to adjudicate, in fulfilment of that promise, inherent in the terms of centrally divested power that all shall be free so long as their freedom is made compatible with the freedom of others. Hence, the state's task is to determine whose autonomy-based claim is superior. Horizontally, as between the parties, we conceive of rights as being of the right-no right variety (as Hohfeld also had it).

The second ambition of this chapter, then, is to demonstrate how the harm principle applies to these two scenarios. Since Mill's harm principle is so heavily criticised in the literature, for its purported insufficiency, the chapter seeks to show how it too can be rehabilitated. Nevertheless, it does so only in abstract terms. The object of part four is to demonstrate how the harm principle applies in particular horizontal scenarios, specifically those relating to digital speech (chapter nine), civil law disputes involving public interest expression (chapter ten), and the employment context (chapter eleven).

Of these, chapter nine is the lengthiest, reflecting both the complexity of the issues involved and its centrality to contemporary discussions about the meaning and nature of free speech. The chapter shows how the conceptual framework of authenticity ought to apply, horizontally, to the digital speech context. The discussion is divided into three distinct parts. In an apparent departure from the general tenor of this enquiry, which has eschewed practical or positivistic expositions of law, it demonstrates that, internationally, there is ostensible confusion between the high-level treatment of the issue (ie whether free speech rights can apply horizontally to digital speech) in the US compared to both Europe and the United Nations. Whereas, at least, some of this apparent incompatibility can be resolved, still there remains important work to be done in conceptualising relations between horizontal actors, in respect of constitutional rights, and in elucidating the liberal formula, of wrongdoing-harm-causation, as it manifests in that space. This initial discussion, then, illustrates the *idea* of a digital speech right as something controversial, at least juridically. It will be shown that the proper jurisprudential (Hohfeldian) relationship between end user and digital speech provider should be understood as one of right–no right rather than right–duty.

Moreover, it will be argued that interferences with digital speech by providers, especially those that are consistent with the terms of use, do not easily map onto that sense of wrongdoing which the liberal formula gives us (of wrongdoing-causation-harm). Accordingly, it is hard to see how such interferences can amount to an undue interference with autonomy, especially when they represent, instead, the autonomy of the provider itself. For although such interferences clearly represent a denial of the will, on the speaker's part, something more is required to satisfy the notion of wrongdoing, as the liberal state understands it.

Thus, when confronted by two conflicting autonomy-based acts, the state requires there to be both a rightfulness (in the claimant's actions) and a wrongfulness (in the defendant's). Quite how this could manifest in a digital speech context is difficult to conceive, although there are multiple suggestions inferable from the literature. Section IV of this chapter demonstrates that, as ingenious as these suggestions are, none is sufficient to count as actionable wrongdoing since all are rooted in a coercive use of the provider's property that is inconsistent with deeply entrenched Lockean norms. Moreover, even if the state could say that wrongdoing is established (because the action – censorship or exclusion – is arbitrary according to the contract), it is hard to see how this would achieve the free speech aims that commentators crave (such as reinstatement of speech or continuation of services) since our contract law traditions generally eschew such draconian outcomes.

Chapter ten is also sceptical about the possibility of horizontal rights to free speech in civil law disputes in which the defendant pleads the existence of a public interest in speech. Such pleadings are relied upon to strengthen the defendant's position and, so, defeat the claimant's claim. Problematically, it seems to me, the term 'public interest' is treated with such reverence by the courts that it overreaches and so protects a greater range of speech than it should. In this way, speech claims attain a trump status that render them both superior and indefeasible to those competing autonomy-based rights-claims of privacy, defamation, etc. This judicial treatment both over-privileges free speech and under-privileges whatever rights stand in its way. As chapter eight argued, free speech ought not to hold trump status as against fellow constitutional rights. Neither should so-called audience interests in speech provide it (the free speech rights-claim) with additional juridical status or power. Much of the problem here results from our apparent inability to better define, or refine, the meaning of 'public interest' (as with 'political speech') to a narrower range of subject matter.

To combat this problem, and achieve a more equitable approach, as between constitutional rights, a dichotomous approach is argued for, along Kantian lines, between the ethical description 'of public interest' and its juridical designation. Recognition of this would mean that the fact of the term's broad coverage, to a wide range of matters, would not, of itself, signify that all speech meeting the description would qualify. It will be argued that the juridical designation should be reserved for 'vertical' speech (ie, consistent with the notion of verticality outlined previously, speech that is directed at the mechanics of the state). Excluded from this category, then, is 'horizontal' speech (ie, consistent also with the notion of horizontality outlined previously, speech that concerns the morality of others). Of course, the 'mechanics of the state' includes speech about people (it is not merely confined to issues in their most impersonal sense). The political performance of Parliamentary representatives would be an obvious example. Likewise, the discussion of criminal activity would count. This includes speech that serves the public interest by signalling state failure to secure justice. However, one notable exclusion from this category is speech that seeks to pre-empt justice by compromising, say, the integrity of a fair trial. Since this represents the usurpation of power, rather than its critique, it is (rightly) excluded from the category (of juridical designation).

Chapter eleven also represents something of a departure from earlier chapters in its support for (greater) recognition of free speech rights horizontally – specifically, in the workplace context. As will become apparent, the basis for this differential treatment of workplace speech is the coercive effect of punitive employer responses to speech it dislikes. Of course, this does not mean that all speech by employees is to be afforded absolute protection. Instead, Chapter eleven demonstrates no more than the possibility that dismissal may amount to an undue interference with the employee's autonomy. When speakers are dismissed for something said that the employer objects to, it will be for the tribunal/court to decide whether the employee's autonomy-based claim is superior to the employer's. The chapter concludes by highlighting conceivable unconvincing claims, including those emanating from the UK's right not to be discriminated against on grounds of philosophical belief.

Finally, returning to the ostensible agreement between my position and Post's, I hope the reader will come to see that the label 'public discourse' is meaningful in the (limited) sense that it conveys the vertical arrangement; that when the state interferes with speech for no other reason than a (misguided) sense of protecting its own interests, that interference is illegitimate and the free speech right must operate as a trump. However, it is unhelpful – misleading, in fact – to apply that label, as if it should protect all contributions to public debate, when speakers in the horizontal setting seek to gain legal protection as against fellow private actors on the (dubious) ground that the speech is identifiable as a contribution to public discourse. Trump status cannot apply here, I maintain, unless, that is, the interference with speech is an unjustified interference with autonomy by that private actor. This analysis, though, applies to *all* speech regardless of its categorisation.

PART II

Methodology

2

Orthodoxy

I. Introduction

Free speech theory is a mess. Its function is indeterminate. Its value in resolving intense and complex practical questions is doubted. Its significance reduced to academic status, of the pejorative kind. I exaggerate for rhetorical effect, but not entirely. If we re-examine the purpose and nature of theory, as this book urges, then we must confront the tensions and confusions that dog free speech theory as an intellectual pursuit by which this sense of failure and inferiority comes to the fore.

As chapter one alluded to, there are two discernible attitudes toward theory. For one group, it seems to have become dysfunctional, such that its basic tenets are mentioned, but only in passing. Whilst this group will note similarities between practice and theory as they arise, the comparison is one of academic interest – a sort of comment on motif. Practical difficulties are driven by questions of historical precedent (sometimes originalism) and intuition rather than philosophical reasoning. For the other group, theory retains its vitality as a significant functionary by which difficult practical matters are to be resolved. For this group, theory offers the best source of intellectual design.

Since these two groups exist, and with contrary views upon theory, certain narrative gymnastics must be undertaken to keep both engaged without alienating either. This is a daunting challenge. The aim of part two of this book, then, is to sketch out this discernible, diverse methodological approach to theory in terms that suit the narrative yet retain the reader's interest. This chapter does no more than outline what I take to be three inter-related problems that dog the attempt to realise an 'authentic' free speech theory. First, I think we must recognise the US-centric nature of theory. This is important because it colours, if not clouds, the attempt at universality that authenticity must achieve. As will become clear in later chapters, the goal of universality is impossible on the autonomy scale because there are discernible political systems that eschew individual autonomy for political hegemony or community cohesion (see part three of this book). Nevertheless, recognition of the US's intellectual dominance of the scene remains significant because, as shall be demonstrated, it is rooted in a local notion of rights – both the specific right to free speech and the relationship between hypothetical/actual rights – that pervades the understanding of both how free speech should be conceived and how it should perform as a legal matter. In this way, free speech operates as a sort of apex predator that defeats other 'rights' existing in statute and the common law, such as rights to privacy and to reputation. The chapter commences, then, with recognition of this US-centricity.

Secondly, and stemming from this localised rights context, emerges the sense that free speech is to be understood in purposive terms. There is, it seems, significant consensus on this point, as section III below highlights. Since the notion of purpose is fundamental to the criticism, which will be explored in greater detail in chapter three, it is worth explaining the term here. In a prosaic sense, the criticism may seem bizarre. All rights must exist to serve some purpose, otherwise they would not exist – how would they have come about if not through agitation to protect a particular group and/or serve a specific end? As I hope will become apparent, the criticism, here, is the way in which purpose emerges.

Taking a step back, it can be said that free speech exists as a product of power by which, through necessity, if not convenience, political functions are organised through concentrations of power at the centre. Since power is granted to the centre to serve the citizenry, freedom of speech is retained so that dissatisfaction, amongst other things, can be communicated. This idea is familiar in political theory and, of course, informs Jürgen Habermas's essential concept of the conduit function that free speech serves.[1]

As we shall see, this notion of delegated power is common to many interpretations of free speech. In this book, it shall be used to justify the Millian understanding of power as the basis for recognising autonomy.[2] Theories derived from autonomy stand in tension with the others for one simple reason. They say nothing about the types of speech that are protected by the free speech clause. The others, though, do say something about those types. They are constructed in such a way that the justification informs the meaning. This inversion has a profound effect upon the discourse. The animating question, informing the disagreement between theorists, is why we should protect speech for its contribution to, or realisation of, political discourse, self-fulfilment and truth discovery (as in, epistemic advance). These are all social goods that the theory of autonomy can endorse, but they are largely irrelevant to the practical question of protecting free speech in a legal system.

As chapter one outlined, the Millian account of autonomy has long since fallen into disrepute. Although it is hardly forgotten, still its finer points tend to be ignored or else substituted with Justice Holmes's marketplace of ideas conception[3] (which differs from Mill's account in significant and fundamental ways)[4] or Milton's notion of truth as a superior and invincible foe of falsehood ('Let [Truth] and Falsehood grapple. Who ever knew Truth put to the worse in a free and open encounter?').[5] Instead, autonomy theory tends to be understood in terms of Thomas Scanlon's account from the 1970s (which, itself, was derived from Mill's account),[6] which even Scanlon himself doubted,

[1] See, eg, J Habermas, *Philosophical Introductions: Five Approaches to Communicative Reason* (Polity Press, 2018).

[2] JS Mill, *On Liberty* in *Collected Works of John Stuart Mill*, Vol XVIII (JM Robson, ed) (University of Toronto Press, 1977) 276.

[3] '[T]he best test of truth is the power of the thought to get itself accepted in the competition of the market': *Abrams v US*, 250 US 616, 630 (1919).

[4] See discussion in ch 6.

[5] J Milton, *Areopagitica* [1644] (JM Dent, 1941) 36.

[6] T Scanlon, 'A Theory of Freedom of Expression' in RM Dworkin, *The Philosophy of Law* (Oxford University Press, 1977) 153.

in a later piece, as unfeasibly broad.[7] The specific contribution that Mill's theory makes, but which subsequent versions of autonomy have either downplayed or else lost, is the value of irrationality. Autonomy can be understood in purposive terms as that which benefits the realisation of one's best self. Understood purposively, therefore, irrational speech – especially that which would denigrate or otherwise harm the self could be excluded. Mill's account, however, has the conspicuous advantage, over these accounts, for its protection of the irrational as an *essential* feature of autonomy rather than some degraded or unworthy part of it.

Although some loss of clarity may arise, the following distinguishes between Millian autonomy and the other accounts on the basis that the latter group is purposive in design. Section III below, therefore, signals consensus amongst commentators of this purpose or teleological design in which the progressive agenda of modern conceptions manifest most plainly. In this way, the questions of 'why protect free speech?' and 'what is free speech?' leads to the same set of answers, and, hence, intellectual confusion, I suggest, in the meaning and nature of the concept. Thus, even autonomy-based accounts, such as Scanlon's, could fall within this purposive grouping if autonomy is understood in consequentialist terms as that which *benefits* realisation of the best self.

The final section of this chapter outlines the confusion over the source or proof of free speech's conceptual design. As will be seen (and explored more fully in chapter four), there is considerable disagreement over whether free speech is a matter of precedent, intuition or history, and hence whether theory ought to be derived from these sources instead of from philosophical reasoning. This division also speaks to the notion that free speech exists to further some specific social or political goal (such as political participation, epistemology or self-fulfilment/self-realisation) rather than being a product of autonomous decision-making by which individuality is preserved.

II. Sources

The established theoretical literature is dominated by scholarship from the United States of America. In a sense, this is unsurprising, given its history. Although the French and American Revolutions occurred contemporaneously, the framers of the US Constitution were driven by free speech concerns in ways that the French were not.[8] Nevertheless, it was not until the early twentieth century that First Amendment scholarship began in earnest, influenced, to a great extent, by Justice Oliver Wendell Holmes Jr's provocative judgments.[9] Although Alexander Meiklejohn was as an early pioneer of free speech theory, it was arguably his contemporary, Zechariah Chafee Jr, who produced the first substantial body of theoretical work through three key publications.[10]

[7] T Scanlon, 'Freedom of Expression and Categories of Expression' (1979) 40 *University of Pittsburgh Law Review* 519.

[8] See LW Levy, *Emergence of a Free Press* (Oxford University Press, 1985).

[9] eg, *Abrams v US* 250 US 616 (1919) and *Schenck v US* 249 US 47 (1919).

[10] Z Chafee Jr, 'Freedom of Speech in War Time' (1918–1919) 32 *Harvard Law Review* 932; *Free Speech in the United States* (Harvard University Press, 1941); and *Government and Mass Communications Vols I & II* (University of Illinois Press, 1947).

Yet it was Thomas Emerson, in the 1960s, who advanced that scholarship through his magisterial book, *The System of Freedom of Expression*,[11] in which, as the title indicates, he called for a more systematic approach to the intellectual design of theory. In his view, 'no really adequate or comprehensive theory of the first amendment has been enunciated, much less agreed upon'.[12] He influenced an intense period of theorising which began in the late 1970s[13] with Vincent Blasi's 'The Checking Value in First Amendment Theory'[14] and Thomas Scanlon's 'Freedom of Expression and Categories of Expression',[15] and concluded in the early 1990s with contributions from Robert Post, in his early work,[16] Cass Sunstein's *Democracy and the Problem of Free Speech*[17] and Owen Fiss's *Liberalism Divided*.[18] This theorising peaked in 1980s, beginning with Frederick Schauer's *Free Speech: a Philosophical Enquiry* in 1982,[19] and ending with C Edwin Baker's *Human Liberty and Freedom of Speech*[20] and Kent Greenawalt's *Speech, Crime & the Uses of Language*[21] in 1989. Influential publications during this time include Martin Redish's 'The Value of Free Speech',[22] Larry Alexander and Paul Horton's extended review of Schauer's book, 'The Impossibility of a Free Speech Principle',[23] Michael Perry's 'Freedom of Expression: An Essay on Theory and Doctrine',[24] Steven Shiffrin's 'The First Amendment and Economic Regulation',[25] Stanley Ingber's 'The Marketplace of Ideas: A Legitimizing Myth',[26] Lee Bollinger's *The Tolerant Society*[27] and Richard Posner's 'Free Speech in an Economic Perspective'.[28]

[11] TI Emerson, *The System of Freedom of Expression* (Vintage Books, 1970). In singling out Emerson's contribution, I do not ignore the work of other contemporaries, such as Harry Kalven, *A Worthy Tradition: Freedom of Speech in America* (Harper & Row, 1988).

[12] TI Emerson, 'Toward a General Theory of the First Amendment' (1963) 72 *Yale Law Journal* 877, 877.

[13] Within this timeframe emerged, as well, a series of influential articles on the conceptual meaning of press freedom, eg, P Stewart, 'Or Of The Press?' (1974–1975) 26 *Hastings Law Journal* 631; NM Nimmer, 'Is Freedom of the Press a Redundancy: What Does It Add to Freedom of Speech?' (1974–1975) 26 *Hastings Law Journal* 639; RP Bezanson, 'The New Free Press Guarantee' (1977) 63 *Virginia Law Review* 731; WW Van Alstyne, 'The Hazards to the Press of Claiming a "Preferred Position"' (1977) 28 *Hastings Law Journal* 761; DA Anderson, 'The Origins of the Press Clause' (1983) 30 *UCLA Law Review* 456. See further, P Wragg, *A Free and Regulated Press* (Hart, 2020) 24–31.

[14] V Blasi 'The Checking Value in First Amendment Theory' (1977) *American Bar Foundation Research Journal* 521.

[15] Scanlon (n 7), which corrected views he had expressed in the early 'A Theory of Freedom of Expression' (n 6).

[16] eg, RC Post, 'Meiklejohn's Mistake: Individual Autonomy and the Reform of Public Discourse' (1993) 64 *University of Colorado Law Review* 1109.

[17] CR Sunstein, *Democracy and the Problem of Free Speech* (The Free Press, 1993).

[18] OM Fiss, *Liberalism Divided: Freedom of Speech and the Many Uses of State Power* (Westview Press, 1996).

[19] F Schauer, *Free Speech: A Philosophical Enquiry* (Cambridge University Press, 1982).

[20] CE Baker, *Human Liberty and Freedom of Speech* (Oxford University Press, 1989).

[21] K Greenawalt, *Speech, Crime & the Uses of the Language* (Oxford University Press, 1989).

[22] MH Redish, 'The Value of Free Speech' (1982) 130 *University of Pennsylvania Law Review* 591.

[23] P Horton and L Alexander, 'The Impossibility of a Free Speech Principle' (1983) 78 *Northwestern University Law Review* 1319.

[24] MJ Perry, 'Freedom of Expression: An Essay on Theory and Doctrine' (1983) 78 *Northwestern University Law Review* 1137.

[25] S Shiffrin, 'The First Amendment and Economic Regulation: Away from a General Theory of the First Amendment' (1984) 78 *Northwestern University Law Review* 1212.

[26] S Ingber, 'The Marketplace of Ideas: A Legitimizing Myth' (1984) *Duke Law Journal* 1.

[27] LC Bollinger, *The Tolerant Society* (Oxford University Press, 1986).

[28] RA Posner, 'Free Speech in an Economic Perspective' (1986) 20 *Suffolk University Law Review* 1.

Whether or not driven by Fish's cynicism[29] or Rorty's pragmatism,[30] American free speech scholarship since then has focused more on the refinement of existing theory than in its renewal. It is not that theory has stagnated entirely. Instead, it exists in a state of augmentation. So it is that the same starting points animate the intellectual agenda, in which certain ideas are fixed points. This is not problematic of itself – after all, the point of this monograph is to revisit old ideas. It is that progress is stymied by this apparent dogmatism. It seems as if modern American literature is doomed to revisit the same questions and produce largely the same answers. So it is that Seana Valentine Shiffrin's 'thinker-based' account follows the contours set by Thomas Scanlon in which both seek to combine the Millian harm principle with the priority of political expression.[31] That C Edwin Baker and Martin Redish, following in the footsteps of Thomas Emerson, should argue that free speech is about self-fulfilment or self-realisation as Brian Murchison should argue that the courts might 'consider the value of the speech in the person's own process of identity development, as citizen and as person'.[32] That Leslie McKendrick[33] (and Shiffrin)[34] should ask if there is anything special about speech, as Schauer did.

What we find, then, is that although the interest in theoretical design continues, especially as new speech contexts emerge, such as through social media, these fixed points I mentioned remain in place as if axiomatic. Specifically, as the following sections introduce, free speech theory is understood in terms of a purposive approach that dictates what free speech means according to a sense of how it should be used. In this way, we find commentators asking why free speech is protected as if that question is all that needs to be asked to know what the term 'free speech' means. Yet essential methodological questions remain unanswered. When we ask how authenticity is evidenced, we find differential standards in play.

These two trends affect the international literature more generally for the simple reason that the global community tends to rely heavily on the US literature for its conceptual understanding of free speech principle.[35] Our shared reliance on this literature is

[29] S Fish, *There's No Such Thing As Free Speech and It's a Good Thing Too* (Oxford University Press, 1994).

[30] R Rorty, *Philosophy and the Mirror of Nature* (Princeton University Press, 1979).

[31] SV Shiffrin, 'A Thinker-Based Approach to Freedom of Speech' (2011) 27 *Constitutional Commentary* 283.

[32] BC Murchison, 'Speech and the Self-Realization Value' (1998) 33 *Harvard Civil Rights-Civil Liberties Law Review* 443, 503.

[33] L Kendrick, 'Use Your Words: On the Speech in Freedom of Speech' (2018) 116 *Michigan Law Review* 667.

[34] Shiffrin (n 31) 306.

[35] See, eg, from Europe: J Oster, *Media Freedom as a Fundamental Right* (Cambridge University Press, 2015) ch 1; A Koltay, *Freedom of Speech: The Unreachable Mirage* (CompLex Publisher Ltd, 2013) ch 1; *New Media and Freedom of Expression: Rethinking the Constitutional Foundations of the Public Sphere* (Hart Publishing Ltd, 2019) 8–14; and *Media Freedom and the Law: The Regulation of a Common European Idea* (Routledge, 2024); E Carolan, 'Promoting Civic Discourse: A Form of Positive Free Speech under the Constitution of Ireland?' in AT Kenyon and A Scott (eds), *Positive Free Speech: Rationales, Methods and Implications* (Hart Publishing Ltd, 2020) 65; and B Török, 'Can religions or religious people be protected against blasphemy?' in A Koltay (ed), *Media Freedom and Regulation in the New Media World* (CompLex Publisher Ltd, 2014) 509. From Canada, see: R Moon, *The Constitutional Protection of Freedom of Expression* (University of Toronto Press, 2000) ch 1; and J Weinrib, What is the Purpose of Freedom of Expression? (2009) 67 *University of Toronto Faculty of Law Review* 165, 174–80. From Chile, see: J Charney, *The Illusion of the Free Press* (Hart Publishing Ltd, 2018). From South Africa, see: D Milo, *Defamation and Freedom of Speech* (Oxford University Press, 2008) 55–79. From Japan, see: J Shimizu, 'Defamation and privacy law in Japan – from a comparative perspective' in A Koltay and P Wragg (eds), *Comparative Privacy and Defamation* (Edward Elgar, 2020) 416

problematic, for the search for free speech's meaning is inextricably ensnared by the task of divining the First Amendment's meaning – that is, as the framers understood it. This problem goes unnoticed, I suspect, because the wording of the First Amendment is so vague and general that it takes universal form. As we know, it says nothing more than that Congress shall make no law abridging freedom of speech and of the press. In that sense, it is merely a restriction on legislative sovereignty when something called freedom of speech (or freedom of the press) is at stake. Since the clause provides no further information about these two rights, there is no immediate reason why US scholarship should not provide, or be taken to provide, a universal conception of the term.

The problem arises due to the nature of US scholarship. Freedom of speech is *not* the universal concept that the rest of us (might) take it to be. That enigmatic quality, of rendering it in terms that the framers would approve of, makes it a parochial event. Accordingly, its nature and parameters mesh with its surroundings in terms that alienate it from other regimes. This is problematic for obvious reasons that (perhaps) we are not sufficiently cognisant of. First, it means that the concept of free speech given to us by the established literature cannot be imported into other jurisdictions without preliminary work to disentangle it from those domestic social, cultural and political values (which may be overt or hidden). As the exemplar of late capitalism, it is no surprise that protection for commercial speech has dominated intellectual thought over the past half century in US scholarship,[36] but whether its inclusion or exclusion is appropriate in other political regimes needs considering afresh. According to Redish, the claim to authenticity is contingent upon the fit with America's political identity:

> It is my view that any model of free speech theory grounded purely in notions of some form of communitarian pursuit of the public interest ignores a real understanding of what America's democratic society is all about. Even casual examinations of American political history demonstrates that it has been pluralism and diversity, rather than some sort of homogeneous consensus on virtually all matters, that inherently characterizes America's form of democracy.[37]

As we shall see, this insularity is apparent across the literature.

Secondly, the US constitutional landscape differs significantly from, certainly, that of Europe and, even, its nearest neighbour, Canada – unlike in those jurisdictions, free speech has no natural competition in this environment. This domesticated version of free speech, then, is not like that found in the wild. Although, in the US, reputation and privacy are recognised by law, they could hardly be called rights given how rarely those causes of action succeed.[38] Whilst it would be wrong to say the US jurisprudence knows nothing of balancing, still the US-centric literature has never had to grapple with the proportionality principles in terms that would be familiar to Europeans. Similarly,

(in which the baseline notion of free speech is taken to be the US position). From Singapore, see: D Tan, 'Freedom of Speech in Singapore: A Living Tree Cannot Thrive Within Four Walls' (2022) 96 *Australian Law Journal* 727, 735–38.

[36] MH Redish, 'The First Amendment in the Marketplace: Commercial Speech and the Values of Free Expression' (1970–1971) 39 *George Washington Law Review* 429.

[37] MH Redish, 'Fear, Loathing and the First Amendment: Optimistic Skepticism and the Theory of Free Expression' (2015) 76 *Ohio State Law Journal* 691, 693.

[38] See discussion in ch 10.

constitutional rights are a cherished part of the American way of life in terms that, say, the British find alien. Not even the Europeans appreciate rights frameworks to the same degree. Although I am sure the French have the same greater cultural appreciation that the Eastern Europeans of the former Soviet bloc would have had, even behind the Iron Curtain, still the history of having rights is different across the continent. Allied to this is the mechanical dimension in which Americans are given inalienable rights by the state (or, more properly speaking, by itself as a free people) as opposed to the Europeans and, in fact, much of the rest of the world, who receive them only by virtue of international treaties which, to lesser or greater extent, renders those rights somewhat precarious. Moreover, that self-same international quality can give rise to some suspicion that those rights are 'alien' in their origin. (This attitude is a source of some frustration to those Britons who have seen this xenophobic reaction in their countrymen: the British were instrumental in drafting the European Convention on Human Rights after all).[39]

Thus, when we think of the balancing act that courts must undertake to reconcile competing rights claims, the European Court of Human Rights is better placed to do so (or, at least, to formulate the mechanics of doing so) than, say, the Supreme Court. Indeed, in some quarters of the US, balancing, as a practice, is treated with disdain. Whilst Emerson recognised that the interplay of rights was a 'particular problem' in need of solution, he was spectacularly vague about how that should be done methodically, saying nothing more than that 'such issues … must be resolved on a functional basis, taking into account the objectives and operation of the system'.[40] This is especially unhelpful given that the two systems he mentions by name – free speech and privacy – are diametrically opposed when they clash, the wants of one to publish personal information being resisted by the other. The solution to this deadlock is typically unrefined utilitarianism – a system that transcends both.

These two features within our collective approach to theory signal something of the need to revisit even its (ostensibly) axiomatic features. To fully appreciate the point, we should examine the impact that these preconceptions have upon the methodology that principle employs. As will become apparent through the course of this book, my interest in methodology stems from a concern about how theory, in its ostensible incrementalism, has been applied, with such little resistance, to horizontal contexts, ie, disputes between citizens and/or private organisations. We have moved with little difficulty from our collective concerns about the totalitarian state restricting speech it dislikes, finds offensive, or else shocking, as it did in, say, *Schenck v US*[41] or *Abrams v US*,[42] to platform regulation of digital speech, or to those private lawsuits labelled 'strategic lawsuits against public participation' (SLAPPs), or to the dismissal of employees for speech that the employer finds distasteful. This is not to say that free speech claims are invalid absolutely in these horizontal settings, but that our theory needs urgent refinement to best understanding when such claims are authentic.

[39] See discussion in AWB Simpson, *Human Rights and the End of Empire* (Oxford University Press, 2004).
[40] Emerson (n 11) 19.
[41] n 9.
[42] n 9.

Arguably, revisions of this sort have been required for some time. For whilst free speech theory, and its proponents, have been acutely sensitive to the position of speakers, we have been less sensitive, sometimes insensitive, to the collateral damage that unfettered speech can cause. So it is that the needless hurt inflicted caused by speech has been explained away as so much caustic medicine, unpleasant at the time but beneficial in the long run to a societal sense of tolerance and, hence (presumably) social cohesion. How else are we to explain the fervour with which even the American Civil Liberties Union clambered to the aid of those neo-Nazis who sought to make the lives of Holocaust survivors miserable in the town of Skokie, Illinois?[43] How else can we explain the English Court of Appeal's finding that:

> Publication may cause needless pain, distress and damage to individuals or harm to other aspects of the public interest. But a freedom which is restricted to what judges think to be responsible or in the public interest is no freedom. Freedom means the right to publish things which government and judges, however well motivated, think should not be published. It means the right to say things which 'right-minded people' regard as dangerous or irresponsible.[44]

Are we so insensitive to the rights of others that freedom of speech cannot be interfered with when real harm is caused to others? For if, as Mill would say,[45] the state owes duties to all, to protect them as they seek to realise their own life goals in pursuit of happiness and fulfilment of their autonomy, then no one can hold the monopoly to either happiness or the infliction of needless harm for their own sake.

The task is not always easy, even on the vertical plane, as between citizen and state, in which we expect the right to free speech to act as a trump. Yet that trump is hard to explain, even in the context of political speech, when the resultant harm to be tackled is not to some inflated, false impression of government, but to other citizens – citizens like those in the Skokie affair, who suffered very real psychological damage by the indulgence of a fascist fantasy, or to the Black family whose persecutor – a youth who burnt a cross on their front lawn – had his conviction overturned because the underlying ordinance might transgress the principle of content neutrality.[46] Or to the grieving family of a US serviceman, whose funeral was interrupted by the homophobic hollering of a Baptist church declaring war on homosexuals in the army.[47] The rights of the Snyder family to bury their kin in peace was inferior, it seemed, to the protest rights of the Westboro Baptist Church.

To be sure, in both cases, the Supreme Court was not insensitive to the plight of those affected families, but what good is the bitter medicine of tolerance to a family terrorised by hate? In the vertical context, it is important that the state does not prefer some messages over others. That much is clear from both courts. In *RAV v City of St Paul* the principle was expressed in this way:

> The reason why fighting words are categorically excluded from the protection of the First Amendment is not that their content communicates any particular idea, but that their content

[43] *National Socialist Party of America v Village of Skokie* 432 US 43 (1977).
[44] *R v Central Independent Television plc* (1994) Fam 192, 204.
[45] n 2, 260.
[46] *RAV v St Paul* 505 US 377 (1992).
[47] *Snyder v Phelps* 562 US 443 (2011).

> embodies a particularly intolerable (and socially unnecessary) *mode* of expressing *whatever* idea the speaker wishes to convey.[48]

Can we not find a way to respect this principle but recognise the autonomy of those families affecting in terms more effective than the mild rebuke of the Court, a rebuke so ineffectual as to be barely worth mentioning: 'Let there be no mistake about our belief that burning a cross in someone's front yard is reprehensible'?[49]

The same can be said of *Snyder v Phelps*, in which, remarkably, the Supreme Court overturned an earlier finding that the Westboro Baptist Church's actions constituted a tortious wrong (intentional infliction of emotional distress). This could not be so, said the Supreme Court, because the speech concerned 'a matter of public concern' and was delivered on public property.[50] This insensitivity to truth was compounded by the Court's conclusion that the funeral service itself had not been unduly disrupted by the angry scenes taking place nearby. Only Justice Alito, delivering the sole dissent, was alive to the grave injustice of the decision: 'Our profound national commitment to free and open debate is not a license for the vicious verbal assault that occurred in this case.'[51]

To my mind, these decisions demonstrate that the US jurisprudence lacks the analytical toolkit by which to properly protect the autonomy of others. These were not protests against state action, as in *Cohen v California* ('fuck the draft'),[52] *Johnson v Texas* (desecrating the flag)[53] or *Tinker v Des Moines* (black armbands symbolising dissent against the Vietnam war).[54] These were specific attacks on specific individuals designed to foster fear and intimidation. The language used by the Supreme Court demonstrates this deficiency. The actions of Westboro Baptist Church are given the imprimatur of respectability – it was not an angry mob attacking a grieving family, but an act of 'picketing' on a matter of 'public concern'. Similarly, the repeated references to 'peaceful' protest and of the picketers simply holding their placards are misleading; the Westboro Baptist Church is well known for its noisy demonstrations in which their offensive messages are broadcast through song or chants. As Krotoszynski observes, the decision in *Snyder* 'constitutes a very distinctly American solution to the problem of reconciling [two competing rights-claims]'.[55] In other words, the decision signals the apparent inability of the court to recognise competing rights-claims in the free speech arena *as* rights-worthy.

Despite widespread recognition that the free speech guarantee cannot be absolute, a sort of absolutism prevails in the US literature such that the 'clear and present danger' test[56] speaks meaningfully to the American mindset on permissible interferences in

[48] *RAV* (n 46) 391.
[49] ibid, 396.
[50] *Snyder* (n 47) 460–61.
[51] ibid, 463–72.
[52] *Cohen v California* 403 US 15 (1971).
[53] *Texas v Johnson* 491 US 397 (1989).
[54] *Tinker v Des Moines Independent Community School District* 393 US 503 (1969).
[55] R Krotoszynski, *Privacy Revisited* (Oxford University Press, 2016) 28.
[56] Per Justice Oliver Wendell Holmes, only words which 'are used in such circumstances and are of such a nature as to create a clear and present danger that they will bring about the substantive evils that Congress has a right to prevent'. *Schenck* (n 9) 52.

all contexts *despite* no longer being the juridical standard. That this sort of thinking should arise in horizontally orientated speech is troubling. In this sense, the detrimental impact of speech on its recipients is either not taken seriously[57] or else is taken to be deserved. We see this in the present SLAPPs debate (the term SLAPP was coined by Penelope Canan and George Pring in 1988)[58] in which harm-causing speech (typically defamation) is treated as a lesser order issue compared to the greater societal harm caused by the aggressor. Whereas the paradigmatic case that Canan and Pring envisaged still resonates – of the archetypal villain hoodwinking society and silencing those who would expose him – the malleability of the underlying terms 'baseless legal action' and 'public participation' has the obvious but unintended effect of encapsulating more than it should. For, given the US Supreme Court's unequivocal insistence that the intentional infliction of emotional distress cannot suppress speech on matters of public concern, can we avoid labelling the *Snyder v Phipps* litigation as a SLAPP? Certainly, it meets Canan and Pring's criteria of:

1. a civil complaint or counterclaim (for monetary damages and/or injunction),
2. filed against non-governmental individuals and/or groups,
3. because of their communications to a government body, official, or the electorate,
4. on an issue of some public interest or concern.[59]

Pring notes that, typically, SLAPPs are for 'staggering'[60] amounts, are time- and resource-intensive, prolonged by (sometimes successive) appeals,[61] and end in defeat for the claimant. The Snyder family issued multiple claims against Phelps and his fellow picketers, in intentional infliction of emotional distress, intrusion upon seclusion and civil conspiracy. The action was commenced in December 2009 but not concluded until April 2011.[62] At first instance, the family was awarded $5m in damages. This was overturned by the Fourth Circuit on appeal, which was confirmed after the Snyder family appealed further to the Supreme Court.

It is not as if the US literature is insensitive to the plight of the Snyder family, nor other private citizens, whose reputational and/or privacy interests have fallen at the altar of the First Amendment. As we saw with Krotoszynski, there is recognition that the juridical treatment of the Snyder family is deeply unpalatable. However, it is not inevitable that a court would designate the Snyder litigation as a SLAPP. Certainly, it would be hard to say that it had been issued 'strategically' so as to intimidate. Nevertheless, this puts pressure on the judge to read the term 'strategic' flexibly (or intuitively).

Critically, the literature lacks the analytical toolkit by which judges might dissect precisely the agreeable First Amendment claims from the troubling ones without

[57] The psychological impact of speech animates the discussion in MJ Matsuda et al, *Words That Wound: Critical Race Theory, Assaultive Speech, and the First Amendment* (Westview Press, 1993).

[58] P Canan and G Pring, 'Strategic Lawsuits Against Public Participation' (1988) 35 *Social Problems* 506. See further discussion in ch 10.

[59] GW Pring, 'SLAPPs: Strategic Lawsuits against Public Participation' (1989) 7 *Pace Environmental Law Review* 3, 8.

[60] ibid, 7.

[61] ibid, 17 fn 50.

[62] www.supremecourt.gov/docketfiles/09-751.htm.

compromising the absolute commitment to viewpoint neutrality. If public protest on a matter of public concern is jeopardised seriously by litigation, then should the intentions of the litigator really matter? In this way, the whole structure of the expression, and its underlying definition, becomes provocative given its value-laden terminology. The literature has sought to provide innovative methods of achieving something like this result by focusing less on matters of protection and more on what Schauer calls coverage, ie, the sorts of activity or behaviour that count as 'speech'.[63] For Emerson, this represented the 'central idea' and it involved drawing a 'fundamental distinction … between conduct which consists of "expression" and conduct which consists of "action"'.[64] For reasons like this, it is no wonder that Baker should lament that the content neutrality doctrine had become a 'land mine'[65] and 'deeply confused'[66] and yet 'a major part of the doctrine' that theory seeks to comply with.[67]

These opening remarks are intended only to signal a problem with the collective approach to theory. Although a few cases have been mentioned, the intention is not to lay the blame squarely upon the positive law. Perhaps there will always be unsatisfactory and troubling cases. It is, instead, to question orthodox theory's ability to influence or otherwise judge standards within the positive law as an independent indicator of authenticity. There are, I think, two methodological failings in particular that need our attention. The first relates to the relationship between justification for the free speech guarantee and the meaning of the term. We are too quick to assign a purpose to free speech usage which both detracts from and otherwise restrains the underlying concept of rights. This problem is explored in the next section. The second issue relates to the source or proof that is used to substantiate the notion. These sources relate to a myriad of items, for which the literature is yet to adopt a sufficiently methodological approach. I introduce this problem in the final section. In an important sense, both of these sections are introductory to the issues to be discussed in the remainder of this part of the book.

III. The Consensus on Function

Despite widespread disagreement amongst commentators about the nature and scope of free speech, there is apparent consensus concerning the method for determining its scope. That method relates to the purpose of the clause, of course, as in the purpose for which it was introduced. The corruption, I say, in this method arises from the academic community's understanding of purpose. For, it seems to me, when commentators ask what purpose the framers had in mind, they are also asking what purpose the framers had in mind for its usage. It is this additional factor, in the question of purpose, that has tainted the method such that it needs revising. We see something of

[63] Schauer (n 19) 89–112.
[64] Emerson (n 11) 17.
[65] CE Baker, 'Is Democracy a Sound Basis for a Free Speech Principle?' (2011) 97 *Virginia Law Review* 515, 528.
[66] ibid, 529.
[67] ibid.

this corruption, I think, in Zechariah Chafee Jr's observation that '[we can] obtain light upon its meaning from the history of the constitutional clauses and from the purpose free speech serves in social and political life'.[68] Asking what purpose free speech serves is to ask what benefit or good it serves, thus elevating it to something worthwhile and essential rather than something inalienable.

This purposive approach affects the scope of the free speech guarantee profoundly. In Alexander Meiklejohn's hands, it led him to conclude that free speech exists, chiefly, to serve the function of communal decision-making. 'The First Amendment is not, primarily, a device for the winning of new truth, though that is very important. It is a device for the sharing of whatever truth has been won.'[69] Thus, he said, 'its purpose is to give every voting member of the body politic the fullest possible participation in the understanding of those problems with which the citizens of a self-governing body must deal'.[70] This led him to a position that was both expansive and restrictive. For although he took the widest possible view on audience rights – that 'no idea, no opinion, no doubt, no belief, no counterbelief, no relevant information, may be kept from them [the people]'[71] – he took a decidedly narrow view on speaker rights: 'What is essential is not that everyone shall speak, but that everything worth saying shall be said.' He resiled from this position in later years,[72] but, according to Redish, in ways that were 'less than persuasive'.[73]

Emerson, of course, adopted a diametrically opposed view, but in terms that rendered the First Amendment incredibly broad. For him,

> freedom of expression is essential as a means of assuring individual self-fulfilment … for advancing knowledge and discovering truth … for participation in decision making by all members of society … and [in] achieving a more adaptable and hence a more stable community [through] healthy [disagreement] and necessary consensus.[74]

Here we also see the meaning of free speech described in terms of what it is to be used *for*. This meaning is also, of course, the familiar justificatory reasons for protecting it. So, as with Meiklejohn's description, we see the justifications for the right being used to describe its meaning in terms of its (societal) value.

This purposive or functional approach to free speech is so deeply engrained as to represent a key methodological feature of scholarship. We see it, for example, in Adrienne Stone and Frederick Schauer's view that 'the only coherent way to approach the question of coverage is by reference to the underlying rationale or rationales for freedom of speech'[75] and in Kent Greenawalt's observation that 'I proceed on the premise that the principle of speech protection for speech covers mainly behaviour to which its underlying justifications apply.'[76]

[68] Chafee, 'Freedom of Speech in War Time' (n 10) 945.

[69] A Meiklejohn, *Political Freedom: The Constitutional Powers of the People* (Oxford University Press, 1965) 75.

[70] ibid.

[71] ibid.

[72] A Meiklejohn, 'The First Amendment is an Absolute' (1961) *Supreme Court Review* 245.

[73] Redish (n 22) 592.

[74] Emerson (n 11) 8.

[75] A Stone and F Schauer, 'Introduction' in A Stone and F Schauer (eds), *The Oxford Handbook of Freedom of Speech* (Oxford University Press, 2011) xvii.

[76] K Greenawalt, *Speech, Crime and the Uses of Language* (Oxford University Press, 1989) 40.

The purposive approach manifests in two forms, one of which is more nuanced than the other. The first, which is a more blatant form, describes free speech in terms of its social value. For example, in *Terminiello v Chicago*, the Supreme Court held that 'a function of free speech … is to invite dispute. It may indeed best serve its high purpose when it induces a condition of unrest, creates dissatisfaction with conditions as they are, or even stirs people to anger'.[77] The second ascribes the notion of purpose to the First Amendment itself, such as the well-known finding in: *Red Lion Broadcasting v FCC* ('it is the purpose of the First Amendment to preserve an uninhibited marketplace of ideas')[78] or *Garrison v Louisiana* ('[there exists] practically universal agreement that a major purpose of [the First] Amendment [is] to protect the free discussion of governmental affairs')[79] or *United States v Alvarez* ('truth is not the *sine qua non* of First Amendment protection … [autobiographical speech] is intimately bound up with a particularly important First Amendment purpose: human self-expression').[80]

In an important sense, this second form may seem unobjectionable – prosaic, even – if it were understood to represent no more than the proposition: the First Amendment serves the purpose of protecting free speech. In other words, if the justification attributed to the free speech clause said nothing about the uses to which free speech is to be put, only the reasons for protecting it, then the corruption described above would be remedied. Yet, as the subject matter of these decisions show, this is not how the courts have applied the notion of purpose. The *type* of speech at stake is relevant to the underlying free speech claim. In other words, purpose is thought to illuminate the difference between speech and *free speech*.

This purposive approach dominates the literature. Certainly, it is central to what the US literature labels the collectivist or communitarian theory of free speech, which limits the free speech guarantee to that *benefiting* public discourse and self-government.[81] Understandably, Post attributes this approach to Alexander Meiklejohn and sees it most clearly developed in the work of Owen Fiss and Cass Sunstein.[82] To my mind, the logic of it is most apparent in BeVier, who said:

> A carefully articulated conception of the basic purposes of the amendment is essential to first amendment adjudication and commentary. Without this firm grounding in principle, the various "tests" can neither summarize nor guide the decisional process effectively. They therefore cannot create a foundation for a theory of the first amendment nor provide adequate justification for first amendment results.[83]

From this position, she went on to say:

> If, as argued above, a central purpose of the first amendment is to protect the democratic process by assuring an unfettered formulation and expression of the will of the majority, then the amendment's force as a check on exertions of majority power ought to be exhausted when free and effective participation in the decision-making process is assured.[84]

[77] *Terminiello v Chicago* 337 US 1, 4 (1949).
[78] *Red Lion Broadcasting v FCC* 395 US 367, 390 (1969).
[79] *Garrison v Louisiana* 379 US 64 (1964).
[80] *United States v Alvarez* 638 F.3d 666, 674 (9th Cir 2011).
[81] Post (n 16) 1110–11.
[82] ibid.
[83] LR BeVier, 'The First Amendment and Political Speech: An Inquiry into the Substance and Limits of Principle' (1978) 30 *Stanford Law Review* 299, 300.
[84] ibid, 311.

Thus, she could say: 'the regulation of non-political speech, which by definition infringes only values other than that of political participation, may often be a quite rational means of attaining objectives that are unquestionably subject to the majority's control'.[85]

Clearly, reasoning of this sort inspired Owen Fiss to say:

> [T]he purpose of free speech is not individual self-actualization, but rather the preservation of democracy, and the right of a people, as a people, to decide what kind of life it wishes to live. Autonomy is protected not because of its intrinsic value, as a Kantian might insist, but rather as a means or instrument of collective self-determination. We allow people to speak so others can vote. Speech allows people to vote intelligently and freely, aware of all the options and in possession of all the relevant information. The crucial assumption in this theory is that the protection of autonomy will produce a public debate that will be, to use the talismanic phrase once again, 'uninhibited, robust, and wide-open.' … The premise is that autonomy will lead to rich public debate.[86]

Similarly, Sunstein argues that 'any well-functioning system of free expression must ultimately distinguish between different kinds of speech by reference to their centrality to the First Amendment guarantee',[87] by which he means 'by reference to [its] purpose'.[88]

For Vincent Blasi, in his well-known 'checking function' account, this purposive function extends to differential assessments of both speech *and* speaker in determining First Amendment protection. Thus, he says: 'Since the argument for protection based on the checking value rests on the social consequences of speech activities, the content of the speech and the speaker's credibility and resources for dissemination would appear to be highly relevant factors.'[89] Accordingly, he argues that 'the checking value can thus be viewed as supporting a distinctive constitutional role for certain specialized countervailing forces in the society and certain specialized speech and press activities'.[90] Further, he says, it 'places a premium' on certain types of speech content, especially that 'concerning the behavior of public officials'.[91]

Although especially prevalent in democratic process accounts, it is apparent even in individualistic conceptions of free speech, such as those found in the work of C Edwin Baker and Martin Redish (who both advocate self-realisation or self-fulfilment as free speech's ultimate value) and Thomas Scanlon (who advocated for autonomy). Accordingly, Baker has written that 'the method for determining the scope of protection proceeds, first, by determining the purposes or values served by protected speech'.[92] Redish, meanwhile, rejects those that conclude 'the sole purpose served by the constitutional guarantee is to aid the political process, and that absolutely no other form of expression can logically be considered to fall within it'[93] on the basis that 'individual self-realization is the sole value furthered by free speech'.[94] As is well known, Scanlon's

[85] ibid, 312.
[86] O Fiss, 'Free Speech and Social Structure' (1986) 71 *Iowa Law Review* 1405, 1409–10.
[87] CR Sunstein, 'Free Speech Now' (1992) 59 *University of Chicago Law Review* 255, 275.
[88] ibid, 302.
[89] Blasi (n 14) 547.
[90] ibid, 548.
[91] ibid.
[92] CE Baker, 'Scope of the First Amendment Freedom of Speech' (1978) 25 *UCLA Law Review* 964, 990.
[93] Redish (n 22) 592.
[94] ibid, 595.

account, although based upon individual autonomy, still placed a firm thumb on the scales for political forms of speech.[95] Finally, Lee Bollinger, despite rejecting these accounts, nevertheless subscribes to this functional analysis by describing free speech as a means of compelling tolerance amongst the populace.[96]

Thus, all of these accounts illustrate a familiar understanding that free speech *usage* has a purpose by which both the justification and, hence, meaning of the right is to be determined. This adherence to purposive analysis is apparent in current free speech theory. Whilst one commentator has noted, recently, that these theories 'explain the constitutional salience and preferred protection of freedom of speech on the basis of one or several external values that the freedom is believed to promote',[97] another has spoken of the First Amendment 'serv[ing] its vital function supporting self-governance'.[98]

It strikes me, however, that this purposive analysis is a fundamental weakness in free speech theory. This claim is defended more substantially in chapter three. In this chapter, I am interested in exploring how it is that theory provides such varied accounts despite the shared view that free speech is a purposive concept. As will be seen in section IV below, this stems from the divergence by which theorists seek to prove the basis of their claim(s).

IV. The Basis of Disagreement

As we know, and have seen, free speech theorists disagree on the ultimate value or values that free speech serves. This disagreement may be said to manifest from an underlying disagreement concerning the source or proof of authenticity by which the value is derived. Whereas value-based disagreement is overtly recognised, this underlying tension tends to be overlooked in the literature. Methodologically, it is rarely, if ever, commented upon in any serious or sustained fashion. Nevertheless, it is problematic, as show more fully in chapter four.

To introduce the problem, consider the different ways in which theorists seek to substantiate their value-based appraisal of authentic free speech claims. Let us begin with Michael Perry's methodological statement: 'How ought the principle of freedom of expression be conceived? I begin, as most commentary on freedom of expression begins, by considering the implications for freedom of expression of certain of our basic societal politico-philosophical commitments.'[99] Although Perry does not say who uses this technique, he may have had in mind Lillian BeVier's claim that 'the only legitimate sources of constitutional principle are the words of the Constitution itself, and the

[95] Scanlon (n 6) 167–68.

[96] n 27.

[97] T Huang, 'A Quadruple Doctrinal Framework of Free Speech' (2022) 53 *Columbia Human Rights Law Review* 467, 469.

[98] DS Ardia, 'Beyond the Marketplace of Ideas: Bridging Theory and Doctrine to Promote Self-Governance' (2022) 16 *Harvard Law and Policy Review* 101, 135.

[99] MJ Perry, 'Freedom of Expression: An Essay on Theory and Doctrine' (1983) *Northwestern University Law Review* 1137, 1143.

inferences that reasonably can be drawn from its text, from its history and from the structure of government it prescribes'.[100]

Whereas Perry and BeVier utilise pre-existing constitutional arrangements as the comparative source, others, like Frederick Schauer, rely on the positive law:

> [T]o ignore what the law has done with respect to freedom of speech would be a mistake, because the law furnishes both doctrine and illuminating examples. The rules of law relating to freedom of speech are in many instances sources of important philosophical principles, and in many other instances illustrative of instructive mistakes.[101]

Meanwhile, others rely upon intuition. We see this in James Weinstein's work:

> In addition to, and in some sense more important than these judicial statements, is the strong intuition, shared not just by lawyers and judges, but by the American public that, regardless of any societal good produced by the speech, people in this country have a basic right to voice their views on matters of public concern.[102]

These four techniques are representative of the broader literature, in which four different sources – political theory, history, positive law and intuition – are used to substantiate the values that theorists attribute to free speech. Thus, these sources are used as proof to authenticate the value-based claims they have in mind.

Methodologically, the relationship between values and sources on definitional matters is, at best, complicated and, at worst, confused. For example, we might say that values determine meaning, and so provide the means of authenticating free speech claims, and sources provide the justification for that meaning over competing meaning, or rather that conception over competing conceptions. In some accounts, this is achieved by retrospective means: meaning is produced by extracting the value is from the source. Sometimes, these sources are used in combination. For example, Leslie Kendrick relies on intuition and positive law: 'Our way of talking about free speech suggests that it is a special right that does not attach to everything, and our jurisprudence suggests the same.'[103] Similarly, Cass Sunstein relies upon a broad range of sources when he says:

> An approach that affords special protection to political speech, thus defined, is justified on numerous grounds. Such an approach receives firm support from history – not only from the Framers' theory of free expression, but also from the development of that principle through the history of American law. There can be little doubt that suppression by the government of political ideas that it disapproved, or found threatening, was the central motivation for the clause. The worst examples of unacceptable censorship involve efforts by government to insulate itself from criticism. Judicial interpretations over the course of time also support a political conception of the First Amendment.[104]

Employing this technique, of either value(s)-based propositions justified by or derived from by source(s), means that tentative definitional propositions are then tested

[100] BeVier (n 83) 304.
[101] Schauer (n 19) x.
[102] J Weinstein, 'Database Protection and the First Amendment' (2002) 28 *University of Dayton Law Review* 305, 325, fn 10.
[103] n 33, 697.
[104] Sunstein (n 87) 305.

against the source to determine compatibility. These propositions may be generalised and abstract – why do we protect free speech? – or specific and practical – what features does an authentic free speech claim possess? These then might produce precise and useful answers about how free speech manifests, what it concerns and when it may be restricted.

However, the literature sometimes presents definitional matters as if the value-based judgement is incidental to source-based propositions. This is especially apparent in process theory. For example, we see it in Weinstein's claim, above, that 'strong intuition' dictates that the American public have the 'right to voice their views on matters of public concern' – a right that exists 'regardless of any societal good produced by the speech'. Perhaps it may be said that the source provides the mode of determining authenticity and the emergent value is the justification for constitutional protection. Certainly, this is an attractive interpretation since, logically, justification should follow definition (a point I shall return to in chapter three). Nevertheless, this does not strike me as adequate explanation, for the value does little or no work as a justification. Both the definition and justification for this proposition is to be found in the constitutional arrangement of democratic participation for all.

The same is true of Schauer's remarks about the significance of positive law. To be sure, Schauer is not saying that positive law is determinative of principle. Instead, as with Weinstein, theory becomes a means of making sense of these sources so as to produce the most convincing story. In this way, the justificatory value becomes an organising principle by which to deduce a 'best fit' scenario and so explain some sources away as inauthentic applications of the overarching superstructure. This explains Sunstein's position and his further remarks that intuition holds strong evidential value: 'This approach seems likely as well to accord with our initial or considered judgments about particular free speech problems. Any approach to the First Amendment will have to take substantial account of those judgments, and adjust itself accordingly'.[105] And:

> Thus, it is not unprincipled or merely convenient to adjust a theory when it proves to deal inadequately with particular cases. Sometimes the adequacy of the theory is itself tested by how well it conforms to initial or considered judgments about particular outcomes.[106]

It would also fit with Magarian's view: 'Our deepest intuitions about the substance and limits of constitutional rights concern individuals' decisions to behave as they choose, and courts' understandings about constitutional rights should reflect those intuitions.'[107]

It is also apparent in Horton and Alexander's claim that 'Deontological theories are perhaps most successful in justifying the bulk of our pre-theoretical intuitions regarding freedom of speech.'[108] So too in Thomas Scanlon's opinion that a theory of free speech too sensitive to competing harm claims, leading to an absolute ban on

[105] ibid, 305.

[106] ibid, 305, fn 156.

[107] GP Magarian, 'The First Amendment, the Public-Private Distinction, and Nongovernmental Suppression of Wartime Political Debate' (2004) 73 *George Washington Law Review* 101, 146.

[108] Horton and Alexander (n 23) 1356.

all parades due to traffic-interference, large public meetings for being unruly, and newspaper publications as a waste of paper or other natural resources, would 'surely strike us as intolerable. That they so strike us is a reflection of our belief'.[109] Value, in this sense, is not a definitional tool so much as a second order means of connecting the dots.

Nevertheless, these various sources seem to hold their greatest propositional power, so far as theorists are concerned, as the principal means of challenging competing value-based claims. We see this clearly in Solum's thoughtful critique:

> The self-realization theory must respond to the following questions: why wouldn't communicative education shaped by government serve the self-realization function as well as individually chosen communication? If the answer has to do with the development of an individual's capacity to choose, then why won't a circumscribed set of choices serve as well as an unlimited set? If an unlimited set is necessary, then how can any limitations on speech be justified? If a limited set will do, does this set fit our *intuitions* about what speech should be protected and the existing law?' (emphasis added)[110]

We see this also in Martin Redish's claim that: 'It is my view that any model of free speech theory grounded purely in notions of some form of communitarian pursuit of the public interest ignores a real understanding of what America's democratic society is all about.'[111]

Similarly, Robert Post employs this strategy to say 'It makes sense to conclude that the scope of the First Amendment extends only to those forms of speech (or regulation) that implicate constitutional values',[112] so as to deny the viability of all except that which furthers democratic self-governance.

These uses of sources also raise questions about the interrelationship between them. For example, is there a hierarchy? Do constitutional arrangement, history and positive law trump intuition? What if I can make my case using one source but not another? Do I need a preponderance of sources to prove my point? The literature is silent on these basic methodological points, suggestive of a haphazard and unsystematic approach at work. No account is taken of the relationship between these sources and that, for example, the reason why Sunstein can find his point about 'unacceptable censorship' in history, political theory and jurisprudence is not because these are three independent sources of information which happen to align but, in fact, the same piece of information, concerning sedition, extracted from three different locations.

Of all these sources, the use of intuition is most fascinating to the academic mind. Historically, its use signalled inferior reasoning. In Chafee's hands, its use provoked trenchant criticism, as when he lamented 'Nearly every free speech decision [by the judiciary] … appears to have been decided largely by intuition.'[113] For Bork, it was the object of scorn, as when he said 'Laymen may perhaps be forgiven for thinking

[109] Scanlon (n 6) 222. See also 222–23: 'Thus there is a part of our intuitive view of freedom of expression which rests upon a balancing of competing goods.'

[110] LB Solum, 'Freedom of Communicative Action: A Theory of the First Amendment Freedom of Speech' (1989) 83 *Northwestern University Law Review* 54, 81, fn 108.

[111] Redish (n 37) 693.

[112] R Post, 'Participatory Democracy and Free Speech' (2011) 97 *Virginia Law Review* 477, 477.

[113] Chafee (n 10) 945.

that the literal words of the amendment command absence of governmental inhibition upon verbal activity, but what can one say of lawyers who believe any such thing?'[114]

That it has gained intellectual respectability is due, surely, to John Rawls's application of it as the basis for what he calls 'reflective equilibrium', in which he urged the formation of principle from a reasoned consideration of initial premises, leading to an end state that is 'reached after a person has weighed various proposed conceptions and he has either revised his judgments to accord with one of them or held fast to his initial convictions (and the corresponding conception)'.[115] According to Horton and Alexander, free speech's popularity amongst philosophers is due partially to its compatibility with reflective equilibrium reasoning, in which 'clear' (as opposed to 'cloudy or conflicting') pre-legal intuitions represent the starting point for principle-construction until reflective equilibrium is achieved.[116] Post also advocates this Rawlsian technique: 'Determining the meaning of this commitment involves reflective equilibrium; it requires us to interpret our history in light of our best ideals while simultaneously re-examining our ideals in light of our actual history.'[117] Similarly, Seana Valentine Shiffrin, one of the current leading thinkers on free speech theory, defends its use in the following terms (discussing the observations of others):

> These are, of course, theoretically informed, provisional starting points that strike me as highly intuitive, secure, illuminating, and important lodestars. Nonetheless, if a plausible theory cannot be found that supports and explains these judgments or if a more plausible theory would reject them for good reason, these judgments should be revised or discarded. That is, I regard their identification as just an early step in a process aimed at achieving reflective equilibrium and not as fixed or immutable 'results' that must be accommodated, no matter what the other theoretical costs.[118]

In Shiffrin's hands, then, intuition is something temporary or transitory, which helps progress the discussion to firmer standing. Schauer signals the same intent when noting that 'our intuitions may be erroneous',[119] as do Horton and Alexander: 'it may well be true that our intuitions, more frequently than not, prove to be trustworthy companions. Intuition, however, is simply not enough for philosophers or lawyers'.[120]

Yet, even they think intuition is more valuable than, certainly, Bork would. For example, Horton and Alexander hold intuition in such high regard that: 'the job of philosophers and lawyers is to follow common intuitions into the articulation of the principle or theory that underlies and justifies them'.[121] This approach resonates with the views of Sunstein and Magarian who, as we have seen, value intuition in similar terms, as though it is, if not actually binding, then certainly something approximating it. Accordingly, there is this profound but unresolved tension, methodologically, in intuition's significance to the construction of free speech principle.

[114] R Bork, 'Neutral Principles and Some First Amendment Problems' (1971) 47 *Indiana Law Journal* 1, 21.
[115] J Rawls, *A Theory of Justice*, rev edn (Oxford University Press, 1999) 43.
[116] Horton and Alexander (n 23) 1320.
[117] Post (n 112) 477.
[118] Shiffrin (n 31) 285, fn 4.
[119] Schauer (n 19) 6.
[120] Horton and Alexander (n 23) 1353.
[121] ibid.

V. Conclusion

From these initial sketches, certain methodological features emerge concerning authenticity. The process of determining what counts as an authentic free speech claim begins with justificatory arguments. Scholars frame the discussion through the lens of the free speech guarantee. Accordingly, authentic claims are those that resonate with the reasons why free speech is protected as a constitutional right. On this point, there is near consensus that free speech theory is a purposive account in that the right exists to protect speech matching or else signifying the justification. Yet, as we know, these justificatory arguments are multifaceted. The question of which value or values best serves these purposes produced, in the 1980s, a rich and abundant source of intellectual disagreement amongst US scholars.

Whilst the basis of this disagreement is attributable to the difference in value (or values) used to justify the nominated free speech theory, it is, in a deeper sense, due to the standard or source of proof used to justify that nomination. For the use of intuition, political identity, history, positivism or syllogistic logic takes the argument in different directions. So it is that Bork (explicitly political speech), Post (deliberative democracy), Redish (self-realisation), Baker (self-fulfilment), Scanlon (autonomy) and Perry (epistemology) can all reach wildly different but deeply entrenched positions on the nature and scope of free speech whilst all maintaining that theirs is the authentic view of the American free speech tradition.

If we are to make progress in consensus-building about authenticity then we must revisit these two key methodological features in the process, first, whether the use of justification as a definitional tool is valid and, secondly, whether these differential standards of proof are justifiable. The reminder of this part of the book concentrates on these two issues, starting with the justification-as-definition method in the next chapter.

3

Justification as Definition

I. Introduction

Methodologically, the description of activity to which the rights-claim attaches should be logically prior to the reasons for attaching rights-status to that activity. If that is true, then the reason why free speech should be guaranteed rights-status should follow from the description of what free speech means. However, free speech orthodoxy does not agree with this statement. Instead, the method is inverted, such that meaning is derived from justification, as the previous chapter sketched out. We see this in C Edwin Baker's comment that 'the method for determining the scope of protection proceeds, first, by determining the purposes or values served by protected speech'.[1] We see it in Zechariah Chafee Jr's view that '[we can] obtain light upon its meaning … from the purpose free speech serves in social and political life';[2] in Adrienne Stone and Frederick Schauer's that 'the only coherent way to approach the question of coverage is by reference to the underlying rationale or rationales for freedom of speech';[3] and in Kent Greenawalt's: 'I proceed on the premise that the principle of speech protection for speech covers mainly behaviour to which its underlying justifications apply.'[4] In this way, the justification becomes the definitional tool in free speech analysis.

This methodology seems mistaken to me. It generates the confused or else confusing arrangement that to understand what free speech *is* we must first identify why it is *protected*. In this awkward transition, the 'it' moves from the indeterminate to the determinate somehow, and so predilection and bias creeps in, apparently unnoticed. Moreover, as this chapter seeks to show, not only intuition but also precedent trumps philosophical reasoning through this arrangement, because the question of what *ought to be* becomes exclusively answered (and answerable) only by what *is*. Political speech becomes the exemplar of a hypothetical free speech claim because political speech is the exemplar according to the courts. Moreover, political speech is the intuitive exemplar because, once inured to the (Western) tradition of political conflict and strife to realise freedom, the (purported) importance of political speech over all else is familiar to us.

[1] CE Baker, 'Scope of the First Amendment Freedom of Speech' (1978) 25 *UCLA Law Review* 964, 990.

[2] Z Chafee Jr, 'Freedom of Speech in War Time' (1918–19) 32 *Harvard Law Review* 932, 945. Chafee also thought 'the history of the constitutional clauses,' ibid, was also an important point of reference (see discussion in ch 4.

[3] A Stone and F Schauer, 'Introduction' in A Stone and F Schauer (eds), *The Oxford Handbook of Freedom of Speech* (Oxford University Press, 2011) xvii.

[4] K Greenawalt, *Speech, Crime and the Uses of Language* (Oxford University Press, 1989) 40.

Political speech is not the only example. Once value is admitted into the methodological lexicon, and the progression from justification to meaning reversed, then the distinction between its alternate meanings of quality and worth collapses, such that the claim to coverage becomes dependent upon demonstrating the *worth* of speech to the *qualities* apparent in the justification. Speech that *benefits* epistemic advance, self-fulfilment or autonomous decision-making has value and can demonstrate its connection to the justificatory-definitional tool much more easily, and with greater persuasive force, than speech that *degrades* these collective and individual goals, which (by this logic) is to be excluded.

Yet, whilst this methodological approach is deeply entrenched, it does not entirely fit the pattern: a principle like content neutrality could not be explained, much less defended, if we were forced to apply the logic of this approach across the spectrum of free speech thinking. With this in mind, this chapter will argue that the inverted logic of determining definition by means of justification ought to be abandoned. The discussion is divided in the following way. Section II provides greater evidential depth to demonstrate this methodological technique at work. Through this, I hope to show that theory has become a sort of programme for progressive agenda-setting, such that theory is not about what free speech is but what it ought to be in terms of how it should be used. Section III assesses this inadequacy in light of its apparent conflict with other fundamental free speech principles, such as that concerning content neutrality, before section IV introduces, in some detail, the problems it generates for the realisation of those principle in a horizontal (that is: disputes involving individuals) setting.

II. Inverted Logic

The use of justificatory arguments as definitional tools is prevalent in the established literature. Robert Bork, for example, was adamant that if free speech is justified on democratic participation grounds, then 'constitutional protection should be accorded only to speech that is explicitly political. There is no basis for judicial intervention to protect any other form of expression, be it scientific, literary or that variety of expression we call obscene or pornographic.'[5] Lillian BeVier was similarly emphatic.[6] Restrictions on any other type of speech are legitimate, she argued, because such decision-making represents the democratic process in action.[7]

Since such an approach denies free speech coverage (let alone protection) to scientific and literary works (especially), it is, say Martin Redish and Michael Perry, 'counter-intuitive'[8] and therefore cannot be correct. According to Redish, 'the moral

[5] R Bork, 'Neutral Principles and Some First Amendment Problems' (1971) 47 *Indiana Law Journal* 1, 20.

[6] See LR BeVier, 'The First Amendment and Political Speech: An Inquiry into the Substance and Limits of Principle' (1978) 30 *Stanford Law Review* 299, 300–01.

[7] ibid, 311.

[8] MH Redish, 'The Value of Free Speech' (1982) 130 *University of Pennsylvania Law Review* 591, 596–97; MJ Perry, 'Freedom of Expression: An Essay on Theory and Doctrine' (1984) 78 *Northwestern University Law Review* 1137, 1160.

norms inherent in the choice of our specific form of democracy logically imply the broader value, self-realization'.[9] For Perry, the normative value is a combination of truth-discovery and self-realisation, which he terms the 'epistemic value'.[10] Like Bork and BeVier, both Redish and Perry employ a sort of circular or inverted logic to derive the scope of the free speech guarantee. Redish, for example, says that since democracy embodies the self-realisation value, it follows that 'all forms of expression that further the self-realization value, which justifies the democratic system as well as free speech's role in it, are deserving of full constitutional protection'.[11] Perry, meanwhile, says:

> Few will deny that it is of fundamental importance, to the flourishing of human beings and to the welfare of society, that people be as free as circumstances permit to exercise their distinctive capacity to pursue and achieve an even better understanding of reality. Conceived in terms of the epistemic value, freedom of expression (presumptively) forbids government to interfere with information or ideas (plausibly) useful to the people in their capacity as seekers after understanding.[12]

Here we see the essential elements of this strategy. If speech is protected because it promotes a value, then speech furthering that value is an authentic instance of free speech claim. The dialogic function of theory becomes a matter of correctly identifying either the true singular value or else the correct proportions of a multi-valued system.

The logic of this strategy is used also to criticise theories. For example, Baker deploys it when he says that since both the Meiklejohnian conception of free speech and the Holmesian 'marketplace of truth' ideal value speech for its contribution to political truth-discovery, both suffer from the same essential weakness. Neither explains why freedom would produce better or more reliable results than a carefully crafted programme of censorship, where speech is 'intelligently and purposefully restricted'.[13] Baker, as we know, favoured a more Millian approach to free speech theory in which the liberty principle is understood in terms of self-fulfilment.[14] Others have criticised this approach and, in BeVier's work, we see the justification-as-definition strategy underpinning the critique: 'Protection of other values [such as self-fulfilment] necessarily devalues the amendment's most important function, to protect and *promote* participation in the political process' (emphasis added).[15] Similarly, Greenawalt has noted that 'the value of free speech for accountable government may be underestimated if only the relationship to self-fulfilment is addressed'.[16]

As these comments suggest, theoretical criticisms are premised on a presumed relationship between free speech claims and the asserted or disputed justification. Since these justifications assume that the free speech guarantee is a social good, so too should

[9] Redish (ibid) 594.
[10] Perry (n 8) 1158.
[11] Redish (n 8) 594.
[12] Perry (n 8) 1158.
[13] CE Baker, *Human Liberty and Freedom of Speech* (Oxford University Press, 1989) 28.
[14] See, eg ibid, ch 3.
[15] BeVier (n 6) 313.
[16] Greenawalt (n 4) 14.

presumed instances (of free speech) demonstrate this good in action. This causality features heavily. Sometimes it is explicit, as when Schauer criticises the argument from truth. Its 'validity', he says, 'turns initially on the legitimacy and importance of its goal'[17] but 'without a causal link between free speech and increased knowledge the argument from truth must fail'.[18] Sometimes it is implicit, as when Meiklejohn claimed the First Amendment 'is not the guardian of unregulated talkativeness' and nor does it require that 'every citizen shall take part in public debate' or have 'the opportunity to do so': 'What is essential is not that everyone shall speak, but that everything worth saying shall be said.'[19] Likewise, we see this implicitly in Baker's exclusion of commercial speech: 'given existing economic structures, commercial speech is not a manifestation of the liberty of the speaker. Market determination breaks the connection between commercial speech and individual choice.'[20] In other words, commercial speech should fall outside the free speech guarantee because it does not/will not benefit autonomous decision-making.

As these examples demonstrate, the stubborn principle has been impregnated into orthodox theory that the meaning or definition of free speech activity in action is that which 'serves these values'[21] taken from the nominated justification (or justifications). This architectural feature translates to the definitional process thus: *value-laden* speech is *valuable* speech – valuable, that is, to furthering the purported free speech goal. We see this, further, in the concerted attacks that theorists make on types of speech that, they argue, are not authentic instances of free speech. Consider, for example, the following from Cass Sunstein, who speaks for the Borkean tradition (by either limiting the First Amendment to political speech or otherwise prioritise such speech):

> The basic problem with an autonomy-based account … is that such an account will make it difficult or impossible to distinguish in the appropriate way among different categories of speech … If we protect speech because people want to talk, it is not easy to come up with standards by which to distinguish among different kinds of talk. And if we cannot come up with such standards, an approach based on speaker autonomy will not be able to do what a theory of free speech is obliged to do, that is, to make distinctions among different kind of speech.[22]

This (presumed) need to distinguish types of speech according to justification leads Sunstein to conclude that 'if we understand the free speech principle largely in democratic terms, we will give less than complete protection to non-political speech'.[23]

Applying this logic, BeVier, as fellow process theorists Robert Post[24] and James Weinstein[25] would, denies protection to commercial speech: 'proposals of commercial

[17] F Schauer, *Free Speech: A Philosophical Enquiry* (Cambridge University Press, 1982) 17.
[18] ibid, 19.
[19] A Meiklejohn, *Political Freedom: The Constitutional Powers of the People* (Oxford University Press, 1965) 26.
[20] Baker (n 13) 224.
[21] Baker (n 1) 990.
[22] CR Sunstein, *Democracy and the Problem of Free Speech* (The Free Press, 1993) 141.
[23] ibid, 121.
[24] R Post, 'The Constitutional Status of Commercial Speech' (2000) 48 *UCLA Law Review* 1.
[25] J Weinstein, 'Fools, Knaves & the Production of Commercial Speech: A Response to Professor Redish' (2007) 41 *Loyola of Los Angeles Law Review* 133.

transactions are so far removed from the context of political debate that the public's keen interest in the messages is totally irrelevant to first amendment values'.[26] Likewise, as we have seen, Baker argues against the inclusion of commercial speech, since 'speech as an expression of the self seems ill-suited for describing the profit-motivated speech of the marketplace of commodities'.[27] In response, Redish claims that the process theorists (and Baker)[28] are wrong to deny rights coverage to commercial speech. Specifically, he decries Meiklejohn's exclusion of 'commercial self-interested speech' as

> a *logical* mistake because it results from his adoption of criteria that are antithetical to his underlying rationale for protecting speech in the first place and a *pragmatic* mistake because it ignores the potential of commercially self-interested speech to deliver information relevant to democratic decision making.[29]

So far as I can tell, no one seriously questions the coherency of this methodological approach by which (free speech) meaning is taken to be the exclusive domain of justificatory delineation (be that one or multiple justifications). It is taken to be a legitimate method of deriving the meaning and scope of the free speech guarantee. Yet, it strikes me that this approach is deeply flawed and ought to be abandoned. Certainly, as a strategy, it seems inconsistent with the general tenor of debate in other rights contexts in two specific ways.[30] First, the insistence that the justificatory values should relate specifically to speech (by, say, distinguishing speech from action or else justifying free speech as a principle independent from more general claims for liberty) (see discussion below). Second, that the meaning and scope is limited, in some way, to furthering valuable social goals, be those to society at large or the individual exercising that right. For example, we can say that rights to a fair trial, to vote, to marry, to exercise our religion, and to privacy are all derivable from the autonomy value. Yet, we do not say that fair trials, voting, marriage and religious observance are instances of the privacy right in action. Neither do we say that there can be no right to privacy because the autonomy value is too broad or that the right to privacy is simply the liberty principle, writ large. The established literature treats each of these rights as sufficiently distinctive despite apparent commonality in the normative value(s) that justify them.

However, freedom of speech is treated differently. Theorists cherish it only to the extent that it furthers some collective end. This pattern is true of all established free speech theories. Tao Huang speaks for all, apparently, in saying 'freedom of speech is protected not for its own sake, but for its relationship with another treasured value'.[31]

[26] BeVier (n 6) 353.

[27] Baker (n 13) 194.

[28] MH Redish, 'Commercial Speech, First Amendment Intuitionism and the Twilight Zone of Viewpoint Discrimination' (2007) 41 *Loyola of Los Angeles Law Review* 67, 87.

[29] MH Redish and AM Mollen, 'Understanding Post's and Meiklejohn's Mistakes: The Central Role of Adversary Democracy in the Theory of Free Expression' (2009) 103 *Northwestern University Law Review* 1303, 1318.

[30] The larger problem of deriving the scope of a right from its justification may be prevalent in other rights contexts. However, that is not my concern here.

[31] T Huang, 'A Quadruple Doctrinal Framework of Free Speech' (2022) 53 *Columbia Human Rights Law Review* 467, 469.

The literature is replete with references to free speech 'goals'.[32] This usage is not to be confused with the goals of speakers or listeners in utilising free speech[33] nor government's specific goals in suppressing speech.[34] Instead, it is an instrumentalist account that values the right of free speech according to its fulfilment of specified goals.

Typically, these take the form of collective goals for the benefit of individuals and society at large. We see this especially, but not only, in process theory, in which 'free speech should be understood in relation to its goal of furthering an informed electorate and promoting political participation'.[35] As Jack Balkin puts it, 'freedom of speech serves the values of political democracy. It enables democratic participation in the formation of public opinion.'[36] The truth argument is also described in such terms, eg, as furthering 'the goal of ensuring that ideas can freely compete with each other'[37] or that 'one of the key purposes of the First Amendment is to advance the search for truth'.[38] The classic example of this goal-orientated account treats the press, for example, as the primary means of achieving social goals.[39]

This sort of reasoning is not confined to the collectivist goals of democratic participation and truth-discovery arguments, but extends to individualistic accounts of free speech, including the self-fulfilment/self-realisation and autonomy arguments. For example, although disagreeing in the final analysis, Weinstein accepts that 'the ability to produce, distribute and consume hardcore pornography arguably promotes autonomy, self-expression and self-fulfillment'.[40] Similarly, Thomas Scanlon conceived of 'equity in the satisfaction of participant interests' as 'one goal of freedom of expression'.[41]

[32] See, eg, Baker (n 1) 1026; RL Lieberwitz, 'Freedom of Speech in Public Sector Employment: The Deconstitutionalization of the Public Sector Workplace' (1986) 19 *University of California Davis Law Review* 597, 603; CR Sunstein, 'Free Speech Now' (1992) 59 *University of Chicago Law Review* 255, 262, 276, 279, 314, 315; WP Marshall, 'In Defense of the Search for Truth as a First Amendment Justification' (1995) 30 *Georgia Law Review* 1, 4, 7, 10; AI Goldman and JC Cox, 'Speech, Truth, and the Free Market for Ideas' (1996) 2 *Legal Theory* 1, 10; D Halberstam, 'Commercial Speech, Professional Speech, and the Constitutional Status of Social Institutions' (1999) 147 *University of Pennsylvania Law Review* 771, 802, fnn 127, 810, 812, 816, 828; WP Marshall, 'The Last Best Chance of Campaign Finance Reform' (2000) 94 *Northwestern University Law Review* 335, 350; TR Piety, 'Heroic Corporation and First Amendment Romanticism: A Response to Professors Redish and Neuborne' (2014) 92 *Texas Law Review See Also* 181, 185 and 191; C Calvert, 'Democracy & the Discourse of Distrust: Explicating the Hypocrisy Exposition Value in First Amendment Jurisprudence' (2010) 32 *Thomas Jefferson Law Review* 177, 180, 182, 190, 200, 201, 205; JM Balkin, 'How to Regulate (and Not Regulate) Social Media' (2021) *Journal of Free Speech Law* 71, 77, 95; G Lakier, 'The Non-First Amendment Law of Freedom of Speech' (2021) 134 *Harvard Law Review* 2299, 2344; DS Ardia, 'Beyond the Marketplace of Ideas: Bridging Theory and Doctrine to Promote Self-Governance' (2022) 16 *Harvard Law and Policy Review* 101, 113, 114, 118, 137, 166.

[33] See, eg, CT Wonnell, 'Truth and the Marketplace of Ideas' (1985–86) 19 *University of California, Davis Law Review* 669.

[34] CM Corbin, 'Mixed Speech: When Speech is Both Private and Governmental' (2008) 83 *New York University Law Review* 605, 643–46; M Ramsay, 'The status of hearers' rights in freedom of expression' (2012) *Legal Theory* 31.

[35] Marshall (2000) (n 32) 350.

[36] Balkin (n 32) 77.

[37] Ardia (n 32) 166.

[38] P Horwitz, 'The First Amendment's Epistemological Problem' (2012) 87 *Washington Law Review* 445, 463.

[39] See discussion in ch 7.

[40] J Weinstein, 'Democracy, Sex and the First Amendment' (2007) 31 *New York University Review of Law and Social Change* 875, 876.

[41] TM Scanlon Jr, 'Freedom of Expression and Categories of Expression' (1979) 40 *University of Pittsburgh Law Review* 519, 545.

Even when theorists recognise that the pursuit of collective goals is inconsistent with rights discourse in a larger sense, still the protection of individuality is but the means for collective ends. We see this, for example, in Jacob Weinrib's thoughtful paper exploring the purpose of free speech from a Canadian, positivistic perspective. Despite his ostensible rejection of such collectivism – 'rights are not instruments for the achievement of collective goals, whether the promotion of truth or the furtherance of majoritarian democracy'[42] – still, his ultimate conclusion embraces the sentiment of collectivism, that hate speech is incompatible with a constitutional framework that seeks to instil mutual respect of human dignity in its citizens. In this way, Weinrib echoes Lee Bollinger's classic account, which of itself echoes Voltaire, in claiming free speech promotes social tolerance.[43]

Accordingly, theory is united in its essential view of free speech as a means of social engineering. Process theory, presently, pushes the boundaries of acceptable interference with speech so as to secure these goals. Thus, Sunstein was moved to say

> the overriding goal of reformulation is to reinvigorate processes of democratic deliberation, by ensuring greater attention to public issues and greater diversity of view. The First Amendment should not stand as an obstacle to democratic efforts to accomplish these goals.[44]

We find the same sentiment expressed in Balkin's programme for social media regulation:

> A healthy system of free expression requires much more than non-censorship … No matter what your theory of free speech might be, realizing the values of free speech depends on the creation, curation, and dissemination of knowledge by intermediate institutions and professions that the public generally trusts.[45]

Sunstein's progressive agenda from the early 1990s – that free speech theory should be 'reformulated' so as to not only permit but encourage greater state interference with speech to enhance democratic participation[46] – has found new adherents. Whereas, for Sunstein, the battleground was broadcast regulation, it is, for modern proponents, the Internet. The pervasive reach of social media, and the insidious opportunities it provides for manipulative disinformation, has prompted a new wave of commentary that insists free speech theory must respond to this problem. It has been suggested that state intervention is not only beneficial but also constitutionally mandated. As one commentator puts it: 'What the Constitution requires is that government take an active role in ensuring that citizens are informed and capable of exercising their right of self-governance.'[47] According to another: 'Courts neither are, nor is it plausible to expect them to be, the only government actors with responsibility for creating the conditions

[42] J Weinrib, 'What is the Purpose of Freedom of Expression?' (2009) 67 *University of Toronto Faculty of Law Review* 165, 190.

[43] LC Bollinger, *The Tolerant Society* (Oxford University Press, 1986).

[44] Sunstein (n 22) 119.

[45] Balkin (n 32) 77.

[46] n 22.

[47] Ardia (n 32) 166.

of expressive freedom under which democratic government can flourish.'[48] These viewpoints speak clearly to Owen Fiss's opinion that

> we may sometimes find it necessary to "restrict the speech of some elements of our society in order to enhance the relative voice of others," and that unless the Court allows, and sometimes even requires, the state to do so, we as a people will never truly be free.[49]

On this view, the 'guarantee' within the constitutional protection of the free speech concept is not a promise that authentic free speech claims will be protected by law, as and when they arise. It is a political vision that the protection of authentic free speech claims will benefit individuals, specifically, and society, collectively, by means of bettering them, either so that they realise the best version of themselves leading, inexorably, to society itself realising its best form. These benefits are not merely the incidental benefits of the system, as Mill had it, but, indeed, the end of the system itself. Authenticity, then, becomes contingent upon demonstrable societal benefit.

This goal-orientated conceptualisation colours the debate so emphatically that theory has become an analytical process by which positive law is judged according to 'how well our system works to *promote* free speech values'[50] (emphasis added). So it is that James Weinstein could be so damning in his assessment of the positive law: 'Unfortunately, the United States Supreme Court has not done a good job of explicating the underlying purpose and values of free speech doctrine.'[51] In this, he echoes Cass Sunstein, who criticised positive law in the following terms:

> It protects more than it should, because it includes, within the category of protected expression, speech that serves few or none of the goals for which speech is protected, and that causes serious social harms. It protects less than it should, because current doctrine does not sufficiently serve the central goal of producing a deliberative democracy among political equals.[52]

As one commentator puts it: 'These critics suggest that there are reasons to be skeptical that our public sphere, as currently fashioned, provides the best – or even a reliable – method for advancing either social knowledge or finding "truth," however we might define that term.'[53] This reasoning inverts the process of determining the justification for the free speech guarantee according to its meaning such that meaning is derived solely by the desired benefits of such protection. Thus, self-fulfilment becomes the perfection of the analytical faculties, democratic participation becomes the betterment of collective decision-making, truth-discovery becomes epistemic advance, and autonomy becomes contingent upon demonstrable rationality.

[48] Lakier (n 32) 2381.

[49] O Fiss, 'Free Speech and Social Structure' (1986) 71 *Iowa Law Review* 1405, 1425. The citation within this quote is taken from the Supreme Court decision in *Buckley v Valeo* 424 US 1, 48–49 (1976) in which the Court dismissed the idea of interfering with speech to achieve greater plurality as being 'wholly foreign' to the US Constitution.

[50] Lakier (n 32) 2345.

[51] J Weinstein, 'Database Protection and the First Amendment' (2003) 28 *University of Dayton Law Review* 305, 314.

[52] Sunstein (n 32) 315.

[53] Ardia (n 32) 114.

III. Methodological Incoherence

This distorted sense of justification (as a definitional tool) creates profound but largely unacknowledged incoherency with the irreducible elements of free speech principle that the community is otherwise committed to. Specifically, the goal of content neutrality in the state's treatment of authenticity is vulnerable. For, if we conceive the state's legitimate interest in securing the free speech guarantee as anything other than protecting authentic free speech claims when they arise then we must accept it is legitimate for the state to interfere with speech that does not fulfil the nominated goal of the free speech concept, be that collective truth-discovery and democratic participation, or individual self-realisation and autonomous decision-making. In other words, if authentic free speech is valuable speech, then such an outcome may be better achieved through careful regulation of debate, not only its form but its content. Yet the long tradition of content neutrality amongst American jurists holds that the state has no such legitimate interest, and, according to Schauer, no competency, in determining questions of truth and falsity amongst competing messages.[54] The apparent disconnect between this injunction and the goal-driven rhetoric within the established literature represents a profound defect within the justification-as-definition strategy, which commentators cannot remedy. Instead, all they can do is distract from this weakness by means of alternate but concurrent arguments that are premised as fundamentals of authentic free speech reasoning.

Emerson, following in the footsteps of Mill, tried, in vain, to preserve the essence of content neutrality by means of distinguishing expression from action. Adopting the widest possible view on justificatory arguments, he reduced the state's task to the more prosaic issue of policing the delivery mechanism, leaving the message itself largely untouched.[55] Emerson had no illusions about the difficulty of this task: 'The line in many situations is clear. But at some points it becomes obscure. All expression has some physical element.'[56] Naturally, this dichotomy has attracted strong criticism (as with Mill's apparent distinction between the same phenomena).[57] Prominent amongst these is Baker's sustained analysis which, to my mind, was more than a little unkind in accusing Emerson of providing 'little specific guidance'.[58] At 754 pages, Emerson's book contains nothing but closely reasoned applications of the dichotomy in every conceivable scenario, from freedom of belief to freedom of protest, from academic freedom to freedom for government officials, from obscenity to libel and privacy.[59]

In the horizontal context, Emerson promotes strong privacy rights in 'action' settings, such as seclusion from intrusion, and decidedly weak (virtually non-existent) reputational and privacy rights in 'expression' settings, such as libel, public disclosure

[54] Schauer (n 17) 73–86.
[55] TI Emerson, *The System of Freedom of Expression* (Vintage Books, 1970) 17–19.
[56] ibid, 18.
[57] See, eg, A Haworth, *Free Speech* (Routledge, 1998) 29–32. See discussion in ch 8.
[58] Baker (n 13) 70–73.
[59] Later on, Baker acknowledges that Emerson's application of the expression/action dichotomy produces 'highly perceptive analyses of concrete situations' which renders his earlier criticism somewhat confusing: ibid, 71.

of embarrassing facts and false light privacy.[60] Emerson's criticisms of legal doctrine remain perceptive. His observation that the 'newsworthiness test'[61] was an exercise in idiosyncrasy, in respect of public disclosure claims, is shrewd and speaks well to the difficulties English courts have encountered in applying the public interest test to determine privacy disputes (see below). Problematically, though, his insistence that the social value of authentic free speech necessitates a narrow reading of privacy and reputation works best in a legal system that treats only the former as a right and latter as mere interests. This sort of ordering does not work in the system created by the European Convention on Human Rights for the simple reason that privacy and reputation are rights under Article 8 and of equal status to freedom of expression under Article 10.[62]

Typically, criticisms of the expression/action dichotomy are driven by the efficacy of realising justificatory goals. We see this, for example, in Baker's response to Emerson. According to Emerson, public protests involving physical manifestations, such as property damage, obstruction or civil disobedience are instances of 'action' and, hence, regulatable by the state.[63] Although sympathetic, Baker feared the sense of pressure emanating from loud, insistent and continuous protest could be too easily mistaken for coercion.[64] Later on, Baker describes these objections in terms of inconvenience or received offence. Protests that attract large numbers communicate that 'the status quo is not responsive to the real concerns or needs of [many] … In these situations, society needs to have the status quo disrupted. Many of us need to be shaken up even if this means being inconvenienced or offended.'[65] Schauer echoes the point:

> There is perhaps 'too much' speech … Under such circumstances it is frequently necessary, literally and figuratively, to shout to be heard. One method of gaining a listener's attention is by … offensive words or pictures. Another … is … placards, large groups of people and all the other attention-getting devices … of parades, picketing and demonstrations. To restrict these methods of communication is *to restrict the effectiveness of speech* … (emphasis added)[66]

Greenawalt makes the same point: 'Often symbolic speech [ie, action] is more effective than verbal speech.'[67]

The emphasis on efficacy of goal realisation has unintended consequences for content neutrality. As we have seen already, Baker saw something of the problem without realising the cause when he asked 'why should we expect better results from non-suppression than from carefully (or democratically) chosen suppressions?'.[68] Despite his insistence on content neutrality, even he succumbed to the underlying paternalism rife in free speech theory in believing that certain forms of speech – for him, commercial speech especially – could be treated differently without betraying the sacrosanct

[60] Emerson (n 55) 517–62.
[61] ibid, 554.
[62] A status that is confirmed in the leading privacy cases of *Campbell v MGN Ltd* [2004] UKHL 22, [134]–[140]; *Re S (a child)* [2004] UKHL 47, [17].
[63] Emerson (n 55) 89–90.
[64] Baker (n 13) 72–73.
[65] ibid, 136.
[66] Schauer (n 17) 202.
[67] Greenawalt (n 4) 56.
[68] Baker (n 13) 20.

principle of content neutrality. Tamara Piety, following in Baker's footsteps, demonstrates the problem by means of her 'skepticism about whether freedom for corporate and commercial speech advances fundamental First Amendment goals'.[69] She seeks to separate content from what she calls 'motivations' for speaking, leading to her conclusion that

> there are structural reasons to conclude that corporations 'cannot be expected to produce truthful or reliable information when it is not in their economic interest to do so' and that therefore, the assumption that robust First Amendment protection for corporate and commercial expression will benefit listeners or society generally is not well-founded.[70]

Like Baker, and Piety, Seana Shiffrin also signals the 'distortive influences' of commercial speech as reason to apply differential treatment. In this, both Piety and Shiffrin (and Baker, as it happens), echo the sceptical view on hardcore pornography that we find in Dworkin and Schauer. Although he defended it on other grounds, Dworkin thought it 'preposterous to think that we are more likely to reach truth about anything at all because pornographic videos are available' on the basis that 'most pornography makes no contribution to political or intellectual debate'.[71] Schauer went further to denounce hardcore pornography as activity, not speech: 'a product for the purpose of inducing immediate sexual stimulation'.[72] In this, both Dworkin and Schauer echo the sentiments of Bork, who thought pornography nothing more than a problem of pollution, comparable to other environmental issues.[73]

Here, then, we see something of the problem in maintaining content neutrality's supremacy. It is preserved only by the insistence that certain categories fall outside the scope of permissible coverage because either they are not 'speech' properly understood or do not further the value(s) associated with authentic free speech claims. Both strategies are apparent in Bork's work.[74] In his critique of the four benefits that Justice Brandeis identified in free speech[75] – self-improvement, happiness, political truth-discovery and the 'safety valve' of expelling obnoxious viewpoints from the body – he argued that these amounted to two –personal gratification and political truth-discovery – of which only the latter was valid:

> The first two benefits – development of individual faculties and the achievement of pleasure – are or may be found, for both speaker and hearer, in all varieties of speech, from political discourse to shop talk to salacious literature. But the important point is that these benefits do not distinguish speech from any other human activity.[76]

This analysis speaks to a common theme in the literature – that the basis for determining authentic free speech claims, be that on questions of coverage or protection, is to be found through the search for either the one true value served by authentic claims or else the perfect blend of multiple values.

[69] Piety (n 32) 185, quoting from her monograph.
[70] ibid, 191.
[71] R Dworkin, 'Women and Pornography' *New York Review of Books* (21 October 1993).
[72] Schauer (n 17) 181.
[73] Bork (n 5) 29.
[74] ibid, 24–26.
[75] *Whitney v California* 274 US 357, 375 (1927).
[76] Bork (n 5) 25.

Here, then, in Bork, we see the basis of what Schauer would call the independence principle – that authentic free speech theory is comprised of elements peculiar to free speech as compared to other claims:

> [I]t is not difficult to justify some freedom of speech by recourse to a broader principle of liberty of which free speech is an instance. But this approach is troubling, for it seems to clash with the frequency with which we talk about 'freedom of speech' in isolation.[77]

Expanding on the point, Schauer concluded 'But if there are no sturdy foundations, if there is no principle of free speech independent of a more general liberty, then free speech is more a platitude than a principle.'[78]

In Schauer's hands, the independence principle has two parts: a) that free speech is justified by reasons distinct from a more general liberty or social contract claim that autonomous beings should be free to do whatever they want unless it causes harm to other; and b) that authentic modes of delivering free speech are distinctive to non-speech and other forms of speech.[79] Thus, 'speech' has a specific meaning (albeit that meaning is yet to be fully realised).[80]

This methodology renders autonomy especially vulnerable to attack. It is a common tactic, amongst theorists, to say that the autonomy value is far too vague and far-reaching to be an authentic free speech value because it captures too many forms of speech and activity that have no bearing on free speech problems. Again, Bork is an archetypal proponent of this view. To his mind, deriving authentic free speech from autonomy would be unprincipled, at least in the court room, because it represents merely the fulfilment of gratification. As such, there can be no scale by which the principled judge can distinguish competing claims of gratification.[81]

We see this sort of criticism elsewhere. Weinstein, for example, is not alone in saying

> a theory that attempts to explain free speech in a terms of a broad, undifferentiated autonomy interest would protect many forms of noncommunicative conduct as well, including drug use, 'deviant' sexual behavior or even more mundane activities, such as travel to foreign lands, meeting new people and choice of occupation.[82]

Likewise, he says: 'the problem with … an autonomy-based argument against obscenity doctrine is that virtually any form of human communication can be seen as promoting these values'.[83] In this, he echoes Bork's complaint that

> the important point is that these benefits do not distinguish speech from any other human activity. An individual may develop his faculties or derive pleasure from trading on the stock market, following his profession as a river port pilot, working as a barmaid, engaging in sexual activity, playing tennis, rigging prices or in any of thousands of other endeavors.[84]

[77] Schauer (n 17) 5–6.
[78] ibid, 6.
[79] ibid, 89–112.
[80] See, eg, L Kendrick, 'Use Your Words: On the Speech in Freedom of Speech' (2018) 116 *Michigan Law Review* 667.
[81] Bork (n 5) 8–11.
[82] Weinstein (n 40) 877.
[83] ibid, 876–77.
[84] Bork (n 5) 25.

Even Greenawalt – who argues that 'the idea that any justification with broader relevance may be written off as not bearing on a principle of freedom of speech is erroneous and must be strongly resisted'[85] – nevertheless succumbs to that perpetual insistence the free speech justification must have some 'special relation to communication'.[86] Accordingly, he dismisses autonomy on the basis that 'if autonomy is to undergird a principle of freedom of speech, a notion of autonomy is required which has some special relation to communication and which helps draw lines between permissible and impermissible regulation'.[87]

These criticisms of the autonomy value bleed into those concerning self-fulfilment. We see this clearly in Stanley Ingber's observation that 'the self-fulfilment theory argues for the value of freedom in all human choices and activities, but fails to explain why choices and activities related to speech conduct deserve unique protection'.[88] We find the same reasoning in the work of Paul Horton and Larry Alexander,[89] Michael Perry,[90] James Weinstein[91] and Risa Lieberwitz.[92]

To be sure, commentators do not advocate direct breaches of the content neutrality rule. There is no appetite for overt state censorship. Instead, they deploy one of two strategies. The first relates to positive speech obligations, in Isaiah Berlin's sense of the term, and has become popular, recently, as a response to the apparent success of mis- and disinformation to colour democratic participation. For example, one commentator has said:

> The response to this disturbing state of affairs, however, is not to grant the government greater leeway to *directly* regulate truth … Instead, the response should be to identify ways that the First Amendment can support the processes underlying democratic deliberation, including the creation and dissemination of speech that advances social knowledge. After all, not all speech is equal in fostering an informed and empowered society.[93]

Andrew Kenyon is in the vanguard of this movement. In his view,

> democracy needs to be democracy of expression to have substantial communicative legitimacy. That requires sustained plural public speech. Issues of enablement, voice, reception and diversity are central to free speech, not peripheral, just as the non-censorship dimensions of the freedom are central.[94]

The second, related strategy maintains content neutrality by demarcating certain types or categories of speech as inauthentic free speech. As we have seen, this would

[85] Greenawalt (n 4) 13.
[86] ibid, 32.
[87] ibid.
[88] S Ingber, 'Rediscovering the Communal Worth of Individual Rights: The First Amendment in Institutional Contexts' (1990) 69 *Texas Law Review* 1, 19.
[89] L Alexander and P Horton, 'The Impossibility of a Free Speech Principle' (1983) 78 *Northwestern University Law Review* 1319, 1355.
[90] Perry (n 8) 1154, fn 72.
[91] Weinstein (n 40) 323.
[92] RL Lieberwitz, 'Freedom of Speech in Public Sector Employment: The Deconstitutionalization of the Public Sector Workplace' (1986) 19 *University of Colorado Davis Law Review* 597, 608, fn 66.
[93] Ardia (n 32) 137.
[94] A Kenyon, *Democracy of Expression: Positive Free Speech and Law* (Cambridge University Press, 2021) 244.

exclude, say, commercial speech and pornography from the realm of coverage. Yet this reasoning leads to dangerous propositions that, although ostensibly confined to autonomy-based thinking, spills into both truth-discovery and democratic decision-making. We see something of the problem in Greenawalt's thoughtful exposition that autonomy arguments call into question the rationality of those receiving the message. To appreciate the point, we must set out Greenawalt's thinking in full:

> But a strong version of a principle that the government must always treat citizens as autonomous by maximizing opportunities for informed choice would be powerfully protective of many kinds of speech. The difficulty with the principle in this strong form lies in its implausibility. The government must protect citizens from social harms, and many fellow citizens do not act in a rational and autonomous way. If some communications are especially likely to lead irrational people to do harmful things, why must the government permit them access to those communications as if they were rational and autonomous, rather than protect potential victims of their irrational actions?[95]

This strategy relies on a differentiated understanding of human reasoning in which some speakers and their audiences exhibit stunted powers of rationalisation. As one commentator puts it, in respect of autonomy and self-fulfilment/self-realisation theories:

> Yet the touchstone of these theories – that individuals are rational self-interested participants – has come under fierce attack by behavioral economists who study traditional markets and by communication scholars who study public discourse, both of whom note that research is showing that human behavior is characterized by bounded rationality, lack of willpower, and distorted self-interest.[96]

As Ian Cram has argued, vociferously, such techniques amount to unbridled elitism that undermines the political ideal of treating the 'demos' as the ultimate sovereign power. This, for him, is ochlophobia – or, fear of crowds – and anti-populism. He is especially critical of those who denigrate Brexiteers as 'racist, irrational, or ignorant'.[97] In this, he reflects, or perhaps embodies, Justice Holmes' belief that democracy is 'an experiment' and, as such, means that bad decisions will be reached by popular decision-making.[98]

IV. Horizontality

Orthodoxy's commitment to both functionality and designation of authenticity by reference to descriptive fit with justificatory arguments obscures the important structural feature of verticality. As chapter one introduced, the incremental approach with which theory has developed has allowed this structural feature to drift out of focus in the intellectual design of the right. Rights are given to citizens by the state. The state is the duty-holder; the citizen is the rights-holder. Free speech, as one such right, has

[95] Greenawalt (n 4) 32.
[96] Ardia (n 32) 114.
[97] I Cram, *Liberal Democracy, Law and the Citizen Speaker* (Hart, 2022) 78.
[98] *Abrams v US* 250 US 616, 630 (1919).

trump status precisely because the state cannot sensibly speak of having rights itself. If a citizen speaks in derogatory terms about the state, the state cannot imprison that individual on grounds that it is offended or to protect its right to a positive image amongst its people. This essential principle is familiar to us from cases like *New York Times v Sullivan*[99] in the US, and *Derbyshire County Council v Times Newspapers Ltd.*[100] Free speech, however, is regularly applied in the horizontal setting – that is, in private disputes and contexts – without much recognition of the shift in context. It is not that the literature and courts are insensible to this shift, but that insufficient attention is given to it. For example, in the US, the state action doctrine recognises the point. Nevertheless, critics of the doctrine will say that the mere presence of the court, as arbiter of disputes, is sufficient, if not quite to overcome the problem, then at least to ameliorate it. Thus, if we briefly revisit *Snyder v Phelps*,[101] discussed in chapter two, it may be said that the award of considerable damages, at first instance, was sufficient to render the appellants rights-claims front and centre in the appeal. There is, of course, merit in this analysis, but more work is needed, I suggest, to intellectualise the availability of vertically-given rights-claims in horizontal disputes. As chapter one makes plain, this book aims to give reason both to doubt that the whole gamut of free speech principle can be applied horizontally, as if the shift in perspective does not matter, or matter much, and to show how this might be done.

This work is necessary, I suggest, because theory is yet to provide a refined position on horizontality. Either the structural feature is overlooked or else its significance is minimised. We see this, for example, in Emerson. In his outline of free speech theory, he expressed no reservation when insisting the state protect 'individuals or groups from nongovernmental interference in the exercise of their right to expression'.[102] The state, he said, must 'eliminat[e] obstacles to, or affirmatively promot[e], effective functioning of the system [of free speech]'.[103] This exclusive focus on the merits of speech itself, without regard to these structural problems, meant that, for Emerson, a fictional account promoted as truthful biography of Warren Spahn, a famous baseball player, was entitled to full free speech protection against a false light privacy claim, despite containing 'a host, a preponderant percentage, of factual errors, distortions and fanciful passages'.[104] That free speech should trump privacy was natural, he suggested, because Spahn's 'right to be left alone does not include any general right not to be talked about'.[105] Expanding upon the point, he declared that 'the right of privacy depends upon guaranteeing an individual freedom from intrusion and freedom to think and

[99] *New York Times v Sullivan* 376 US 254 (1964).

[100] *Derbyshire County Council v Times Newspapers Ltd* [1993] AC 534.

[101] *Snyder v Phelps* 562 US 443 (2011). See discussion in ch 2.

[102] Emerson (n 55) 19.

[103] ibid.

[104] *Spahn v Messner, Inc*, 43 Misc.2d 219, 232 (1964). In fact, Spahn won his claim and the subsequent appeal was dismissed. The New York Courts of Appeal held that 'The present case deals neither with public officials nor official conduct. The free speech which is encouraged and essential to the operation of a healthy government is something quite different from an individual's attempt to enjoin the publication of a fictitious biography of him. No public interest is served by protecting the dissemination of the latter. We perceive no constitutional infirmities in this respect': 18 N.Y.2d 324, 329–330 (NY 1966).

[105] Emerson (n 55) 556.

believe, not freedom from discussion of his opinions, actions or affairs'.[106] Accordingly, he was unsympathetic to Spahn's plight: 'Insofar as the biography put him in a false light he was in the same boat as thousands of others who attract public attention. He could not expect a system of privacy to protect him from such comments.'[107]

Emerson's approach, I will suggest in parts three and four, is wrong because the trump status he attaches to free speech here is a product of (and should be confined to) the vertical setting in which the state has no right, as such, to enforce. Whereas in the vertical setting, the state can rely upon other obligations – such as public safety or national security – to resist the trump status of free speech, these obligations apply only if others are implicated by the rights-claim at stake. In the horizontal setting, these obligations are not merely implicated, they describe the entirety of the state's function. After all, the court's function in these disputes is to decide between clashing rights-claims. It is the arbiter of competing autonomy-based claims. On occasion, free speech will succeed over, say, privacy or the right to a fair trial, but not because it is special.

This essential structural difference in horizontal free speech claims seems insufficiently recognised or else too easily explained away. Consider, for example, Michael Perry's treatment of the problem. He argued that free speech trumps privacy because audience interests in truth-discovery outweigh private rights, even in property. In his view, a court could 'authorize communicative access to physical areas *not* within its control to which the public is otherwise admitted', such as a shopping centre.[108] A weaker form of such reasoning can be found in Vincent Blasi's classic essay, in which the monitoring of state power constitutes the ultimate free speech value.[109] Whereas, for example, Blasi criticised the expansion of the public figure doctrine to include those exercising no state power, still he resisted the logical conclusion that free speech claims had no or lesser application to purely private contexts. Instead, he thought the standard of liability should be stratified according to the plaintiff's standing, such that the law might 'provide absolute protection for communications critical of public officials, a qualified privilege defeasible upon proof of reckless disregard for the truth applicable to speech about public figures, and a negligence standard for all other defamatory utterance'.[110]

Whilst Schauer expressed scepticism about the application of free speech principle to horizontal disputes, his doubt related to its societal value, rather than its structural legitimacy.[111] Generally, he accepted that free speech claims concerning individuals were authentic according to the degree of 'risk' that the individual had assumed in entering public life, such that legal principles for defamation and privacy should reflect 'the degree to which an individual assumes the risk of unfavourable and erroneous publicity'.[112] However, for 'purely private individuals', free speech claims may be denied

[106] ibid.
[107] ibid, 557.
[108] Perry (n 8) 1206.
[109] V Blasi, 'The Checking Value in First Amendment Theory' (1977) *American Bar Foundation Research Journal* 521.
[110] ibid, 582.
[111] Schauer (n 17) 173–77.
[112] ibid, 174.

if they had no bearing 'on any issue as to which public truth is important or public error harmful'.[113] Similarly, he thought 'knowledge as to the affairs and past of purely private persons serves little if any private purpose'.[114]

Conversely, Redish argued that his self-realisation theory explained why the courts should treat even private defamation suits (that is, claims made against purely private persons) as a First Amendment issue: 'Comments about a private individual may be relevant to numerous life-affecting decisions of others, such as whether they should deal with him socially, enter into a business arrangement with him, or buy in his store.'[115] Thus, although, like Schauer, he thought differential treatment of public and private persons was justifiable according to the 'risk' in entering public life, he saw no issue in treating defamation as an authentic free speech matter in all instances.[116]

It seems to me that these opinions are all connected by the sense of free speech given to us in the vertical context – of a right with trump status in which the state's power is resisted, and resistible, by the history, nobility and significance of that right, in which its application to the horizontal setting is driven by that importance, character and strengths. There is no real recognition that this unalloyed application to a differential context might be problematic or in need of revision.

One notable exception to this treatment can be found in a much-berated article by Thomas Scanlon, who discusses it explicitly. Nevertheless, even here there is equivalence, for Scanlon notes only that the logic of what he calls 'the Millian principle' applies exclusively to the vertical plane. Since it rests, he says, 'on a limitation of the authority of states to command their subjects', it applies only 'to governments rather than to individuals, who do not have such authority to begin with'.[117] Scanlon does not claim that this structural feature applies to all conceptions of free speech; only Mill's.

If, as Perry suggests and others follow, property rights are inferior to free speech claims on the horizontal setting, then there can be little resistance to the idea that social media platforms are obligated to respect free speech as if it were an emanation of the state. Increasingly, this sort of argument has become popular in the literature. Timothy Garton Ash's book, *Free Speech: Ten Principles for a Connected World*, proceeds on the basis that 'the main limits to our effective freedom of expression are set by the state in which we are currently located, the companies and organisations that control our mediums of communication and the interaction between [them]'.[118] Using an approach that seems commonplace, Garton Ash switches between ethics and law, description and norms, such that, as with this quote, the ability to communicate and the right to do so are not clearly demarcated much less separated. Thus, criticisms of states and companies are aggregated such that the rights of citizens to speak freely are directed against both without differentiation.

[113] ibid, 175.
[114] ibid, 176.
[115] Redish (n 8) 644.
[116] ibid, 640–45.
[117] T Scanlon, 'A Theory of Freedom of Expression' republished in RM Dworkin (ed), *The Philosophy of Law* (Oxford University Press, 1977) 153, 167.
[118] T Garton Ash, *Free Speech: Ten Principles for a Connected World* (Atlantic Books, 2016) 31.

This pattern is familiar in the academic literature, and understandably so. If free speech is known by speech that fits the profile given by the justification, then there is no reason why the rights-claim cannot be made against the corporation as well as the state. After all, if, say, political speech is regulated in ways that defy content neutrality and which effectively neutralise meaningful dissent, why should it matter that the censor is the corporation, not the state? This line of reasoning is apparent in the work of Jack Balkin, for example, who has long decried excessive platform regulation as a serious free speech problem. In his view, free speech rights must be fully protected on social media because:

> Freedom of speech helps to produce a *democratic culture* ... Because cultural power is even more pervasive than state power, individuals need to have a way of participating in the construction and development of the cultures that constitute their identities and affect their lives. Freedom of speech allows widespread participation in the forms of meaning-making that construct us as individuals.[119]

Here, then, we see the purported beneficial effects of free speech rights trumping all else. This type of argument, which has its origins in Jürgen Habermas's work, is prominent elsewhere in the literature. For example, Damian Tambini says that 'without common spaces and trusted, verified truths, democracy fragments and fails to provide the deliberative environment necessary for legitimate collective decision-making'.[120] Timothy Zick has also spoken of the importance of ensuring social media 'serve the interests of democracy'.[121] Although cognisant of the horizontality problem – 'Government officials, who unlike social media are bound by the free speech and press provisions of the First Amendment, will have to tread carefully when addressing the "truth" or "falsity" of online speech.'[122] – still, he insists that the positive moves by prominent social media platforms to tackle hate speech 'raise delicate questions about the extent to which private intermediaries will be able to control and restrict public discourse'.[123]

In this way, social media is treated as if not only public property – free to access and enjoy – but also a public institution. According to Balkin, the state must create 'incentives for social media companies to become such responsible institutions' such that they become akin to 'state actors or public utilities'.[124] This sleight of hand renders the property owner subject to duties and responsibilities equivalent to those found in the state. In this way, the horizontality problem disappears because the owner is treated as an actor on the vertical plane. This strikes me as deeply problematic. There is no tradition of regarding publishers as vertical actors owing duties to would-be authors. A rejected manuscript, for example, is not held aloft as egregious instance of censorship or a threat to democratic participation. Publishers, with commercial and reputational interests at stake, are assumed to be masters of what they will publish. Similarly, despite Jerome Barron's claim that democratic process values necessitated newspapers carrying

[119] Balkin (n 32) 77.
[120] D Tambini, *Media Freedom* (Polity Press, 2021) 143.
[121] T Zick, *The First Amendment in the Trump Era* (Oxford University Press, 2019) 88.
[122] ibid, 89.
[123] ibid, 88–89.
[124] Balkin (n 32) 71.

rights of reply,[125] the Supreme Court struck down such a statute as an unconstitutional violation of the First Amendment.[126]

A related horizontality problem arises in an employment context. Can authentic free speech claims arise in workplace disputes or do the property rights and employer duties of the business owner prevent such? Elsewhere, I have argued that free speech rights are insufficiently protected in the workplace,[127] which would suggest I am committed to the former. How, though, can that be squared with the objections to horizontality in both the social media and civil suit contexts? One plausible explanation to distinguish, say, the social media setting from the employment context is the absence of the state in the dispute. When platforms remove content or block access, the state is uninvolved in the process, whereas when employers dismiss, the state has a presumptive interest in the worker's unemployment, not only in terms of the prospective financial burden upon the welfare state, but also in the political capital derived from high employment rates.

Nevertheless, this argument only goes so far. Process theorists, as we have seen, argue that the state has a genuine interest in the health of the public sphere, with both Habermas and Balkin being exemplars of this sort of reasoning. Moreover, even if the argument were extended to say that the state's interest is legislative (because the state regulates the fairness of dismissal by means of various statutory instruments such as, in the UK, the Employment Rights Act 1996), the same interest would emerge should the state legislate on social media regulation, as Balkin urges (as, for example, the UK and Germany have). Similarly, even if we were to limit the comparison to scenarios when workers complain of unfair or wrongful dismissal in tribunal proceedings, such that we might argue the state is directly involved, this would lend credence to the presumptive legitimacy of horizontality in court proceedings.

The distinction, as shall be argued more fully in part four, lies in the nature of the competing autonomy claims at stake in these different scenarios. The disgruntled social media user, censored for breach of policy, has no grounds to complain if the social media owner acts in accordance with the contract between them. Yet, even if there is a breach, the claim is one of contractual obligations not constitutional rights. Similarly, if the disgruntled object of media interest complains and her complaint is upheld, then the outcome is vindication of her no-right claim, ie, that her rights to privacy or reputation has been unduly interfered with and the publisher has no right to disseminate information that damages those rights. If she fails, then the outcome reflects the limits of her autonomy. The same logic applies in the employment setting. If the dismissal relates to expression attacking the employer or another employee, to put it simply, then the employer has not exceeded her autonomy. Yet, if it does not and if the dismissal is due to nothing more than employer dislike of that speech, let us say, then she exceeds her autonomy.

[125] JA Barron, *Freedom of the Press for Whom?* (Indiana University Press, 1973).

[126] *Miami Herald Pub Co v Tornillo*, 418 US 241 (1974). *cf* C Calvert, 'First Amendment Battles Over Anti-Deplatforming Statutes: Examining *Miami Herald Publishing Co v Tornillo*'s Relevance for Today's Online Social Media Platform Cases' (2022) 97 *New York University Law Review Online* 1. See discussion in ch 9.

[127] P Wragg, 'Free Speech Rights at Work: Resolving the Differences between Practice and Liberal Principle' (2015) 44 *Industrial Law Journal* 1.

Ultimately, I shall argue that the employment setting is more akin to state scenario due to the presence of coercion, or a coercion-like outcome, by the employee suffering in ways akin to a fine or imprisonment by the state. This, it seems to me, is the strongest, most plausible reason to recognise free speech rights in the horizontal setting of employment. The same cannot be said of the digital context. There is nothing (at least, not presently) that the digital speech provider does which impacts upon the user in this same way when properly promulgated policies are enforced. In those settings, the free speech claim is superfluous – nothing turns on it. In fact, free speech is asserted as an additional reason to give leverage so that the claim becomes a trump. In the employment scenario, free speech is central. This, at least, indicates the direction of the arguments presented later in the book.

V. Conclusion

Orthodox theory's approach to free speech principle is backward. It determines the meaning of free speech by asking why free speech is protected. Not only does this result in an awkward transition, in which the indeterminate 'it' of the first part becomes the determinate 'it' of the second, but it also negates the significance of theory as an analytical tool. For if theory can only answer the question of normativity by reference to descriptive practice, then the positive law has hegemonic hold over our understanding of the term. This seems wrongheaded to me. Theory should be our most useful tool in evaluating practice's approach. Specifically, theory offers an external point of evaluation whenever a decision is made concerning a free speech claim. In this way, theory is more valuable than precedent for although inconsistency with previous decisions offers an important means of deciding whether that decision is correct, still it cannot tackle much less overcome the situation whereby all previous decisions were wrong, and the instant decision correct. Indeed, it is meaningless to talk of the instant decision being 'correct' if precedent is all that one can rely upon.

On this method, by which the definition is understood by the justification, we are left to dispute the results of practice according to what is rather than what should be. We are robbed of an independent means of judging practical understandings of free speech and left, instead, in the position that Steven Smith have previously warned about:

> Among disparate theoretical proposals, one point upon which many first amendment scholars seem to agree is that an adequate theory of free speech has yet to be articulated. One consequence of this theoretical impasse is that freedom of speech may come to be seen less as a rationally-based principle than as an article of 'faith.'[128]

This sense comes through strongly from the method by which the source of free speech principle is defended. As the following chapter demonstrates, these sources are taken to be history, political identity, positive law and intuition.

[128] SD Smith, 'Skepticism, Tolerance, and Truth in the Theory of Free Expression' (1987) 60 *Southern California Law Review* 649, 651–52.

4

Proof

I. Introduction

To demonstrate the persuasiveness of their justification-derived elucidations of free speech, commentators rely upon one or more of four specific sources: intuition; the positive law; political theory; and history. This chapter interrogates the merits of this methodology.

To best understand the issues arising in this regard, we must revisit chapter one briefly. As we saw there, the established literature conveys the strong impression that theory is a product of practice. To my mind, this is wrong-headed. Theory has the greatest value if it is independent of practice, such that we may use theory to judge the coherency of practice. If, however, theory is beholden to practice, then this aim is defeated. As should be familiar by now, this book seeks to establish that theory should transcend practice otherwise we shall be robbed of an invaluable method by which to judge the inadequacies of practice. For this reason, chapter one argued that theory ought to be the sole means by which to determine authenticity.

Presently, the question of normativity – ie, what counts as authenticity in free speech terms – is determined by four techniques used individually or in combination. In other words, if we ask what free speech ought to be, then orthodoxy gives us an answer that locates the ought-ness in one (or more) of these four places. Thus, as we shall see, there are those that identify normativity through intuition – what we think, instinctively, free speech should represent. Others construct normative principle from a selective reading of the positive law. In this way 'ought' is derived from aspects of the 'is'. Others still read ought-ness from the political traditions and historical moments of a nation. For ease, I shall treat these last two as interchangeable sources of proof.

This practice of normativity is distinctive from what this chapter argues for. It is, specifically, a form of normativity rooted in the world as it is. It seeks to find coherent patterns in descriptive accounts of law and convention (the positive law, shared history and political experience) or else from the world of practical experience (intuition). The normativity I argue for is that which aims for independence from practice; that sees positive law and convention as evidence of nothing philosophically interesting and which is suspicious of the cognitive biases to which intuition is susceptible. This sort of normativity treats theory as first order, and so determinative, rather than second order, as, say, Robert Post would, by regarding theory only as a means of collating patterns of coherency within practical settings (be that positive law, political mechanisms or history). As chapter one explained, what makes this latter method distinctive is that if practice departs too far from the logic of theory, then it is theory that shall need revising.

With these distinctions in mind, then, the object of this chapter is to criticise the basis on which these distinctive normative 'ought' propositions are determined (as opposed to the descriptive 'is'). This criticism argues for the unsuitability of certain experience-derived propositions informing the 'oughtness' of normativity. As will become apparent, I argue that normativity should be independent of practice rather than beholden to it. In criticising these experience-derived propositions of 'ought,' I am not suggesting that experience has no place in normativity. If we accept Kant's distinction between the phenomenal (the world of experience) and the noumenal (the world beyond that which can be experienced), then some sort of experience must determine normative principle. Free speech, as an abstract concept, is a product of the phenomenal. It is not in that limited category of things beyond our comprehension, such as God, death and the consciousness of others.

Nevertheless, there is much to be said for Wittgenstein's claim, in the *Tractatus*, that: 'the sense of the world must lie outside the world'.[1] Too often, free speech theory resides within 'the world'. It seeks both inspiration and approval from values apparent in that world. This is a mistake – and one which the commentary is not sufficiently cognisant of. To appreciate the error, we should reflect more upon Wittgenstein's criticism of seeking 'sense' from within 'the world':

> In the world everything is as it is, and everything happens as it does happen: in it no value exists – and if it did exist, it would have no value.
>
> If there is any value that does have value, it must lie outside the whole sphere of what happens and is the case. For all that happens and is the case is accidental.
>
> What makes it non-accidental cannot lie *within* the world, since if it did it would itself be accidental.
>
> It must lie outside the world.[2]

Obviously, as creatures of experience, we cannot entirely escape 'the world', for we cannot pretend that there is no such thing as free speech and start again, as it were. Some of our 'ought' propositions are bound to reflect 'the world' of experience. But that is not the point of the criticism. It is that in conceptualising free speech, commentators are too attracted by 'the world' of experience, such that principles have resonance, not for their likeness with experience but their fit. In that way, abstraction is treated as inferior to the world of the 'is'. It is this gravitational pull that we should be cognisant of and actively seek, therefore, to resist it. This idea of stepping outside the known world is one that animates the overarching purpose of this chapter and the next. Specifically, I hope to demonstrate the problem of externality or independence in the relationship between theory and practice in terms that utilise this idea.

The first step is to show that orthodox methodology *is* rooted within the world of the 'is'; that it relies for its authority upon the existence of free speech as an established legal principle. Accordingly, articulation of its finer points is also dependent upon

[1] L Wittgenstein, *Tractatus Logico-Philosophicus* [1922] (Routledge, 2001) 86, [6.41], emphasis in original.
[2] ibid.

this pre-existing conception. The ambition to refine principle, though, is constantly thwarted by this dependence. It cannot produce abstract principles of 'oughtness'; it can only reproduce doctrinal principles of 'is-ness', whether the 'is' is derived from intuition (section II), the positive law (section III), or political traditions and shared history (section IV). In this world, authenticity is merely an artefact of what cognitive biases, predilections and traditions we already possess concerning the concept. If we are to escape 'the world' and produce normativity that transcends description, then we must rely upon a logic that is not derived from the 'is-ness' of a shared experience of free speech. That will be the object of the following chapter.

II. Intuition

A. Differential Expectations

As we saw in chapter two, commentators sometimes use intuition as a means of deriving or proving free speech principle. Intuition, for our purposes, is an intellectual seeming that bears the ring of truth without demanding substantiation. It is something familiar to us by reason of common experience. Yet, herein lies the first significant problem with the use of intuition in normative reasoning in free speech principle. Our intuitions are not the product of universal experience as, say, gravity, time and space are. Intuitions, then, are not of equal value. There is an underpinning to them – a background noise – to which we should be attuned if we are to accept intuitions as proof of oughtness. Thus, intuitions can be distinguished by the influences that give rise to the underlying expectations which inform the 'ought'. The most apparent are those that speak to some professed or apparent practical knowledge, culture, context and time.

Intuitions appearing in the established literature seem sometimes to speak to premises found in the positive law and sometimes not. There is an opacity about them at times, such that the identity of the 'we' and of the 'our' is not immediately apparent. For example, we see this method in action when Frederick Schauer dismisses the claim that free speech is justified by some broader notion of liberty. This proposition, he says, is 'troubling, for it seems to clash with the frequency with which we talk about "freedom of speech" in isolation'[3] and 'we *believe* there is something special about free speech, for otherwise we would not refer to it as we do'.[4] Who is the 'we' here? Is it the legal community, the academic community, the American public, or all of the above? When someone like Daniel Farber refers to 'the intuitive belief that commercial speech is somehow more akin to conduct than are other forms of speech',[5] he refers, presumably, to a pre-legal intuition that may be shared by the American public and philosophers but not practitioners, whose knowledge of the subject tells them that commercial speech *is* protected, at least to some degree, by the First Amendment. Alternatively, he may

[3] F Schauer, *Free Speech: A Philosophical Enquiry* (Cambridge University Press, 1982) 5–6.

[4] ibid, 6.

[5] DA Farber, 'Commercial Speech and First Amendment Theory' (1979) 74 *Northwestern University Law Review* 374, 389.

be saying that this tenet of positive law is counterintuitive *even* to practitioners, who, whilst recognising that the law protects commercial speech, tend to think it should not. Similarly, when Leslie Kendrick says 'our way of talking about free speech suggests that it is a special right that does not attach to everything, and our jurisprudence suggests the same',[6] she may be speaking only of practitioners, of academics, or of the American public too. Rarely do we find the intellectual honesty that Thomas Scanlon projects when he answers his own question – 'to what extent does the [concept of free speech] rest on natural moral principles and to what extent is it an artificial creation of particular political institutions?'[7] – with the admission: 'it seems clear to me that our (or at least my) intuitions about freedom of expression involve both natural and artificial elements'.[8]

Clearly, there are those, in the non-academic and non-practitioner community, who believe that free speech is not a concept as such or, if it is, its meaning is literal and to be found through no greater intellectual inquiry than the plain meaning of two words – 'freedom' and 'speech'. *Free Speech and Why It Matters* by Andrew Doyle[9] is paradigmatic. Despite its pretension to illustrate the importance of ensuring free speech is fully protected, it contains no detailed statement of what the author takes the term to mean. The fullest statement resides on the book cover: 'Unless we are able to speak our minds we cannot innovate, or even begin to make sense of the world.'[10] This is an odd claim given that the author's chief preoccupation is not with innovation, democracy or liberalism, but, instead, with why hostility directed against, specifically, the trans community should be met with either total submission or otherwise fulsome agreement.[11] We see something of this in the specious complaint that 'A new identity-based conceptualisation of "social justice" has brought with it a mistrust of unfettered speech and appeals for greater intervention from the state.'[12] The book is premised on an underlying but unsubstantiated belief that the meaning of free speech is not an intellectual matter as such. We see this elimination of intellectual ambition in the journalist Mick Hume's words: 'The first thing that seems to have been forgotten … is that it's supposed to be Free. The second thing … is that it's simply Speech.'[13]

This, then, begs questions about the epistemological standing of these intuitions. Sometimes scholars are more explicit that the intuition is pre-legal and speaks to what might be called 'common sense'. For example, Steven Smith asserts that 'intuition and common sense … [dictates] that the first amendment … clearly cannot permit a speaker to imprison his or her audience and force the audience to listen'.[14] Other examples of

[6] L Kendrick, 'Use Your Words: On the Speech in Freedom of Speech' (2018) 116 *Michigan Law Review* 667, 697. See, also, AA Mondal, 'The Shape of Free Speech: Rethinking Liberal Free Speech Theory' (2018) 32 *Continuum* 503, 509.

[7] T Scanlon, 'A Theory of Freedom of Expression' (1972) 1 *Philosophy and Public Affairs* 204, 205.

[8] ibid, 206.

[9] A Doyle, *Free Speech and Why It Matters* (Constable, 2021).

[10] ibid, 6.

[11] For criticisms of Doyle's book, see P Wragg, 'Andrew Doyle: Free Speech and Why It Matters' (2021) 58 *Society* 319.

[12] Doyle (n 9) 2.

[13] M Hume, *Trigger Warning*, concise and abridged version) (William Collins, 2016) 11.

[14] SD Smith, 'Skepticism, Tolerance, and Truth in the Theory of Free Expression' (1987) 60 *Southern California Law Review* 649, 717.

this sort include 'the intuition that no one should go to jail for opinions peacefully expressed';[15] the 'intuition … that sometimes government has good reason to regulate content to prevent harm';[16] 'Intuition teaches us that consensus cannot be reached in free-floating talks or chats';[17] and 'the intuition that a silenced speaker is wronged'.[18]

To my mind, these sorts of intuition are not intended to represent unsubstantiated propositions of law, but some deeper, cultural expectation that may well indicate or else contain ethical propositions. This might explain Doyle and Hume's insistence upon a literal interpretation of the term 'free speech' – that mere speech, despite being offensive, provocative or outrageous ought not to carry legal, financial or social consequences because otherwise (they would say) it is not 'free'.

However, these expectations might be more problematic than we imagine. Consider, for example, Eric Barendt's view, in his second edition of *Freedom of Speech*, that, threats of violence apart, 'almost everyone would agree that a verbal or printed attack on the government or other institutions of the state should be immune from legal regulation … [otherwise] it is difficult to see its point at all'.[19] As a statement of 'ought' rather than 'is', this strikes me as a cultural expectation about mature democracy that is peculiar to our time.

Certainly, it is not an expectation shared in antiquity. When, in 1523, Sir Thomas More petitioned Henry VIII for freedom of speech,[20] he did so in temperate terms that recognised Parliament as the King's court in which 'he may be displeased with what members say; and as discipline is his to maintain, he may punish the too bold or too rash for their speeches'.[21] The tolerance that More begged for had clear limits. He did not ask that members should be free 'to frame a form of Relligion, or a state of gouernment as to their idle braynes shall seeme meetest'.[22] According to Neale, if he had, the response would have been: 'no King fit for his state will suffer such absurdities'.[23]

Thus, no one in Henry VIII's court, let alone outside, would have had a legitimate expectation that they might freely 'attack' the Government, for this would have been thought licentious (by which I mean, improper). Something of this remains today: the 'absolute' right to free speech that Parliamentarians enjoy exists only on the premises of Westminster Palace[24] and, even then, is constrained by standards of civility. Parliamentarians cannot use 'any language [that] is intended to bring the House into disrepute, or is insulting to another Member, particularly in respect to accusations of lying'.[25] A failure to retract such remarks may be punished by the Speaker by suspending

[15] E Simpson, 'Responsibilities for hateful speech' (2006) *Legal Theory* 157, 158.

[16] RL Brown, 'The Harm Principle and Free Speech' (2016) 89 *Southern California Law Review* 953, 957.

[17] T Huang, 'A Quadruple Doctrinal Framework of Free Speech' (2022) 53 *Columbia Human Rights Law Review* 467, 487.

[18] M Ramsay, 'The status of hearers' rights in freedom of expression' (2012) *Legal Theory* 31, 51.

[19] E Barendt, *Freedom of Speech*, 2nd edn (Oxford University Press, 2004) 74.

[20] According to Sir John Neale, More was the first to petition for free speech, in terms we would recognise, JE Neale, 'The Commons' Privilege of Free Speech in Parliament' in EB Fryde and E Miller, eds, *Historical Studies of the English Parliament*, vol 2, (Cambridge University Press, 1970) 147, 158–59.

[21] ibid, 157.

[22] ibid, 158. 'Meetest' in this archaic sense means 'suitable' or 'right'.

[23] ibid.

[24] Art 9, Bill of Rights 1688.

[25] 'MPs' Guide to Procedure' (UK Parliament, 2023).

that Member from the House.[26] In this way, the Parliamentary expectation must reflect what Machiavelli said of princes (or, at least, sentiments attributed to him): that they 'must be talk'd of with Reserve and Respect'.[27]

A popular expectation of freedom to 'attack' government by speech must also be a recent phenomenon. Certainly, the American experience, under colonial rule, demonstrates graphically that there could be no such expectation, as Leonard Levy has shown[28] – although the fact of a restrictive and censorious regime by the English over the colonials does not disprove the existence of a contrary expectation. The Americans may have known not to expect the law to protect them, but that does not prove that they did not think it should. Indeed, the jury's decision to find John Peter Zenger not guilty of seditious libel, for exposing the corrupt practices of a New York governor, would rather suggest that the public *did* have such an expectation.[29] Nevertheless, the point should not be stretched too far; even in pre-revolutionary America, there was no great appetite for the sort of unrestricted freedom that we now associate with the term 'attack', for, as Levy also tells us:

> The persistent image of colonial America as a society in which freedom of expression was cherished is an hallucination of sentiment that ignores history. The evidence provides little comfort for the notion that the colonies hospitably received advocates of obnoxious or detestable ideas on matters that counted.[30]

This sentiment finds judicial expression in a 1900 case cited by Zechariah Chafee Jr (albeit with some disapproval): 'The liberty protected is not the right to perpetrate acts of licentiousness … Freedom of speech and press does not include the abuse of the power of tongue or pen'.[31] Indeed, it has been argued, persuasively, that, in England and New Zealand, judicial decision-making in public discourse cases is animated by a requirement for civility.[32]

Similarly, the expectation of a freedom to attack government must be geographical and, perhaps, a distinctly Western idea. Wilbur Schramm's claim, in 1956, that the (Soviet) communist thinks himself 'blessed with the only true freedom of the press'[33] may still be accurate. The ideas of plurality, compromise and opposition are alien to the authoritarian mindset, such as that of Marxist-Leninist communism, for the simple reason that political dissent compromises realisation of the collective vision. Anything short of complete submission to political vision of the state's absolute authority is intolerable. As Putin's repressive regime in Russia demonstrates, 'attacks' on government are

[26] ibid.

[27] J Addison, *The Thoughts of A Tory Author Concerning the Press: With the Opinion of the Ancients and Moderns, about Freedom of SPEECH and WRITING* (London, 1712) 8.

[28] LW Levy, *Emergence of a Free Press* (Oxford University Press, 1985).

[29] See discussion, ibid, 38–44.

[30] ibid, 16.

[31] *State v McKee*, 73 Conn 18, 28, 46 At. 409 (1900) (Chafee's reference). Z Chafee Jr, 'Freedom of Speech in War Time '(1919) 32 *Harvard Law Review* 932, 942.

[32] A Geddis, 'Free speech martyrs or unreasonable threats to social peace? – "Insulting" expression and section 5 of the Public Order Act 1986' (2004) *Public Law* 853; 'Freedom of expression and civility in the New Zealand Supreme Court' (2013) *Common Law World Review* 324.

[33] W Schramm, 'The Soviet Communist Theory of the Press' in FS Siebert, T Peterson, and W Schramm, *Four Theories of the Press* [1956] (University of Illinois Press, 1974) 105.

not tolerated; they are regarded as subversive and destabilising. Journalists who criticise the illegal invasion and occupation of Ukraine, for example, are routinely imprisoned for the 'crime' of spreading 'fake news'.[34] Our instinct that such treatment is barbaric, then, may be a product of Western thought that does not quite explain the popular vilification of Julian Assange, Edward Snowden or Chelsea Manning.

The differential nature of intuitions about authentic free speech raises a significant issue about the ordering or priority to be afforded to intuition, as propositions of 'oughtness', especially when they compete or otherwise sit in tension. As evidence of authentic free speech principle, intuition's apparent but unquantified subjectivity, depending upon differential epistemic, cultural and temporal expectations, renders it incoherent. How are we to distinguish between them? This strikes me as a serious methodological concern that has received little or no academic attention.

For example, if we distinguish between the intuitions of the initiated and the uninitiated, then we might project some sort of crude spectrum in which literalism sits at one end and rationalism at the other. The problem with this – if it is not obvious – is that an informed intuition is oxymoronic on its terms. It is not intuition – properly understood – as something instinctive; it is something learned through experience. Specifically, it is something understood through experience of practice, be that knowledge of the positive law, political science or history. In that case, we do theory a profound disservice if we do not recognise informed intuition for what it is: an unsubstantiated proposition founded upon practice. However, this is a poor source of oughtness; the 'ought' represents a set of two unrelated types. One type, though presented as an 'ought', is but an unsubstantiated assertion of an actual or imagined 'is.' It is an actual 'is' if it represents a proposition found currently or previously in the positive law or in political convention. It is an imagined 'is' if it represents some garbled or misconstrued representation of an actual 'is'. The other type is an 'ought' but an 'ought' derived from political or legal theory. If we say that intuition p dictates that practice should be x and that p is but an unsubstantiated proposition drawn from x, then the whole claim is but a truism.

However, if we are to adopt the opposite position, and treat literalism as a more proper or authoritative source of intuition, then we solve the problem, or perhaps lessen the grip, of practical experience's influence upon the resolution of the task. In this way, intuition is not masquerading as practice but instead challenges it as a form of proof. Yet, its credentials as a kind of proof surely weaken as practical experience the more that practical experience's influence is loosened. For what is an intuition devoid of experience? It becomes Intuitionism – that branch of philosophy that treats certain propositions as self-evidently true without further need of logical inquiry. Free speech seems an unlikely candidate for Intuitionism given its status as an artificial construct borne of abstract reasoning rather than immediate apprehension by the senses.

[34] A Roth, 'Russian journalist Ivan Safronov sentenced to 22 years in prison' *The Guardian* (5 September 2022); W Preussen, 'Russian journalist Maria Ponomarenko sentenced to 6 years in jail over post on Mariupol strike' Politico EU (15 February 2023), www.politico.eu/article/russia-ukraine-anti-war-journalist-maria-ponomarenko-sentence-6-year-jail; K Jochecová, 'Russian journalist gets 8 years in prison over Ukraine coverage' Politico EU, (1 February 2023), www.politico.eu/article/russia-alexander-nevzorov-ukraine-war-oppposition-sentenced-to-8-years-in-jail.

B. Differential Purposes

The second issue is in the method itself of using intuition. It is not used uniformly. We can identify three such usages. First, intuitive statements may be nothing more than, to use a phrase common to contract scholars, mere 'poofs'. They are literary flourishes intended to have no evidential or argumentative value but, instead, give colour to the discussion, as, perhaps, Barendt's statement on political 'attacks' is meant to do, or for the purposes of demonstrating personal values. For example, when Richard Posner says that 'forbidding all Nazi advocacy would do less harm to society than suppressing all scientific discussion or, for that matter, all price advertising',[35] he speaks to personal conviction rather than sociological or psychological empiricism.

Secondly, intuition can be used as juxtaposition, ie, as transition between what we might think authentic principle should be as compared to what it is. In this sense, it serves a performative function as that initial step demanded by Rawls' process of reflective equilibrium: that 'state … reached after a person has weighed various proposed conceptions and he has either revised his judgments to accord with one of them or held fast to his initial convictions'.[36] This performative use functions as a helpful device by which to signal the counterintuitive, as when Xiangnong Wang says, 'While it may be intuitive to assume that the First Amendment extends to all expressive and communicative acts, this claim is demonstrably inaccurate.'[37] In this way, Wang gives polite expression to Robert Bork's stinging rebuke (mentioned in chapter three): 'Laymen may perhaps be forgiven for thinking that the literal words of the amendment command absence of governmental inhibition upon verbal activity, but what can one say of lawyers who believe any such thing?'.[38]

If intuition serves no more than this performative role, then we can perhaps say, with Seana Shiffrin, that there exist:

> Theoretically informed, provisional starting points that strike me as highly intuitive, secure, illuminating, and important lodestars. Nonetheless, if a plausible theory cannot be found that supports and explains these judgments or if a more plausible theory would reject them for good reason, these judgments should be revised or discarded. That is, I regard their identification as just an early step in a process aimed at achieving reflective equilibrium and not as fixed or immutable 'results' that must be accommodated, no matter what the other theoretical costs.[39]

The only caveat that might be added is to question the significance of those theoretically informed lodestars bearing comparison with intuition.

My hesitancy stems from the third, and final, usage of intuition, in which it is treated as determinative or otherwise persuasive to the construction of authentic free speech principle. For these commentators, intuition is more than a performative tool;

[35] RA Posner, 'Free Speech in an Economic Perspective' (1986) 20 *Suffolk University Law Review* 1, 10.
[36] J Rawls, *A Theory of Justice: Revised Edition* (Oxford University Press, 1999) 43.
[37] X Wang, 'De-Coding Free Speech: A First Amendment Theory for the Digital Age' (2021) *Wisconsin Law Review* 1373, 1379, fn 21.
[38] R Bork, 'Neutral Principles and Some First Amendment Problems' (1971) 47 *Indiana Law Journal* 1, 21.
[39] SV Shiffrin, 'A Thinker-Based Approach to Freedom of Speech' (2011) 27 *Constitutional Comment* 283, 285, fn 4.

it is either a proof of itself, perhaps in need of refinement, or else a presumption to be rebutted. In this way, intuition must be taken seriously. Theory must 'fit' intuition by adhering to it or demonstrating the exception. In this sense, intuition is more than a provisional step in the process of reflective equilibrium. It is not a rhetorical device; it holds a stubborn form of evidential value that, whether proven or disproven, cannot be ignored. We see this, for example, in several of the claims quoted in the last chapter. We see it, for example, in Lawrence Solum's claim that self-realisation theory, if it is to be taken seriously, must 'fit our intuitions about what speech should be protected';[40] in James Weinstein's view that intuition is 'in some sense more important than … judicial statements';[41] and in Cass Sunstein's endorsement of theories which fit 'our initial or considered judgments about particular free speech problems. Any approach to the First Amendment will have to take substantial account of those judgments, and adjust itself accordingly'.[42]

This sense of intuition as determinative is also apparent in Gregory Magarian's claim that 'our deepest intuitions about the substance and limits of constitutional rights concern individuals' decisions to behave as they choose, and courts' understandings about constitutional rights should reflect those intuitions'.[43] Rival accounts are deficient, by this method, if they do not accord with intuition: 'Autonomy theory … is in danger of merging into a general argument for individual liberty *that does not explain our intuition* that there is something about expression that makes it especially deserving of constitutional protection' (emphasis added).[44] This statement mirrors Kendrick's and Schauer's sentiment above that there is something in 'our way' of speaking about free speech that authentic theory, if it is to deserve the name, must either reflect or otherwise overcome.

C. Confirmation Bias

These observations move us to a position where we might see intuition as a contaminant in the principle-construction process. Ultimately, it operates as a form of confirmation bias. The intuitions most often relied upon are stubborn, monolithic influences that hinder the rational process. For example, if we start from the assumption that political speech is a crucial type of free speech activity then the thought is bound to dominate our thinking to the exclusion of all else. All subsequent propositions will be examined through this lens such that exceptions or alternate explanations will be disregarded as false.

Barendt's statement, above, illustrates the point. Attacks on government or state institutions should receive legal immunity, he said. The intellectual design of this

[40] LB Solum, 'Freedom of Communicative Action: A Theory of the First Amendment Freedom of Speech' (1989) 83 *Northwestern University Law Review* 54, 81, fn 108.

[41] J Weinstein, 'Database Protection and the First Amendment' (2002) 28 *University of Dayton Law Review* 305, 325, fn 10.

[42] C Sunstein, 'Free Speech Now' (1992) 59 *University of Chicago Law Review* 255, 305.

[43] GP Magarian, 'The First Amendment, the Public-Private Distinction, and Nongovernmental Suppression of Wartime Political Debate' (2004) 73 *George Washington Law Review* 101, 106.

[44] M Crawford, 'Regimes of Tolerance: A Communitarian Approach to Freedom of Expression and its Limits' (1990) 48 *University of Toronto Faculty of Law Review* 1, 6.

assumption attributes absolute protection to written or verbal 'attacks'. The qualifier 'almost all' operates as a synonym for 'all right-minded people'; it presupposes that there are no good reasons to deny its propositional validity. If we are in the grip of confirmation bias then we are predisposed to accept it without critical thought. After all, it speaks clearly to the verticality of that essential rights-based structure outlined in chapter two. Moreover, it resonates with initiate understandings of practice, in which, at both a normative and descriptive level, our laws are assumed to protect speakers in these circumstances. Obnoxious public protest is outlawed only at the point it constitutes, to borrow a phrase, a 'clear and present danger' to public order or national security. Similarly, sedition, to the extent it still exists, gains purchase as reason to interfere only when the threat of violence is real. In the US and the UK, and for Council of Europe members, access to libel law is severely curbed for public officials. In the UK, the restriction is even more pronounced: the state, collectively, cannot sue for libel. When a local authority sued a newspaper for accusing it of serious maladministration of a pension fund, the House of Lords, then the apex court of England and Wales, held that it had no right to do so.[45] The common law, it said, was clear that:

> It is of the highest public importance that a democratically elected governmental body, or indeed any governmental body, should be open to uninhibited public criticism. The threat of a civil action for defamation must inevitably have an inhibiting effect on freedom of speech.[46]

Accordingly, the local authority was powerless to prevent or otherwise cure the damage done by these allegations, regardless of the truth in them.

However, the logic of the essential premise – that there are no good reasons to deny absolute free speech protection in these circumstances – is more doubtful than these statements acknowledge. Anecdotal evidence abounds to demonstrate as much. Consider, for example, the state of English social services, which is terminally demoralised by the vitriolic attacks it routinely receives from the British tabloid press. One such instance is particularly striking. A 17-month-old infant, Peter Connelly, known as Baby P, died from the brutal maltreatment and abuse inflicted by his mother, Tracey Connelly, her violent partner, Steven Barker, and his brother, Jason Owen. A damning public inquiry identified serial failings across a range of public services, including social services, the police and health workers, which, had they not occurred, could have saved the infant.[47] The death of Baby P subsequently became a political football in which the opposition of the day – then the Conservatives – used it to attack the beleaguered party in power, Labour, for political gain. It led to a public scapegoating of Sharon Shoesmith, the director of children's services in Baby P's constituency, championed by Rebekah Wade, then editor of *The Sun*, which resulted in her sacking, on live television, by then Secretary of State for Children and Families, Ed Balls. Not only did this have serious mental health repercussions for Shoesmith personally,[48] it inculcated a public

[45] *Derbyshire County Council v Times Newspapers Ltd* [1993] AC 534.

[46] ibid, 547.

[47] Department for Education, 'Haringey Local Safeguarding Children Board, First and Second Serious Case Review "Child A"' (26 October 2010).

[48] P Butler, 'Sharon Shoesmith on Baby P, child protection and the tabloid media: "I came very close to not standing up again"' *The Guardian* (19 August 2016).

mentality of blaming social services for undetected child abuse that continues today. In 2023, Prime Minister Rishi Sunak, for example, blamed social workers for 'ignoring' allegations of serious sexual child abuse due to 'cultural' oversensitivity and 'political correctness' – a view condemned by the British Association of Social Workers as 'irresponsible, misrepresentative, and damag[ing to] the profession's reputation'.[49] Since this public misapprehension cannot be corrected through libel laws, and since governments of the day are happy to rely on it for cheap political gain, the pervasive harm caused to public institutions deepens inexorably.

It is not only social services that are scarred by demonstrable falsehood. The judiciary is also prone to such malicious and inaccurate reporting. Sometimes those attacks are deeply personal, as when a sitting judge, Mr Justice Eady, was publicly abused by the *Daily Mail* for his part in developing the misuse of private information tort.[50] These *ad hominin* attacks have continued apace. In the aftermath of the disastrous Brexit referendum, when public campaigners sought to ensure, through judicial review, that the final exit settlement reflect Parliament's, rather than the executive's, intentions, the Lord Chief Justice and two other judges were castigated as 'Enemies of the People' by the *Daily Mail* when they agreed.[51]

Students of history are well aware that the phraseology behind 'enemies of the people' and the scapegoating of sections of society is but propaganda utilised by the fascist to serve his end. Yet free speech principle is inept to recognise the difference if it slavishly follows its confirmation bias to believe such attacks on public institutions are not only necessary but also, perversely, a *healthy* display of the right in action. The apparent but untrammelled harm that this reporting does to those institutional workers goes unaddressed in the balance. This outcome is especially acute if, as those commentators above urge, intuitions such as this *must* be recognised, in the final analysis, as authentic free speech principle.

This confirmation bias produces strong inclinations to favour certain principles, and they are not easily overcome. Consider, for example, the view of Ashutosh Bhagwat and James Weinstein, that 'it can hardly be denied that freedom of political expression is an indispensable means by which the people in contemporary democracies control their government',[52] or David Richards's explanations that 'the political process model of free speech conceives the core function of such speech to be the protection of the democratic political process from the abusive censorship of political debate by the transient majority who has democratically achieved power'.[53] We find the same in Joseph Raz's bold claim that 'freedom of expression is an integral part of a democratic regime'.[54]

[49] 'PM criticised for 'offensive' comments about social workers' *Professional Social Work magazine* (5 April 2023), www.basw.co.uk/resources/psw-magazine/psw-online/pm-criticised-offensive-comments-about-social-workers.

[50] Q Letts, 'As cold as a frozen haddock, Mr Justice Eady hands down his views shorn of moral balance …' *Daily Mail* (25 July 2008); P Dacre, 'The threat to our press' *The Guardian* (10 November 2008).

[51] J Slack, 'Enemies of the people: Fury over "out of touch" judges who have "declared war on democracy" by defying 17.4m Brexit voters and who could trigger constitutional crisis' *Daily Mail* (4 November 2016).

[52] A Bhagwat and J Weinstein, 'Freedom of Expression and Democracy' in A Stone and F Schauer, *The Oxford Handbook of Freedom of Speech* (Oxford University Press, 2021) 87.

[53] DAJ Richards, 'Free Speech as Toleration' in WJ Waluchow (ed), *Free Expression: Essays in Law and Philosophy* (Oxford University Press, 1994) 34.

[54] J Raz, 'Free Expression and Personal Identification,' (1991) 11 *Oxford Journal of Legal Studies* 303, 308.

Both the attitude ('it can hardly be denied') and the elemental parts resemble John Stuart Mill's concern that:

> [N]ot only the grounds of the opinion are forgotten in the absence of discussion, but too often the meaning of the opinion itself. The words which convey it cease to suggest ideas, or suggest only a small portion of those they were originally employed to communicate. Instead of a vivid conception and a living belief, there remain only a few phrases retained by rote … it will be held as a dead dogma, not a living truth.[55]

It is not that these views are inherently objectionable, but that they leave too much unexplained and unsubstantiated. They call to mind Stanley Ingber's concerns about indoctrination[56] brought about by state educational processes, which the mechanics of doctrinal free speech serve to legitimate. For him, individual autonomy and the neutrality of the marketplace of ideas concept are mythical because the educational process, reinforced by cultural norms, weaken, if not eliminate, true individuality by the socialisation programme it engenders, such that certain propositions become instinctively accepted and resistant to analytical scrutiny. We find similar scepticism, of course, in Stanley Fish's radical pragmatism, in which he dismisses the ideal of free speech as but that which is leftover when society has eliminated that which it refuses to entertain.[57]

D. Conclusion

The dominance of intuition in free speech orthodoxy sullies its intellectual ambition. It denigrates theoretical accounts as, at best, instinctively known by virtue of some learning and, at worst, easily knowable to anyone possessing a dictionary. Intuition may serve *some* valuable purposes in the construction of free speech principle, but only if used to tease out common misapprehensions about its nature and ambit. If it forms the basis of the principle, then it denigrates free speech as something trivial or else something not worth serious intellectual inquiry.

Intuition is not the irreducible form of experience; it is contingent experience masquerading as the universal. We should be more attuned than we are to this limitation. Our intuitions contain unacknowledged experiences of the world. One of these, of course, it is that it reflects our expectations for the term which is derived from our wider experiences of the world as we know it. Inevitably, it is tainted by unacknowledged influences upon this expectation, including privileged perspectives upon that world. These contingent experiences are derived, or derivable, from established practices of positive law, shared political identity or culture, and deeper but unrefined reflections of historical circumstance. The remainder of this chapter examines the suitability of these sources as propositions of authenticity. My essential point is this: if intuitions are unsubstantiated propositions drawn from practice, then their persuasiveness should be determined by reference to these underlying propositions.

[55] JS Mill, 'On Liberty' in JM Robson (ed), *Collected Works of John Stuart Mill*, vol XVIII (University of Toronto Press, 1977) 243 and 247.

[56] S Ingber, 'The Marketplace of Ideas: A Legitimizing Myth' (1984) *Duke Law Journal* 1.

[57] S Fish, *There's No Such Thing As Free Speech and It's a Good Thing Too* (Oxford University Press, 1994).

III. Positive Law

The positive law is also presented, by the established literature, as a source of oughtness, either directly or indirectly, as the ultimate source of intuition. In this endeavour, two types of positivistic account can be identified. There are those that are not theoretical as such, but which make general statements of principle derived directly from the positive law. The use of normative language in these accounts can mislead. The 'ought' refers to internal matters of consistency rather than external matters of morality. Thus, although the 'ought' directs the decision-maker and, in that sense, concerns law's development, it is the law of the 'is' and not the law of the 'ought'. We readily encounter such usage in technical accounts of law. For example, after enactment of the Defamation Act 2013, but before any decided case law on it, the editors of the 12th edition of *Gatley on Libel and Slander* could write that '[section] 1(1) should be read as meaning that a statement is not *actionable* unless its publication has caused, or is likely to cause, serious harm to the reputation of the claimant', not by reference to some larger moral purpose, but because 'the intention of the drafters' required it.[58] Here, then, we see normative language used as HLA Hart[59] or John Austin[60] do in their descriptive enterprises. The preoccupation with rules of recognition in legal positivism means that such accounts have no pretensions of oughtness in the moral sense. The question of bad or wrong decision-making does not arise if the posited law is legitimate according to underlying constitutional norms. On this basis, authenticity is a procedural but not a substantive question.

The second kind of normative language use is also concerned with consistency. Yet, here the moral language of value-derived definitions or justifications acts as a critical lens by which to view the positive law. It is this sort of normativity I am concerned with in this section. We see it, for example, in Robert Bork's claim that: 'Constitutional protection should be accorded only to speech that is explicitly political.'[61] This is radically different from the first type of positive normativity because, as Bork states, 'this theory departs drastically from existing Court-made law'.[62] We find this method in Chafee's work too. For example, he says: 'In war time, therefore, speech *should* be unrestricted by the censorship or by punishment, unless it is clearly liable to cause direct and dangerous interference with the conduct of the war' (emphasis added).[63] This is not a purely descriptive account because, in the preceding paragraph, he tells us that the law does *not* routinely apply such a high threshold. As proof, he offers[64] the following principle applied in *United States v "The Spirit of '76"* by Justice Bledsoe: 'No man should be permitted … to do that which will *in any way* detract from the [US war] effort'[65] (emphasis added). Instead, he relies upon a series of arguments, drawn largely

[58] A Mullis and R Parkes, *Gatley on Libel and Slander*, 12th edn (Sweet & Maxwell, 2013) [2.5], 40.
[59] See, eg, HLA Hart, *The Concept of Law*, 2nd edn (Oxford University Press, 1994) 57, 86 and 117.
[60] See, eg, J Austin, *The Province of Jurisprudence Determined* [1832] (Prometheus Books, 2000) Lecture V, esp 159–71.
[61] Bork (n 38) 20.
[62] ibid.
[63] Z Chafee Jr, 'Freedom of Speech in War Time' (1919) 32 *Harvard Law Review* 932, 960.
[64] ibid, 959.
[65] *United States v 'The Spirit of '76'* BULL DFPT JUST, No 33, 2 (S D Cal, 1917) (Chafee's reference).

from practice (including political history, which I shall refer to in the next section) to support, and augment, his point concerning the limits of political expression in war time. The critical elements of his argument – that rights cannot be dispensed with in war time[66] albeit free speech is not an absolute;[67] that the criminal law imposes a high threshold for punishment;[68] that war time powers are subject to free speech rights;[69] and that political speech is afforded primacy[70] – are all based on supportive readings of the positive law.

This kind of normativity seeks to extrapolate a prevalent moral norm or value from the positive law and, in turn, craft this into an overarching, coherent theory that explains past outcomes, predicts future ones, and, most importantly, distinguishes good from bad reasoning. The obvious limitation with this approach is that it does not, and does not aim to, explain all positive law according to this value. Instead, it seeks to provide the best account. This methodology is pervasive in the legal academic literature. Robert Post speaks for most – but not all – when he says that:

> '[I]nterpreting the First Amendment involves explicating our national dedication to freedom of expression. The task is not to determine what is 'in the abstract' the best possible theory of freedom of speech but instead to offer the best possible account of our actual historical principles.[71]

In this way, Post discards theories that, he says, do not fit with established doctrine. Thus, he says 'the structure of First Amendment doctrine is responsive to a value other than autonomy';[72] 'the purpose of fostering a marketplace of ideas is an implausible goal of First Amendment doctrine';[73] and, 'historically speaking, the theory of democratic self-government has been preferred'.[74]

This methodology seeks coherence in the macrocosm – the larger picture – as it appears from the microcosm of individual principle found in the positive law. Accordingly, coherence is a matter of 'best fit' which describes the positive law in the most cohesive form. For example, Lawrence Solum tells us that Jürgen Habermas's process-based theory of communication 'provides the best justification for the first amendment while simultaneously providing the best fit with the existing case law'.[75] Or, as Cass Sunstein puts it: 'No other approach unifies initial or preliminary judgments about these matters as well as a political conception of the First Amendment.'[76] Similarly, Vincent Blasi has it: 'Some of the strongest intuitions registered by the [Supreme Court] Justices seem best understood in terms of the checking value'.[77]

[66] Chafee (n 63) 937.
[67] ibid.
[68] ibid, 948.
[69] ibid, 956.
[70] ibid, 960–69.
[71] R Post, 'Participatory Democracy and Free Speech' (2011) 97 *Virginia Law Review* 477, 477.
[72] ibid, 482.
[73] ibid, 487.
[74] ibid, 489.
[75] Solum (n 40) 56.
[76] Sunstein (n 42) 305.
[77] V Blasi, 'The Checking Value in First Amendment Theory' (1977) *American Bar Foundation Research Journal* 521, 620.

Rival accounts to process-based theories are also defended, in the main, by their consistency with the positive law (or wider practice, as I have defined it above). Martin Redish, for example, is explicit on this point. His self-realisation model, he says, 'can be proven, not merely by reference to some unsupportable, conclusory assertions of moral value, but by reasoning from what we in this nation take as given: our democratic system of government'.[78] Likewise, Michael Perry argues that his theory, which furthers the epistemic value aspect in the truth argument, is consistent with judicial reasoning in the Supreme Court (more so than process-based accounts, he says), especially where protection has been afforded to non-political forms of speech such as pornography, commercial speech and advocacy of illegality (short of violence).[79] Even Edwin Baker, who, as we shall see, urged caution in the reliance on doctrine to elucidate theory, felt that the autonomy value 'best explains many results that I, and I believe most First Amendment commentators, approve'[80] of the positive law.

In this way, commentators treat the positive law as not only the ultimate source of proof for their value-based definitions. More than that, they treat it as determinative of all that free speech *can be*. For them, the positive law is but a jumbled mass of discordant principle – some faulty, some competing, some conflicting – that needs normative values to reorder and rationalise it. In the words of Eric Morecambe, these are all the right notes but not necessarily played in the right order. This approach is, if not driven by then certainly, consistent with Bork's argument that certain restrictions limit the principled judge from acting on sentiments that strike her as morally right. Seen in that light, we might regard a theory built from the positive law as both appealing and persuasive to those judges who wish to bring normative clarity to apparent descriptive confusion.

Nevertheless, it seems to me that this approach is fatally flawed in its limited, and limiting, ambitions for theory. Normative positivism, of this kind, may create an overarching narrative of coherence but only of a fragile type. There can be no hope of consensus or definitive view precisely because this methodology permits a variety of coherent accounts to be constructed. Accordingly, it is no wonder that Redish, Baker, Perry and Post (or anyone) can disagree so vehemently despite the commonality in their approach. Having selected a value that fits a substantial – but not total – portion of the positive law, each is bound to conclude that their champion is the one true source. Each seeks to find coherence through commonality so that patterns which fit the asserted value are deemed authentic and those which do not as discarded as inauthentic. For Post, and his ilk, the dominant pattern is embodied by that which enables public decision-making. For Redish, Baker and Perry the pattern is larger but only to the extent it promotes self-realisation (Redish), self-fulfilment (Baker) or epistemic advance (Perry). Thus, commercial speech is a battle ground for Redish and Baker because the former's conception of informed private decision-making would include it whilst the latter's would not. Yet, according to the rules of their own game, only the

[78] MH Redish, 'The Value of Free Speech' (1982) 130 *University of Pennsylvania Law Review* 591, 594.

[79] MJ Perry, 'Freedom of Expression: An Essay on Theory and Doctrine' (1984) 78 *Northwestern University Law Review* 1137, 1210–11.

[80] CE Baker, 'Autonomy and Free Speech' (2011) 27 *Constitutional Comment* 251, 270.

judiciary (or legislature) can decide and they refuse to do so. Steven Shiffrin recognises as much when he says:

> [The] commentary argues that some or many Court decisions implicate the particular value discussed. In short, the Court has been generous about the range of value relevant in first amendment theory, and unreceptive to those who ask it to confine first amendment values to a particular favourite.[81]

In the final analysis, each is hamstrung – unable to land that telling blow – because they have left themselves beholden to a regime that refuses to arbitrate.

This approach to authenticity is misguided, I argue, for its failure to appreciate that practice ought to be beholden to theory and not the other way around. There is a deep-rooted methodological opacity to this approach which resides in its constant selectivity to the material. Yet, rather than see this opacity as an essential weakness, theorists seem, instead, to embrace it as a necessary feature. Sunstein, for example, is one such theorist, for he recognises this situation, albeit without questioning its coherence. Arguing that the primacy of political speech is justified by a variety of sources, including First Amendment jurisprudence, he sees the need for continual revision but claims:

> [I]t is not unprincipled or merely convenient to adjust a theory when it proves to deal inadequately with particular cases. Sometimes the adequacy of theory is itself tested by how it conforms to initial or considered judgments about particular outcomes.[82]

Post hints at the same: 'it requires us to interpret out history in light of our best ideals whilst simultaneously re-examining our ideals in light of our actual history'.[83]

What seems to go unnoticed, or otherwise unexplored, is the perpetual theoretical uncertainty produced by this constant dependency upon practice. Chief amongst this is the realisation that this kind of normative positivism cannot find positive law to be absolutely incoherent. I do not mean to suggest that the positive law is, in fact, utterly incoherent. My point is that since theory ought to be independent of practice, it should be able to reach this conclusion. As set out in chapter one, ideally, practice should follow theory. At the very least, theory should not be reliant upon practice to articulate authenticity; to explicate the essential elements of authentic free speech principle free from interference from practice.

To make my point clear, consider the ultimate aim of theory, as it lies in the hands of the established literature. That aim is to produce a moment for a grand readjustment or realignment; a kind of universal reset, if you will. The theorist says, in effect, I have examined the entirety of positive law and, from this rigorous endeavour, I can demonstrate that, previously, *these* cases (whatever they might be) were authentic instances of free speech principle at work and *these* were not. From this point in time on, the theorist concludes, only those decisions that conform with my overarching theory are authentic. In this way, the theory purports to independence from the positive law, for the theorists says I *was* beholden to practice but no more. Yet, this is a fallacious claim precisely because any future incongruous decision (in conflict with that overarching

[81] S Shiffrin, 'First Amendment and Economic Regulation: Away from a General Theory of the First Amendment' (1984) 78 *Northwestern University Law Review* 1212, 1252.

[82] Sunstein (n 42) 305, fn 156.

[83] Post (n 71) 477. 'Historical principles' equates to 'practice' as I have defined it above.

theory) represents not a moment of inauthenticity but a necessity to revisit theory. The claim of independence is thus fictitious. If these purported deviations create, in effect, coherency from a new or different point of view, then it is theory that must be rewritten rather than practice.

This methodology cannot escape from the gravitational pull of its own logic – that it is constantly bound by the coherency to be found from within the positive law. It is tethered, permanently, to the world of the 'is' despite its pretensions to exist in the world of the 'ought'. Accordingly, Post's account that public decision-making is the most constant form of positivism would be undone if the First Amendment gave greater protection to private decision-making than it did public. So too Baker's account would need substantial revision if the First Amendment consistently protected commercial law for its benefits to private decision-making. Whilst it is true that Baker could fall back upon the argument that this is philosophically incoherent, his and Post's accounts would become products of a sort of historical originalism rather than manifestations of a collectively discernible principle derived from case law.

This would not be the case if theory were the first order premise, rather than the second. For if practice were beholden to theory, then, certainly, applications of theory may vary according to social and technological developments but not the theory *itself*. This would be so even if the underlying conditions that dictate theory were to alter radically. If that were so, we should no longer be able to say there is such as thing as free speech in practice. But we could still talk meaningly of free speech in principle.

So too, normative positivity is premised on another unacknowledged fiction – that it is a species of esotericism: it presupposes that there *is* coherence to be found in the mass of positive principle, if only one possesses the Rosetta Stone by which to decode it. Inevitably, I think, this projects the fiction that judges and legislators possess a 'true' sense of authenticity, even if only dimly or inconsistently. This faith is implausible or, certainly, questionable for, as we know, the founders themselves had no such pretensions. If judges and legislators do possess this Rosetta Stone then they, as a sort of Illuminati, have been remarkably successful in concealing it from public view. Of course, no theorist really believes this to be the case, but few have been as perceptive as Schauer, whose self-confessed 'motivation' in striving for normative clarity was the 'gradual realization that the legal system takes freedom of speech as a given, devoting little if any attention to the philosophical foundations of the principle it seeks to enforce'.[84] Yet, Schauer is not entirely true to this insight. Whereas he recognised that practice should not be ignored entirely, since it provides 'illuminating examples' and may be 'illustrative of instructive mistakes', he felt compelled to construe its rules as 'sources of important philosophical principles'.[85] In the final analysis, Schauer's philosophical approach deserted him. On the question of why free speech could not be construed by the autonomy value, he resorted to positivism: 'it is freedom of speech and press, and not freedom of liberty in general, that is specifically set forth in the text for special protection'.[86] There is, according to Schauer, no 'mandate' to seek to understand

[84] Schauer (n 3) ix.
[85] ibid, x.
[86] F Schauer, 'Must Speech Be Special?' (1984) 78 *Northwestern University Law Review* 1284, 1297–98.

free speech on a greater scale than the plain text of the constitution allows. Accordingly, 'what makes speech special … is the very fact that the constitutional text says it is'.[87] In this, he is firmly with Bork, who also said 'the first amendment indicates that there is something special about speech'.[88]

However, Baker stands apart. In his final works before his untimely death, he glimpsed the inadequacy of the positivistic approach to theory when he lamented that:

> Academic thought sinks to its lowest depths when its methodological ambition is to be an apologist for the status quo … The measure of the appeal of a First Amendment theory should not be the extent that it conforms to existing doctrine.[89]

From this insight, he saw that:

> A theory could be measured by how well it casts light on what is good about portions of doctrine that are good and what is bad about portions that are bad, and we should be as morally and ethically insightful as possible at distinguishing the two.[90]

In chapter five, I will examine what it means to stand 'outside' of the known world for the purposes of construing authenticity. Before that I explore reliance on practice in its widest sense by considering the influence of political history in the construction of authenticity.

IV. Politics and History

This form of proof may be used on its own or otherwise in conjunction with the other forms discussed above. Typically, it takes the form of a narrative in which major moments of political or constitutional upheaval are said to have shaped or else reformed the national commitment to free speech. In the USA, of course, this moment is independence. In Europe, it may be the French revolution but more likely the downfall of totalitarianism, which, in the West, is marked by World War II's end and the creation of the European Convention on Human Rights in 1950 and, in the East, by liberation from Soviet suppression after the Iron Curtain fell.

In the American literature, then, we see frequent reliance upon the Madisonian ideal that 'public opinion sets bounds to every government, and is the real sovereign in every free one'[91] to animate, usually, whatever process theory is being asserted. Bhagwat and Weinstein do this,[92] as Alexander Meiklejohn did,[93] before them. However, the evidential weight of history is opaque. Sometimes, as Bhagwat and Weinstein do,

[87] ibid.

[88] Bork (n 38) 23.

[89] Baker (n 80) 270.

[90] CE Baker, 'Is Democracy a Sound Basis for a Free Speech Principle?' (2011) 97 *Virginia Law Review* 515, 525.

[91] RA Rutland and TA Mason (eds), *The Papers of James Madison*, vol 14 (6 April 1791–16 March 1793) (University Press of Virginia, 1983) 170.

[92] Bhagwat and Weinstein (n 52) 85.

[93] A Meiklejohn, *Political Freedom: The Constitutional Powers of the People* (Oxford University Press, 1965) 102–06.

it is presented as, if not conclusive, then certainly persuasive where demonstrative of the framer's intentions. Since the constitutional text itself is but a bald statement, some knowledge of the framer's understanding of free speech is thought to be illustrative of its meaning. Of course, this sentiment has obvious limits because, as Bork says, 'the framers seem to have had no coherent theory of free speech and appear not to have been overly concerned with the subject'.[94] Moreover, as Barendt argues, it would be 'absurd' to constrain conceptions of authentic free speech to enquire what the framers would do with new technologies, etc, given that 'political and social circumstances will have changed so radically'.[95]

Nevertheless, an historical approach has its advantages. If we are to accept Wittgenstein's invitation to leave 'the world' of the 'is', then historical sources provide us with a rich data set of the 'outside'. There are two different approaches to history and we should be careful to distinguish between them. To ask what free speech meant prior to modernity captures a range of intellectual processes in need of analytical scrutiny. To simplify, there are the underlying conditions that prompt the conclusion and there is the conclusion itself. That conclusion is the product of intellectual thought that gives us the conception of authentic free speech as the ancients understood it. Those ancients may be the Romans, as embodied by, say, Cicero, Cato or Seneca. Alternatively, they may be the Parliamentarians of the Tudor age, such as Sir Thomas More. Or, more recently, they be James Madison or Alexander Hamilton, defending Peter Zenger from the strictures of seditious libel. When scholars rely on the conception of free speech as these notables understood and practised it, they rely upon the *conclusion*. That conclusion is bound to be an expression of political and/or religious freedom (the two being broadly similar at various times in our history). However, these conclusions remain firmly in the world of the 'is', but the 'is' as it was. To escape the world of the 'is', we must inquire further into the conditions that prompted these conclusions. We must understand what caused or prompted these conclusions. It is these conditions that enable us to construct normativity, as the next chapter will show. In this way, we can say, with Bork, that 'logic has a life of its own, and devotion to principle requires that we follow where logic leads'.[96]

For the 'is' is deeply misleading if we focus only upon the conclusion. Compare, for example, the free speech claims discernible in, say, ancient Greece and Rome, Tudor England, Colonial America with modernity. Undoubtedly, we shall find something resembling political speech as the common form of free speech claim (followed, closely, by religious persecution). Commentators that focus only on this surface appearance to prove some point about, typically, political speech's priority in the free speech concept neglect the deep, intractable differences underpinning those conceptions. Often these references to antiquity are brief, especially in the popular literature, and presented selectively, to prove a point that it cannot bear. Timothy Garton Ash does this when he says 'it remains astonishing how [*sic*] the essence of our modern idea of free speech

[94] Bork (n 38) 22.

[95] Barendt (n 19) 3. Nevertheless, there are those that ask these sorts of questions, meaningless though they are, eg, C McGlynn and I Ward, 'Would John Stuart Mill Have Regulated Pornography?' (2014) 41 *Journal of Law and Society* 500.

[96] Bork (n 38) 6.

as a democratic good is to be found almost fully formed 2,500 years ago, in Athens'.[97] Specifically, he has in mind *parrhesia*, which he translates as 'speech that was both free and fearless' so as to conclude 'free and equal speech would allow deliberative democracy and that, the ancient Athenians believed, would produce better government'.[98] So too, Andrew Doyle refers to ancient Athens and *parrhesia*, but without the same intellectual rigour that Garton Ash achieves. He translates *parrhesia* as 'speaking truth with candour' and, like Garton Ash, concludes that 'the open and honest expression of viewpoints, however, was deemed essential to the business of Athenian governance'[99] It is unclear which period he has in mind, but the reference, in the following sentence, to the Socratic method is suggestive. Nevertheless, the reference to Socrates, in Doyle's work, and the absent reference to him in Garton Ash, is unfortunate, for if the Athens of his time did recognise free speech in the fulsome terms that both Garton Ash and Doyle encourage, then, clearly, it did not do Socrates himself much good, judging by his end.

Doyle also refers us to ancient Rome where, he says, 'the right to free speech in matters of politics was rarely extended beyond the Senate, although anyone familiar with Shakespeare will know that the plebeians could find ways to make their voice heard'.[100] Commentators like Doyle do not seem to appreciate the underlying culture that would, as of choice if not compulsion, have placed natural limitations on both the Roman and Athenian understandings of their 'rights' to political freedom. As Larry Siedentop says, without hyperbole, if we lived in antiquity, we should 'find ourselves [in] an utterly remote moral world'.[101] This is a world devoid of equality in which strict hierarchical structures prevailed. This is a world which practiced elaborate forms of slavery and, in which the concept of property had application to the family dynamic. The father was not merely the symbol of domestic authority, but a power in his own right by which to control the family and to dispense justice as he saw fit. The *ius vitae necisque* gave him the right to execute his children. They were bound to paternal authority as the wife was to her husband. According to Siedentop, this was not subjugation as we would understand it; there was an innate rightness, a moral virtue, that the family itself would embrace.[102] It was a good in an intrinsic sense, but also instrumental in its association with a good reputation being vital to ensure the family name remained untarnished – that they did not become outcasts.

This unquestioning obedience and subservience runs through the vertical arrangement of society. In Rome, the division was not, as Doyle's clumsy distinction might suggest, between senators (or, more accurately, patricians) and plebeians, nor citizens and slaves. It was more finely graded such that plebeians, as citizens other than patricians, could possess differing legal rights and privileges (and these classifications were known as *Cives Romani*, *Latini*, *Socii*, *Provinciales* and *Peregrini*). These peoples belonged to the polis and were not 'of the people', as Siedentop explains.[103] This hierarchical structure

[97] T Garton Ash, *Free Speech: Ten Principles for a Connected World* (Atlantic Books, 2016) 76.
[98] ibid, 77.
[99] Doyle (n 9) 9.
[100] ibid.
[101] L Siedentop, *Inventing the Individual: The Origins of Western Liberalism* (Penguin, 2014) 9.
[102] ibid, 15.
[103] ibid, 29.

in which the patricians ruled and were themselves, as all mankind was, subservient to the gods severely restricts the content of speech that could inform the term 'political'. To associate this severely limited sense of political freedom with our modern conceptions is so misleading as to be fallacious, for this was a world in which individual autonomy had no meaning. Accordingly, the appeal to *parrhesia* as an emblem of free speech is absurd.

As Siedentop argues, it is only after the fall of Rome and Athens, and, he says, the death of Christ, that individual autonomy, as a concept we would recognise, can exist.[104] Even then, however, the various understandings of autonomy, as it related to a freedom to speak, vary across time. As suggested above, neither the parliamentarians of Tudor England nor the inhabitants of colonial America would have recognised that freedom in the terms that modern commentators seek to impress upon them. It is not simply that the freedom to criticise was unavailable to them; it would have been unthinkable. The simplistic idea, of Doyle's, that free speech is denied by 'preventing individuals from expressing themselves as they see fit',[105] even if this means being offended or caused psychological harm by the speech, would appal these historical characters. We have seen this above. Sir Thomas More was not calling for a right to insult the trans community[106] or make racist jokes.[107] James Madison and Alexander Hamilton were not fighting against cancel culture or 'wokeness'.[108] Propriety, as a concept, was not forced upon the Middle and Victorian ages; it was actively embraced by the god-fearing folk of that time. As proof of an authentic free speech principle, then, this selective treatment of historical examples suffers clearly from its distinct failure to distinguish superficial conclusion from underlying conditions. These selective treatments, then, read the historic world of the 'is' through the lens of modernity without appreciating the gross distortion that this lens imposes.

Moreover, these selections mislead in the conclusions drawn from them. For they speak to a predilection that treats those content types with historical pedigree as proof of some undeniable priority in the normative framework of authentic principle. Thus, process theorists think it important to say that the best examples of free speech controversy in our shared past all speak to the significance of political (and religious) freedoms. Colonial America, they say, attests to this significance by the rebellions against pernicious seditious libel foisted upon them by their British overlords. These arguments are utterly meaningless. What do they prove? Our history, stretching into antiquity, is a litany of political and religious persecution precisely because it can be nothing else. What else are commentators hoping to find? That the ancient preferred to political speech to commercial or pornographic speech? Pornography as we know it could not exist until the invention of the camera, which happened in the late-nineteenth century. Likewise, commercial advertising could not exist until the establishment of capitalism, which is roughly the same period. Perhaps we can find instances of labourers admonished for saucy woodcuttings of nubile maidens or merchants whose notices

[104] ibid. See, esp, 51–66.
[105] Doyle (n 9) 5.
[106] ibid, ch 1.
[107] ibid, ch 10.
[108] ibid, ch 6.

of sale attracted negative attention, but these are hardly the same thing. To say that there is no established culture in our history of championing protection for anything other than speech of religious or political significance is to say nothing at all. It is but a straw man.

V. Conclusion

Authentic free speech theory is a normative proposition. It is the world of the 'ought'. Yet, if the world of the 'ought' is but intuition, then it is nothing but fallacy. For intuition, once interrogated, reveals itself to be a thinly veiled description of the 'is' as given to us by experience – either the epistemic experience of the initiate or the familiar experience of the uninitiated coloured, as it must be, by local political, social and cultural traditions. Likewise, oughtness derived from the practical experience of the positive law tells us no more than what our shared traditions reveal. While we can tell interesting and coherent stories by these traditions, which conform to overarching propositions espousing moral values, we are given only what the is-ness provides. We see a coherent but not cohesive picture of the world of the ought as a 'best fit' to describe the world of the 'is'. In this way, practice begets theory and not vice versa. Theory, in this way, becomes hostage to fortune; it must bend its will, as Post's or any other process theory must, should the ratio of non-political to political cases change in the future. This picture remains unchanged by the use of history as an evidential source of oughtness. For history is bound to tell us that political speech is important because it can say nothing else. Yet freedom of political speech is not the constant that these commentators imagine, for it speak not to one overarching concept but distinct conceptions according to variations in the underlying moral and political conditions of the time.

Theory, if it is to achieve its independence from practice, must seek authenticity from outside the world of this 'is'. As the next chapter argues and previous sections allude to, this requires greater scrutiny of the underlying conditions that inform our claims to free speech. What is it about those conditions that produce meaningful, and persuasive, conceptions of free speech to impose themselves? It is only in these conditions that we can begin to differentiate the world of the 'is' – a world in which a free speech tradition exists – from the outside world in which we may achieve objective observation.

PART III

Restatement

5

The Problem of Individuality

I. Introduction: Choices in Intellectual Design

The design parameters for free speech theory championed in the previous chapter may be summarised as follows. Authentic free speech principle is a derivable set of premises. It is to be derived not from intuitive experience, nor the informed experience of (positive) law and political tradition as such, but from a vantage point that Wittgenstein described as being 'outside the world'. Since we are creatures of experiences, and cannot transcend the limitations of our own intellectual faculties, we must accept, following in the Humean and Kantian tradition, that we cannot eliminate the problem of experience altogether in our formulation of this external viewpoint. Thus, we must construct free speech theory from scratch, as it were, as if free speech were an alien concept in our world, whilst being cognisant of the evident fiction within that constraint. This aim has two practical aspects to it. First, to describe the parameters of free speech theory in this way requires us to consciously abandon our preconceptions about what free speech entails. We must therefore avoid our innate presumptions about its value, significance, or most poignant manifestations as, say, a monument to political ambition. Accordingly, authentic free speech is only that which we can derive from this programme and not that which we carry with us through intuition, shared history and innate knowledge of positive law. Secondly, and relatedly, we must construct this world prospectively, from meaning to justification, rather than retrospectively, from justification to meaning.

One issue that remains unaddressed in the preceding chapters is whether this programme aims to be a statement of the universal or the particular. If it is universal then its logic applies not only to any culture but also to any time period. In *A Theory of Justice*, John Rawls also sought to escape the world through the device of the hypothetical contract agreed in the original position. However, his ambition did not to seek to limit the influence of experience in the same way. From what he called his Archimedean point, he sought to derive a notion of justice that was 'not contingent upon existing desires or present social conditions'[1] but which described the universal position, ie, one that any race would arrive at, at any point in time. Yet one of the telling criticisms of this project, made by Alastair MacIntyre amongst others, has been to reveal the edifice of universalism as but a façade; that the actions of his

[1] J Rawls, *A Theory of Justice*, rev edn (Oxford University Press, 1993) 232.

disinterested actors in the original position betrays a particularism firmly rooted in liberal democracy.[2] This prompted him to revise his position in *Political Liberalism* to the extent that he acknowledged the influence of liberalism upon those actors, at least in terms of their political morality, and sought to defend it.[3]

Moreover, MacIntyre in *After Virtue*[4] signals a second problem with the universalistic ambition. According to him, any attempt to elucidate justice – or any other rights-based account, it may be said – is implausible due to the problem of individualism upon which such concepts are ultimately reliant. Such accounts, in the modern era, overlook the problem that individualism, by its nature, conflicts, in obvious ways, with community ideals and the larger framework of co-operative existence upon which civilisation depends. From this insight, of course, he champions the importance of community as a necessary constraint upon individuality-based constructs, which, of course, must include the elucidation of human rights.

We can confine MacIntyre's insights to their natural home of ethical norms. In this way, we might say, with Joseph Raz, that whilst I may have a moral (ethical) interest in prosperous, harmonious, enlightened society, 'it is difficult to imagine a successful argument imposing a duty to provide a collective good on the ground it will serve the interests of one individual'.[5] Accordingly, we can separate the legal from the ethical so as to say that the construction of free speech as an individualistic account, expressed in juridical terms, does not preclude its realisation in ethical terms that recognise the importance of community. Thus, we can say that press freedom is a legal right specific to individual newspapers, journalists, etc, but with communal ambitions and implications, such as to inform others and assist them in making good public decisions.

Nevertheless, to proceed on the basis of this separation alone would not be entirely intellectually satisfying, for MacIntyre is surely right that the universal must admit the communal into its conceptualisation of the individual. Accordingly, since, as will become apparent presently, this book aims to separate the individual from the communal, it can be acknowledged that it has no pretensions at universalism. Instead, it seeks only to describe the particular, as it relates to individuality. In this way, individuality and community will be treated, in the spirit of MacIntyre, as two separate units of currency by which to construe constitutional arrangements. Since this distinction seems (and is) peculiarly 'Western' in its orientation, it needs some explanation, and defence, which the remainder of this (lengthy) introduction will partially provide.

To begin, some clarification on the meaning of 'individuality' is called for. Specifically: given that the book aims to rehabilitate the Millian account of individuality, but relies heavily upon Kant at times, recognition of the profound difference between the two is necessary. As Rawls saw clearly, the Kantian agent starts from a specific metaphysical position. She wants to live a perfectly good life, in which her actions – actual or prospective – always meet the objective standard of right (as in correct or just). This deontological account presents autonomy in its most strained form, for the Kantian agent is *not* free to do the wrong thing. She is forever constrained

[2] A MacIntyre, *After Virtue* [1981] (Bloomsbury, 2011) 283–95.
[3] J Rawls, *Political Liberalism* (Columbia University Press, 1996).
[4] MacIntyre (n 2) 283–95.
[5] J Raz, *The Morality of Freedom* (Oxford University Press, 1986) 203.

to do what is right. Moreover, her *subjective* understandings of right also amount to the wrong thing, given, amongst other things, the strictness of the supreme principle in the doctrine of virtue (*Tugendlehre*) – 'act in accordance with a maxim of *ends* that it can be a universal law for everyone to have'[6] – which follows from the categorical imperative of the *Groundwork of the Metaphysics of Morals*, which establishes the nature of moral duties according to the Formula of Universal Law (act on principles that could through will be universal)[7] and the Formula of Humanity (treat others as ends and never means).[8] The motivation to do what is right for no other reason than that it is right informs the autonomous nature of right conduct; otherwise, if right conduct were enforced, heteronomously, from above, it would be not a categorical but a hypothetical imperative: we should do what is right because we wish to avoid state punishment.

Kant's doctrine of right (*Rechtslehre*) differs significantly from his doctrine of virtue (*Tugendlehre*), and so provides a fuller sense of autonomy. For, unlike in the *Tugendlehre*, the supreme principle of right – by which he means a system of juridically legislated duties paired with rights – is that: 'any action is right [ie, just] if it can coexist with everyone's freedom in accordance with a universal law, or if on its maxim the freedom of choice of each can coexist with everyone's freedom in accordance with a universal law'.[9] Admittedly, 'right' or *recht*, has connotations that extend beyond legal theory to also encompass the moral, as can the word 'law' or 'rule' when used figuratively rather than literally, as when it has predictive power.[10] This ethical sense of law can be seen, for example, when Kant speaks of morality as the 'laws' that a person ascribes to herself.[11] Moreover, as Kant acknowledges, the language of ethics and law can both speak of duties. The duty to fulfil promises under a contract are both of an ethical and legal kind. The difference lies in the externality that separates the two, ie, the power of coercion: 'It is no duty of virtue to keep one's promises but a duty of right, to the performance of which one can be coerced.'[12] Thus: 'Ethical lawgiving (even if the duties might be external) is that which *can* not be external; juridical lawgiving is that which can also be external.'[13]

Kant was a man of his day. Despite his open support of the French Revolution,[14] he operated under a regime of state censorship, in which he had already earned the King's displeasure, prior to publication of *The Metaphysics of Morals*,[15] and further

[6] I Kant, *The Metaphysics of Morals* [1797] (L Denis, ed, M Gregor, trans) (Cambridge University Press, 2017) 168 [6:395].

[7] I Kant, *Groundwork of the Metaphysics of Morals* [1785] (M Gregor and J Timmermann, eds and trans) (Cambridge University Press, 2012) [4:420–1].

[8] ibid, [4:429].

[9] Kant (n 6) [6:230].

[10] See Translator's note on the text in Kant (n 6) xli–xlii.

[11] ibid, [6:224].

[12] ibid, [6:220].

[13] ibid, [6:221].

[14] See discussion in M Kuehn, *Kant: A Biography* (Cambridge University Press, 2001) 342.

[15] Kuehn reports that on 1 October 1794, the King, Frederick William II, wrote to Kant, noting that Kant's continued 'misuse [of] your philosophy' corrupts the youth in his charge and contravenes his duties 'as a teacher of the youth against our paternal purpose … We expected better things of you as you yourself must realise.' Failing immediate atonement, there would be 'unpleasant measures for your continued obstinacy': ibid, 378–79.

disobedience 'would certainly have meant dismissal or forced retirement without pension … includ[ing] banishment.'[16] Accordingly, the greater part of his scheme deals with private (or horizontal) rights, rather than public (vertical) rights. The relationship between the state and its citizens, is both brief and conservative, in outlook. Alongside his narrow, chauvinistic view of voting rights,[17] he denies that the people have either a right to rebel or spread sedition against unjust rulership.[18] His scheme produces a striking rights regime, in which rights with corresponding duties arise only on the horizontal plane, in private relations of external lawgiving. On the vertical plane, Kant is clear that 'the sovereign has only rights against his subjects and no duties (that he can be coerced to fulfil)'.[19] In the Hohfeldian analysis, this is known as the right/no-right relationship.

This dynamic introduces a further feature in our intellectual design, which relates to the orientation of the right/no-right and the right/duty relationship to the horizontal and vertical planes. For, in our time, I will suggest, the Kantian model is inverted, such that right/duty exists between citizen and state with the right/no-right model confined to the horizontal plane in the context of authentic free speech claims, such that talk of 'rights' and (corresponding) 'duties' in the horizontal plane is mistaken unless, that is, we refer only to the state's (ie, court's) inalienable obligation to hear disputes and secure autonomy against undue coercion.

Since, essentially, the claimant argues that the defendant's actions amount to an undue harm, she asks the state to: a) declare that her right has been unduly interfered with by the defendant; and b) order the defendant to compensate her for her losses. This is analogous to the criminal context. If, as part of the social contract, I have a right to be safe in public, it is the state that has the duty of fulfilling this obligation; it is not a duty owed to me from my fellow citizen. Thus, it is the state that secures this right by punishing those who injure me. Accordingly, it is not the defendant that owes me the duty of safeguarding my reputation or privacy, any more than I owe her a duty to speak freely. It is the state that must decide whether her actions constitute an unlawful interference with that right or not. Once it has so decided, we can then speak sensibly of intra-party duties, but these relate to the obligation to compensate losses, not to safeguard rights. At all times, the coercive power to compel obedience lies with the state. It is a right/no-right scenario because either she has a right to free speech or I have a right to privacy/reputation. This feature, therefore, relates to the way we articulate the relationship between the parties in a free speech dispute. The state has the duty to protect the right; citizens have no such right against each other.

Individuality, then, in the conception and realisation of rights sits in tension with community – or, rather, the strict language of collective decision-making. The purpose of part three of this book, therefore, may be summarised in terms of justifying this premise. Specifically, it seeks to show that authentic free speech theory is to be understood either in the language of individuality or the language of community – but not both. If we choose individuality as our base unit, then we are committed to a world in

[16] ibid, 379.
[17] Kant (n 6) [6:315].
[18] ibid, [6:321].
[19] ibid, [6:319]–[6:320].

which individuals choose to co-operate for mutual benefit (whether material, spiritual, etc), but cannot be forced to (ie, to submit to communal interest over self-interest); or, we choose the world of communitarianism in which the pursuit of a common goal is predetermined, irrevocable and enforceable in spite of any conflict with, and denial of, individual rights.

As will be apparent from previous chapters, it strikes me that this stark choice goes, if not unnoticed then certainly unresolved, in the established literature on free speech. Worse, it seems, the literature speaks the language of individuality only superficially; that instead it pursues a communitarian agenda of essentially epistemic advance above all else. This tension reveals itself in the apparent commitment to content neutrality in juridical decision-making as against the underlying commitment to realising a kingdom of ends producing an optimal, ultimate epistemology, manifesting in something like the scientists of HG Wells' benevolent Dictatorship of the Air in *The Shape of Things To Come* that is more akin to Plato's Kallipolis (rule by the philosopher-king) in *Republic* than Marx's dictatorship of the proletariat.

Whereas epistemic advance, and all that it entails, is possible through the language of individuality, it cannot be guaranteed, for the prosaic, and depressing, reason that individuals, *qua* individuals, can reject it, living, instead, through decisions formed from superstition, instinct and myth. Thus – and perhaps this is the most significant feature of all – individuality is not an ideal – or, rather, no more of an ideal than communitarianism is. It is, in every sense, a problem. In defending a particular (rather than universal) conception of free speech, based on individuality, I argue for a specific understanding of individuality based on irrationality. Otherwise, if individuality stands for rationality, it would be communitarianism by another name.

This chapter therefore introduces the subject matter of part three (to demonstrate the incompatibility of individual with communal interpretations of free speech) and focuses, specifically, upon irrationality as the essential premise of individuality and, hence, authentic free speech principle. To demonstrate that – and that it is an idea derived from the radical thought of John Stuart Mill – two conceptions of freedom are compared: Hegel's and Mill's. By comparing Hegel's freedom-as-rationality with Mill's freedom-as-irrationality, I argue, in the final section, that, when individuality is the base unit, freedom of speech cannot be understood positively, in terms of its personal or social value, only negatively, in terms of (Kant's) noumenal self and its impact on the world. Thus, to regulate speech we must speak the language of harm, not value.[20] I leave, until the remaining chapters of this part of the book, the larger question of why the communitarian base unit is incompatible with the concept of free speech.

II. Hegelian Freedom

Lenin's additions to Marxist thought provides an important antithetical view of individuality. Following the October Revolution, the Central Committee, led by Lenin, decided that the two-stage process of realising the ideal communist state would, at its

[20] The harm principle is defended in ch 8.

first stage (the dictatorship of the proletariat), require all political decisions to be taken centrally. Yet, only Lenin could direct this critical operation because, unlike Marx, only he had devised the practical steps necessary to realise the Marxist ideal. Thus, dissent was not merely intolerable, but it imperilled Marx's triumph and compromised its actualisation. Dissenters within the Central Committee, therefore, had to be removed for the sake of the revolution. As Leszek Kołakowski says,

> in this way, by a natural progression, the dictatorship first exercised over society in the name of the working class, and then over the working class in the name of the party, was now applied to the party itself, creating the basis for a one-man tyranny.[21]

Under Stalin, of course, this tyranny assumed epic and terrifying proportions, and the withering away of the state, promised first by Engels and then Lenin, was indefinitely suspended. The death of individuality under this repressive regime is both well known and obvious. Again, as Kołakowski tells us:

> When the party is identified with the state and the apparatus of power, and when it achieves perfect unity in the shape of a one-man tyranny, doctrine becomes a matter of state and the tyrant is proclaimed infallible. Indeed, he really *is* infallible as far as the content of Marxism is concerned, for there is no Marxism but that which the party asserts in its capacity as the mouthpiece of the proletariat, and the party, having once achieved unity, expresses its will and its doctrine through the leadership embodied in the dictator's person.[22]

The communal goal is prioritised above all else, and those who do not subscribe to the communal goal, as it is given, are to be exiled or worse.[23] In this climate of absolute repression, Trotsky could say, with feeling, that individual rights were 'irrelevant nonsense':[24] 'The State, before disappearing, assumes the form of the dictatorship of the proletariat, ie, the most ruthless form of State, which embraces the life of the citizens authoritatively in every direction.'[25] This premonition was to have an ironic end for Trotsky: eventually, even he was wrong and had to be purged.

That this is a misrepresentation of Marx's thought is, again, both well known and obvious, for 'the 'dictatorship of the majority' was supposed to be exercised through a political organization imbued with a scientific understanding of history'.[26] Individuality was not anathema to Marxist thought – at least, not as Marx himself understood it, for he believed the tensions between individuality and community would be resolved, or otherwise dissipated, when the individual was free to put her individuality to use in socially useful ways.[27]

Nevertheless, freedom of expression under Soviet rule could but assume attenuated form. There could be no political dissent, for to dissent was to doubt the truth of

[21] L Kołakowski, *Main Currents of Marxism* [1978] (Norton, 2005) 747.
[22] ibid, 791.
[23] Memorably, Stalin's show trials were chillingly retold in A Koestler's novel, *Darkness at Noon* [1940] (Vintage Classics, 2020).
[24] Kołakowski (n 21) 764.
[25] ibid, 766.
[26] ibid, 757.
[27] ibid, 132–34.

the Marxist-Leninist ideal and so undermine the Soviet state. There could be no freedom of art, for what is art but the frivolous bauble of the bourgeoisie? There could be no literature but that which preserved the *status quo*. There could be science but only successful science, for unsuccessful science was anathema to historicism; it would mean that communism was not historical progress and that could not be correct.[28]

Both Hannah Arendt[29] and, notoriously, Karl Popper detected the origins of this totalitarianism in Hegelian thought (amongst others). Totalitarianism, in the spirit in which both Popper and Arendt meant it, is not the scenario in which community comes before self-interest, for otherwise all religious texts, certainly of the dominant and established kind, would be totalitarian. It is, instead, those circumstances in which the community is *made* to come first; where the national interest trumps not only personal interest but where the individual has no existence except as of an element – a living cog – of the state machine. Individuality is not purely self-interest, for the altruistic and the ascetic are both symbolic of individuality. Neither is individuality the descent into the Hobbesian nightmare of all against all. But when individuality is denied in the totalitarian state, so non-conformity assumes the appearance of an intolerable existential threat to community itself.

It should be said that for both Arendt and Popper (specifically), the attack on Hegel as an architect of twentieth-century totalitarianism, especially as it manifested in Stalinist Russia, is not to say, as some have argued,[30] that they thought Hegel, the man, championed fascism; the evidence, in his writings and lifestyle, suggests strongly that he (Hegel) did not.[31] Hegel is clear that all human beings have civil rights by virtue of their humanity, regardless of race or religion.[32] Instead, it is to say, as Allen Wood acknowledges, that Hegel 'presents a communitarian rather than an individualistic rationale for modern economic and political institutions and of the freedom they seek to actualize'.[33] For the notions of 'unity' (as a dialectical process), 'the scientific understanding of history' and the collision of individuality with community in the manifestation of socially useful production are all Hegelian ideas. Thus, although Popper polemicises unfairly when he dismisses Hegelianism as but the esoteric mysticism of alchemy by any other name,[34] still he is not wrong to conclude that, as a political theory, it signifies 'the state is everything, and the individual nothing; for he owes everything to the state, his physical as well as his spiritual existence'.[35]

[28] Vadim Birstein, a Soviet scientist, attests to this in VJ Birstein, *The Perversion of Knowledge* (Basic Books, 2001). He shows that continual Party and KGB interference both conflicted with and undermined the consistent claim that Soviet science was the envy of the world.

[29] H Arendt, *The Origins of Totalitarianism* [1951] (Penguin, 2017) 456.

[30] Stephen Houlgate expresses the point strongly, in his introduction to Hegel's *Outlines of the Philosophy of Right*: 'the relative obscurity in which Hegel's political philosophy still languishes is also due partly to the ill-informed but influential prejudice of philosophers such as Karl Popper' GWF Hegel, *Outlines of the Philosophy of Right* (TM Knox, trans) (Oxford University Press, 2008) vii. As will become apparent, I think Houlgate is too critical of Popper and too generous toward Hegel, but he is not alone in attacking Popper.

[31] A point that Houlgate also makes firmly: ibid.

[32] GWF Hegel, *Elements of the Philosophy of Right* (AW Wood, ed, HB Nisbet, trans) [1821] (Cambridge University Press, 2017) §§209 and 270R.

[33] AW Wood, 'Editor's Introduction' in ibid, xxviii.

[34] K Popper, *The Open Society and Its Enemies, vol 2: Hegel & Marx* (Routledge, 2003) 30–33.

[35] ibid, 34–35.

Yet, in taking the quick steps that he does, Popper does disservice both to the complexity of Hegelian thought and to the fate of individuality within it. For, despite Popper's hyperbole, Hegel, like Marx, insists that individuality *survives* the prioritisation of the communitarian ideal in an interesting and meaningful sense. Given that this is the self-same belief we see in modern thought, with the fusion of communitarian ideal and individual free speech right, it is worth scrutinising Hegelian thought in much more detail than Popper was prepared to do, to show why Popper is both right (*and* wrong) in important ways.

To describe Hegelian thought, in short order, as a coherent scheme with specific meaning must be a conscious misrepresentation of his work, for Hegel is neither concise nor consistent nor clear in his meanings. Moreover, as a visionary of the first order, comparable only to Plato, Kant (who preceded him) and Arthur Schopenhauer (who followed),[36] his meaning can be discerned only by reference to the grand, overarching scheme animating his entire work, for Hegel, like those others, is a system-builder. Therefore, his political theory must be posited in that system, in which everything – from the life of the mind to the universe, from religion to the progress of history, and from the nature of God to the legitimacy of the state – is connected and infused with purpose. That purpose is represented by the word *Geist*, in all its subtle forms, and its progress through dialectical movements (ie, that unity which results from sublation, typically represented, crudely, as thesis combined with antithesis forming synthesis and hence new theses in search of antitheses).[37] All is unified and all is working toward unification of its bifurcated representations. The dialectical is an inexorable progression toward a singularity in which not only the dichotomy of objectivity and subjectivity collapses but so too the barriers between the phenomenal and the noumenal. Only through this movement, does absolute knowledge arise:

> The *goal*, Absolute Knowing, or Spirit that knows itself as Spirit, has for its path the recollection of the Spirits as they are in themselves and as they accomplish the organization of their realm … the two together [History and the Science of Knowing], comprehended History, form alike the inwardizing and the Calvary of absolute Spirit, the actuality, truth, and certainty of his throne, without which he [God] would be lifeless and alone.[38]

To see the Hegelian treatment of individuality as an attack that undermines any sensible understanding of the term, we must begin with this understanding of mind or spirit (*Geist*), from which his sense of freedom stems. The mind seeks to understand both itself and the world around it. If all problems have solutions, and all questions have answers, then there comes a point when there is nothing mysterious left in the world. The mind, through reason, has conquered all as a continual progression of dialectical movements. Choice must disappear in this final analysis. There is nothing left to choose because there is nothing left to discover. All is solved. Individuality, at this point,

[36] Albeit Schopenhauer thought Hegel to be a 'flat-headed, insipid, nauseating, illiterate charlatan, who reached the pinnacle of audacity in scribbling together and dishing up the craziest mystifying nonsense': ibid, 36.

[37] Hegel sets out his meaning of the dialectical, as it relates to the discussion, in *Elements of the Philosophy of Right* (n 32) § 31.

[38] GWF Hegel, *Phenomenology of Spirit* (JN Findlay, ed, AV Miller, trans) [1807] (Oxford University Press, 1977) §808, but see §788–808.

collapses in upon itself. It is not only pointless; it is subversive and destructive, for it would deny the absolute truth, which now comes from the collapse of the noumenal (God) into the phenomenal (the apprehension or perception of experience).

This progression is confusing if limited to finite experience for the individual cannot achieve absolute knowledge, for this absolute knowledge is obtainable if not by the infinite being (or God), then by a mind that could exist longer than the individual body can survive. Artificial intelligence points in this direction, for our (collective) epistemological advances may yet create the sort of immense super-computer powerful enough to digest all knowledge and so understand God in terms that Kant denied but Hegel promised. Yet whether this mind – this *Geist* – could ever communicate this absolute knowledge to humankind is also surely doubtful for, it follows, the mind is incapable of digesting it, even if the initial (time-consuming) processing has been completed for it. It would be the language of the lion, in the sense that Wittgenstein gives us.[39] The mind could repeat but it could not comprehend; it could not know, it could only trust. It would be, to paraphrase Douglas Adams, to find that the answer to the meaning of life is 42. Moreover, we would be returned to our original state, of the phenomenal world and the noumenal other, but with a new godhead (AI) to replace the old (the Divine) and yet still in our state of individual ignorance and, ultimately, bounded capacity for knowledge.

These essential difficulties persist, I maintain, when we examine Hegel's political theory, given to us in the *Elements of the Philosophy of Right*.[40] Like Kant, Hegel locates 'right' in 'freedom' via the 'will':[41] 'Will without freedom is an empty word, just as freedom is actual only as will or as subject.'[42] The will is, thus, '*individuality* [*Einzelheit*], the *self-determination* of the "I".'[43] Yet the will is not mere subjectivity. It begins as such but must progress, through its meeting of objective, to the third moment, ie, unity between the two concepts.[44] This unity is rationality[45] (for 'what is rational is actual and what is actual is rational'):[46] 'A will which resolves on nothing is not an actual will; the characterless man can never resolve on anything.'[47] Freedom as impulsiveness – as '*being able to do as one pleases*' – is immature;[48] it is 'a delusion' to think that this is true freedom.[49] It cannot be for the simple reason that it (the mind driving the will) lacks rationality:

> When I will what is rational, I act not as a particular [*partikulares*] individual, but in accordance with the concepts of ethics in general: in an ethical act, I vindicate not myself but the thing [*die Sache*]. But a person who does something perverse gives the greatest prominence to his particularity [*Partikularität*]. The rational is the high road which everyone follows and no one stands out from the rest.[50]

[39] L Wittgenstein, *Philosophical Investigations* (GEM Anscombe, trans) (Basil Blackwell, 1958) 225.
[40] Hegel (n 32).
[41] ibid, §4.
[42] ibid, §4R.
[43] ibid, §7.
[44] ibid, §§7–9.
[45] ibid, §§10–13.
[46] ibid, Preface, 20.
[47] ibid, §13R.
[48] ibid, §15.
[49] ibid.
[50] ibid, §15R.

Freedom as mere choice is an inadequate explanation, for Hegel, not least because the individual's apparent decision to choose may be motivated by unconscious or subliminal factors that have not been properly accounted for in her decision. Arbitrariness is freedom of a literal, but only superficial kind:

> If we stop our enquiry at arbitrariness, at the human being's ability to will this or that, this does indeed constitute his freedom; but if we bear firmly in mind that the content of what he wills is a given one, it follows that he is determined by it and is in this very respect no longer free.[51]

However, free will is to be realised through the perfection of the will, from instinct to (emotional) intelligence,[52] a state of nature to a civilised state,[53] from evil to good through Christ.[54] Thus, the will aims to the 'universal' and achieves it when 'all limitation and particular individuality [*Einzelheit*] are superseded within it';[55] 'the universal which has being in and for itself is in general what is called the *rational*'.[56] Accordingly, the '*free will which wills the free will*' is the subjective or individual spirit which seeks to 'make its freedom into its object' and so actualise the objective or general will to live rationally.[57]

The foregoing discussion has dwelt on Hegel's sense of the free will at some length to illustrate the complexity (and verbosity) of his scheme and to demonstrate the recurrent theme of the will as a dialectical movement, in which the subjectivity of arbitrariness or immaturity combines with the objectivity of rationality or higher purpose. To be sure, even for Hegel, the will *can* be understood as arbitrariness, but only in its first moment. This manifests in the sublation of subjectivity into objectivity or, when transposed to the political, of individuality into community. Subjectivity and individuality are both still visible, says Hegel, through this sublation,[58] but the extent of that visibility and the meaningfulness of an independent conception, I would suggest, is highly doubtful. The problem, to my mind, is that whereas Kant insists on neat separation between ethical and juridical lawgiving, Hegel, in the spirit of dialectical progression, folds them together.

These points must serve as the critical lens by which to examine Hegel's claim that the 'right is something *utterly sacred*, for the simple reason that it is the existence [*Dasein*] of the absolute concept, of self-conscious freedom'.[59] For freedom is not the apparent (or empty) concept we find in Kant's political theory, it is a contingency that hangs on this deeper ethical understanding of the will. Thus, right itself is contingent.[60] The state has such significance in Hegel's system because it is freedom made manifest and so represents the accumulated progression through the dialectical movements (as given to us by history) of the state of nature, the tyranny of the family, and the end of

[51] ibid.
[52] ibid, §21.
[53] ibid, §§18–20.
[54] ibid, §18.
[55] ibid, §24.
[56] ibid, §24R.
[57] ibid, §27.
[58] ibid, §28.
[59] ibid, §30.
[60] Only the 'right of the world spirit is absolute', says Hegel (ibid) §30R.

civic society. Yet, at the third moment of the dialectical progression, the state is the superior manifestation of freedom because it is the subjective and objective unified (thus, says Hegel, the 'states of classical antiquity' could not qualify because they recognised only 'universality' and no 'particularity' – ie, they recognised no such thing as individuality).[61] Hence, Hegel can say 'the state is the actuality of the substantial *will*, an actuality which it possesses in the particular *self-consciousness* when this has been raised to its universality; as such, it is the *rational* in and for itself'.[62]

As a result, freedom, in the Hegelian sense, is achieved through reconciliation of the individual mind, and its place in the world, with the general will through obedience to the absolute or infinite wisdom as it manifests in the idealised state. This combination, of the *Einzelheit* or individuality of the subjective with the universality of all in a state of civilised society, manifests as rationality, which is a key concept in Hegelian freedom. Hegel defines his understanding of rationality in the following terms:

> Considered in the abstract, rationality consists in general in the unity and interpenetration of universality and individuality. Here, in a concrete sense and in terms of its content, it consists in the unity of objective freedom (ie, of the universal substantial will) and subjective freedom (as the freedom of individual knowledge and of the will in its pursuit of particular ends). And in terms of its form, it therefore consists in self-determining action in accordance with laws and principles based on *thought* and hence *universal*.[63]

It is only when the individual mind ceases its resistance to the general will that it achieves peace and, hence, freedom. This general will is not simply despotism or, even, acquiescence to majoritarian rule[64] (as Mill would have it, the tyranny of the majority), but rather that which is given by the end of history or, what Hegel calls the will of historical or universal reason (ie, when subjectivity and objectively achieve unity).[65] At this point, the subjective will (ie, individuality) and universal reason (as it manifests in the political and legal institutions of the state) coincide such that there is no longer any inner conflict between the senses of freedom and reason and, thus, no external conflict either. Individuality loses itself to collective humanity when individual contribution to reason ends, such as when maximal knowledge is both achieved and beyond individual understanding. At this point, the individual can reason only that the superior entity – the infinite state – has achieved its end.[66]

Let us consider some concrete examples to show the difficulties inherent in Hegel's system as a means of protecting individuality. As we have seen, individuality is not mere caprice or impulsiveness. It is the urge to be independent of external influence; the oneness between mind and action despite external influence. What does this look like? Imagine my employer warns me that to speak out against trans-exclusionary radical feminism (TERF) is a disciplinary offence, for it is, they say, a brand of misogyny or else, at the very least, may upset colleagues who, unbeknownst to me, may be TERFs themselves or are otherwise supportive of that movement. My employer fears that my

[61] ibid, §260R.
[62] ibid, §258.
[63] ibid, §258R.
[64] ibid, §§261 and 261R.
[65] ibid, §260.
[66] ibid, §§259 and 259R.

outburst will chill their (the TERFs') freedom of speech (perhaps, even, their freedom of thought). Or, imagine, my employer imposes restrictions on my ability to criticise the human rights records of certain international regimes because the university depends on income (as student fees) from them. Or, let us say that I am instructed not to broadcast my experience of bullying in the university hierarchy because, I am told, it damages my employer's external reputation as a place of harmonious industrial relations. So, disobediently, I use social media to show my support for the trans community as an ally; I sign open letters condemning the human rights record of those countries; and I signal the toxic managerial practices of my university to the wider world. I do so despite the external influence because I am driven by an immanent sense of the right and the good.

Am I exercising my Hegelian freedom? Certainly, my actions satisfy that initial sense of the free will as the impulse to resist external factors. Yet, my actions are arbitrary rather than rational. Generally speaking, notions of rationality resonate, ultimately, with ideals of self-preservation – that is, preservation of the human race, and preservation of the self within that race. Self-appointed goals that enhance one's chances of optimal self-preservation, that is phenomenal existence for as long as possible, register highly on the scale. Thus, healthy living, dedication to career goals and successful parenting are all emblems of rationality. If we achieve material success at work, we shall be able to care for ourselves for as long as possible. If we maintain a healthy lifestyle, we maximise our chances of a long life. If we succeed in parenting, we shall have someone to care for us in our dotage, and ensure our lineage/heritage continues after we die. Self-destruction, though it lost the theological label of 'sinfulness', still retained that communal sense of undesirability, post-Enlightenment, by being called irrational.

My actions, therefore, are irrational, whether we label them 'impulsive' (because, they objective observer will say I have not thought them through) or 'principled' (because I have, and *still* choose to act on my instincts). Why irrational? Because I have mouths to feed (including my own). I have children, whose happiness and security depend upon my income to help sustain them in our mortgaged home, to pay the bills, to provide food. I jeopardise their happiness and security by angering my employer and risking dismissal. I can obtain alternative employment, of course, but my options are limited by a specialised skill-set that is not easily transferrable to another sector offering comparable pay. Accordingly, my choice would be to accept lesser paid employment or else seek academic employment at a university located elsewhere, which not only diminishes my disposable income but also represents lost opportunity to spend time with my children and to be a good father as I waste additional travel time getting to and from my new employer's location. And, in the final analysis, what good do my actions do? It matters not one jot to the collective happiness of the trans community, the international community, or to improving my bullied colleague's lot if I keep quiet or speak out, for, putting rampant egotism aside, what difference can I possibly make? My actions, therefore, constitute a grave risk to my immediate community (family life) in pursuit of contributing a highly minimal or contingent good to the larger community (civic society). This is pure irrationality that cannot possibly count as freedom in Hegel's ultimate sense. And yet I would choose to make that same choice (of speaking out) every single time.

Perhaps this is mere eccentricity on my part, but then what was rational about Sir Thomas More's decision to defy his King, to risk death, for his religious beliefs? His belief could have survived, untouched, if he had but recanted. The King could not disturb his inner life, only the phenomenal manifestations of the external, so why did he choose to die than compromise if he was rational? What was rational about Galileo's decision to provoke the Catholic Church, after it had lambasted his work as foolish, by repeating his views in the *Dialogue Concerning the Two Chief World Systems*, and attacking Pope Urban VIII too? He was forced to recant and was held under house arrest – if he had but recanted earlier, he could have avoided this. If he had not angered the church, he could have pursued a much fuller and richer existence than he did. What was rational about defying the will of Nazi Germany? Martin Heidegger survived by acquiescing; Sophie Scholl died because she would not. Heidegger lived to be 86; Scholl was dead before she was 22. What was rational about Martin Luther King's decision to lead the Civil Rights Movement and, in the process, anger bigoted white Americans? They killed him for it. What is rational about agitating for change or defending the rights of others (or even oneself) against known and hostile resistance? English MP Jo Cox defended the immigrant's humanity; she was murdered for it. Peter Tatchell defends gay rights vociferously, for which he has been beaten and castigated; still, he continues.

From the schoolground to the workplace, from pop culture to mass media, conformity is presented as the rational choice. Phrases like 'pick your battles' and 'don't make waves' abound. We are inculcated into a way of life that encourages 'normalcy' and discourages 'eccentricity'. It is only when non-conformity is successful, and meaningful changes follows, that it is celebrated – but this is done by *normalising* it, thus robbing it of its essential meaning. Pride marches and Black History Month, for example, remain important institutions of themselves because they challenge this process of normalisation and so remind us of the struggle with normalcy without which non-conformity could not have gained acceptance (as well as reminding us of the precarious nature of 'acceptance' and the constant challenges faced to be accepted).

Hegel is clear that the idealised state is not a despotic state. The unity of subjectivity and objectivity is not achieved if its members are compelled to identify with it through fear, deception or ideology.[67] As Wood puts it, 'freedom is actual … only in a rational society whose institutions can be felt and known as rational by individuals who are "with themselves" in those institutions'.[68] Nevertheless, in the spirit of the dialectical, freedom comes with responsibility, and rights with duties. As Wood also recognises, the Hegelian state is harmonious but highly regimented. Individual self-interest must be balanced with collective good: this is the path to freedom – of individuality, rationally construed, combined with the duty to serve the community: 'the only real guarantee of freedom is a well-constituted ethical life, which integrates the rights of persons and subjects into an organic system of customs and institutions providing individuals with concretely fulfilling lives'.[69] In this environment, the

> more serious threat to freedom … is what [Hegel] calls the 'principle of atomicity', the tendency in modern life for individuals to be only abstract persons and subjects, *who fail to actualize their personality and subjectivity in a fulfilling social context*.[70]

[67] ibid, §§268 and 268R.
[68] Wood (n 33) xii.
[69] ibid, xvi.
[70] ibid, xvii.

Accordingly, 'if people insist too stubbornly on their rights or withdraw too far into their subjectivity, Hegel believes that they become alienated from the common social life, without which nothing they do has any significance for them'.[71] Did More or Galileo do this when they insisted on their interpretation of the world? Or King and Scholl? Or Cox and Tatchell?

To be sure, Hegel could not agree that the slaughter of dissidents is justifiable; it remains 'evil'.[72] Nevertheless, the sense of 'choice' in leading a life of one's choosing, in the Hegelian system, is heavily constrained by: a) rationality (as Wood says, and as we have seen, 'freedom is possible to the extent that we act rationally');[73] b) duty (to family life, to civic society, and to the state, which Hegel labels as the constituent parts of the ethical life or *Sittlichkeit*, ie, 'the duty to support [oneself] through labour which benefits the whole');[74] c) patriotism (which, as Wood says, he defines as 'a habit of leading one's normal life and doing one's ethical duty, while taking the state as one's "substantial basis and end"');[75] d) the priority of public good over self-interest ('We cannot be free … unless we successfully pursue ends larger than our private good, indeed larger than anyone's private good'[76] since the state has 'the highest right in relation to individuals, whose *highest duty* is to be members of the state');[77] and e) the rejection of experimental ways of living (as Wood says 'he thinks [our] choices must be between recognized ways of life, systematically integrated into the organic system of modern ethical life; the various ways of life should be known to provide dignity and fulfilment to those who lead them').[78] Accordingly, it can be seen why we can say, with Marina Bykova, that 'freedom for Hegel is not a momentary act; it is a long and complex practical achievement, taking shape in and through human activity over historical time'.[79]

What, then, can we say about freedom of speech in a Hegelian system? If we return to my example, of being disciplined for my outspokenness in respect of trans rights, of human rights abuses in the international community, and of bullying in the workplace, can we say that this coercive action amounts to an interference with my freedom of speech? I argued above that although this represented a manifestation of my internal will, free from the influence of external expectation, which would satisfy the Hegelian sense of freedom distinct from arbitrariness, still the irrationality or irresponsibility of my actions (to the family life and to the immediate civil society of my colleagues) would discount it as an expression or manifestation of freedom. Disciplinary action leading to dismissal would represent alienation from the *Sittlichkeit*, but my irrationality would be the material cause of that. I could, then, have no reason to complain since I was the victim only of my own incorrigibility.

[71] ibid, xvii.
[72] Hegel (n 32) §140R.
[73] Wood (n 33) xii.
[74] ibid, xix.
[75] ibid, xxv.
[76] ibid, xxiv.
[77] Hegel (n 32) §258.
[78] Wood (n 33) xx.
[79] MF Bykova, 'Will and Freedom' in A De Laurentiis and J Edwards, *The Bloomsbury Companion to Hegel* (Bloomsbury, 2013) 269.

Am I unfair to Hegel? Am I engaging in the sort of 'shockingly superficial and selective'[80] treatment of Hegel that, Houlgate says, Popper indulged in? Perhaps. Yet, as Wood states, 'the element of truth' in the liberal critique of Hegel as an enemy of human rights lies in the fact that 'Hegel thinks personal right, apart from a developed system of ethical life, is an empty abstraction'.[81] As we have seen, Hegel has no fondness for a return to antiquity, in which individuality had no meaning let alone no identity in the communitarianism of the state. Clearly, he believes, as modern free speech scholarship seems to, that, when properly done, the synthesis of individuality with community will retain a sense of individuality in a meaningful way. Yet, in the final analysis, what assurance does that give us? The imposition of communal goals on individual enterprise is bound to compromise the sense of freedom that individualism gives us precisely because the Hegelian world is so regimented that unproductive, speculative, and contingent manifestations of individuality are but alienation and waste.

Moreover, at an atomistic level, the demand for rationality radically alters the meaning of 'choice' and of 'choosing', both in terms of immediate decision-making and the technique practised by the individual in doing so. For, to select, according to the Hegelian schemata, is to discern the rational from the irrational, and then, once that group has been discarded, the more rational from the less, and so on. In this way, when presented with choice, the Hegelian is not choosing as such; she is identifying the authentic outcome (maximal rationality) from imposters (irrationality and inferior rationality). This, then, is not choice as preference, for the sense of competition is entirely illusory.

Likewise, if my freedom must be reconciled with your freedom, so that your right is my duty, etc, then decisions of choice become a numbers game of a crudely utilitarian kind. If the exercise of my freedom would benefit less of those in my immediate *Sittlichkeit* than it would burden, then I can have no freedom to choose that outcome even if my irrationality sensibility (my desire) tells me that that is what I want most. This is why, it seems to me, Hegel's faith in individuality's survival in the dialectical process is either misplaced or disingenuous for how can individuality (my *Einzelheit*) survive if idiosyncrasy and other such immature understandings are tolerable but inessential in the final form of the state, in which general will and universal will agree on freedom's meaning?

There is an inescapable group dynamic to Hegel's system of freedom which cannot condone *ir*rationality. The sublation of the individual into the community is to recognise community as not only a collection of individuals, but of *like-minded* individuals, for whom freedom is a reconciliation of subjectivity within a common enterprise (of objectivity). This is not the totalitarian eradication of diversity necessarily, but it is an eradication nevertheless. In other words, it is eradication by necessity. In this system, full realisation of the self's potentiality is an obligation; it is also an obligation in the Kantian system. Yet, in a Kantian system, this obligation can be contained within ethical lawgiving, whereas in a Hegelian system, that distinction is much harder to

[80] Houlgate (n 30) vii.
[81] Wood (n 33) xvi.

preserve – at least, to my mind. For, in the Hegelian system, the ethical collapses back into the juridical, either by means of dialectical progression, or by virtue of rationality's appeal to ethical lawgiving (which may amount to the same thing).

Einzelheit could manifest as dereliction (of the duties given by the *Sittlichkeit*), as willed destitution, as extreme introversion, as servility, as sloth, as wasted talent, as scepticism, as wilful ignorance, as contempt, but not as Hegelian freedom. This freedom cannot be the freedom to *escape* or shirk responsibility. It cannot be the freedom to be *ir*responsible. Neither can it be the freedom to be *ir*rational. This greater sense of freedom is that which we find in Mill. For Mill, freedom from responsibility was *not* freedom from consequence nor freedom from liability. It is this larger sense of freedom, as Mill had it, that we shall now scrutinise since, I shall argue, it is this Millian sense of freedom that authentic free speech theory should embrace.

III. Millian Freedom

Inspired by Mill's own brush with ignominy (resulting from his controversial relationship with Mrs Harriet Taylor,[82] his sustained advocacy against the subjugation of women,[83] his aversion to the despotism of empire[84] and his support of universal education),[85] *On Liberty* is a monument to irrationality as the symbol of individuality. For a book so well known, and so well referenced, its low reputation in the established literature is surprising. For *On Liberty* is taken to be a sort of consequentialist treatment that justifies the state's guarantee of free speech only for its demonstrable contribution to epistemology. Typically, it is dismissed in short order: 'Pollyannaish', says Lee Bollinger;[86] the haughty pretensions of 'the seminar room', says Alan Haworth;[87] 'paradoxical', says Rawls;[88] unduly 'optimistic', says Bernard Williams;[89] '[in]accurately portrays reality', says Frederick Schauer;[90] 'carefully disguised intolerance'

[82] Harriet Taylor was a married woman that Mill maintained a close relationship with, of the type that Victorian England frowned upon, and for which he was ostracised. After her husband's death, they became a couple, only serving to confirm earlier suspicions amongst the gossips. See, eg, MS Packe, *The Life of John Stuart Mill* (Martin Secker & Warburg, 1954) 129–52; G Himmelfarb, *On Liberty and Liberalism* (Alfred A Knopf, 1974) 187–279; N Capaldi, *John Stuart Mill: A Biography* (Cambridge University Press, 2004) 227–32; R Reeves, *John Stuart Mill: Victorian Firebrand* (Atlantic Books, 2007) 238–61.

[83] JS Mill, 'The Subjection of Women' in *Collected Works of John Stuart Mill*, vol XXI (JM Robson, ed) (University of Toronto Press, 1984). Mill was castigated, mocked and vilified for these views – and roundly ignored by Parliament in the process. See Reeves (ibid) 413–48.

[84] This manifests throughout his work, but notable examples include his abject rage against the overt racism of Governor Edward John Eyre, for his brutal suppression of a riot in Jamaica, in which Mill doggedly pursued the death penalty (see Packe (n 82) 470); and his concern about the treatment of the Irish, see, eg, 'What Is to be Done with Ireland?' in *Collected Works of John Stuart Mill*, vol VI (JM Robson, ed) (University of Toronto Press, 1982).

[85] See Reeves (n 82) 413–48.

[86] LC Bollinger, *The Tolerant Society* (Oxford University Press, 1986) 74.

[87] A Haworth, *Free Speech* (Routledge, 1998) 27, 38, 53, 63, 66, 142–43, 208.

[88] J Rawls, *Justice as Fairness: A Restatement* (Harvard University Press, 2001) 34.

[89] B Williams, *Truth and Truthfulness* (Princeton University Press, 2002) 212.

[90] F Schauer, *Free Speech: A Philosophical Enquiry* (Cambridge University Press, 1982) 25.

and 'a peculiarly exclusive, peculiarly insinuating moral doctrine', says Maurice Cowling;[91] etc.

To my mind, the only peculiarity about Mill is that he should be so profoundly misunderstood by some of the greatest minds of the twentieth century (Cowling excepted). For, when it comes to Mill, there is a kind of mass delusion at work that would have us believe that Mill is but an imitation of Milton. Nothing could be further from the truth, for Mill is *not* espousing the sort of romantic fiction that Milton did when he said, in the *Areopagitica*, that truth would always win in a fair fight with falsehood. He dismisses this idea, explicitly, as 'a piece of idle sentimentality … Men are not more zealous for truth than they often are for error'.[92] I shall not rehearse what I have said elsewhere about this, except to say, emphatically, that there is no causality in Mill's complex position on truth of the sort that commentators continue to ascribe to him.[93]

Instead, *On Liberty* represents two related but separate (or, rather, separable) arguments to advance one solitary proposition or, as he puts it, 'one very simple principle',[94] which, by distinguishing self-regarding actions (that which affects only the self) from other-regarding actions (that which affects the interests of others), says, in effect, that harm to others is the sole (but not sufficient) justification the state can have in interfering with one's actions; when a person acts only in terms that affect themself, that person has absolute dominion.[95] Accordingly, the strength, and focus, of *On Liberty*, is in defending this absoluteness even when it amounts to irrationality. It says more than this, of course, but not with the same intensity.

Its first premise, in support of irrationality, is, in Kant's language, a hypothetical imperative (ie, a conditional proposition). It speaks to the realisation of human potentiality as a thinking entity, capable of deploying her critical faculties to good effect. This argument is the source of the confusion concerning Mill for, aping Mill's own claim about the emergence of 'dead dogma' from rote learning without critical engagement,[96] too much attention is given to the specifics of his argument concerning the role of fallibility in epistemological advance without recognition of its context. For Mill's argument against state determinations of truth is not an absolute prohibition on the state pronouncing upon the truth of things.[97] It is an argument *against* the deployment of the state's coercive apparatus (imprisonment, fines, legal liability, etc) when things are said that the state finds to be wrong.[98] This hypothetical argument is simply this: if we (the state; civic society) want citizens to realise themselves as critical thinkers in their best possible form, then the use of coercive measures to do so is self-defeating for it leads, inevitably, to the dead dogma scenario: citizens will have information but not

[91] M Cowling, *Mill and Liberalism* (Cambridge University Press, 1963).

[92] JS Mill, *On Liberty* in *Collected Works of John Stuart Mill*, vol XVIII (JM Robson, ed) (University of Toronto Press, 1977) 238.

[93] See, eg, P Wragg, *A Free and Regulated Press: Defending Coercive Independent Press Regulation* (Hart, 2020) 136–45.

[94] Mill (n 92) 223.

[95] ibid, 223–24.

[96] ibid, 243.

[97] ibid, 229–32.

[98] ibid.

knowledge; they will be capable of repetition but not understanding. To assume something is true because it comes from an authority is 'not knowing the truth. Truth, thus held, is but one superstition the more, accidentally clinging to the words which enunciate a truth'.[99] Moreover, 'he who does anything because it is the custom, makes no choice … gains no practice' and, hence, does not improve her mental faculties which, 'like the muscular powers, are improved only by being used'.[100]

The reason for Mill's hypothetical imperative becomes apparent in the (much neglected) latter part of *On Liberty*, in which we see, especially in Chapter V, that his argument is really about the limits of state action as it relates to intellectual improvement of the masses, not only for the purposes of universal franchise, but also for realising a profitable economy.[101] His point, which, again, has its roots in irrationality, is that whereas the state has duties to educate children – duties that mirror, and so embody, the duties of parents to care for a child's intellectual as well as physical needs – those duties end (abruptly) when the child achieves majority. This, then, is an argument of its time, which had to be grappled with in an era in which children were thought, literally, an extension or manifestation of the father, who served the household, through the patriarchy, first and foremost. To remove a child against not only her will but also the family's in service of an education was, to many households, financially detrimental, for it deprived that child of earning household income through farming, mining and other child labour schemes.

Hence, Mill's lifelong belief that enhancement of the faculties, from an early age, held the key to developing both the earning potential and opportunity for greater happiness that a greater range of employment opportunities would surely bring, which would benefit the individual, directly, and society at large, indirectly. As if responding directly to Hegel, Mill says

> where, not the person's own character, but the traditions or customs of other people are the rule of conduct, there is wanting one of the principal ingredients of human happiness, and quite the chief ingredient of individual and social progress.[102]

Yet, whereas the newly minted adult might be encouraged to pursue further intellectual development, and would be incentivised to do so where lucrative employment demanded higher qualifications, she could not be *forced* to, by the state or society. Since adults cannot be forced to enhance (or even maintain) their critical faculties, they must have a right to use those powers as they see fit (except to the extent that that usage is other regarding, in which case the harm principle – qualified as it is – comes into effect).

The contingency apparent in the hypothetical imperative is at its clearest when Mill discusses enhancement of the critical faculties. Only the moral agent can choose for herself not only whether but also how she will develop her own critical faculties.[103] Here we see shades of the Kantian thought that Mill was most attracted to – that, in terms of

[99] ibid, 244.
[100] ibid, 262.
[101] This paragraph relies on those passages contained in ibid, 301–05.
[102] ibid, 262.
[103] ibid.

noumena, the only thing-in-itself that a person can know for sure is her own mind.[104] For anyone else, the experience of her mind is of a phenomenal kind, ie, the physical or sensual manifestations of her thought, as they appear in her actions and speech. Since, as an adult, she will become the product of nurture, not nature, her intellectual development is contingent to the fact of having critical faculties. But once she does, and it can be assumed she does, she attains absolute sovereignty over her life choices and goals. For the state, or anyone else, is singularly unable to determine, for her, what would amount to a positive development of her faculties.[105] Of course, others (the state included) might *think* it knows how best to improve her (by, for example, close scrutiny of her phenomenal life), it cannot know for sure because it cannot know her mind: the noumenal thing-in-itself. Thus, we see in Mill the natural progression of Kant (which we do not find in Hegel): that life is, and *must be*, an experiment in which the moral agent is the conductor, even when responding to events beyond her control.[106] No one can live her life for her, for no one can enjoy or suffer its consequences as she does.

In determining her life choices, there is, of course, some similarity here with Hegel, in that both writers imagined civic society as a productive means of generating the 'options' inherent in individuality – the different ways of living – which prove valuable to the moral agent's sense of choice. Both thought that the state should have no direct control over how these options manifested, nor that the state should be capable of selecting which type of living or lifestyle should be understood as more valuable or good than any other. The difference, with Hegel, as we have seen, is that he thought these choices were limited to those that are 'rational'. This constrains the *Sittlichkeit* to established ways of living and so precludes the experimental method that Mill's irrationality principle firmly endorses.

However, the hypothetical imperative is but one aspect of Millian thought. The second premise – which, since it informs the first, I regard as the major one – is a categorical imperative (ie, an unconditional proposition), binding on the state as a

[104] Mill's appreciation of Kantian thought appears throughout his work and differs, dramatically, from his father's view. He thought Kant (and those who followed) spoke 'dogmatically, and convey[ed] no clear ideas': J Mill, *Jurisprudence* (J Innes, 1825) 4–5. In 'Utilitarianism,' Mill calls Kant 'a remarkable man, whose system of thought will long remain one of the landmarks in the history of philosophical speculation': *Collected Works of John Stuart Mill*, vol X (JM Robson, ed) (University of Toronto Press, 1969) 207. He relies on Kant's noumenal/phenomenal dichotomy in his 'A System of Logic' (*Collected Works of John Stuart Mill*, vol VII (JM Robson, ed) (University of Toronto Press, 1973) 59), and in 'An Examination of Sir William Hamilton's Philosophy' in *Collected Works of John Stuart Mill*, vol IX (JM Robson, ed) (University of Toronto Press, 1979). *cf* FEL Priestley's criticisms of Mill's understanding of Kantian thought in 'Introduction' in *Collected Works of John Stuart Mill*, vol X (ibid) xxx: 'one feels that his comprehension is so faulty as to suggest that he has not taken the metaphysical and epistemological parts … very seriously'. Certainly, by his own admission, Mill did not think himself expert in either Kant or Hegel, for that matter, confiding to Auguste Comte on 13 March 1843 that he knew nothing of either (see *Collected Works of John Stuart Mill*, vol XIII (FE Mineka, ed) (University of Toronto Press, 1963) 576). Whether this was false modesty or not is a matter of opinion, but in an April 1829 letter to Thomas Wirgman, he speaks of having read Wirgman's *Account of the Philosophy of Kant* and of finding it to be an excellent summary. In the same letter he also endorses the Kantian system, which he hopes will become better known through Wirgman's work (Letter 24, *Collected Works of John Stuart Mill*, vol XVII (FE Mineka, ed) (University of Toronto Press, 1969).

[105] Mill(n 92) 269.

[106] ibid, 260–62.

juridical obligation, and on society (that tyrannous majority)[107] as an ethical one. It is, as I have indicated, that the realm of individuality extends beyond simply rationality to encompass the irrational as well. This categorical imperative does not lend itself to neat classifications like 'intrinsic' or 'instrumental', for whether we recognise this right as one given to each by reason of her 'noumenality' (ie, as a being-in-itself) as Kant, Hegel and modern-day scholars would,[108] or whether we recognise it as a species of contingent good, as Mill hints at (that her irrationality is a necessary and indivisible part of her capacity for self-improvement), but others are more committed to,[109] we miss the point. For Mill's recognition of irrationality is a profound statement about the human condition. It recognises the immanent uncertainty of being; that life is fragile, temporar and unpredictable. The noumenal self exists as a precarious thing, which can no more assert that its next decision will not be its last than it can predict the moment of its own ending.

Central to Millian freedom, then, is an absolute rejection of externally imposed efficiencies to optimise the lived experience of each (the individual) and all (civic society; the state). Knowledge is a product of experience, discussion and the critical faculties that can critically analyse both types of phenomena. Given that experience (of life and discussion) is bounded, so too is rationality. 'There are many truths of which the full meaning *cannot* be realized, until personal experience has brought it home';[110] and, as we have seen above, that the intellectual faculties are a 'muscle' like any other, in need of exercising if they are to be honed. This aspect of Millian thought is often neglected, for which Mill himself is to blame. For, unlike Kant and Hegel, his is not the haughty language of German idealism or realism. It is plain speaking which is easily (and often) dismissed as simple;[111] and yet it is as rich and complex of anything that, if not Kant then certainly, Hegel ever produced. For Mill was not the stuffy academic of Haworth's and Cowling's imagining; he was the radical 'firebrand' that Richard Reeves clearly perceives.[112] Nevertheless, if we read *On Liberty* closely, we see that the noumenal self cannot be subjected to externally given programmatic optimalisation: 'human nature is not a machine to be built after a model'.[113] Our immanent irrationality means that life is not, and cannot be, an efficient economy of optimally productive agents fulfilling their own material ambitions and serving, as if mere machinery, the optimisation of the state's ambition as a global power-grabbing agency on the world stage. The state can, and does, exist to serve individuality; but individuality does not

[107] ibid, 219.

[108] 'Fundamental human rights ... are not concerned with protecting a person's interests, but with expressing his nature as a being of a certain sort, one whose interests are worth protecting. They express the worth of the person rather than the worth of what is in the interests of that person': FM Kamm, *Intricate Ethics: Rights, Responsibilities, and Permissible Harm* (Oxford University Press, 2007) 271, cited in R Cruft, SM Liao and M Renzo, *Philosophical Foundations of Human Rights* (Oxford University Press, 2015) 17. James Griffin says much the same in *On Human Rights* (Oxford University Press, 2008) ch 2.

[109] See discussion in chs 6 and 7.

[110] Mill (n 92) 250.

[111] As CL Ten has pointed out, '*On Liberty* is a more complex piece of work than is generally supposed': CL Ten, *Mill On Liberty* (Oxford University Press, 1980) 144. Alan Ryan makes much the same point: A Ryan, *The Making of Modern Liberalism* (Princeton University Press, 2012) 257.

[112] n 82.

[113] Mill (n 92) 263.

exist to serve the state (through, as Hegel had it, dialectical movements). This insight places important restrictions on the state's ability to optimise its own efficiency as a world power. As far as the state's ambitions are concerned, there can be only what *is*; that is, the state as the product of a disenchanted group of disparate ends, which has world power only as a moral force (committed to the irrational processes that drive the noumenal self's realisation of herself in which she realises the best but imperfect version of herself, if committed to that end).

Clearly, this irrationality is not an ideal and is, therefore, problematic; it manifests in actions and behaviour that not only society (objectively) determines to be bad for her, but that she herself may eventually come to think of as a mistake or detriment to her life goals and sense of accomplishment or satisfaction. Smoking,[114] gambling,[115] drunkenness,[116] fornication[117] and idleness[118] are all recognised by Mill as actions that society may disapprove of but which belong to the realm of individuality in their entirety.[119] Free speech also belongs in this category:

> I acknowledge that the tendency of all opinions to become sectarian is not cured by the freest discussion, but is often heightened and exacerbated thereby; the truth which ought to have been, but was not, seen, being rejected all the more violently because proclaimed by persons regarded as opponents.[120]

Accordingly, Mill does not pretend that individuality as irrationality is an ideal, ie, something to aspire to. Mill is not advocating irrationality as some utopian state, as if he wishes to see a society emerge in which all have taken leave of their senses and are committed to nothing but their own moral and physical destruction by any and all means necessary. He is driven, instead, by the insight that the 'truth' of the proposition – that constant drunkenness or other illicit debauchery is unsatisfying in the longer run – is something that only the noumenal self can discover by her own means, through experience and discussion.[121] Hence, for Mill, irrationality is a natural state. The noumenal self, bounded by her own impending mortality, is driven to make the best of her life, as it is and as she can conceive it to be through her own willing. In this, she is accountable only to herself, not the state.[122] To do otherwise, to forgo her own autonomy permanently, by making herself a slave, is not something she can contemplate and remain free.[123] By the same token, she cannot let the state decide for her, by coercive means, for that would be to suffer a state of 'despotic, or what is called

[114] ibid, 296. For Mill, of course, smoking was but 'a choice' that some enjoy and others not. He would not conceive of it as self-harm as we would. Likewise, although he does not mention it, the practice of 'opium-eating' (*laudanum*) would be viewed by Mill as a choice (albeit an immoral one) rather than an illicit act, as we would understand it. See, eg, T De Quincey, *Confessions of an English Opium-Eater* [1821] (Oxford University Press, 1998).
[115] ibid, 296.
[116] ibid, 295.
[117] ibid, 296.
[118] ibid, 295.
[119] ibid, 295.
[120] ibid, 257.
[121] ibid, 231.
[122] ibid, 292.
[123] ibid, 306–08.

paternal, government'[124] not least because, to do so, would be patronising, in its fullest sense, for her alternate, eccentric, or, as Mill calls it, 'spontaneous'[125] lifestyle may prove to be satisfying despite the external reservations of others. In this way, we see what Mill means when he says, for example, 'originality is the one thing which unoriginal minds cannot feel the use of'.[126]

Accordingly, this insight (of individuality) places important but irreconcilable imperfectability on the state. For there can be no such thing as the utopian state. The state, as a representation of imperfect individuality is but, even in its best possible form, a constant state (condition, situation, or circumstance) of indeterminate ends striving toward the improvement of itself and its members but never quite fulfilling its own ends because life is both finite and unpredictable. Thus, humanity's lot is frustrated and frustrating in its continual striving toward perfection and satisfaction tempered by its own profound realisation of imperfectability and dissatisfaction – a life of failure and mistake that repeats without ever quite realising the lessons of its own shared history. The fecundity of Mill's insight, then, is in its profound realisation of this immanent imperfectability; of the noumenal self as a frustrated, and frustrating, being.

This sense of living without judgement, and of being true to oneself, manifests in the *motif* of the tree (or other flora) that Mill uses repeatedly.[127] This gives emphasis to the sense of individuality as variety of organic life that, through its own innate sense of wants and needs, develops, literally and metaphorically, through unencumbered growth. The tree needs only the fertile soil in which to grow (compulsory state education for the infant or infantile) and should be left to its own devices once established (ie, of age), without interference.

Thus, a commitment to individuality is a commitment to the essential irrationality of humankind. It is a commitment to inefficiency – for a life of experiment is, by its nature, suboptimal.[128] Whereas the noumenal self can always discover better ways of living, and try to impart this wisdom to others, still she cannot rectify her own mistakes absolutely (she cannot ensure they never happened; only that they do not again). Moreover, because of her own sense of mortality, hers is always a sense of decision under pressure; that her time is diminishing, constantly. Likewise, it is never an informed choice in an absolute sense, for she can no more eradicate her own mistakes than she could lead multiple lives at once and so determine which route is best in the final analysis. Hence, even her best, most refined sense of rationality is bounded by her own mortality and the constant limitations that the space/time continuum imposes upon her.

None of this is to deny that Mill uses the language of consequentialism to describe the intellectual progress of the noumenal self, none more so than when he defends

[124] ibid, 299.
[125] ibid, 261 and 264.
[126] ibid, 268.
[127] ibid, 263–65.
[128] For example, Mill discusses truth in relative, not absolute, terms, eg, when he argues that if we can freely debate the grounds of a proposition then 'we may hope that if there be a better truth, it will be found when the human mind is capable of receiving it; and in the meantime we may rely on having attained such approach to truth, as is possible in our day. This is the amount of certainty attainable by a fallible being': ibid, 232.

free speech as a 'necessity to the mental well-being of mankind'.[129] And of course, his argument takes a Hegelian turn, when he declares that because, in the past, truth has emerged despite brutal persecution, that it will again[130] (which is the point that many commentators seize upon). However, this consequentialism is apparent only on a superficial reading of Mill. As it relates to self-improvement and, therefore, societal progress, his argument is always conditional (the hypothetical imperative) and never categorical. For example, Mill says 'in proportion to the development of his individuality, each person becomes more valuable to himself, and is therefore capable of being more valuable to others'.[131] The appearance of causality, therefore, – that the individual *will* improve and society *will* benefit from legal recognition of individuality – is always contingent upon the will (the determination to improve) and the skill (the ability to do so). This is why Mill speaks of 'bring[ing] human beings … nearer to the best thing they can be'.[132] Mill is under no illusions about the capacity of mankind, not only to achieve its best possible form, nor the motivation to do so. The best possible version of a person is always a relative term known only to the noumenal self. This means, of course, that even the best possible version may be unachievable – since the noumenal self does not know what she does not know, her conception of relative perfection is, itself, a relative and conditional state. This is yet one more manifestation of irrationality's grip on individuality. Indeed, her best self may be in the past; she may have achieved her optimal self without ever perceiving it until it is beyond her, to be left with nothing but regret at this missed opportunity.

Yet, to be sure, a life of irrationality is not a life of irresponsibility. Emphatically, Mill is *not* saying that freedom is an absolute term so that the irrational noumenal self may do as she pleases without consequence. In railing against the eradication of choice through externally imposed duty and conformity, Mill was not imagining a world of rights without duties. On the contrary, he recognised the importance of duty as both an ethical and juridical obligation. Neither was he arguing that his ideal of life without judgement should be understood, literally, to mean a life free from criticism. Others are bound to feel a compulsion – a duty, even – to criticise her if they think she is being foolish. That compulsion may be driven by positive sentiments, such as love or friendship, and not simply the sort of malice or meddling that the tyrannous majority exhibits. He meant, instead, that the noumenal self should feel impervious to criticism when her actions are purely self-regarding, for it is for her alone to judge whether this advice should be acted upon.

Mill's explication of the harm principle is the weaker part of his argument, although, as said above, this is understandable given the terms of his 'very simple proposition'. He was not seeking to determine the parameters of the harm principle in the realm of other-regarding behaviour, only to recognise its existence. He describes its nature only for the purposes of counterpoint; how it differs from the world of self-regarding behaviour. For all Mill wants to say is that the harm principle cannot apply to self-regarding

[129] ibid, 257–58.
[130] ibid, 239.
[131] ibid, 266.
[132] ibid, 267.

behaviour because either I cannot harm myself as the external world understands it for self-harm is a relative term understandable to each only as a being-in-itself (ie, only as a noumenal concept) or else that even if my actions are self-harm, both objectively (phenomenally) and subjectively (noumenally) understood, that is a matter for me, and me alone. My pain is unique to me and you cannot experience it as I must. Nevertheless, we can make progress – and more progress than his critics accept – with Mill's harm principle as it relates to the other-regarding, if we recognise its operational context given to us by the nature of the juridical world we inhabit. For when my actions are other-regarding, and when those actions cause harm to the legitimate interests of others, then – but only then – it becomes a social 'problem' for which coercive measures may be legitimate.

This does *not* mean that freedom from responsibility is freedom from consequence. Freedom has consequences, not least on the ethical plane. The freedom to offend others does not mean that those offended cannot *complain* that they feel offended. For this expression (of feeling offence) is, of itself, freedom of speech. If freedom of speech is freedom to criticise, then it cannot be a freedom from being criticised. If it is freedom to judge, then it cannot be freedom from being judged. If it is freedom from compulsion, then it cannot be a freedom to compel others to think as we think. If it is a freedom to demand, then it cannot be a freedom from being the subject of demands. If it is a freedom to rationalise, then it cannot be a freedom to be free from irrationality.

IV. The Argument Revisited

It is time to revisit the claims set out in the introduction of this chapter. In this final section, I seek to defend them by means of the distinctive notions of individuality that Hegel and Mill give us and so anticipate the arguments that the remainder of part three provides. As the introductory remarks suggested, my aim is to understand free speech as a product of its surroundings. If free speech is not yet 'in the world' and our ambition is to bring it into that world, then meaning emerges through, and from, this environment. In this way, I set myself against the orthodox approach of defining it by retrospective means: by asking *why* we protect it. For since the 'it' is the thing to be defined, 'its' justification cannot provide its definition without obvious circularity.

History provides us with two types of surroundings which are governed by an ultimate end. One imagines mankind as a social being, which, first, through tribes then, eventually, nations, groups together to defend itself against external threats. Its ultimate end, therefore, is the good of the community. This community or collective standard is, itself, capable of (at least) two forms. The first imagines the community's interests as paramount, so much so that individuality has no meaning. Here, the individual is not so much a cog in the machine as a non-entity, which gives the machine its power but is, ultimately, meaningless in its expendability. This is the system of antiquity, as it existed in Rome and Greece, and as it appeared in Hitler's Germany and Stalin's Russia. In these totalitarian systems, the only beings that matter are either the nobles (of the senate, for example) or the figurehead (Führer, Chairman, General Secretary) – and even then are secondary to the glory of Rome, the Reich or the Soviet dream.

The second form of collective ideal at least recognises the existence of individuality, as a social value, yet renders it inferior, in the final analysis, to the desired communal goal. Thus, individuality's value is contingent upon the realisation of those communal goals that are served, demonstrably, by individuality. Libertarianism, or neoliberalism, portrays elements of this consequentialism, for here we see the term 'individuality' deployed often with a meaning that is, really, innovation by a different name. Individuality-as-innovation is of vital importance to the libertarian goal of economic success. The pioneers of America's global dominance were all individuals in a meaningful sense, whose names, even today, are synonymous with material success, from Rockefeller to Carnegie, Vanderbilt to Ford. Clearly, these men were innovators – renegades, even – of the first order in their relentless pursuit of material success. Capitalism, in its neoliberalist form, mistakes innovation for individuality and so hails entrepreneurialism as the height of autonomy. The neoliberalist state lauds the John Galt character[133] and seeks to interfere only minimally with economic life in the hope that some 'invisible hand' of Adam Smith's imagining will permit maximal entrepreneurialism to thrive. The material success of the entrepreneur will, they believe, reward both the state and the community's indulgence through the employment opportunities it creates, the philanthropy it tends to inspire (of which Rockefeller, Carnegie, Vanderbilt and Ford are, again, exemplars) and, if not, the large tax receipts it produces, which will serve the (typically, limited) socialist inclinations of capitalist government, and the enhanced level of global power that national material wealth provides. State interference with this delicate system, then, is tolerable only to the extent that it might (and does) produce efficiencies in optimising this entrepreneurial spirit.

It is, of course, not only the machinery of state that creates this bounded sense of individuality. For the undercurrent of conformity that drives it is to be found in civil society, through the language of shame that established religion cherishes and the cult of patriotism or nationalism that civic pride cultivates. In America, these symbols of conformity are everywhere, from following the flag to serving God, from gun culture to the materiality of consumerism, these fixed cultural points project the image clearly of what it means to be American – and America is hardly alone in this. These expectations of conformity find expression at a macro level in the perpetual struggle amongst nations to dominate; constantly driven by the will to power for power's sake. This contest envisages the planet not so much as singularity anymore than it regards the refugee as a brother, but as a series of isolated systems incapable of entropy. This struggle demands constant success which, in the battle for limited resources, can be achieved only through greater and greater efficiencies in the system. In this way, the non-conformist creates unbearable tensions that must be driven out, through the language of shame utilised by the tyrannous majority or else the coercive power of the state, embodied by its police force, if it is to preserve its place on the international pantheon. This struggle can only intensify should the overtly communitarian states achieve the sort of material success that shakes the pantheon

[133] A Rand, *Atlas Shrugged* [1957] (Signet, 1996).

of its established order, for it demands that individualist states of traditional Western democracies take drastic steps to enhance their efficiencies through eradication of individual choice and so maintain the appearance of liberal politics only to the most tolerably superficial level.

When we look to our surroundings, then, what do we see? If it is rampant communitarianism, manifesting as authoritarianism or totalitarianism, then free speech can be understood only as a tool of the efficient machine, in which information is *valued*. That value is predetermined by the political climate. If it is a theocracy, then only that which agrees with orthodoxy is tolerable. If it is fascism, then only that which *champions* the entrenched party of power is tolerable. If it is the authoritarianism of the Kallipolis, then only that which is approved is tolerable. In each of these systems, there may be procedures in place which either restrict what may be published, by means of the censor, or else allows only certain types of people to speak, such as the high priests, the *politburo*, or the philosopher-king, for it is only these entities that can channel the divine purpose of God or of the system itself.

If, however, we see individuality as the base unit of the political system, then we must ask ourself which sort of individuality is at work. Here, then, we must ask whether freedom is value-laden or not. For if any freedom (including free speech) is protected only to the extent of serving some nominated value, then it is categorisable only as a manifestation of Hegelian freedom and not of Mill's. The Western (and American) tradition of prizing free speech for its contribution to collective goals is, therefore, something of a mystery. For this tradition manifests Hegelian freedom through its adoration of rationality as the ultimate social good. Whereas, of course, we can trace this celebration of mankind's essential rationality back to the Enlightenment thought of, amongst others, Kant, we cannot attribute the modern fascination with it to Kantian thought, as I have indicated in the opening remarks to this chapter. For, like Mill, Kant says that self-improvement through continual usage of rational thought is not something that we can demand, let alone force, the individuals of our community to do. Hence, the Enlightenment stands not for the coercion of self-optimisation but as the *freedom* to do so *if we choose to*.

Accordingly, Hegel's freedom is but communitarianism by another name. To be sure, it is *not* the communitarianism of ancient Greece and Rome and neither is it the communitarianism of Soviet Russia or Nazi Germany. Yet it is communitarianism nevertheless. This is because it insists upon rationality as the standard by which individuality is understood. Whereas Hegel insists that individuality survives the dialectical movement by which community and individuality unite, this is but wordplay. In the final analysis, one of these must be prioritised when the juridical machinery is unleashed.

This is why Mill's radical thought is so important. He saw, much more clearly than his critics admit, that once we understand the Kantian dichotomy that separates the phenomenal world of sensory experience from the noumenal world of mind and being, then it must follow that true individuality adopts the irrationality standard in its final analysis. This does not mean, of course, that Mill *wants* people to be irrational; he is no anarchist. Neither does it mean that manifestations of rationality cannot count as instances of true freedom – that would also be ridiculous. Instead, it means that since only the being-in-itself – the noumena of the 'I' – knows itself (and is the only being that can), then external standards of rationality cannot be imposed upon her, for only she knows what is rational as it relates to her. Moreover, since she *is* a mind – an unknowable entity so far as external minds are concerned – then it is for her to decide for herself how she lives her life as it relates to her (ie, the self-regarding element).

Whereas, at first glance, the world around us appears to be conformist in nature, this sentiment is superficial, at least as it relates to America and the liberal democracies of Europe and the Commonwealth. For although the conformist spirit drives much of our cultural life, it has less resonance with our system of law. National or civic pride, religious orthodoxy and community spirit may be cherished ethical norms, but they have little or no place at a juridical level. The coercive power of law has little purchase on individuality and none as it relates to the noumenal being and her self-regarding actions. Thus, if, as the opening remarks suggested, we separate the ethical from the juridical then, it seems to me, the standard of individuality that liberal democracy adheres to better fits Mill's freedom-as-irrationality than it does Hegel's sense. Accordingly, it can be argued that countries aspiring to liberal democracy must embrace the Millian sense of freedom. Hence, in these countries, freedom of speech must be designed according to the irrationality standard. This, I must stress, is not a question of what is best, for as I have said individuality is problematic; it is a question of what fits. It is a question of coherence and not of self-congratulation.

The problem of irrationality is, if not overcome, then at least abated by adherence to the harm principle, which Mill also gives us, and which Kant hints at. Irrationality, as it directs self-regarding action, is the noumenal being's sovereign domain. When it impacts on others, it exposes itself to potential external control. To give the clearest example, the noumenal self may hold bigoted beliefs of the worst kind. The law has no power to prevent this, if it is to be consistent with itself. It cannot stop bigoted thoughts from arising in the mind, for these are truly self-regarding. It may interfere with the dissemination of those ideas but only when their expression causes undue harm to the interests of others. Now, we may say that the very idea of bigotry existing, and of spreading, is intolerable, for it hurts those that it attacks, and so corrupts harmonious society by the division and hatred it spreads. We have lived with, and continue to live with, this sort of bigotry gaining prevalence (and, therefore, an undeserved sense of respectability). It happened (and continues to happen) to the black community, throughout America's history, from the unrest that prompted the Civil War to the lynchings in the South, from the Civil Rights Movement to, in our time, the backlash against the Black Lives Matter movement. It happened in Nazi Germany, with the vilification of Jews. It happened to the gay community with the AIDS virus. It happened after 9/11, and still happens, with the vilification of Islam. It is happening now to the trans community. The same destructive misuse of reason that would treat Holocaust denial as but 'the other side of the debate'[134] continues to dog popular debate by which the most insidious forms of hatred towards minorities is given ostensible respectability by being labelled 'political' speech. This is perhaps *the* most problematic issue that individualist society faces and, yet, it is one that cannot be solved through law.

[134] See discussion in D Lipstadt, *Denying the Holocaust* (Penguin, 1993).

The liberal has no difficulty in recognising bigotry, in all its forms, as ethically wrong. Yet the liberal cannot condone coercion to force the bigot to change. For the idea of using force to drive the bigotry out of the bigot is nonsensical. Taken literally, that end could be achieved only through the most barbaric processes. It is for this reason that Mill says:

> [I]f all mankind minus one, were of one opinion, and only one person were of the contrary opinion, mankind would be no more justified in silencing that one person, than he, if he had the power, would be justified in silencing mankind.[135]

Invariably, Mill's point is understood. He is not saying that the contrary opinion is valuable or tolerable. He is not, as I think he so often said to be, championing the lone pamphleteer as the ultimate heroic figure. Neither is he speaking purely of censorship, for even the most draconian measures of the Star Chamber could not compel silence. To silence is not merely to quieten or to object; it is to eradicate. It is to suppress with such power that the opinion cannot be expressed again, at least, not by that person.

Perhaps it might be said that, surely, tolerance of bigotry offends the harm principle. Clearly, it causes harm to the valid interests of others in terms of both the collective goal of realising a harmonious society and to the individual's quiet enjoyment of life, free from prejudice. Although this viewpoint is attractive, it lacks coherency. The suppression of bigotry through coercive means is the suppression of non-conformity. It is the enforcement of morality. So far as it goes, we can say, with Patrick Devlin: 'punishment will not cure'.[136] Nevertheless, we see in Devlin – specifically, his singular view[137] that homosexuality is a form of deviancy – the reasons why the enforcement of morality according to community standards is deeply unattractive. For it allows, in Devlin's words, 'right-minded people', to decide what viewpoints are to be penalised by society according to its own sense of propriety. Hence, we invite the view, as Devlin expressed it, that since 'there is … a general abhorrence of homosexuality'[138] in which these unspecified 'right-minded people' feel, and think themselves entitled to feel, 'disgust' at these practices, homosexuality, as with other forms of immorality, becomes a public interest matter that the law can, and should, take into account when determining the boundaries at which self-regarding behaviour becomes other-regarding.[139] Whereas there is nothing controversial about Devlin's general view that 'the law exists for the protection of society', it becomes troubling when developed to say:

> It [the law] does not discharge its function by protecting the individual from injury, annoyance, corruption, and exploitation; the law must protect also the institutions and the community of ideas, political and moral, without which people cannot live together. Society cannot ignore the morality of the individual any more than it can his loyalty; it flourishes on both and without either it dies.[140]

[135] Mill (n 92) 229.
[136] P Devlin, *The Enforcement of Morals* (Oxford University Press, 1965) v.
[137] HLA Hart's response remains essential reading, of course: *Law, Liberty, and Morality* (Oxford University Press, 1968).
[138] Devlin (n 136) 17.
[139] ibid, 15–18.
[140] ibid, 22.

Given its application to homosexuality, in Devlin's mind at least, it is repugnant. Nevertheless, it is Hegelian freedom in action. This is what freedom-as-rationality stands for; this is the natural end that the unity of individuality and community, through dialectical movement, ends. When tensions between individuality and community arise, it is the community's view that decides.

We begin to see, then, why an insistence upon 'rationality' as the standard for determining protection for autonomy is a dangerous idea. 'Right-minded people' and 'reasonable men' are superficial expressions that stand, in large part, for the subjective ideologies of the judge as emblem of the 'objective' spirit. In Devlin's hands, we see it as but repression by another name. As Devlin shows, any argument that can be made against bigotry, for example, as a corrupting influence in need of state suppression, can and will be used *against* those who call for it. We have seen how Drill music, a genre which 'functions as a culturally and politically-conscious voice that broadcasts the patterns of inequality and social exclusion that disproportionately affects young black Britons', has been castigated as a material cause of increased knife crime in inner-city London.[141] We also find, too readily, that 'exploitation' and 'corruption' are the animating tropes that provoke that special kind of moral panic which the right-wing press serves up constantly. Thus, they are applied to the words of the Iman, to the lobbying for greater recognition of gender dysphoria, and the call for protection of political refugees.

V. Conclusion: The Irrationality Standard

What can we now say about authenticity?

First, free speech cannot be universalised for, as we have seen, there are ineluctable (or else irreducible) dichotomies at work. These tensions are given to us by history and by reason in the conflict between individuality and community that they generate. Whilst we can say, with Hegel, that antiquity recognised no such thing as individuality – and neither did the totalitarian regimes of Stalin and Hitler – still the Hegelian system does not eradicate that tension through dialectical movements.

Secondly, in discerning the impact of communitarianism and individualism on living, we must distinguish ethical from juridical lawgiving. In ancient Rome or Greece, as in the totalitarianism of the mid-twentieth century, juridical lawgiving denied individuality's authority. Instead, in antiquity, those essential decisions of life were taken for the individual. There was no choice to become soldier or serf, slave or senator. These were given. In our time, ethical lawgiving prevails, to varying degrees. There are, it is said, distinctions here between West and East. Still, in the West, although we say that such lifestyle choices are ours to make, this may be a fiction, after a fashion. The *Sittlichkeit* may give us those roles, for our religion may take decisions away from us (such as sexual orientation), our parents or friends may (seek to) limit our choice of life partner, directly or indirectly, and our socio-economic environment may direct our eventual job or career.

[141] See, eg, C Allen, 'The Criminalisation of Drill Music and Article 10 of the European Convention on Human Rights' Inforrm blog (5 March 2021).

In the East, these tensions may be more pronounced through the distinct philosophical and spiritual beliefs given by tradition. From the *hsiao* or filial piety of Confucius to the *Nirodha* (with its emphasis on good toward others) of Siddhartha Gautama, from the *seva* or selflessness of Sikhism to the *Zakat* or almsgiving of Islam, community influences may have greater purchase on *Einzelheit*. This may give parents greater say over essential lifestyle choices than individualism would prefer, manifesting, say, as a practice of parents influencing marriage decisions, as in the Indian sub-continent,[142] or careers, as is the tradition in parts of Asia.[143] In this way, we can detect different understandings of individuality, and of a sublation of individuality into communitarian decision-making, which may resonate in ethical lawgiving, from the middle East to South Asia, from Singapore to Japan. Allied to this, of course, has been the influence of communism on Eastern politics, from Russia to China, Vietnam to North Korea, whose doctrine, at least in the Leninist-Marxist tradition, has been the eradication of individuality. This preference for the prioritisation of community is well captured by Singapore's former Prime Minister, Lee Kuan Yew, who is reported to have said: 'Asians are in little doubt that a society with communitarian values where the interests of society take precedence over that of the individual suits them better than the individualism of America.'[144]

Yet, thirdly, in distinguishing individualism from communitarianism, it would be unwise to speak of ideals. Individuality is not an ideal; it is a problem. It creates tensions that are not easily resolved and, in fact, may not be resolvable. Hegel's solution to this problem (which he seemed more aware of than Kant)[145] is the unity of individuality and community. Yet, this sublation of individuality into communitarian decision-making, of the state and the *Sittlichkeit*, does not remove the dichotomy so much as disguise it. For, in the final analysis, community preferences are bound to dominate. Whereas it is possible that individuality will triumph, still that seems unlikely, in a meaningful sense, for Hegelian freedom adopts the rationality standard as its metric of choice. Thus, as Devlin shows, this standard has ugly connotations, in which individualism may be subjected to pejorative/prejudiced castigation as 'irrational' behaviour in need of correction/elimination.

Fourthly, then, objectivity, reason and rationality have no real purchase on the conception of rights. Whereas Mill, and then Hart, demonstrated that this so-called 'objectivity' is but tyranny by another name, still the argument needs restatement. For Millian freedom, specifically, is so much misunderstood that many may conclude, at least intuitively, that it *also* represents the rationality standard at work. Yet, as the above has sought to show, the purpose of *On Liberty* is to demonstrate the exact opposite: that individuality is *ir*rationality. Hence, Mill's one 'very simple principle' was to demonstrate why society has no legitimate interest, let alone right, to correct the individual of her 'delusions', of her bad choices, of her bounded rationality, when her actions are

[142] See, eg, T Jaiswal, *Indian Arranged Marriages: A social psychological perspective* (Routledge, 2014).

[143] See findings and literature discussed in A Ghosh and NA Fouad, 'Family Influence on Careers Among Asian Parent-Child Dyads' (2016) 24 *Journal of Career Assessment* 318.

[144] D Lague, 'Singapore; Still Playing by Lee's Rules' *Australian Financial Review* (7 December 1990).

[145] It is for reasons like this that Hannah Arendt insists we should dismiss Kant's political philosophy as the product of an unsound mind: H Arendt, *Lectures on Kant's Political Philosophy* (University of Chicago Press, 1992) 7–8.

merely self-regarding. Moreover, even if properly understood as other-regarding, the legitimacy of external interference, by the state or civil society more generally, requires proof of harm as a necessary but not sufficient reason to act. It is Kant's noumena, the being-in-itself, that has priority. As against this, the state has no right to its own maximal optimisation. It has no right to demand that individuality is sacrificed so that it may maintain, or enhance, its international standing as a world power that may manipulate and exploit its material success to achieve greater bargaining power in global relations.

Conceived this way, authenticity as the irrationality standard has a profound effect upon the persuasiveness of popular and academic thought as it holds free speech theory to be a rational system that benefits, ultimately, democratic participation and epistemic advance. I have demonstrated no such thing as yet. As previous chapters show, the overarching ambition of this book is to demonstrate the fallacy, in orthodox theory, that constructs authentic free speech principle according to the societal benefits to be derived. Chapters six and seven aim to show that free speech as epistemic advance (chapter six) or democratic participation (chapter seven) is unsustainable given the irrationality standard though it is sustainable as a product of communitarianism. To persist with the notion of free speech as a communitarian ideal, then, is to forsake individual agency as a meaningful limit on the state's power to optimise its standing. Part three concludes, in chapter eight, by explicating Mill's harm principle, as it relates to free speech, so as to realise the essential tenet of Kantian (juridical) freedom as: '*freedom* (independence from being constrained by another's choice), insofar as it can coexist with the freedom of every other in accordance with a universal law, is the only original right belonging to every other human being by virtue of his humanity'.[146]

Hegelian freedom is but positive freedom. It is the freedom to do good. It is individuality used productively to serve the community. Free speech can be understood as such. The work of one woman can enrich the community's civic life by providing them with sufficient information to make those critical, informed decisions when voting. It can help empower a nation, through its development of epistemically optimised individuals, who can realise their own career ambitions, achieve material success, and so, through tax receipts, enrich the state's coffers and buy political power on the world stage. Yet, freedom in this positive sense has no need of individuality in the final analysis, for if serving one's community is to serve oneself, then the community can rightly expect these positive contributions without further reference to the benefits that individuality receives. Individuality survives this dialectical movement but only in the thinnest sense. In any competition between the two, community triumphs.

Moreover, Hegelian freedom poses no real difficulties in the practical arena. The notion of a free speech 'problem', as we have understood it so far, does not arise in any meaningful sense. For if freedom is the final dialectical movement of the 'individual will' and the 'general will' united, then there is no dispute between personal rights to resolve. The freedom that is in tension with the communitarian goal is no freedom in the Hegelian sense and therefore poses no real problems. Free speech that serves the

[146] Kant (n 6) [6:237].

communal end, of enhancing democratic participation and of furthering epistemic advance, is freedom in action, but there can be no problem of how to resolve conflict involving harmful speech, at least not in a juridical sense, for harmful speech is irrational speech that has not yet achieved its final dialectical form and, therefore, does not qualify as freedom. Such speech is excluded from the realm of right altogether and, so, cannot form the basis of legal problem requiring judicial resolution, for it cannot establish itself as a problem deserving of legal attention in the first place.

As these concluding remarks signify, Hegelian freedom is an incomplete notion. It conflicts with our ambitions in this chapter. This does not mean that positive speech – speech that contributes to community meaningfully – cannot belong to our Wittgensteinian aim of conceptualising free speech from outside the world. What it does mean is that our sense of freedom must be broader than simply the Hegelian sense. It must also capture the negative sense of freedom if it is to be meaningful. That negative sense is given to us by that which Hegel excludes, and which Mill includes. Negative freedom is the irrational and the irresponsible. Freedom, in this sense, is not driven by concern for others. If it has rational form, it is a sense of self-preservation. Yet, since it is irrational, it has a form that reason cannot fully account for. It is impulsiveness. It is fearful. It is of escape. It is of running amok. It is of cowardice. It is of sentimentality. It is not productive – that is the point.

Recognition of freedom in its fullest sense, then, impacts upon the nature of the ultimate juridical question. In a free speech problem, individuality manifests and the community responds. The judge is asked to choose between the two. In the Hegelian system, averse to personal rights, the juridical position is driven by questions of value (ie, productivity, rationality, benefit, etc). Does the community benefit from that manifestation? In the Millian system, though, it is driven by questions of harm. Is the community's (negative) response justified? It is only in the second system – the Millian – that freedom is realised absolutely, for questions of value are irrelevant. For the Millian question is not in positive form – does the community benefit from this individuality? – but entirely negative – is the community burden intolerable?

6

Epistemology

I. Introduction

The premise that free speech advances epistemic prowess, individually or communally, unifies all four traditional justifications as they are given to us by the orthodox literature.[1] We find it in the work of John Stuart Mill[2] and in Justice Holmes' well-known 'marketplace of ideas' dissent[3] as well as in the post-Meiklejohnian thought of the modern age, as we shall see. Accordingly, it may be said that this commonality gives it, surely, the necessary pedigree by which we can say it is an authentic principle in free speech theory.

Yet, to design theory according to this epistemology premise is more problematic than the established literature acknowledges. Chief amongst these problems is the ambition, amongst theorists, to construe the premise in such terms that the ultimate end of free speech is the collation of an ideal repository of information that is demonstrably valuable to certain social goals – most notably, democratic participation, but also self-realisation/self-fulfilment, 'truth discovery' in its broadest sense, and autonomous modes of living. This emphasis upon value (as in worth) creates an insurmountable problem in intellectual design such that epistemology must be abandoned as an animating principle. Whereas with Mill and Holmes we can say that epistemic advance, individually or collectively, would be impossible (or deeply improbable) without the freedom to challenge received wisdoms and, so, to learn from hearing falsehoods as much as accepted truths, still the insight is meaningless to the juridical task of constructing a rights-based principle.

While it is true that if we were to construe authenticity according to the base unit of community, then the epistemology premise would be useful, to construct theory in this manner would run contrary to the rights-based account by which both vertical and

[1] This premise is apparent in the work of, eg, A Meiklejohn, 'The First Amendment is an Absolute' (1961) *Supreme Court Review* 245, 255: free speech is concerned with the acquisition of 'intelligence, integrity, sensitivity, and generous devotion to the general welfare'; MJ Perry, 'Freedom of Expression: An Essay on Theory and Doctrine' 78 *Northwestern University Law Review* 1137, 1155: 'An essential characteristic of human beings is their need for, and their capacity to pursue and achieve, an ever better understanding of reality … Freedom of expressions facilitates [this] enterprise'; and SV Shiffrin, 'A Thinker-Based Approach to Freedom of Speech' (2011) 27 *Constitutional Commentary* 283, 288: 'Each theory shares the presupposition that the autonomous thinker fundamentally matters.'

[2] JS Mill, *On Liberty* in *Collected Works of John Stuart Mill*, Vol XVIII (JM Robson, ed) (University of Toronto Press, 1977).

[3] *Abrams v US* 250 US 616 (1919).

horizontal disputes depend. Thus, the community base unit (discussed in the previous chapter) must be jettisoned, also, in the intellectual design of free speech theory for a democratic society.

These, at any rate, are the key arguments to be established in this chapter. Section II establishes the introductory point concerning epistemology's ubiquity within orthodox theory. Within this section, the literature's preoccupation with free speech as a tool for realising valuable social or communal information emerges. From this, the picture emerges of free speech as a means to realising an ideal repository. Nevertheless, the significance of epistemology to intellectual design can be understood in minimal and maximal terms. Section III illustrates this point, with a special focus on process theory. This section emphasises the problem of using epistemology maximally to improve the quality and conditions by which epistemologically beneficial speech is provided (and epistemologically detrimental speech is denied) to the community. If we accept this sort of consequentialism into our system of free speech design then we must abandon, or otherwise denigrate, the content neutrality principle. Whereas it is one to thing to exclude such speech according to the harm principle, it is quite another to do so on the basis of individual or communal value. These observations lead to the final section, in which the ultimate epistemological ambition of the ideal repository is critiqued most fully in which the descent into rampant consequentialism is most noticeably observed. Here, the choice between a valued-based or harm-based approach to free speech design becomes most apparent, being between the community base unit or the individuality-based one.

II. Reach

Thomas Emerson understood free speech in epistemological terms. Notably, though, he made no attempt to divide its epistemological benefits according to types of knowledge. Instead, he described its value in broad, sweeping terms. Free speech, he said, 'assured' individual self-fulfilment; was 'an essential process for advancing knowledge and discovering truth', was 'essential' to providing 'participation in [public] decision-making' and of 'achieving a more adaptable and hence a more stable community'.[4] In terms of his approach, Emerson followed Justice Brandeis, who had earlier said that free speech provided four valuable benefits: as a means of optimising cognitive faculties, achieving happiness, acting as a 'valve' for the safe discharge of pent-up negative emotions, and of discovering and spreading 'political truth'.[5] The safety valve function apart, these benefits bear obvious relevance to epistemology.

This expansive treatment of epistemologically derived benefits sets both Emerson and Brandeis apart from the subsequent literature, which has sought to pick off the more suspect candidates in these lists for free speech's beneficial value. Consequently, orthodox theory is known more for either its isolation of (one specific) value or else its attempts at ranking these values in a sort of hierarchy of beneficial value. Typically, as we know, the literature encourages judges to use these preferred or nominated beneficial

[4] TI Emerson, *The System of Freedom of Expression* (Vintage, 1970) 6–7.
[5] *Whitney v California* 274 US 357, 375 (1927).

values as a sort of critical lens by which to isolate the meaning and nature of free speech. Nevertheless, despite this jockeying, the literature displays if not consensus then a broad agreement that free speech is valuable primarily for its contribution to epistemic advance. Whereas this interpretation is most pronounced in democratic process theory, it is apparent across the spectrum, as the following will seek to demonstrate.

We see this clearly, for example, in Robert Bork's analysis of Justice Brandeis's elucidation of its beneficial values. For, in his spirited defence of the 'explicitly political' as the only defensible type of speech covered by the First Amendment, he agreed with Brandeis that free speech provides meaningful epistemic benefits in the discovery and dissemination of 'political truths'. Specifically, Bork said that whilst that category includes a wide range of speech *forms* such, 'as evaluation, criticism, electioneering and propaganda', it is exceptionally limited in terms of *content*: 'It does not cover scientific, educational, commercial or literary expressions as such',[6] nor even that which might be called 'political speech' *per se*, but only that which concerns 'governmental behavior, policy or personnel'.[7] Accordingly, it is not concerned with political speech in a general, hypothetical or philosophical sense, only that which critiques the government of the day. There must be, then, some causal relationship between that speech and the government's actions (or inaction).

Although Bork does not pretend that the distinction between political and non-political speech is problem-free, still he thinks that any concerns about the separating line will be pragmatic rather than principled.[8] The difficulties with Bork's position have been explored by several scholars.[9] As Michael Perry says, the argument is 'seriously flawed', not least because the term 'political' includes more than it excludes.[10] We find much the same criticism throughout the literature. C Edwin Baker, for example, has said that since the political extends to the personal, 'once the insight is … fully accepted, the category of politically relevant speech could be virtually unlimited'.[11] Moreover, 'like the difference between lyric and vulgarity, the identification of politically relevant speech depends on the eye of the beholder'.[12] Similarly, Lee Bollinger argues 'When we turn to open-ended, ambiguous words … we create the opportunity for distinctions to be drawn later that we did not originally intend.'[13] Likewise, as Kent Greenawalt maintains, the concept of political expression is not 'hermetically sealed'; 'speech that is not explicitly political often has political implications'.[14] To tolerate distinctions on this narrow category alone is to permit state meddling that could be put to nefarious ends or else raises questions of competence of the sort that Schauer addresses.

Accordingly, persuasive critique of government decision-making requires not only the speaker but the audience to understand something of the reasoning underpinning it. This epistemological task cannot be confined simply to something called 'political'

[6] R Bork, 'Neutral Principles and Some First Amendment Problems' (1971) 47 *Indiana Law Journal* 1, 28.
[7] ibid, 27.
[8] ibid, 28.
[9] See, eg, MH Redish, 'The Value of Free Speech' (1982) 130 *University of Pennsylvania Law Review* 591, 598–99; S Shiffrin, 'The First Amendment and Economic Regulation: Away from a General Theory of the First Amendment' (1983) 78 *Northwestern University Law Review* 1212, 1234.
[10] Perry (n 1) 1149.
[11] CE Baker, *Human Liberty and Freedom of Speech* (Oxford University Press, 1989) 26.
[12] ibid.
[13] LC Bollinger, *The Tolerant Society* (Oxford University Press, 1986) 36.
[14] K Greenawalt, *Speech, Crime & the Uses of the Language* (Oxford University Press, 1989) 45.

unless it is recognised that since political decision-making applies to all human interactions across all sectors and/or disciplines, there is very little to be excluded from its ambit. As a result, Bork's attempt to exclude 'scientific, educational, commercial or literary expressions as such'[15] is less meaningful than he supposes, unless we are to accept that political critiques are protected by free speech principle but the underlying knowledge on which they stand (or fall) is not.

Other process theorists are not so stringent. Alexander Meiklejohn came to accept, albeit late in life, that the definition had to capture more than 'political speech', narrowly understood.[16] Anticipating Post,[17] he argued that political freedom had to be understood as 'self-government' and not merely 'the absence of government'.[18] This sense of self-government, he said, 'can exist only insofar as the voters acquire the intelligence, integrity, sensitivity, and generous devotion to the general welfare that, in theory, casting a ballot is assumed to express'.[19] Here, acquisition clearly speaks to an epistemic process in which specific faculties, relating to emotional intelligence as much as informational prowess, are to be developed. This is reflected in the greater range of speech that Meiklejohn would protect as compared to, say, Bork. His non-exclusive list includes education 'in all its phases', philosophy and science, literature and the arts, 'public discussions of public issues, together with the spreading of information and opinion bearing on those issues'.[20]

Despite its breadth, Meiklejohn did not claim that *all* speech should enjoy protection under the First Amendment, only that which is 'utilized for the governing of the nation'.[21] He identified three specific elements to this function: that the people 'must try to understand the issues which, incident by incident, face the nation'; 'must pass judgment upon the decisions which our agents make upon those issues'; and 'must share in devising methods by which those decisions can be made wise and effective or, if need be, supplanted by others which promise greater wisdom and effectiveness'.[22] It is, he said, 'these activities, in all their diversity, whose freedom fills up "the scope of the First Amendment." These are the activities to whose freedom it gives its unqualified protection.'[23] Accordingly, he concluded: 'we must recognize that there are many forms of communication which, since they are not being used as activities of governing, are wholly outside the scope of the First Amendment'.[24]

Yet, one obvious and immediate problem is the position of speech that is *not* used for such purposes but which might be so utilised in the future. Even his own list protects such speech. For example, education is protected not for the specific purpose of 'governing the nation' but the larger object of cultivating the mind. Clearly, there is a causal connection between development of the critical faculties and that objective; but it is not

[15] Bork (n 6) 28.
[16] n 1.
[17] See, eg, R Post, 'Participatory Democracy and Free Speech' (2011) 97 *Virginia Law Review* 477, analysed in ch 7.
[18] Meiklejohn (n 16) 254.
[19] ibid, 255.
[20] ibid, 257.
[21] ibid, 256.
[22] ibid.
[23] ibid.
[24] ibid, 258.

a limiting connection. It need hardly be said that cultivation of the mind allows for much more than civic participation alone. Even if so limited, proponents of Meiklejohnian thought would not be assisted by such limitation: that free speech protects only that education which aids democratic participation, for it is surely impossible to say what sorts of cultivation that categorical imperative would capture. Mathematics is vital to understanding the budgetary constraints in managing the nation's finances, but, obviously, not only that.

As we saw in earlier chapters, commentators such as Owen Fiss[25] and Cass Sunstein[26] have sought to move the Meiklejohnian position back to its origins, retaining that sense of democratic discourse as a narrower exercise in evaluating political discourse, which excludes the tools for doing so, *per se*, and focuses instead on the event of political machinations itself. In this way, they have sought to rehabilitate the Meiklejohnian view of free speech as a critical tool in the democratic experiment of governance by mass participation. This move allows them to say that the juridical task necessitates moderation-type interventions such that not all is protected, only that which benefits or enriches public discourse and so permits 'wise' decision-making.

However, other scholars (notably Perry, Baker, Martin Redish and Thomas Scanlon) have sought to take advantage of the weakness in Meiklejohnian thought by arguing, on semantic grounds, for a vision of free speech that pushes the envelope of its reasoning to the limit. In effect, they argue that the Meiklejohnian position either must extend beyond political speech, narrowly understood, or else that the reasons for protecting such speech are greater than Meiklejohn allows for. For example, Meiklejohn's (ostensibly) absolute protection of the arts and literature would suggest that the value at stake is not democratic participation at all – at least not for the purposes of 'governing the nation' – but epistemology in its broadest sense. In effect, these scholars argue that once the beneficial value of *knowledge* is recognised, it becomes impossible to place meaningful limits on the *type* of knowledge to be admitted to the free speech concept without permitting the juridical task to descend into overt paternalism.

Nevertheless, these scholars do not abandon the value of typology altogether as a means of demarcating the parameters of free speech principle. Instead, they use typology to doubt the epistemic credentials of certain kinds of speech. The most notable use of this approach has been to say that the exclusion of commercial speech from First Amendment protection does not offend the content neutrality principle since the distinction applies not to the value or worth of the message itself. Essentially, this has been both Baker's[27] and Robert Post's[28] response to Martin Redish,[29] who champions commercial speech's inclusion.

[25] OM Fiss, *Liberalism Divided: Freedom of Speech and the Many Uses of State Power* (Westview Press, 1996).

[26] CR Sunstein, *Democracy and the Problem of Free Speech* (The Free Press, 1993).

[27] See, eg, CE Baker, 'Realizing Self-Realization: Corporate Political Expenditures and Redish's *The Value of Free Speech*' (1982) 130 *University of Pennsylvania Law Review* 646; *Human Liberty and Freedom of Speech* (Oxford University Press, 1989) 194–224.

[28] See, eg, R Post, 'The Constitutional Status of Commercial Speech' (2000) 48 *UCLA Law Review* 1.

[29] His responses to both include 'Self-Realization, Democracy and Freedom of Expression: A Reply to Professor Baker' (1982) 130 *University of Pennsylvania Law Review* 678 and (with AM Mollen) 'Understanding Post's and Meiklejohn's Mistakes: The Central Role of Adversary Democracy in the Theory of Free Expression' (2009) 103 *Northwestern University Law Review* 1303.

For Redish, commentators are wrong to deny the epistemological value of commercial speech. His starting point, of course, was to challenge the logic of the Borkean/Meiklejohnian treatment by which political speech is the pinnacle of valued expression:

> [W]hen an individual only has an indirect say in governing his life [by voting], he has a right to information that will enable him to exercise his power more effectively; but when the individual has full and total authority to make the very same decisions [affecting only himself], his right to the information mysteriously vanishes.[30]

This, says Redish, creates an untenable situation because the logic of self-rule requires uniformity of access to all information that speaks to individual decision-making, whether of a private or public form.[31] For him, the overt epistemology inherent in orthodox formulations of free speech theory prevent distinctions between the type of speech – or type of speaker – that would provide epistemologically valuable speech. Hence, Redish maintains. Post's attempts to exclude commercial speech from the ambit of 'public discourse'[32] must fail.

Post's response is, of course, that since individual autonomy is retained 'only to the extent that citizens seek to forge (quoting Habermas) "a common will, communicatively shared and discursively clarified in the political public sphere"',[33] it is not only appropriate but *necessary* that commercial expression should be so excluded. This is so, Post says, because 'unlike various forms of liberalism, democracy does not focus on the protection of individual autonomy outside of participation within this public sphere'.[34] This 'public opinion'-focused account limits speech to that which gives 'democratic legitimation' to corresponding, or prospective, state action.[35] This distinction allows Post to make the semantic move that differentiates 'communications that seek to sell toothpaste … from communications that seek to influence the formation of democratic public opinion'.[36]

However, this move is not as convincing as Post suggests. If the state regulates commercial speech, including dental hygiene products, it does so legitimately only if certain 'harm' type factors emerge, such as the presence of misleading or dangerous claims. The advert that claims bleach is a suitable alternative to regular toothpaste but with the additional benefit of better whitening is ripe for regulation because, if followed, death or serious injury would follow. The type of regulation is distinctive from that of orthodox political expression (eg, 'a vote for X is a vote for a better tomorrow') because, typically, the causality between claim and any subsequent 'harm' type that follows is too remote. Where that causality is apparent, because public disorder will follow its dissemination, then the fact of its political expression status cannot save it

[30] Redish (n 9) 607.
[31] ibid.
[32] See RC Post, 'Democracy and Equality' (2006) 603 *Annals of the American Academy of Politics and Social Science* 24, 26.
[33] RC Post, 'Viewpoint Discrimination and Commercial Speech' (2007) 41 *Loyola of Los Angeles Law Review* 169, 176, quoting J Habermas, *The Theory of Communicative Action*, vol 2 (T McCarthy trans) (Beacon Press, 1987) 81.
[34] Post (ibid).
[35] ibid.
[36] ibid, 177.

from regulation.[37] Thus, the generalisable point that arises is in the nature of the underlying harm and the causal connection between it and the speech. Whilst Post sees that the regulation of advertising is concerned with consumers being misled,[38] he does not see, or otherwise address, the category mistake that this admission makes for his argument. For if we accept that the reason for more readily acceptable interference with commercial speech over political speech is due to the differential nature of harm and causality in one type of speech than the other, then we can explain why commercial speech is not entitled to what Redish calls 'full' protection without any reference to the public discourse ambitions of process theory. Recognition of this point does not 'undermine',[39] as Post says, the regulatory apparatus in place to tackle harmful commercial speech; instead, it justifies that system.

The weakness in Post's position, then, is that it ignores rather than overcomes Redish's larger point that commercial speech can, and does, contribute to public discourse by providing reasons for private action. Others have sought to do this by doubting the intentions of commercial speakers in private decision-making. For example, Lawrence Solum has argued that since 'commercial advertising is almost invariably the product of the profit motive in a market economy, we have reason to suspect [it]'.[40] This position suffers from the obvious difficulty that corrupt or disingenuous motives may also be present in the public sphere, from the politician whose will to power is rooted in self-promotion or self-gain, to the press whose independence from government depends upon its profit margin, to the social media outlet whose success also hinges on its commerciality, and, of course, in public discourse actors themselves whose political opinions may be engineered or controlled by external forces. If motive is a relevant consideration, then it transcends taxonomical differentiation.

Baker's position on this is more nuanced. Although connected to the topic of profit-motivation, his point is that for the commercial speaker – unlike, say, the political actor – there is no operative choice in the matter. In effect, what Baker says (but without the Kantian terminology) is that whereas the political actor is driven by a potential multiplicity of reasons, as a noumenal being, the commercial speaker is not, for the simple reason that the corporation lacks noumenal status (or, as Baker calls it 'individual or collective visions about … humanity')[41] and exists only to survive as a commercially-viable entity. As a phenomenal enterprise, it is, then, an entity without a self; it is driven by what Baker calls a 'forced profit orientation'.[42] Even if it could be understood as such by, for example, distinguishing the corporate entity from the owner/employee who creates and disseminates the speech, any discernible contribution to self-discovery is compromised by the strictures placed upon that act (of speaking). For the objective, in

[37] See, for example, a fact pattern such as *Hammond v DPP* [2004] EWHC 69 in which a street preacher's homophobic speech and placards were clearly agitating the gathering crowd. Since the police constable present feared a serious disturbance of the peace was imminent, he arrested the preacher, removed him from the scene and so de-escalated the tension.

[38] Post (n 33) 177.

[39] ibid.

[40] LB Solum, 'Freedom of Communicative Action: A Theory of the First Amendment Freedom of Speech' (1989) 83 *Northwestern University Law Review* 54, 125–26.

[41] Baker (n 11) 219.

[42] ibid, 196.

speaking, is impaired by the market forces that drive that speech. It is not that the corporate speaker is driven by self-interest (be that as an owner or employee) since speech is often self-interested in nature. It is that the corporate speaker is compelled to say only that which maximises profits.[43] This analysis allows Baker to exclude commercial speech even if, taxonomically, it serves overt political ends: the forced profit orientation would still rob the message of any noumenal quality that could otherwise enhance or contribute to public discourse debate on the meaning and nature of existence in all its many forms.

Baker's position leaves him in a tricky position, as he recognises. If corporate speech is suspect because it is but profit-maximising activity disguised as noumenally self-interested speech, then speech emanating from the commercial press must be equally tainted. For its ostensibly altruistic premises, to further the democratic participation interests of its readership, must be compromised for the exact same reasons that the corporate advertiser is – it exists only to the extent that it is commercially viable. If it does not turn sufficient profits to meet its ownership, it ceases to exist. Hence, when altruistic instincts conflict with profit motivation, such as when, say, a story would offend its advertisers, its public-spirited intentions must give way.

Baker, of course, recognises this difficulty (of his own making) and offers a solution, albeit not an especially gratifying one. In fact, he offers two. The first abandons abstract principle for pragmatism: press speech is different from commercial speech because the Constitution says as much.[44] The second abandons the speaker-based self-fulfilment principle for a separate model, applicable only to the press, that would protect as a source that the Government does not control.[45] Baker's commitment to the exclusion of profit-orientated enterprises is maintained, he argues, because the difference between, say, whiskey producers looking to protect comparative advertising under the First Amendment and newspaper owners looking to secure profits and satisfy shareholders is that the former produce whiskey *and* speech whilst the latter produce *only* speech.[46]

However, this differential approach ultimately relies upon the constitutional status of the press as an apparently separate rights-holder. This only works in those jurisdictions that would treat it as such. It does not work especially well in, say, the European context since Article 10 of the European Convention on Human Rights refers only to a solitary or unified 'freedom of expression' which expressly applies to 'everyone'. Moreover, the Strasbourg jurisprudence is clear that there can be no difference in speaker status as between the press and other speakers. The press is *not* a superior speaker.[47] In this jurisdiction, it seems, the critical element concerns what is *said* (ie, is it public interest speech?) and not *who* said it. Interestingly, Baker seems cognisant of this problem, for he states, in passing, that 'of course, the [whiskey] advertiser could also serve the checking function'.[48]

[43] ibid.
[44] ibid, 225.
[45] ibid 229–34.
[46] ibid, 234.
[47] See *Steel & Morris v UK* [2005] EMLR 15, [90]; *Magyar Helsinki Bizottsag v Hungary* app no 19030/11, [168].
[48] Baker (n 11) 234.

Similarly, Scanlon's autonomy-based theory takes its lead from Mill's argument from truth but with notable concessions to process theory, such that although all 'acts of expression' qualify, regardless of content,[49] for coverage, such that protection is subject only to the harm principle, still, he maintains, political speech enjoys a 'special' status: 'there are clearly cases in which individuals have a right to information necessary to make informed choices and can claim this right against the government'.[50] Consequently, although Scanlon dismisses the idea that the parameters of coverage can be drawn according to typology (since, he says, there can be 'no theoretically interesting … definition of the class of acts'),[51] still, when reasons to interfere reflect 'competing goods', a difference is bound to emerge that would, say, distinguish artistic expression from scientific expression.[52] These differences would be greater 'still for expression of political views'.[53] Accordingly, Scanlon's theory is a compromise between Mill's and Meiklejohn's position which, it transpires, satisfies no-one, not even Scanlon himself.[54]

What we see, then, across the entire spectrum of free speech thought, is an affinity to epistemology as an explanation, partial or complete, of the value of speech to human development, be that in the narrow sense of societal progress or the broader (and fullest) sense of noumenal self-development. Whilst this insight leads commentators in different directions, according to the specific value to be protected by the free speech guarantee – be that democratic participation, truth discovery, self-fulfilment/self-realisation or autonomy – there is tacit agreement that it is permissible to use epistemology as an analytical tool by which to determine the meaning and nature of free speech. The following section explores this apparent consensus in more detail so as to scrutinise the differing degrees by which epistemology gains its hold on free speech principle's design.

III. Minimal/Maximal Uses of Epistemology

The benefit (or detriment) of typologically preferred speech to epistemology is sometimes expressed minimally and sometimes maximally. Whereas we may encounter this approach in any formulation, it is especially apparent in process theory, in which the value of political speech to epistemic advance dominates. Understood minimally, it manifests as a right to know about activities of the state and to critique them. Robert Bork's interpretation is the exemplar of this approach. The First Amendment is not a tool of epistemology in its broadest sense – that is, to enable the noumenal being to make sense of herself and the world around her since. As we have seen, Bork thought

[49] T Scanlon, 'A Theory of Freedom of Expression' republished in RM Dworkin, *The Philosophy of Law* (Oxford University Press, 1977) 153, 155–56.

[50] ibid, 168.

[51] ibid, 156.

[52] ibid, 168.

[53] ibid.

[54] See TM Scanlon, 'Freedom of Expression and Categories of Expression' (1979) 40 *University of Pittsburgh Law Review* 519.

this sort of broad interpretation – of the kind that Brandeis gave it – would be so unprincipled as to require all forms of human gratification to be evaluated ('these benefits do not distinguish speech from any other human activity')[55] or else, in respect of the 'safety valve' function, confuse the political with the juridical ('decisions involving only judgments of expediency are for the political branches and not for the judiciary').[56] Hence, for Bork, political speech was sufficiently distinctive from all else because it separated 'human gratification'[57] from state governance.[58]

The epistemic ambitions of this analysis, then, are muted. Although Bork promotes a right to discover and spread 'political truths', he says nothing more that speaks to epistemology in a broader or deeper sense. The distributive aspects inherent in the task are qualified only by a need to avoid violence of the sort that would amount to violent overthrow of government, and action of that kind. Otherwise, he is uninterested in the deeper epistemological concerns of political truth. Accordingly, Bork can be understood to set the justification by the limitations that the Constitution places upon the state's use of coercive power.

Indeed, Bork's account may be said to represent two such constitutional limitations that speak to America's distinctive colonial experience under oppressive British rule. The first of these prohibits the state from immunising itself against criticism either internally (through censorial measures against the party in opposition) or externally, from the press or other sources of popular opinion. The second aspect, which is less pronounced in Bork's account but discernible nonetheless, prohibits the state from controlling, influencing or otherwise manipulating the discovery of 'truth'. This prohibition can manifest in different ways but, above all, it coalesces around notions of state indoctrination or thought-control[59] that are antithetical to freedom in a democratic political system. Again, the revulsion toward such control, especially when enforced through coercive force, speaks powerfully to the American tradition, as given to it through its colonial heritage, but also the broader experience of religious persecution that the Pilgrim Fathers sought to escape by leaving Europe behind. An argument such as this speaks most to malign influences misusing coercive powers to retain or otherwise enforce political control. Yet it extends also to the benign, if we accept Frederick Schauer's essential claim that the state is a blunt instrument that is simply too incompetent to make the correct determinations in this sphere.[60]

Given Bork's restrictive typology of valid free speech claim, this reasoning cannot be given its full force in Bork's case, as it could with, say, Frederick Schauer's 'distrust of government' analysis, Redish's self-fulfilment theory or Baker's self-realisation theory, since it would clearly extend to questions of 'human gratification' with equal effect. Nevertheless, the state's capacity to censor speech based on truth must be limited by those other constitutional values of tolerance and pluralism which give democracy its distinctive traits. Whereas it can contribute to public discourse by expressing its view on

[55] Bork (n 6) 25.
[56] ibid, 26.
[57] ibid.
[58] ibid, 27–28, 30.
[59] The theme of indoctrination figures highly in S Ingber, 'The Marketplace of Ideas: A Legitimizing Myth' (1984) 1984 *Duke Law Journal* 1.
[60] F Schauer, *Free Speech: A Philosophical Enquiry* (Cambridge University Press, 1982) 86.

the veracity of information, it cannot use its coercive power to enforce that position if it wishes to retain its credibility as a democracy.

Bork's account, then, represents a minimalist interpretation of epistemology's role within the process theory, which concentrates only on the limitations imposed upon the state to control public discourse. This may be contrasted with maximalist accounts that seek to introduce a programmatic dimension. Such accounts are typified by their treatment of free speech as a purposive account that seeks to enhance or else enrich the *quality* of democratic participation, such they focus upon the beneficial value of speech. Something of this optimisation can be seen in Vincent Blasi's checking value account: 'The abuse of official power is most likely to be checked effectively when the public has a sophisticated sense of what government actually does and what realistically can be expected of public officials'.[61]

For a minimalist such as Bork, this type of insight has no real juridical value. Whereas it might be accepted that such enlightenment will occur in the manner described, the principled judge can make no use of the sentiment given that its realisation requires overt regulation of public discourse. Such interventions would risk malevolent or incompetent interferences with speech that project an unjustified sense of infallibility in distinguishing epistemically beneficial from epistemically detrimental contributions to collective cognitive development. Also, such interventions would be inconsistent with the state's inability to suppress criticisms of its performance (by, for example, distinguishing between well-founded and inaccurate, misleading, or exaggerated criticisms).

Understood maximally, free speech is not about simply *protecting* epistemologically valuable speech as it arises; it is about *improving* the quality and conditions of epistemologically beneficial speech as well as *denying* or otherwise limiting the protection of epistemologically detrimental speech. This has a profound impact upon the juridical task. Maximalists seek to overcome, or otherwise ameliorate, the problems that Bork identifies by introducing motive into the equation. This allows for a narrative in which good and bad motives for interfering are recognised, such that US heritage is preserved but distinguished. This allows for a sort of 'functionality' dynamic to creep into the commentary. This element is present, and highly significant, in Meiklejohn. The First Amendment, he said, is not 'the guardian of unregulated talkativeness'.[62] Instead, it facilitates the making of 'wise decisions' on public issues: 'what is essential is not that everyone shall speak, but that everything worth saying shall be said'.[63] An authentic act of free speech, therefore, is that which enhances public discourse. Accordingly, this analysis permits such interferences with speech that represent 'moderation' of debate, as seen in a classic 'Town Hall meeting' on community matters. Obviously, this analysis assumes, or is otherwise contingent upon, the presence of noble intentions in such regulatory activity. This is a complex machinery. It is not simply a distinction between content and structure, since the content of the debate is controlled in an

[61] V Blasi, 'The Checking Value in First Amendment Theory' (1977) *American Bar Foundation Research Journal* 521, 603.
[62] A Meiklejohn, *Political Freedom: The Constitutional Powers of the People* (Oxford University Press, 1965) 26.
[63] ibid.

obvious and powerful way. Yet, if it is conducted in business-like fashion, to ensure timely progression of matters, taking in the key or significant points, then the insidiousness of content interference is less than content discrimination, if not entirely content neutral, of the type scholars promote.

Meiklejohn's reasoning found favour with both Owen Fiss and Cass Sunstein who, separately, have argued that free speech has a specific, confined epistemic ambition to optimise the cognitive faculties of the populace, at least in respect of public decision-making. In keeping with Blasi's views (above) about the positive impact upon public discourse of civic enlightenment, they imagine the juridical task to be focus on questions of epistemic advance on political topics, such that the principled judge should ask if speech 'enrich[es] public debate'[64] or would 'best promote democratic deliberation'.[65] This is because, says Sunstein, the constitution manifests 'a structural commitment to deliberative democracy'.[66] Thus, 'the free speech principle should be understood to be centered above all on political thought. In this way [it] should be seen through the lens of democracy'.[67]

Accordingly, it may be said that these accounts are predicated upon a purposive interpretation of free speech in which epistemic *optimisation* figures highly. For these commentators, the notion of free speech as an expression of government incapacity or invalidity in respect of speech, or certain speech, is an inadequate explanation. Instead, the right is an ambitious social tool for maximising the cognitive faculties of the people, such that the juridical question becomes one that examines the *effect* of (contested) speech in achieving this social goal. State interferences are still subject to judicial scrutiny but the introduction of motive caters for discerning tastes. Interference, then, becomes acceptable *if* it can be said it has positive epistemic impact, and is motivated only by such (so that 'wise' decision-making or an optimised public discourse will emerge).

As Post says, this interpretation has unintended consequences. Instead of strengthening public discourse, it jeopardises it. It adopts a regulatory position that is contrary to its aims

> because public discourse is precisely the site of political contention about the nature of collective identity, and it is only by reference to some vision of collective identity that speech can be categorized as relevant or irrelevant, abusive or not abusive, high or low value.[68]

Meiklejohnian logic is fatally flawed, then, because there is no 'possible neutral position' by which to moderate public discourse.[69] Hence, juridical optimisation of public discourse is achieved, and only achieved, by compromising 'the integrity of processes of collective thinking'[70] and causing 'alienation or disaffection'.[71]

[64] Fiss (n 25) 19.
[65] CR Sunstein, 'Preferences and Politics' (1991) 20 *Philosophy and Public Affairs* 3, 28.
[66] Sunstein (n 26) 249.
[67] ibid, 252.
[68] RC Post, 'Reconciling Theory and Doctrine in First Amendment Jurisprudence' (2000) 88 *California Law Review* 2353, 2369.
[69] ibid.
[70] ibid, 2369.
[71] RC Post, 'Meiklejohn's Mistake: Individual Autonomy and the Reform of Public Discourse' (1993) 64 *University of Colorado Law Review* 1109, 1134.

The Meiklejohnian position, then, demands or otherwise permits a consequentialism to creep into judicial decision-making that runs contrary to the essence of content neutrality. Such consequentialism would allow for interferences with speech which does not benefit epistemic advance in demonstrable or, even, ostensible ways. Both mis- and disinformation would be prone to censorship on the ground that the epistemic agent might reach the *wrong* conclusions and so adopt positions that are false. This insight leads Post to also say that First Amendment jurisprudence is unsuited to such determinations since it 'recognizes no such thing as a "false" idea'.[72] Consequently, he says further that the free speech concept cannot be understood in terms of (what he calls) a 'cognitive value' since epistemological practices demand such censorship and since the First Amendment has no workable methodology of making the required distinctions it must be treated as entirely 'unsuited for the creation of new knowledge'.[73]

Post's is an extreme position, which will shall revisit in the following chapter. Nevertheless, there are parallels between his view and Bork's. Part of the reason why Bork is so keen to eliminate speech beyond the 'explicitly political' is his profound concern that otherwise the principled judge would otherwise lapse into moments of unprincipled Lochnerism, in which her own social and political values would dominate and lead her astray.[74] Yet even Post succumbs to a sort of consequentialism in his view that commercial speech is irrelevant to democratic participation in any meaningful sense.[75] Likewise the position of both Scanlon and Seana Valentine Shiffrin is also prone to the problem of consequentialism. Although both eschew purposive typology as means of determining coverage, still both cannot escape the problem altogether in their insistence that speech is 'necessary' for epistemic advance. For this 'necessity' dynamic introduces a causality that could be overcome through contrary empirical states. Again, this is a problem that we shall address more fully in the following section.

Redish sees this problem clearly. If self-realisation meant only self-government, then it would protect only that which *will* 'aid an individual in making decisions about how his or her life will be conducted'. Accordingly:

> [A]dvocacy of unlawful conduct cannot be deemed relevant, because the individual is not allowed to undertake the conduct urged by that form of expression. Nor is the dissemination of undisputedly false factual information a valid means of aiding private self-government, since such information cannot be thought to provide legitimate guidance to individual decisionmaking A mere stream of obscenities must also be deemed irrelevant to the goal of private self-government.[76]

Here, then, we see the concern that free-speech-as-an-epistemic-concern invites the judge to make consequentialist decisions. For if the claim is that free speech aids, say, self-fulfilment or individual autonomy, then problems arise, at least intellectually, if the disputed material is too unwholesome to benefit such a worthy pursuit. Hate speech and pornography are two obvious examples that serve only to denigrate the participant and her subjects/opponents.

[72] *Hustler Magazine v Falwell* 485 US 46, 51 (1988).
[73] Post (n 17) 479.
[74] ibid, 28.
[75] Post (n 28) 47.
[76] Redish (n 9) 627.

Redish overcomes this problem, at least partially, by rendering self-realisation to be a methodology that protects speech both instrumentally and intrinsically. This intrinsic element he describes in broadly Millian terms that values speech as a means of protecting 'the development of one's human faculties':[77]

> There is more to self-realization, however, than private self-government. For it is highly doubtful that fine art, ballet, or literature can be thought to aid one in making concrete life-affecting decisions, yet all three seem deserving of full first amendment protection. This is because of the other branch of self-realization: the development of one's human faculties, recognized as an end in itself. Once this form of self-realization is acknowledged, it becomes significantly more difficult to exclude many of the categories of expression deemed irrelevant to the private self-government branch.[78]

Redish is not alone in making this claim: both Scanlon and Shiffrin value speech in this way. The difference, at least ostensibly, is that if speech is valued intrinsically then the opportunity to interfere is severely curtailed. Strictly, no interference with speech is tolerable, rendering free speech entitled to protection *absolutely*.

Of course, this is *not* a move that Redish seeks to make. Emphatically, he is not saying that protection should be afforded by the state whenever it encounters something that fits the description of 'speech'. Redish, like all other commentators, would permit interference when speech causes intolerable, or rather undue, harm. In this respect, Redish's account bears little difference from either Mill's or Holmes's account since neither of these applies a purposive typology to the treatment of speech at the coverage stage of juridical treatment. This aspect of both Mill's and Holmes's conceptions of free speech are often overlooked, as if both are concerned with nothing more than the success of epistemic advance.

Certainly, this is untrue in respect of Mill. Indeed, given the conclusions of the previous chapter, we can go further than John Gray, who said that 'truth itself is *sometimes* regarded by Mill as but the upshot of open debate',[79] to say that it is *always* incidental, for Mill's concern is not with epistemic advance but the proper protection of autonomy. However, Mill obfuscates on this point because, unlike, say, Kant, he does not provide neat distinctions between the ethical and juridical in his moral reasoning. This confusion is not aided – in fact, is compounded by – the opening quotation, taken from Wilhelm Von Humboldt's *Sphere and Duties of Government*,[80] 'the grand, leading principle, towards which every argument unfolded in these pages directly converges, is the absolute and essential importance of human development in its richest diversity'.[81] This, of itself, would seem to suggest that Mill's scheme for free speech principle is firmly rooted in epistemology. Yet, if that were so, the irrationality proviso, so carefully crafted in those lesser read parts of *On Liberty*, especially chapters three to five, would be rendered nugatory. Of course, undoubtedly, there *is* a clear epistemological theme to *On Liberty*. Nevertheless (in common with Kant),[82] it is a matter

[77] ibid.
[78] ibid.
[79] J Gray, *Mill on Liberty: A Defence*, 2nd edn (Routledge, 1996) 110.
[80] Otherwise known as *The Limits of State Action* (W Von Humboldt, *The Limits of State Action* (JW Burrow, ed), [1792, 1854] (Cambridge University Press, 1969).
[81] Mill (n 2) 215.
[82] See discussion in ch 8.

only for the noumenal being herself, for whom free speech (amongst other things) helps develop those critical faculties necessary to separate reason from unreason, and not the state as such. Certainly, epistemic advance is not to be achieved by compulsion. Hence, we are given his four well-known reasons for tolerating irrationality – the assumption of infallibility in penalising error, the value of counter-speech to counteract falsehood, the inevitability of truth to become dead dogma if not capable of being contested, and the loss of new insights into truth if experiments in living that truth are not tolerated.[83] Whereas his position on coercion is rooted in the juridical, his commitment to the value of epistemic advance upon individual well-being belongs to the ethical realm.

Likewise, the connection between free speech and epistemic advance in Holmes's rationale might be disputed too. The central tenet of his dissent in *Abrams v US* that 'the best test of truth is the power of the thought to get itself accepted in the competition of the market'[84] seems, incontrovertibly, to be epistemological. Certainly, it is often understood this way. Perhaps it too has become a dead dogma of the kind that Mill warned of – not because we are prevented from discussing it but from constant repetition of this short statement alone. Nevertheless, the underlying context of his dissent demonstrates that he was far from believing there was anything meaningful to ascertained from the prosecuted speech. After all, he is emphatic that the speech is a mere 'silly leaflet'.[85] Moreover, he is fairly damning in his view that the leaflet espouses a 'creed of ignorance and immaturity when honestly held'.[86]

Like Mill, Holmes's position is disserved by the language of 'truth' which, it seems, signifies not verifiable (or non-falsifiable) fact as such, but belief in a course of (political) action. Instead, it is meant to convey the liberal nexus of wrongdoing–harm–causation as the means by which the state, through Congress, is entitled to regulate the actions of citizens in pursuit of preserving, in this case, democratic will through laws of sedition. On the facts of the case, clearly, Holmes was unconvinced that the defendants in the prosecution had acted in ways that should meet the high threshold by which incitement to undermine the war effort – imploring factory workers to 'sabotage' the war effort by refusing to make or else supply the bullets by which Russian revolutionaries may be stopped in realising their own political will by overthrowing the state. The words complained of – to Holmes's mind – were merely earnest attempts at persuasion and not sedition: 'Congress certainly cannot forbid all effort to change the mind of the country.'[87]

Accordingly, when Holmes speaks of a 'free trade in ideas',[88] he speaks not of the speaker's position but that of the state. Hence, Holmes says:

> Persecution for the expression of opinions seems to me perfectly logical. If you have no doubt of your premises or your power, and want a certain result with all your heart, you naturally express your wishes in law, and sweep away all opposition.[89]

[83] See recapitulation at end of ch II (n 2) 259.
[84] *Abrams v US* 250 US 616, 628 (1919).
[85] ibid, 628.
[86] ibid, 629.
[87] ibid, 628.
[88] ibid, 630.
[89] ibid.

Yet, says Holmes, this is not the constitutional constraint that the US has made for its Government through the First Amendment. Whilst this provision could be understood as suggesting that mere words alone are 'impotent' or else cannot conceivably convey the sense that those in power are weak if they reconsider their decisions or reasons for action, this is still not the logic underpinning the First Amendment – it represents a profound commitment to rule by popular will, even if that will is proven to be misconstrued or ill-founded. Hence, he says:

> But when men have realized that time has upset many fighting faiths, they may come to believe even more than they believe the very foundations of their own conduct that the ultimate good desired is better reached by free trade in ideas – that the best test of truth is the power of the thought to get itself accepted in the competition of the market, and that truth is the only ground upon which their wishes safely can be carried out.[90]

In other words, the 'they' is those in power. It is they who act 'safely' when they allow the basis upon which they act to be determined by the 'free trade in ideas'. Of course, 'best' is a relative term. Moreover, Holmes is not saying that this is an incontrovertible proposition, only that this 'at any rate, is the theory of our Constitution. It is an experiment, as all life is an experiment.'[91]

Holmes concludes his point in strong terms:

> Every year, if not every day, we have to wager our salvation upon some prophecy based upon imperfect knowledge. While that experiment is part of our system, I think that we should be eternally vigilant against attempts to check the expression of opinions that we loathe and believe to be fraught with death, unless they so imminently threaten immediate interference with the lawful and pressing purposes of the law that an immediate check is required to save the country.[92]

Accordingly, it seems to me, US commentators are wrong to reject the 'marketplace of ideas' theory, at least as Holmes conceived it, as a flawed means of deriving epistemically valuable speech. This is not what Holmes is saying. Instead, he is conceiving the means by which the state can regulate speech-as-opinion and does so in terms that resonate with Mill's theory: that other-regarding speech should be regulated according to the harm principle, ie, the liberal nexus of wrongdoing-harm-causation. This proposition is explored in greater detail in chapter eight.

IV. Feasibility

For the process theorist, the ultimate epistemological ambition for free speech is the collation of an ideal repository of information containing verified factual material and the most diverse range of opinions concerning those materials.[93] In this way, the

[90] ibid.
[91] ibid.
[92] ibid, 630.
[93] See, eg, AT Kenyon, 'Positive Free Speech: A Democratic Freedom' in A Stone and F Schauer (eds), *The Oxford Handbook of Freedom of Speech* (Oxford University Press, 2021) 233.

citizen has, at her disposal, optimised epistemic tools by which to fulfil her duties as a responsible agent of democratic participation. Those espousing the autonomy-based claims of Baker, Redish and, to a lesser extent, Scanlon and Shiffrin, also seek to use free speech in this way. Yet, despite the epistemological overtones of both Mill and Holmes, the same is not true for them. This is because Mill and Holmes recognise, to a greater extent than, certainly, Baker, Redish and Scanlon/Shiffrin, that epistemic advance is a contingent event over which the state can have no dominion. Although epistemology has a relationship with the free dissemination of speech, especially in the ability to challenge received wisdoms, it is, for Mill and Holmes, a byproduct. As such, epistemology is irrelevant to the juridical task (of determining its parameters). In other words, the free speech guarantee is not about knowledge or thinking, as Shiffrin has it. Here we see free speech conceptualisation as a forward-orientated rather than backward-looking process: the free speech guarantee may well lead to epistemic advance but that is not its purpose. This section, then, is a defence of Mill's and Holmes's position. It advances three connected arguments: that relate to the state's interest in cognitive faculty development, to the meaning of epistemology, and to the role of censorship in epistemic advance. Each claim is taken in turn.

To begin with, a clarification is in order. Meiklejohn did not pretend that the state had a legitimate interest in correcting epistemic failings within the voting public: 'A citizen may not be told what he shall or shall not believe. In that realm each citizen is sovereign.'[94] Other scholars have sought to undermine or at least modify this position by introducing a specific epistemic failing within the general populace – that, although the state cannot *control* belief, it is still justified in some level of epistemic interference since the people lack the requisite rationality to separate truth from falsity when falsehood is alluring. This is sometimes presented as a problem of irrationality or, more generously, a question of 'bounded rationality'. The necessity of intervention, then, could resemble the form of a 'correction' in the speech or else counter-speech, if not outright censorship.

Talk of 'bounded rationality' is, perhaps, unproblematic as a purely sociological observation, but becomes so if used to justify interference, for it presupposes that freedom of speech is a matter of epistemological perfection. However, to justify this conception requires the theorist to adopt, or otherwise endorse, the communitarian standard as the base unit of constitutional design. If that is so then the word 'freedom' becomes either redundant or else severely enfeebled. The noumenal being would have the 'freedom' only to disseminate known or accepted truths which, at best, can only serve to stunt cognitive development and, at worst, would render her an agent of state-endorsed dogma. She could 'contribute' only in this very narrow sense. She could not develop, enhance or elucidate state dogma unless she had authority to do so. In theocratic and authoritarian contexts, this limitation is the necessary norm because only certain institutions (synod, caliphate, politburo) are empowered to interpret them.

[94] Meiklejohn (n 1) 257.

In a system in which individuality is the base unit, such interferences are illegitimate because, as the last chapter made clear, they conflict with the irrationality proviso. In at least partial recognition of this problem, Post argues that the epistemology value has no role to play in understanding the free speech principle, as noted above. However, Post is unconvincing on this point in his insistence that those regimes of epistemic advance that we find in, say, academia, especially in the context of scientific knowledge, depend upon practices of censorship. We can distinguish between those contexts in which epistemic credentials, as we find in not only academia but also in the professions, depend upon those credentials for the purposes of professional recognition and advancement. In these contexts, the interference speaks not to epistemology as such but, rather, the trade in epistemic credentials. Since the person who claims to be a solicitor, accountant, doctor, etc, professes to have aptitude to perform certain operations, government interference speaks to simple harm analytics. The state's concern, here, is that the purported professional who has insufficient knowledge is likely to cause physical and psychological harm to her patient or client. This reasoning applies also, after a fashion, to the academic context. The publisher of learned journals, etc, has a legitimate interest in ensuring its standing in the marketplace is maintained through mechanisms such as peer review. Strictly speaking, this is not the epistemic value in operation. It is a contingency that speaks to risk management in the publication of material that furthers this legitimate (profit-orientated) market-based interest.

As Mill (and Holmes) saw clearly, epistemic advance can occur even in contexts where the autonomous agent is subject to demonstrably false information. To appreciate this insight requires a deeper grounding in the nature of epistemology as a philosophical concern. The empiricists, David Hume and John Locke, for example, were given to understand that knowledge required more than simply acquaintance with accepted facts or norms. Thus, Locke was driven to say that 'the floating of other Men's opinions in our brains makes us not a jot more knowing though they happen to be true'.[95] Hence for Hume and Locke, true knowledge was a sensory or cognitive matter that required something in the order of direct experience. According to Hume, knowledge as justified true belief requires both the cognitive apparatus to discern truth and the relevant sensory event to experience it. Without these, the autonomous agent possesses only a contingent belief (a probable opinion) that is subject to change (ie, Humean scepticism). For the Humean sceptic, received information is contingent upon further and better particulars – what Popper would call the prospect of 'falsification'.[96] In other words, the autonomous agent operates on the basis of healthy distrust in what she is told, because its verifiability (or non-falsifiability) is subject to her epistemic limitations. For the empiricists, then, knowledge acquisition, as the pursuit of certainty (about truth), cannot be a passive process. Whereas the epistemic agent can recall what they have been told, they cannot claim to possess knowledge without more. That the world is spherical, that gravity stops us from floating off into space, and that water is a compound comprised of hydrogen and oxygen, are

[95] J Locke, *An Essay Concerning Human Understanding* [1689] (Hackett, 1996) I, iv, §23.
[96] K Popper, *Objective Knowledge: an Evolutionary Approach* (Oxford University Press, 1979).

epistemologically sound positions to adopt but they rely upon a deeper level of epistemic advance than recollection alone. What is acquired through experience depends as much upon epistemic luck as cognitive ability. Such reasoning led Mill to conclude that to tolerate only the repetition of accepted opinion subdued and jeopardised the cognitive faculties of the epistemic agent for if she could only repeat what was known rather than to test or question its essential proposition, she would possess only dead dogma and not true knowledge.

Epistemologists have sought to ameliorate the strictness of Humean scepticism by means of an ethical–epistemological hybrid claim in which certain sources of information may be said to have an epistemic purpose, such that the 'epistemically dependent' public may rely upon them.[97] The ethical dimension manifests, then, in the 'trust' that is apparent in, or common to, everyday situations in which reliance is placed upon the apparent epistemic superiority of another person's claims. This scenario might arise in a social setting, as when a stranger is entrusted to give directions[98] or an academic setting, as when scientists collaborate to produce joint papers.[99] On this basis, it has been said that 'trust is often epistemologically even more basic than empirical data or logical arguments'.[100] This argument has been developed to admit institutional contexts, of which the press is taken to be an exemplar. Thus, in conveying information to furtherance of the grand repository ideal, they are said to have an obligation not to deceive[101] or to display greater intellectual honesty in speculative or compromised truth-claims,[102] or that newspapers should eschew 'the profit-maximizing pressures of sensational reporting' in favour of 'high quality science journalism',[103] or that the selection of expert sources is an ethical concern.[104] Similarly, one commentator has argued that journalism can be distinguished from 'fake news' by 'the *motivation* to convey accurate information, rather than in outcome-oriented terms'.[105]

Central to this trust-based dynamic is the pragmatic concession necessitated by distinct resource-based limitations within the autonomous agent relating to time, opportunity and cognitive ability. If it is taken to be no more than an ethical observation – ie, a means of labelling the epistemologically indifferent journalist as unethical – then it is of no significance for our purposes. The problem arises if (and when) commentators seek to pivot from this claim to make demands upon the juridical task of determining

[97] See, eg, J Hardwig, 'Epistemic Dependence' (1985) 82 *Journal of Philosophy* 335.

[98] J Lackey, Testimonial Knowledge and Transmission (1999) 49 *Philosophical Quarterly* 471, 484.

[99] Hardwig gives the example of a paper about particle physics with an incredible 99 joint authors (n 97) 346.

[100] J Hardwig, 'The Role of Trust in Knowledge' (1991) 88 *Journal of Philosophy* 693, 694.

[101] O O'Neill, *A Question of Trust* (Cambridge University Press, 2002) 96–100. See also C Schwarzenegger, 'Personal epistemologies of the media: Selective criticality, pragmatic trust, and competence-confidence in navigating media repertoires in the digital age' (2020) 22 *New Media & Society* 361–77, 366.

[102] Z Soysal, 'Truth in Journalism' in JE Katz and KK Mays (eds), *Journalism and Truth in an Age of Social Media* (Oxford University Press, 2020) 103–16, 110.

[103] G Irzik and F Kurtulmus, 'What Is Epistemic Public Trust in Science?' (2019) 70 *British Journal for the Philosophy of Science* 1145, 1163.

[104] M Carlson, 'Dueling, Dancing, or Dominating? Journalists and Their Sources' (2009) *Sociology Compass* 526.

[105] D Pritchard, 'Good News, Bad News, Fake News' in S Bernecker, A Flowerre and T Grundman (eds), *Epistemology of Fake News* (Oxford University Press, 2021).

free speech: then it could be said that the state might interfere with inaccurate speech without betraying free speech principle so as to ensure the audience receives the (quality of) information that it is entitled to.

Something of this reasoning can be found in Andrew Kenyon's work on free speech as a positive right. His position, built upon the *necessity* of public discourse to democratic participation, differs from that of Post[106] (which will be examined in the next chapter). Specifically, he says, 'what one can hear is central to democratic choice, not only what one can say … the law can require state action in pursuit of communicative freedom'.[107] This is not merely desirable or beneficial to democratic participation, says Kenyon; it is essential: 'to express opinions and have political effect … people need to form opinions, and, for that to be substantially legitimate, it *needs* sustained plural political speech'.[108] Thus, 'sustained plural public speech is required for democracy to have communicative legitimacy'.[109]

However, this presupposes the existence of 'epistemic workers'[110] (not Kenyon's phrase) who can be compelled to provide this type of speech, if necessary. Obviously, such coercion runs contrary to the individuality dynamic (but not the communitarian one) such that it demands greater justification than Kenyon's rhetoric provides. As we saw in the previous chapter, the argument transgresses the sharp divide between the ethical and the juridical. Kenyon avoids this difficulty by limiting the practical ambition that the normative position would otherwise permit, for he is not (or not necessarily) arguing that individual autonomy be sacrificed on the alter of audience prerogative. Instead, he argues that the state's obligation, as he sees it, to facilitate plurality informs the allocative choices made by publicly owned broadcasters when determining content. To that end, Kenyon makes much of media ownership laws (which can be explained, of course, in competition terms without any reference to free speech ideals at all). Further, he argues that the judiciary should take this plurality obligation into account when called upon to supervise this allocative decision-making. This curbs individual autonomy only to the same degree that managerial instruction would in an employment context. The autonomous being chooses to forego some degree of individual autonomy in exchange for the work–wage bargain.[111] The state, as paymaster, can issue directions in favour of democratic values, such as plurality, so long as there is no conflict with others, including, chiefly, the right to criticise. In this regard, he points to the experiences of German and (albeit to a lesser extent) French courts.[112]

[106] By his own admission, see A Kenyon, *Democracy of Expression* (Cambridge University Press, 2021) 217–18.
[107] ibid.
[108] ibid, 214.
[109] ibid, 217.
[110] H Örnebring, 'Epistemologies and Professional Roles' in C Mellado, L Hellmueller and W Donsbach (eds), *Journalistic role performances: Concepts, context and methods* (Routledge, 2017) 75.
[111] Although see discussion in ch 11.
[112] See Kenyon (n 106) 139–208.

Even if we put the existence and justification for epistemic workers aside, we should scrutinise the (intuitively appealing) claim that democratic society *needs* epistemically rich speech relating to political scenarios. Kenyon's work is a case in point. As seen above, in arguing for the necessity of pluralism, he argues that receipt of information (access to the debate as an audience member) is central to the concept of democracy he has in mind. This access is so important that the audience *needs* it. Of course, no one would question that democracy *wants* such speech as it would also want engaged, inquisitive citizens. However, 'need' presupposes some prerequisite. In an epistemic sense, there is no conditional link between the capacity to vote (or belong to the *Sittlichkeit*) and cognitive faculty. Neither the epistemic credentials of the voter nor the cogency of voting intentions is tested prior to voting. There is no ongoing assessment of cognitive capacity between voting opportunities. What then is the basis of the term 'need'? There is nothing in the formal requirements of democratic participation that would justify the term. Neither can it be said that the state cannot function without an epistemically optimised electorate.

For Kenyon, clearly, necessity is linked to the speaker function itself: 'To express opinions and have political effect … people need to form opinions.'[113] However, this modification does not alter the tenor of the criticism. The equality value eliminates the advantage (or disadvantage) of the contribution. If we follow Meiklejohnian logic, clearly 'wise voting' will follow, we hope, from the most elaborate, comprehensive and incisive analysis of whatever social problem is under consideration. Yet, there is nothing in the formal structure of democratic participation, as it relates to voting, that would dictate, or otherwise justify, this insistence upon necessity. Poorly formed, ill-judged opinions are as valid to democratic discourse as careful, reasoned ones. That is but an inevitability of the 'one person, one vote' underpinning of the democratic state. Moreover, the implication of 'effectiveness' in public discourse runs contrary to the tenor of anti-elitism that signifies democracy. As a majoritarian process, at least in terms of voting, the effectiveness of political debate is not, or should not be, in the wisdom of the vote but its popularity. Subject to important qualifications, relating to those other values of a democracy relating to pluralism, tolerance and equality, the appeal of a political position centrally is not necessarily that it is the wisest course of action but that it represents the democratic will of the people. This clamour for epistemic perfection is admirable but it cannot claim to be a basic minimum (a precondition) in the way that Kenyon (and others) say.

Allied to this is the problem of epistemic misunderstanding. Even if we could say that access to the debate, as an audience member, is essential, and so holds the status that Kenyon attaches to it, what is to be done to ensure that the message is received as it should be? In the dialogical scenarios illustrated above – of receiving directions from a stranger or of collaborative work to achieve epistemic advance – the opportunity exists to clarify understanding such that the epistemic transfer of information is more or less perfect (or perfectible). In these scenarios of high-level interactivity, the parties

[113] ibid, 214.

will alternate, constantly, in their role as speaker and listener (audience). In a purely audience context, though, the dialogic function does not arise. The audience member receives information to which she must apply her own cognitive faculties. In circumstances of low information content, such as a news bulletin, she may find the speech is ambiguous or speaks to an epistemic gap in her knowledge/experience such that she misunderstands or otherwise cannot comprehend the message. Such is the nature of language that this scenario may be said to arise frequently and leads to epistemic failings that the (good faith) speaker neither intended nor foresaw. Even if there are no such failings within the transmission itself, there can be no guarantee that the epistemic agent will receive it or, moreover, accept it. This then alters the generality of the necessity claim. If the audience 'needs' (rather than 'wants') this information, for the purposes of opinion formation, etc, then the disquieting implication is that the state can force the audience, willing or not, to both receive it and accept it.

In a political system where individuality is the base language of constitutional design, then no such move is possible. The audience member is entitled to form her own opinions, whether rational, accurate and reliable, or not. Where community is the base language, such moves are permissible, but result not in internal acceptance but the mere external impression of such. In such systems, denial of a political truth is not tolerated and is punishable. Accordingly, it must be the case that epistemic deficiencies – ranging from ignorance to wilful refusal to accept the truth – in audience understandings are an unavoidable, inescapable feature of the democratic freedom to vote according to conscience alone. Thus, Mill's argument must stand for the legitimacy of falsehood within the noumenal being's reasoning, not because it is social valuable but because correction requires, in the final analysis, force of a kind that would be both morally repugnant and inherently incompatible with the ideal of a free state.

Understandably, then, Kenyon's position speaks to no such coercion. It is instead limited to a purported 'right to hear' – that is, an appreciable desire on the part of engaged and compassionate voters to hear all sides, including the underrepresented. This presents a further problem for Kenyon, which relates to the question of how this audience makes their intentions known to the state. It is one thing for the state to act from an intuitive or reasoned sense of what values democracy stands in furtherance of them (ie, equality and plurality); it is another to claim that this initiative is driven by audience intentions – for if such intentions exist, then why not leave it to the market to respond? Kenyon's point is that the market cannot be trusted to meet this demand because, for example, owner intention, in pursuance of specific world views, may prevent it. This is a compelling argument only in so far as it goes. Stubborn owner resistance to market demands can last only for as long as the owner's financial resources do. If there is, in fact, a market for pluralistic viewpoints, then others can be expected to cash in on this lucrative source of revenue. The idea that such a lucrative market exists but is stubbornly ignored by all entrants to the market defies what we know of human nature in a competitive capitalist environment. Nevertheless, Kenyon's point is surely not that such markets do not exist, but that they are not popular or, perhaps, not sufficiently mainstream.

V. Conclusion

To varying degrees, the epistemic value is put to work by commentators in pursuit of a grand repository by which society might achieve the ultimate source of epistemically valuable information. In this way, free speech is pressed into the service of a political agenda, as if theory is but a form of social engineering for the realisation of a collectively valuable goal. This sense of politicalisation is so widespread that it separates the modern (orthodox) approach to free speech theory design from the past. For, whereas, since Meiklejohn, at least, theorists have sought to explicate the free speech guarantee in terms of its (nominated) beneficial value to society – be that democratic participation, truth discovery, self-realisation/self-fulfilment or else the benefits to autonomous ways of living – the Millian tradition (of which Holmes's 'marketplace of ideas' is an example) exemplifies a detached sense of the guarantee's benefits to communal living. Whilst Mill (and Holmes) could freely acknowledge that epistemic advance would be impossible without the freedom to challenge received wisdoms, that fact alone still meant little to the intellectual design of authentic free speech principle.

In keeping with the radical past, it has been argued in this chapter that epistemology is not a viable candidate for authenticity in the construction of free speech principle. It is a byproduct of freedom, not a design component. Specifically, it has sought to show that we cannot be faithful to democracy if we co-opt the free speech right into some grand design for realising the ideal repository of epistemologically valuable information. In the final analysis, the state can have no real interest in the cognitive perfectibility of its citizens. It follows that epistemology is a meaningless metric in evaluating free speech principle. We cannot say that the free speech guarantee exists to *ensure* epistemic advance any more than we can use it as the basis of free speech's meaning or definition so as to detect instances of free speech in action. Neither can we seek to differentiate the epistemically valuable or beneficial from the epistemically suspect or detrimental. For if we say that free speech means epistemologically valuable expression, then we must, by logical necessity, say that it excludes epistemologically detrimental speech in the final analysis. Otherwise, if we are *not* saying this about free speech's meaning – if we are ackmnowleging that even epistemologically detrimental speech might be protected by it – then we concede that epistemology is *not* an authentic principle for free speech theory's design but, as Mill and Holmes would have it, a byproduct or unrelated feature.

We must, then, discard epistemologically from the list of candidates for authentic design and look to the next. In doing so, the following chapter examines alternate uses of information in the programme of process theory. This alternative arises from another interpretation or, perhaps, notable feature of the way in which commentators use epistemology is to attach a formal role to free speech in the experiment of communal living that Holmes describes democracy as. As we have seen, this formality ascribes specific purpose to protected speech itself, as if the free speech guarantee is there only to ensure that society benefits from the realisation of this specific individual right. There is something of this formality, as we have seen, in Kenyon's work on positive freedom, in its exploration of how public finances might be used optimally for communication purposes. However, it is much more present, in terms of both significance and comprehensiveness, in the work of Jürgen Habermas, and, to a lesser extent, Robert Post, whose Habermasian influences are abundantly apparent. For them, the formality of free speech manifests both in symbolic terms, as a signifier of the individual's inherent worth as a valued stakeholder in democratic participation, and, in (perhaps) more material terms, as an enabler of the conduit function by which both the (central) state and (dispersed) participatory stakeholder might readily communicate the efficiency of the economy (or, in more Hegelian terms, health of the *Sittlichkeit*).

7

Democratic Participation

I. Introduction

Robert Post's conception of free speech is notable for its rejection of the epistemic value in the construction of authentic principle. Accordingly, his work represents the ideal lens by which to scrutinise democratic participation as an alternative candidate for authenticity in (narrower) terms that transcends epistemological considerations. For, according to Post, free speech manifests not in the extent to which speech is *valuable* to democratic self-rule but in the *opportunity* to influence collective decision-making through contributions to public discourse. Thus, the free speech right enables the citizen to feel *valued* in, rather than alienated or isolated from, the (political) world she inhabits.[1] It is, he says, this participatory value, and not epistemology,[2] that provides the most compelling reason to protect free speech (at least, that is, as the US judiciary understands the term). Hence, he argues that forward movements in advancing free speech theory should be governed by this participatory value, which represents a marriage of individual will with collective self-determination.[3]

In this regard, Post's work evokes Hegel's conception of the ethical life (the *Sittlichkeit*). Although Hegel's term represents a generality (if it represents anything at all),[4] its political dimension speaks to an ideal civic community whose search for the right or best solution to collective problems or dilemmas is occasioned by their individual needs and the availability of protection for their (individual) rights and interests by the state.[5] This collective is guided by a common 'conscience'[6] (and conscionability)[7] in which 'ethics is the interpenetration of the subjective and the

[1] RC Post, 'Democracy and Equality' (2006) 603 *Annals of the American Academy of Political and Social Science* 24, 27, 'must experience the state as in some way responsive to [her] own values and ideas'.

[2] RC Post, 'Reconciling Theory and Doctrine in First Amendment Jurisprudence' (2000) 88 *California Law Review* 2353, 2371: 'the participatory approach does not focus on the cognitive cogency of speech, but rather on its facilitation of democratic participation'.

[3] Post (n 1) 27.

[4] See, eg, EF Carritt, 'Hegel's Sittlichkeit' (1936) 36 *Proceedings of the Aristotelian Society* 223, for whom the term means merely obedience to the state (235–36), or HC Gutteridge, 'Abuse of Rights' (1933–35) 5 *Cambridge Law Journal* 22, who described it as 'impossible to translate … into English' (37).

[5] GWF Hegel, *Elements of the Philosophy of the Right* (AW Wood, ed) (Cambridge University Press, 1991) §157.

[6] ibid, §141.

[7] ibid, §§142–57.

objective'[8] culminating in a 'customary morality'.[9] As chapter five demonstrated, Hegelian freedom differs significantly from its Millian counterpart in its preference for rationality over irrationality in individual decision-making. Cultural identity (as a sort of obedience to the communal goals of the state) and the dialectical movement that integrates particularism with universality, subjugates individual idiosyncrasy to group-determined rationality. Thus, both freedom and the *Sittlichkeit* become manifestations of an objectivity in which subjectivity survives only when compatible with a common sense of reason, duty, welfare, etc.

The focal point of Post's theory lies in the communicative process that allows citizens to see themselves as active participants in centralised decision-making. In this respect, of course, Post owes an intellectual debt to Jürgen Habermas, whose theory of communicative action envisages the same scenario – and, in this, Habermas is directly influenced by Hegel. Like Post, Habermas is concerned with the communicative structures by which civic society (as a community of noumenal beings) and centralised government (as a manifestation of collectively given power) are mutually responsive. For both, the notion of democratic legitimacy is centrally important. Habermas's is a broader vision of the participatory value which contains the epistemic quality (the idea of the grand repository discussed in the previous chapter) that Post eschews (at least to the extent of formulating free speech principle). For both, of course, access to public opinion, for the purposes of collective will-formation is critical.

In an important sense, the idea of the participatory value as *the* animating principle in conceptualising authentic free speech theory dominates the literature. Nevertheless, this conceptualisation takes different forms. In this chapter, I identify three different (albeit related) forms of the argument. The most obvious form is explored in section II. This may be understood in terms of conceiving free speech as an independent principle which rejects, say, autonomy (and, in fact, all other value-based interpretations of free speech principle) for its ostensible failure to distinguish, adequately, free speech from all other liberty-based assertions of freedom. This claim will be disputed on its own terms – that, in fact, this conceptualisation fails to distinguish free speech from all other aspects of democratic participation (such as the process of voting) and so does not render free speech to be independent, in the final analysis, but, instead, a subset of the principles by which democratic participation is realised.

However, this insight does no more than equalise the competition between the participatory value and all others for the title of animating principle. Certainly, it does not defeat the authenticity claim of participatory value. Sections III and IV seek to do so by scrutinising the *Sittlichkeit* claim (as Habermas and Post might understand it) in greater depth. The problem, as chapter five foreshadows, concerns the relationship between the *Sittlichkeit* and juridical law-making. Whereas Hegel could collapse the hard division between ethics and law, through the dialectical, neither Kant nor Mill could. Harm is the only language they understood, not good or righteousness, for the purpose of legitimising state intervention. Accordingly, the political system in which community is the base language of constitutional design can move with Hegel such that centrally imposed mandates override the individual autonomy underpinning human rights; but

[8] ibid, 404.
[9] ibid.

the individuality-based system cannot. Accordingly, the Habermasian dynamic that Post employs must break down. Habermas knows this, which is why his communicative action remains firmly within the grip of the *Sittlichkeit*; law cannot enforce the ethical duties he has in mind. This argument is set out in section III.

Nevertheless, one move remains, which both Habermas and, to some extent, Post take, which is to eliminate the autonomy problem by dehumanising the conduit that serves the 'feedback loop'. Whereas Habermas ascribes an epistemic function that Post does not, still both are faced by a dilemma that tests their commitment to the automaton status of the conduit. For if the conduit *is* non-autonomous, then it must provide either the epistemically optimised repository of information (Habermas) or else such *access* that enables contributions to that repository as would satisfy the participatory value in which particular noumenal experience feeds into the collective understanding of the world and its problems. The challenge for Post, specifically, is whether this privileged access right can be realised without compromising the individuality-based constitutional language that democracy is founded upon. This problem is explored in section IV.

In this way, the chapter is divided in three distinct parts that explore whether, in the formation of authentic free speech theory, the participatory value is to be understood as a self-contained principle (section II), an organising principle (section II), or else a contingent principle (section IV).

II. As a Self-Contained Principle

The rhetorical attachment to the participatory value in free speech cases is prevalent in judicial reasoning globally. For the Australian High Court, free speech is of 'fundamental importance' to democratic participation.[10] For the US Supreme Court, it is 'indispensable'.[11] For the English and Welsh, it is the 'lifeblood'.[12] For the Canadians, 'a democracy cannot exist without' it.[13] For the European Court of Human Rights, it is the 'very core of the concept of a democratic society'.[14] For the United Nations Human Rights Committee, it is the 'foundation stone for every free and democratic society'.[15] As we saw in the previous chapter, this exuberance also extends to the academic literature. Even stripped of its epistemic function, free speech is recognised symbolically as a manifestation of an individual's inherent status as a co-author and co-authority figure in the formation and exercise of centralised power by virtue of her humanity alone.

This symbolic treatment of participation is as apparent in Alexander Meiklejohn's and Robert Bork's work as it is in, say, that of Thomas Emerson, C Edwin Baker, Martin Redish, and Thomas Scanlon. For Vincent Blasi, for example, it allows the people to monitor exercises of state power in their name, such that malignity within

[10] *Australian Capital Television Pty Ltd v Commonwealth* [1992] HCA 45, [41].
[11] *Smith v Daily Mail Publishing Co* (1979) 443 US 97, 106.
[12] *R v Secretary of State for the Home Department ex parte Simms* [2000] 2 AC 115, 126.
[13] *Edmonton Journal v Alberta* (1989) 2 SCR 1326, 1336.
[14] *Lingens v Austria* (1986) 8 EHRR 407, [42].
[15] United Nations Human Rights Committee, General Comment No 34, 12 September 2011, [2].

state office can be addressed as well as to ensure state decision-making corresponds to the political mandate.[16] Thus, according to Ashutosh Bhagwat and James Weinstein,[17] free speech is not only the precursor to state power (through voting), it is the lever – the 'primary mechanism', they say – by which the body politic 'controls' the government. This is achieved, they argue, through the creation of public opinion. In this way, through its facilitative and supervisory dimensions, freedom of speech symbolises the continuing power of the people over the servile state; it demonstrates the contingent, temporary transference of power from its popular origin to central state organs.

Yet, as we have also seen, for Baker, Redish and Scanlon, this facet of free speech speaks to the autonomy principle (as they each interpret it) rather than the participatory value as such. This explains why Baker, Redish and Scanlon would protect speech broader than 'explicitly political speech' (as Bork has it) or 'public discourse' speech (as Post claims).[18] Clearly, the autonomy value has serious explanatory power in this context. The body politic, as a collection of autonomous beings, has no power to give nor retain unless the autonomy value is recognised constitutionally. This autonomy prevails in a democratic state in ways that would be unthinkable in, say, a socialist or authoritarian state. Why, then, is it not the autonomy value that explains this sense of power transference? Why is it the process value instead?

For some process theorists, led by Post, the autonomy value is relevant but subordinate to what Rawls would deem the 'lexical priority' of the participation value.[19] For others, the autonomy value is excluded altogether because it is too large and uncritical to distinguish speech from non-speech nor to set meaningful distinctions between a meaningful free speech right and a more generalised notion of liberty. Owen Fiss, for example, has spoken at length on this point,[20] as has Frederick Schauer.[21] According to Fiss, those that argue for the autonomy value fail to recognise that autonomy is not protected as 'an end in itself' in this scenario, 'nor as a means of individual self-actualization', but only instrumentally to the extent it furthers specific political ends.[22] Yet, to this end, they say, autonomy is a poor tool for it cossets the individual in a protective environment that tolerates little or no state interference.[23] No improvements in the quality of public discourse may result from this; instead, the power imbalances inherent in the status quo will remain such that minority voices are drowned out and powerful (corporate) influences prevail. Interferences with discourse, so as to enhance democratic participation, therefore, conflict with autonomy but satisfy the underlying political structure of the US Constitution, according to Fiss. Such interventions

[16] V Blasi 'The Checking Value in First Amendment Theory' (1977) *American Bar Foundation Research Journal* 521.

[17] A Bhagwat and J Weinstein, 'Freedom of expression and democracy' in A Stone and F Schauer (eds), *The Oxford Handbook of Freedom of Speech* (Oxford University Press, 2021) 85.

[18] ibid, 2371.

[19] RC Post, 'Meiklejohn's Mistake: Individual Autonomy and the Reform of Public Discourse' (1993) 64 *University of Colorado Law Review* 1109.

[20] OM Fiss, *Liberalism Divided: Freedom of Speech and the Many Uses of State Power* (Westview Press, 1996).

[21] F Schauer, *Free Speech: A Philosophical Enquiry* (Cambridge University Press, 1982).

[22] Fiss (n 20) 37.

[23] Such criticisms are typical of Scanlon's thesis; see E Barendt, *Freedom of Speech*, 2nd edn (Oxford University Press, 2004) 16–18.

as are necessary will help 'save democracy' in ways that the autonomy value alone could not.[24]

Fiss's position is an extreme, but by no means isolated, conceptualisation of the participation value.[25] Its ubiquitous quality resides in its admiration of the participation value's conceptual neatness. It is, process theorists say, self-contained in ways that the autonomy value or any other alternative values are not. For example, James Weinstein notess: 'a theory that attempts to explain free speech in terms of a broad, undifferentiated autonomy interest would protect many forms [of speech]' and so represent not a free speech principle as such but free speech as an element of some larger principle.[26] Likewise, Stanley Ingber says: 'the self-fulfillment [sic] theory argues for the value of freedom in all human choices and activities, but fails to explain why choices and activities related to speech conduct deserve unique protection'.[27] Post also shares this view. Autonomy, he says, 'is not unique to speech but instead extends to the full libertarian protection of personal action'.[28] This view – that the authentic value of free speech principle should be self-contained – is so widespread in the literature as to be almost axiomatic.[29] The process theory, scholars say, meets what Frederick Schauer calls the 'independent principle' test[30] – that is, it explains the meaning and nature of free speech without resort to some larger principle, such as general liberty.[31] Certainly, process theory is attractive for what Eric Barendt calls its relative simplicity and ready comprehensibility.[32]

Then again, we might question how firmly the self-containment argument holds. It seems to require certain accommodations to be made that are not readily admitted by its proponents. For if the autonomy and other values suffer from their applicability to action, then surely the process value does too. After all, democracy entails much more than speech alone as a conceptual construct. It extends to matters that are more action than speech, especially in the realisation of political decision-making. Even if we confine our gaze to the participatory element, then we find it admits many facets that are unrelated to the free speech claim, from the administrative aspects (eg, registering to vote, opting out of appearance on the open electoral register, nominating the preferred choice of voting, ie, in person or through postal vote), to the representational aspects (eg, access to representatives through surgeries, correspondence, etc), to

[24] Fiss (n 20) 42–46.

[25] See also CR Sunstein, *Democracy and the Problem of Free Speech* (Free Press, 1995).

[26] J Weinstein, 'Democracy, Sex and the First Amendment' (2007) 31 *New York University Review of Law and Social Change* 865, 877.

[27] S Ingber, 'Rediscovering the Communal Worth of Individual Rights: The First Amendment in Institutional Contexts' (1990) 69 *Texas Law Review* 1, 19.

[28] RC Post, 'Participatory Democracy and Free Speech' (2011) 97 *Virginia Law Review* 477, 479.

[29] Which is not to deny that important contrary positions exist: see, eg, P Horton and L Alexander, 'The Impossibility of a Free Speech Principle' (1983) 78 *Northwestern University Law Review* 1319, SV Shiffrin, 'A Thinker-Based Approach to Freedom of Speech' (2011) 27 *Constitutional Commentary* 283, 288.

[30] See, eg, Schauer (n 21) 5–12; 'Must Speech Be Special?' (1984) 78 *Northwestern University Law Review* 1284, 1293 and 1302–03; 'Free Speech on Tuesdays' (2015) 34 *Law and Philosophy* 119.

[31] Schauer was not entirely convinced by the process theory, but his essential criticism was that he thought it derivative of, and inferior to, the best aspects of Mill's argument from truth. Schauer (n 21) 44–46.

[32] Barendt (n 23) 18.

the procedural aspects (of holding elected officials accountable). These elements involve action as well as speech, understood simplistically.

Likewise, the strong rhetorical attachment of the judiciary, globally, to free speech's significance to democracy seems prone to exaggeration. Certainly, we might question whether the notion of democracy cannot be understood without reference to freedom of speech. For if free speech *is* essential to democracy, then no such account should be possible. And yet, it strikes me, it can be so understood. Just as there are no formal conditions by which voting eligibility is subject to epistemic evaluation (as discussed in the previous chapter), so too there is no mechanism that tests levels of political engagement as a condition of voting. Accordingly, votes are cast, legitimately, regardless of whether the voter takes her civic duties seriously or not. Her vote is just as valid if influenced by malignity. Indeed, she can spoil her ballot paper if she wishes, without consequence. She can ignore any or all literature concerning the candidate and still her vote counts. Since our system of democracy neither contains nor permits the monitoring of voter activity, at least not as it occurs in the ballot room, then it cannot be said that free speech has a causal connection with the process of voting itself.

Moreover, although commentators, such as Ashutosh Bhagwat and James Weinstein, speak of public opinion as a 'primary' means of 'control' over government,[33] the accuracy of this position is surely doubtful. Certainly, Post must disagree, in an important sense, since, he says, 'democracy is distinct from popular sovereignty and majoritarianism'[34] because the latter denies or otherwise easily overcomes those critical democratic values of equality, pluralism and tolerance,[35] especially as it relates to those other terms or concepts thought to be immune to popular control: justice and the rule of law. The term 'control', then, is in need of modification despite the assertion that 'it can hardly be denied that freedom of political expression is an indispensable means by which the people in contemporary democracies control their government'.[36]

This logic, although perfectly intuitive, is incompatible with the self-containment proposition that it seeks to emulate. The idea that the state *must* respond to public opinion is a rule, if it exists at all, that is properly categorised as a basic tenet of democratic principle, not freedom of speech. It represents a rule about power itself and the circumstances in which power, if it is to be legitimately exercised, must represent the popular will. The notion of democratic legitimacy is, of course, one that fascinates both Habermas and Post, albeit both have somewhat different ideas about it. For Habermas, following Hannah Arendt, state action corresponding to popular will is 'communicatively generated power', as opposed to 'administratively employed power'.[37] If this is all free speech is – a source of power for others to employ – then it is stripped of its vitality. It is but a degenerative form that preserves the vehicle – speech – but not the essence by which individuality recognises itself in the locution 'freedom'. It is a freedom, of sorts, but only in authorising *others*. Even so, it is a rather flimsy sort of freedom in that the

[33] Bhagwat and Weinstein (n 17) 85.

[34] Post, 'Democracy and Equality' (n 1) 25.

[35] See, eg, Schauer (n 21) 41; RM Dworkin 'Introduction' in RM Dworkin (ed), *The Philosophy of Law* (Oxford University Press, 1977) 15–26; *cf* Bhagwat and Weinstein (n 17) 87–88.

[36] Bhagwat and Weinstein (n 17) 87.

[37] J Habermas, *Between Facts and Norms* (W Rehg trans) (Polity Press, 1996) 483.

authority comes not from the noumenal being but the collective spirit of 'noumenality' as it manifests in the phenomenality of perceivable 'consensus' or 'majority'. It is but a delegation, or worse, an abandonment – an admission of an opportunity to influence others that is now lost, whether that moment of influence was successful, on its own terms, or not. This is a trivial sort of freedom for speech.

This power-derived conception of free speech is also unconvincing as a self-contained principle in another important sense. For what, beyond its theatrical exuberance for the Madisonian ideal of popular rule, justifies the claim of 'indispensability' as a means of controlling political power? If free speech has such power then it is but one of many competing or complimentary forms of control. Indeed, once these other forms of control are considered, the suggestion of primacy surely falls away. For, from the abstract idea of the separation of powers, to concrete procedures, the uses of power are monitored and controlled by a broad range of constitutional levers in which free speech as democratic participation figures only tenuously, if it figures at all. For example, the ruling party of the day is elected on its manifesto promises which set, in broad terms, the political mandate. Deviations from that mandate generate compelling reasons for opposition criticism which, in times of strong opposition government, has strong claims to be the primary mechanism by which state power is controlled. This mechanism does, of course, involve the notion of free speech in a strong and important sense, but public opinion figures only tangentially (to the extent that opposition forces are influenced by constituent issues in addition to party politics).

Free speech as an essential facet of democracy has a more obvious connection to Blasi's checking function, in which an active press, as champions of the voting public, monitors the uses and abuses of power, which, for Blasi, is a 'special' kind of wrong because of the state's 'unique' capacity to 'employ legitimized violence'.[38] Yet, even here the 'necessity' of free speech may be doubted. In the Kingdom of Ends, the (Kantian) autonomous being is driven purely by the categorical imperative. They are driven to moral purity not by fear (ie, the threat of corrupt activity being exposed by a virtuous press), nor by self-interest (ie, the prospect of re-election), nor, even, the sense of fulfilment that virtuosity brings, but purely because abuse of power – in fact, any deviation from the political mandate on which they were elected – is wrong and, therefore, incompatible with the ethical duty that the categorical imperative demands. This ascetic agent of moral purity, then, has no need of oversight and neither do those other ascetic agents that she works for. Theirs is a world in which moral goodness is guaranteed because it is the right thing to do and moral corruption is therefore non-existent.

Of course, this is not a real world; it is hypothetical. Yet it illustrates that the causative link between political life and free speech, as the participatory value evaluates it, is driven by a cynical distrust in the goodness of humankind to resist corruption when given power. If that is the essential value of free speech, there are other means by which the wrong can be governed – and, in fact, such alternate processes are common, relating to, as they do, internal (that is, Parliamentary) mechanisms for accountability, transparency, and strong ethical oversight whose reporting function is but one facet of the mechanism. Again, the dilution of 'free speech' as a critical functionality

[38] Blasi (n 16) 538.

either weakens the claim to necessity or else radically alters it, for the publicity element central to the policing of corruption resides purely in the reporting of those processes in operation – that suitable punishment has been meted out by the responsible body – rather than in any opinion concerning that process and the reasons which prompted it. While one can point to the value of free speech as a monitor that watches the ethics body as it watches the politician for signs of corruption, that really is to reduce, or otherwise transform, speech to a regulatory functionally which, again, can be achieved through ever greater chains of critical oversight. The body that watches the body that watches the body that watches the body *ad infinitum*. This is not to deny that one is entitled to question the operation of these bodies, nor challenge their effective; it is to question whether supervision against corruption is achievable *only* (or even mainly) through free speech.

We might say, with Blasi, that the point is not about the effectiveness of oversight as such but merely in the fact of recognising the populace as the ultimate overseer. Nevertheless, even here, we might say that the 'controlling' aspect of public opinion must be subject to scepticism not least because, in addition to the problem of opinions incompatible with the underlying constitutional values, we have the very real pragmatic concern of identifying the scope and nature of public opinion with precision. Whereas it may be said that a vociferous and ubiquitous message across the spectrum of political press outlets has some claim to representing such, still we should recognise the manipulations that the press can and do exercise in furtherance of their own partisan enterprises. Similarly, social media tends to project the loudest voices but not (necessarily) the full spectrum, or even extent, of national feeling. Polling is useful but still prone to misrepresentation especially given the obvious limitations that arise from restricted sample sizes. Finally, in this regard, we should also recognise the manipulations that politicians themselves can make of discernible public opinions, which twists and spins social and cultural reality to suit political ambition.

Conventionally, democracy, in its electoral manifestations, involves *some* level of, if not discourse, then publicity so that engaged citizens can know what they are voting for (assuming that their voting intentions are contingent and responsive to circumstance rather than simply given like some religious affiliation according to political colours). This conventionally does not exhibit the categorical imperative of a 'must' inherent in 'necessary' and 'vital' but, still, this correspondence, between electoral prospect and citizen, if only unilateral, suggests some form of free speech function is operative, if only in very weak form. Yet this is a very different and more modest claim than the grander idea of a public discourse that includes all citizens. This more modest enterprise requires only the transmission of information rather than the feedback loop that process theories argue for. Neither does it require an active public watchdog to haunt the viewing gallery of the Parliamentary chamber.

Of course, the symbolism of free speech transcends both conventionality and the pragmatic concerns, expressed so far, with the idea of 'necessity' as a causative connection between that concept and democracy. The prospect of malign influences controlling legislative and executive processes lurks menacingly if the free speech claim is diminished in this way. Partly, the popular clamour to venerate free speech's importance to democratic participation is motivated by our shared history in which dark forces gathered when authoritarianism ruled. The right to decry state policy publicly is, of itself, a symbolic, powerful agent against repression. The government that can freely deny popular dissent is one to be feared. Nevertheless, the moral wrong inherent in the state suppressing dissent can be articulated as clearly and persuasively through the doctrine of ultra vires as it can the concept of free speech. For the wrong is in the state's overreach of power. This wrong is not confined to matters of speech; it would emerge as clearly if the state, by reason of capriciousness, banned marriage, outlawed religious observance, trespassed on private land, stole property, etc. The wrong resides in the conflict with individual autonomy; it does not need a special principle of free speech to explain it.

None of this is to doubt the importance, let alone existence, of free speech principle. It is, instead, to question whether a meaningful conception of democracy necessitates a corresponding free speech principle and, thus, to question the causal connection between the two. For if there is no such causal connection, then the self-containment appeal of process theory dissolves away, either because it renders free speech an elementary part of some larger principle or else its significance to democratic participation is much more modest than previously advertised. Accordingly, if the participatory value is the authentic essence of free speech principle, it must be for some other reason than its purported novelty or uniqueness in separating free speech from some larger concept. One such argument, mentioned above, is found in the work of Post, derived from Habermas, that treats free speech as an organising principle in the concept of democratic legitimacy.

III. As an Organising Principle

In his powerful critique of process theory, Post argued that commentators, since Meiklejohn, had failed to sufficiently account for individuality in their teleological understanding of the First Amendment.[39] This failing, he argued, is both inconsistent with actual First Amendment decision-making and incoherent for the purposes of strategising its development since it cannot account, for example, for the essential wrong of censorship.[40] Censorship of individual contributions would cause no First Amendment difficulties – would be necessitated, in fact – if the *quality* of public discourse were the ultimate end of the free speech guarantee. Yet since censorship *is* a wrong, according to the positive law, and since all debate, even the nature of what it means to discourse publicly, must be socially constructed, the essence of free speech must reside in the possibility of 'access' to the great debate and not in any epistemic qualities of the contribution itself.[41] Thus, Post says: 'The state ought not to be empowered to control the agenda of public discourse, or the presentation and characterization of issues within public discourse, because such control would necessarily circumscribe

[39] Post (n 19).
[40] ibid, 1116.
[41] ibid, 1115.

the potential for collective self-determination.'[42] The juridical task, then, is only to separate contributions to public discourse from those that are not (which may or may not be a straightforward task). Once satisfied that it is, the juridical task is complete and protection must follow.

Central to Post's analysis is the protection of individual autonomy not for its own sake, but as the first step in the balletic movement by which it meets, intertwines and converges with collective will. Since democratic legitimacy resides in centralised power responding to collective will, free speech, as the source of this communicatively generated power, to borrow Habermas's phrase, must be valued for its recognition of individuality, at least to the extent of individuality's integration with community. In this way, says Post: 'Democracy attempts to reconcile individual autonomy with collective self-determination by subordinating governmental decisionmaking to communicative processes sufficient to instill in citizens a sense of participation, legitimacy, and identification.'[43] Clearly, there are strong echoes of Habermas (and Hegel) in this analysis. Nevertheless, Post and Habermas move from this first step in different directions.

Since Habermas and Post hope to terminate their journey in the land of individualism rather than communitarianism, it is important to trace the distinctive steps each take so that we might better understand the implications for the participatory value. To best understand the distinctive steps that each takes, it is worth reiterating something of Hegel's position, set out in chapter five. In the Hegelian scheme, the particulate of individuality is problematic when its idiosyncrasy runs contrary to both communal success and the sovereignty of rationality – hence the arbitrariness of particularity when met by the opposition of universality must be ameliorated. This need not the overt denial of individualism, of course, for in its dialectical movement, individualism and communitarianism are conjoined such that elements of both are retained.

Nevertheless, it is individuality of an especially anaemic variety, for the individuality of the 'concrete person'[44] 'gains satisfaction … through the exclusive *mediation* of the form of *universality*'.[45] The most 'satisfying' forms, then, are those that survive this transition to the communal scheme. Hence: 'particularity, limited by universality, is the only standard by which each particular [person] promotes his welfare'.[46] Accordingly, freedom is not the supremacy of individuality over community; 'the ethical life is freedom, or the will which has being in and for itself as objectivity'.[47] More starkly put, 'the *right of individuals* to their *subjective determination to freedom* is fulfilled in so far as they belong to ethical actuality; for their *certainty* of their own freedom has its *truth* in such objectivity'.[48] Thus, each noumenal being gives itself to the *Sittlichkeit* in pursuit of both communal goals and the inner truth of realising self-conscious righteousness. Hence, 'ethical life is the *Idea of freedom* as the living good which has its knowledge

[42] ibid, 1118.
[43] ibid, 1115.
[44] Hegel (n 5) §182.
[45] ibid.
[46] ibid.
[47] ibid, §145.
[48] ibid, §153.

and volition in self-consciousness, and its actuality through self-conscious action'.[49] Since each noumenal being is committed to this end of ultimate self-realisation, the *Sittlichkeit* is both 'a system of social institutions'[50] such as civic life, and a representation of the concrete person's 'moral attitude'. Since the particular and universal progress, in the third phase, as a dialectical movement, so community leaves it indelible mark upon individuality.

The sovereignty of rationality that we find in Hegel's treatment of individuality remains manifest in Habermas's work and, to that extent, dominates the meaning of communal success. That success means neither the homogeneity nor hegemony that Hegel's scheme can be understood to promote, not least in Hegel's insistence upon obedience to the state. Habermas can make these adjustments, such that individuality is more enlivened, because he is as much – in fact, more so – a Kantian than he is a Hegelian in his conceptualisation of the *Sittlichkeit*. This combination creates a dynamic interplay, which we see in Habermas's treatment of the *Sittlichkeit* in its political setting. Here, Habermas's theory of communicative action as a rich and complex superstructure speaks powerfully to the dynamics inherent in a *Lebenswelt* (or lifeworld) of noumenal beings that must make sense of themselves, the phenomenal world around them, and the other noumenal beings within it. Given this ambition, there is much in Habermas that extends far beyond the subject of free speech. Nevertheless, the aspect most relevant to our purposes is that which explains the dialogical interactions of civic society and the state.[51]

This structure recognises the dual existences of the citizen within the *Lebenswelt* of the everyday and the *Sittlichkeit* of civic society. This duality is sufficiently dynamic that the autonomous agent may operate within one or both in fluid movements. The question is not (necessarily) whether the agent wishes to engage with the *Sittlichkeit* so much as how events within the *Lebenswelt* influence the *Sittlichkeit* and vice versa such that problems, as they emerge, are mediated or else dissolved. Central to this is the problem of publicity. The state must know of these events if it is to respond effectively and the *Lebenswelt* must know that the state is cognisant of the problem (and is formulating, or else has conceived, a plan to tackle it). It calls for a dynamic interplay of reciprocal, constant communication between the two such that the performance of one can be evaluated by the other. Yet, it also requires the inherent deficiencies within the noumenal *Lebenswelt* to be overcome. As Habermas says, civic agreement on political decision-making must overcome 'individual egocentrisms [by] anchoring the moral point of view in the substrate of communicatively structured forms of life [which] takes up Hegel's idea that morality is embedded in ethical life'.[52]

These two related phenomena – the need for a communicative conduit and to overcome the egocentrism of the noumenal self – set criteria for the condition of optimal communication to be achieved. The solution, as Habermas sees it, is a carefully curated repository to exist which manifests diverse opinions generated from accurate

[49] ibid, §142.
[50] ibid.
[51] See, esp, *Between Facts and Norms* (n 37) chs 7–8, and 'Political Communication in Media Society: Does Democracy Still Enjoy an Epistemic Dimension? The Impact of Normative Theory on Empirical Research' (2006) 16 *Communication Theory* 411.
[52] ibid, 109–10.

trustworthy information. This fact-opinion dynamic is given further expression by the three functions that Habermas ascribes to the conduit:

> As an essential element of the democratic process, deliberation is expected to fulfil three functions: to mobilize and pool relevant issues and required information, and to specify interpretations; to process such contributions discursively by means of proper arguments for and against; and to generate rationally motivated yes and no attitudes that are expected to determine the outcome of procedurally correct decisions.[53]

Into this dynamic interplay emerges the (self-regulated) media which, as a good faith actor, strives to realise this repository (of accurate information on the underlying social problem(s) and the plurality of opinions upon which (political) action is formulated). Self-regulation here aims at creating the conditions of independence from both state and societal interests such that a sort of neutrality is achieved. Only in this way can the media act 'as an intermediary system between state and society'.[54] This independence is significant, not only to prevent the corrupting effect of regulatory capture by the state (such as being condemned to client journalism) but also to overcome the inherent intersubjectivity at work in the kingdom of noumenal beings in which the experienced world differs and the moral landscape shifts, causing language to lack essential uniformity. Only if this condition is satisfied can the dialogical conduit function between good faith political actors and engaged public citizenry be realised. Here, then, we see the dialectical movement in Hegel's political theory given expression within Habermas's theory.[55] As with Hegel, Habermas connects the health of democratic life with the degree of participation by its citizens in public life.[56] For Lawrence Solum, Habermas gives voices to Hegel's critique of Kantian autonomy, that Kant's categorical imperative rang 'hollow' because it could not 'generate concrete norms of action',[57] whereas Habermas's can, says Solum, because it allows for agreement of norms through the ideal speech situation (unlike Kantian autonomy, which is driven by an ascetic sense of duty that eschews wants and needs, understood as interests, desire, or beneficial advantage).[58]

As is apparent from this discussion of Kantian autonomy, Habermas's theory of communicative action is a discourse *ethics*. Uses of the categorical imperative (and the hypothetical) are limited to their Kantian (moral) sense of what the ethically good agent would do. His aim is to problematise the issues arising in a political system that envisages itself as a deliberative democracy. Since this is his aim, his concern is not with solutions, as such. This is not to deny that Habermas offers solutions. Instead, it is to recognise that those solutions are framed solely in terms of incentive and encouragement, not force.

Consequently, Habermas identifies (at least) three ideals that would need to exist to realise his perfect(ible) state. These ideals relate to, first, the quality of political (or, rather government) actors, who are driven as much by the will to remain in power as

[53] Habermas (n 51) 416.
[54] ibid, 412.
[55] See, eg, Habermas (n 37) 342–51.
[56] See, eg, J Habermas, *Philosophical Introductions: Five Approaches to Communicative Reason* (Polity Press, 2018) 109–10.
[57] LB Solum, 'Freedom of Communicative Action: A Theory of the First Amendment Freedom of Speech' (1989) 83 *Northwestern University Law Review* 54, 117.
[58] ibid, 103.

by the need to satisfy core party membership (usually represented by donor or strong lobbying influences); second, the cognitive functions and good faith intentions of the electorate, who may be driven by prejudice, intuition, and (party) loyalty as much as reason and open-mindedness; thirdly, the inhibitions upon the epistemological and ideological intentions of the media, driven, as it is, to retain its independence from (undue) state interference through private financing, be that the predilections of subscriber interests or else the power ambitions of its ownership.

Obviously, these dynamics take us beyond the narrow question of how rights to speak are formulated at an abstract level. For example, the ethical behaviours of political actors can be addressed through parliamentary rules on, say, the transparency of lobbying and/or financial interests. Likewise, the concentration of media power raises issues of competition or corporate laws whilst the capacity for civic engagement in the populace raises questions about levels of education. Thus, to put it simply, Habermas is not saying that the ideal political (democratic) state is wholly contingent on our conceptual understandings of free speech. His systematic appraisal of the whole scheme is much more complicated than that. Nevertheless, much hangs upon the overarching rights-based apparatus, for if the citizenry is unfree to access, let alone influence, public debate then the responsive dynamic of public sphere is jeopardised in obvious ways. Habermas describes this as the problem of 'privileged access'.[59] Simply put, if universal access to the conduit is illusory then we shall revert to the nineteenth-century predicament in which political decision-making is a closed loop whereby one elite (wealth) speaks to another (state functionaries) through a third (the press barons' newspapers) such that the voting populace is but a token or otherwise inferior group of no real significance.

Habermas's vision, then, is of great explanatory power. It provides us with the critical ethical language by which to scrutinise, evaluate and criticise failings within each link of the chain. In this way, Habermas expands upon – or, rather, populates – the Kantian categorical imperative by which we can say what each of these actors (political, citizen, media) *must* do to fulfil their moral duties to realise the ideal democratic state.[60] Although this involves a powerful normative juridical theory, the relationship to law is not as straightforward as it might seem. Habermas is not saying that the state is, or would be, justified in deploying its coercive powers to *force* these actors to fulfil their duties, ie these ethical duties do not *become* legal obligations which, if not performed, could be punished by the state – at least, not as far as the palpable free speech dimension is concerned. In his explanatory introductions, he rejects that possibility in unequivocal terms: 'the democratic constitutional state depends on motivations oriented to the public interest that cannot be legally enforced, however modest their scale may be'.[61] What is required, then, is a

> pre-political source of 'solidarity' that is relevant for the political consciousness of the citizens and that, as a medium through which society as a whole is integrated, serves as a counterbalance to the other media of integration, the 'market' and 'political power'.[62]

[59] See Habermas (n 37) 334–35.
[60] See Habermas (n 56) 100–04.
[61] ibid, 130.
[62] ibid, 133.

This cannot be imposed 'as it were "from above", from the point of view of a philosopher king'[63] but, instead, must come through collective self-consciousness – that 'in each case "freedom" [is] the sense of self-obligation at work'.[64]

Given the Kantian influences on Habermas's work, this stark conclusion is understandable. As set out in chapter five, the division between ethical and juridical obligations is so strict in Kant that the purely ethical tenor of Habermas's communicative action theory cannot bridge the gap. Accordingly, Habermas clearly recognises both the reality of, and the limitations imposed by, the irrationality proviso. As he says, 'the literature on "public ignorance"' paints a rather sobering portrait of the average citizen as a largely uninformed and disinterested person'.[65] Obviously, this presents serious problems to the deliberative democracy model given that an engaged and informed citizenry is a central condition. Nevertheless, Habermas maintains a belief that such a community can be encouraged – though not guaranteed – by adjustments to the 'feedback loop' (the conduit) between state and citizen by means of a self-regulated media whose good faith commitment to creating the ideal repository of accurate information and diverse opinion is assured.

Habermas's work on the role of communicative action as a means of legitimising state decision-making is, of course, an important influence on Post's participatory value. As with Hegel, Post sees public discourse as the union of individuality and community in terms of his recognition of the participatory actor as a valid co-author of law and policy *despite* both her alienation from power *and* her latent inability to influence collective decision-making. For Post, free-speech-as-contribution is symbolic, not in its pejorative sense as tokenism (although it could be understood that way), but as a meaningful signifier of individual civic power of the kind, it may be said, that Hegel gives us: that the participant in the *Sittlichkeit* is an authority figure holding real but latent power to determine collectively-realised outcomes.[66]

Post's position is appealing to the extent that this symbolic contribution to law and policy resides not in the actuality of agreement amongst competing interests, but in its latency. In this way, free speech is about non-alienation or 'identification with the state'.[67] Accordingly, free speech (or, rather, the First Amendment) is the pivotal tool by which this state is achieved. Through it, the individual achieves full satisfaction of her status as a co-author of law and policy, even if it is not *her* political viewpoints that triumph in the end. Through this symbolic process, her sense of authority is retained.

Here, then, we see the influence of Rousseau upon Post's thinking: that the state's power is but an aggregated levy of that power invested in all citizens as free and equal members of a democracy. Although they disburse that power to the centre, still they retain some part of it. This retained power manifests in their right to speak about uses (and abuses) of their delegated power. This symbolism relates that sense of democracy that Rousseau and Madison exemplify in their adoration of the people as worthy

[63] ibid, 116.
[64] ibid, 115.
[65] Habermas (n 37) 420.
[66] See discussion in ch 5.
[67] Post (n 1) 28.

ultimate rulers and sources of coercive power, such that the state is but their servant. This 'authority' status animates Post's understanding of the participatory value. It explains why the *fact* of participation rather than the *substance* of it is the telling element of his free speech design.

Although both Habermas and Post see the conduit as the functionary by which centralised state and diffuse public co-ordinate, their differing viewpoints on its purpose and nature put their positions in sharp tension. For Post, it must be that the conduit can generate the grand repository of perfect information and most diverse opinion, for, by necessity, he must tolerate the imperfections, of both factual and opinion-based material, generated by the epistemologically flawed contributions that the autonomous agent, as co-author of law and policy, is to be permitted to make. Even if Habermas does not authorise direct interventions with these contributions, still their impact will be ameliorated by the demand for rationality that his Hegelian ideals necessitate. This rationality will drive out the imperfections from the conduit system. This is a move Habermas can make, but Post cannot, for rationality has no greater dominion over the conduit than irrationality, for it is the sort of tool of epistemology that he banishes from the realm.

Another reason why Post is prevented from embracing this corrective is that the functionaries within the conduit – those epistemic workers encountered in the previous chapters – are themselves noumenal beings whose engagement with will-formation are to be valued as equally as any others. This also sets him apart from Habermas in an important sense. Nevertheless, this tension, if it exists, may be illusory, for Habermas and Post are not operating on the same plane of semantic design. Habermas's conception is an ambitious work of ethical law-giving. He is not presupposing that the state can regulate the conduit in the ways he has in mind for ethics. Indeed, he is emphatically opposed to the idea, as we have seen. His sociological agenda, then, is to find empirical data that would suggest human beings do conform to patterns of behaviour that speak to his discourse ethics in meaningful ways.[68] Meanwhile, Post *is* concerned with the limits of juridical law-giving. His denial of epistemology's role in the constitutional design of free speech stems explicitly from the limitations of law as he sees them, especially in the necessity of censorship that, he believes, epistemological perfection must entail.

Thus, Post moves beyond Habermas in three important ways. First, he is less enamoured with the grand repository ideal, for that would suggest free speech has a pronounced epistemological value which at times he denies outright and at other times accepts, but only as an inferior item in the juridical toolkit. Moreover, there can be no 'special' speakers within the conduit, and so no privileged speakers such as the institutional press. Second, relatedly, he eschews the progressive element within Habermas's belief that his discourse ethics both explains and prefigures the sort of teleological march of history that characterises the extreme elements of Hegelian thought. Free speech is not a tool for rendering society better; it is but the promise that speaks to inherent entitlement regardless of qualification. Third, resultantly, he treats access as the essential element in free speech design. It is the *capacity* to contribute to collective

[68] See, eg, 'Political Communication in Media Society' (n 51).

will-formation, not the contribution itself, that counts. Accordingly, although the idea of the conduit remains vital, even after his reconfiguration of its properties, in his intellectual design, it is for very different reasons than Habermas provides.

IV. As a Contingent Principle

A. Contingency in the Habermasian Conduit Function

If we think of the participatory value in free speech theory as a contingent principle, then, at least, some of the difficulties apparent in Habermas's and Post's theories are ameliorated. For Habermas, this contingency arises in respect of the conduit function that bridges the gaps in knowledge as between state and citizenry, such that both can participate effectively in the roles that democracy assigns to them. In this way, citizens, as individuals within the *Sittlichkeit*, retain their rights to participate without any additional burden to provide epistemically valuable speech to the grand repository. Instead, their free speech rights are separate to the grand repository which exists only to benefit them, as participants in a vibrant democracy, at both national and local levels, regardless of whether they are active, engaged contributors to that community or not. In fulfilling their (ethical) duties as members of the voting class, citizens can access this grand repository at any point, either solely for the purpose of, and at the moment of, voting, or else in the periods between voting opportunities.

Yet, in Habermas's case, there remains the problem of both populating and collating the information – verifiable (or non-falsifiable) information combined with the widest diversity of opinion concerning it – that constitutes the grand repository. Moreover, if epistemically suspect or suboptimal speech is to be tolerated (juridically, if not ethically) in Habermas's scheme, then someone is required to provide sufficient 'corrective' discourse by which to counteract the damage done to the grand repository. For, although, ethically, all can be taken to be required to contribute to the health of the grand repository, no one can be expected, let alone compelled, to do so juridically. How, then, is the grand repository to be established, maintained, and its quality preserved if no one can be compelled to contribute, etc, without violence to her rights as a (autonomous) member of the community?

One move available to Habermas (but not Post) is to render the conduit function as a non-autonomous body to whom obligations can be placed without (burdensome) rights being established or, rather, to afford it such rights as are parasitic upon the audience's. This has notable advantages for the Habermasian scheme in terms of the feedback loop between *Sittlichkeit* and central government. As noted above, both groups use this conduit as a means of measuring the performance of the other. From central government's perspective, if the feedback loop is defective or else disadvantaged by structural and/or qualitative problems, then it will not receive the proper impression of society's performance. In this way, the conduit relays those key performance indicators upon which central government relies if it is to retain power. These inform that executive action by which social, political and economic levers are pulled to effect meaningful course corrections. Likewise, ineffective or inaccurate monitoring of central government's performance disadvantages the electorate, both at the time of election and in between, especially if the inaccurate data set leads to unrest or community tension.

This contingent approach to free speech principle is not peculiar to Habermasian thinking. As I have written elsewhere, there is an entire body of literature that would solve the epistemic shortfalls in public discourse, not by insisting that individual free speech is protected (or protectable) by reason of its epistemic virtue, but by assigning the problem of correcting epistemic shortfalls in public discourse to the press industry as a quasi-public sector body, lacking in noumenality.[69] In this way, the press is expected to carry the burden of serving the *Sittlichkeit*'s 'right to know', such that the conduit is not populated by individuals, campaigners, etc, as Habermas envisaged but, more or less, by the press exclusively. As both a philosophical principle and practical expectation, it strikes me that this expectation is fallacious. Whereas interferences with press speech are justifiable if the object is to protect the individual rights of others, ie, when civil wrongs are committed, but are not if it is to protect so-called societal rights, as audience interests, in furtherance of optimised democratic participation. Hence, the press cannot be obliged to do good, only to make good any unjustified harm caused to individuals in its way.[70]

Since the justification for this position are relevant to our consideration of the conduit function, I set them out here briefly. In *A Free and Regulated Press*, I took as my starting point the findings of the Leveson Inquiry into the Culture, Practices and Ethics of the Press, a government-initiated, independent inquiry which heard testimony from multiple stakeholders in the press industry, from owners, editors and journalists to victims, campaigners and academics.[71] Of relevance to our discussion here is the conception of press freedom that Lord Justice Leveson, the presiding judge in this inquiry, was most taken by – that, in keeping with Habermas, the press has obligations to the public that are essentially different to that of individuals. Amongst other things, he described press freedom as 'an instrumental good, to be valued, promoted, and protected to the extent that it … serve[s] its important democratic functions'.[72] Although there is nothing unusual in this statement – after all, we find much the same in case law (as noted above), and in, say, the work of the self-styled (US) Commission on Freedom of the Press of 1947, which thought the press to be a sort of public trust with 'responsibilities to the general spread of information [analogous] to those of a … trustee'[73] – still, Leveson's rationale is striking. He was taken by Onora O'Neill's claim that the public has a right to an 'adequate' press.[74] Cognisant, perhaps, of the autonomy problem inherent in expecting members of the press to perform services for the

[69] P Wragg, *A Free and Regulated Press: Defending Coercive Independent Press Regulation* (Hart, 2020).
[70] ibid.
[71] Lord Justice Leveson, An Inquiry into the Culture, Practices and Ethics of the Press: Report (HC 780, 2012).
[72] ibid, 63, [3.7].
[73] WE Hocking, *Freedom of the Press: A Framework of Principle* (University of Chicago Press, 1947) 150 and 225.
[74] webarchive.nationalarchives.gov.uk/20140122192219/http://www.levesoninquiry.org.uk/wp-content/uploads/2012/07/Witness-Statement-of-Professor-Baroness-ONeil.pdf, [2d], [5], [6], [8] and [9]. Leveson (n 71) 61, [3.2].

general public, Leveson gave voice to O'Neill's idea of press freedom as parasitic upon audience interests of the voting public:

> Freedom for commercial mass media businesses ('corporate speech') is a very different proposition from the freedom of individual self-expression ('personal speech'). The latter is discussed further below, and has its roots in a very personal conception of what it is to be human. Take, for example, John Stuart Mill's argument from *On Liberty*, that freedom of speech serves a central function in promoting individual autonomy and self-fulfilment. This argument has no direct relevance to press freedom because, put simply, press organisations are not human beings with a personal need to be able to self-express. In any event, "*an argument for free speech for the powerless will not make a case for free speech for a powerful organisation.*"[75,76]

This statement resonates powerfully with the Habermasian ideal and yet is clearly taken from O'Neill's witness statement, which echoes Kantian morality in a more obvious sense. For example, O'Neill is convinced that press freedom cannot be explicated from Millian principle, and she is damning of those that would:

> Contemporary claims about *freedom of expression* are quite often confused with J.S. Mill's much more specific claims about *individual rights of self expression*. This simple error often leads to confusion, and claims about media freedom based on this error have no value. Mill argued that individuals should enjoy *rights of self expression* because these are needed to protect individuality, and that individual self expression should be curtailed only where likely to harm others. His argument for rights of self expression still has great cultural resonance, but shows little, if anything, about the speech rights of organisations, including the media, as opposed to those of individuals.[77]

O'Neill offers three grounds in defence of her position: first, that: 'An argument for free speech for the powerless will not make a case for free speech for powerful organisations. If (unlike other powerful organisations) the media are to enjoy extensive freedom of speech, other arguments are needed.'[78] Second, that 'Mill's argument from the need to protect individuality applies only to beings that *can* express themselves. Organisations, including media organisations, are not in the business of self expression: they are not selves in the relevant sense.'[79] Third, that 'Mill's argument for limiting freedom of self expression only when likely to harm others has unclear implications.'[80]

In other words, then, O'Neill argues that whereas individual free speech is speaker-orientated, press freedom is audience-orientated. This is so, she claims, because the protections afforded by the free speech guarantee, as given by Mill's argument, apply *only* to those that are power*less*. Both empirically and philosophically, this argument does not quite stack up. There is nothing in Mill's *On Liberty* to suggest that free speech should be so understood. Moreover, the empirical data suggests that the institutional press is *not* powerful, as a whole, especially at a local level. Instead, there is a

[75] O'Neill (n 74) [2].
[76] Leveson (n 71) 62, [3.3] (emphasis in original).
[77] O'Neill (n 74) [2b].
[78] ibid.
[79] ibid (emphasis in original).
[80] ibid.

distinct power imbalance as between certain national titles and others. This is not a purely UK-perspective; it is true across the globe, as a general rule. (Her final, alternative, ground that Mill's harm principle has 'unclear implications' is tackled in the next chapter.)

O'Neill concludes that press freedom is 'a public good because it is *needed* for civic and common life' (emphasis added).[81] In this way, 'adequate (or better than adequate) standards of public communication, that allow readers, listeners and viewers to gain information and form judgements, and so to participate in social, cultural and democratic life'. This argument is strange in that it presupposes the public can *demand* that a private sector organisation/industry performs services, justification-wise, that might be expected of the public sector. The argument seems to be that because the press *can* (and sometimes *does*) provide benefits to voter thinking, etc, it *must*.

O'Neill's position here, as an exclusively audience-orientated, parasitic conception of press freedom is epistemic in nature. In this way, she argues, her theory is superior to those speaker-orientated conceptions 'that ignore the importance of communication that does not aim at truth'.[82] In doing so, she is exposed to at least some of the criticisms of epistemological conceptions of free speech principle that were discussed in the previous chapter. Nevertheless, if the juridical task is confined to audience interests, such that the press freedom right is but parasitic upon the *Sittlichkeit*'s interests in epistemic advance for participatory purposes, then at least some of the difficulties faced in the previous chapter are ameliorated. This reasoning, for example, would permit regulatory interference with speech deemed inaccurate or else insufficiently diverse for grand repository purposes. In this way, the press industry becomes the epistemic drone that serves the participatory value inherent in the *Sittlichkeit*, which represents the ultimate symbol of power.

Nevertheless, such reasoning must confront a serious problem. For, despite arguments to the contrary, the press is not some impersonal entity or quasi-public sector body; it *is* the *Sittlichkeit*. Each organisational level – owner, editor and journalist – is populated by noumenal beings. These noumena cannot be compelled to adopt an end, if individuality is the ultimate language of constitutional design, and not community. Of course, no one could seriously argue otherwise (albeit O'Neill's position appears to). The point seems to be that by virtue of belonging within the conduit community, if it may be put that way, the press occupies a special position that requires noumenal interests in self-fulfilment, etc, to be forsaken (or otherwise, deprioritised) in favouring the (claimed) audience interest in epistemically rich speech (for grand repository purposes).

To the extent this problem – of treating a series of private organisation as if it were some quasi-public body – is recognised, O'Neill's intellectual design is justified by the concept of 'need', which, in Habermasian terms, would conform to the expectations that both the *Sittlichkeit* and the central state have for the conduit as that body which shuttles performance-related information back and forth between the two. We have already seen how the necessity argument is unpersuasive in the context of

[81] ibid, [2d].
[82] ibid.

individuality – amongst other things, that citizens do not *need* information to vote; they can vote perfectly legitimately without any information at all. How then is this supposed necessity in the conduit function to be rationalised juridically? In an important sense, the problem will not always arise. If conduit speech is of obvious relevance to the conduit function (because it serves the public interest explicitly) then no conceptual difficulties arise as such. The problem arises, then, in the regulatory setting, in which it may be said that speech is defective because what is produced is said not to serve the conduit function *well enough*. Moreover, it presupposes, further, that demands could be made, by either the *Sittlichkeit* or central state, that information is provided, either in the form of factual material or diversity of opinion, to address epistemic gaps in the grand repository.

The literature contains several strategies by which to defend the legitimacy of these expectations. One of the more ambitious says that the press is not forced so much as incentivised to accept this burdensome arrangement through the benefits it receives consequently.[83] This view can be traced back to, at least, Theodore Peterson's claim, in the mid-1950s, that 'freedom carries concomitant obligations; and the press, which enjoys a privileged position under our government, is obliged to be responsible to society for carrying out certain essential functions of mass communication in society'.[84] This claim, of itself, has its heritage in the work of the Commission on Freedom of the Press which, as we have seen, thought the press had duties to the general public as trustees do to beneficiaries of the trust. We see modern echoes of this in O'Neill's claim that there can be no 'rights without counterpart responsibilities'.[85] In keeping with these views, Judith Lichtenberg, in the US, has long argued that if special rights for the press exists, as she thinks they should, then they are contingent upon fulfilment of the conduit function: 'if press institutions or their agents have special rights, it is because the people as a whole have granted them; if the people have granted them, it is because doing so is to the benefit of us all'.[86] In the UK, Geoffrey Robertson has argued the point more emphatically: the British press *does* benefit from special rights and, accordingly, he says:

> There is no reason why the press should not be given corresponding duties to ensure that factual errors are corrected, that privacy is not invaded in order to obtain stories of no importance, and that certain ethical standards are generally observed.[87]

For Robertson, these special rights exists in respect of 'copyright, contempt, defamation, court reporting, rehabilitation of offenders, official secrecy, elections, local council meetings, matrimonial proceedings, race relations – to name but a few'.[88]

However, Robertson's list is striking in that these special rights, if they do exist,[89] all relate to the *performance* of the conduit role itself. They are not, as such, *incentives* to the bargain, applying, as they do, only to the role once operative. Consequently, there

[83] See discussion in Wragg (n 69) 112–19.
[84] FS Siebert, T Peterson and W Schramm, *Four Theories of the Press* (University of Illinois Press, 1956) 74.
[85] O O'Neill, *A Question of Trust* (Cambridge University Press, 2002) 96.
[86] J Lichtenberg, 'Foundations and limits of freedom of the press' in J Lichtenberg (ed), *Democracy and the Mass Media* (Cambridge University Press, 1990),128.
[87] G Robertson, *People Against the Press* (Quartet Books, 1983) 157–58.
[88] ibid.
[89] *cf* Wragg (n 69) 113–19.

remains something unexplained or unexplainable about the asserted bargain; these privileges do not explain why the initial transaction should be entered into. In other words, the bargain – benefits for burdens – does not contain benefits *in exchange for* burdens. It is, instead, benefits *within* burdens – special terms that apply to the burden itself which *might*, in some circumstances, ameliorate the harshness of the role. Still, though, we are left to beg the question of *why* the press, as a collection of private organisations with shareholders to satisfy, should want to expose themselves to the burden of servility to public demand that the literature seeks to impress upon them.

One move available to proponents of the benefits-for-burdens argument is to point to tax exemptions or qualifications for press outputs. For example, in the UK, newspapers are zero-rated for the purposes of value added tax (VAT). Yet, in the UK at least, this is hardly a benefit for the press itself. It simply means that the purchase price of newspapers is less than it would be if full-rated VAT were added. If that happened, the consumer, rather than the newspaper, would suffer the burden. It may be that an increase in cost would affect newspaper sales, which would, of course, affect newspapers detrimentally. Yet the rationale for zero-rated status is not for the newspaper's benefit; it has always been that society would benefit from the promotion of reading that the diminution in price that the status is meant to promote.[90]

An alternative move is to argue that this burdensome notion of press freedom is precisely what journalism means in a democratic society. Yet, this moves the argument no further along. The meaning of journalism, and the aims of press freedom, cannot be imposed, as if some fixed notion, from above. It must be an ethical position, to be proposed, contested, and debated, from within the *Sittlichkeit* itself. It is in recognition of such thinking that Post says Meiklejohnian logic is wrong to assume communal decision-making can be improved through artificial interferences with the quality of speech since such intervention will either prevent specific citizens from full participation, which would be wrong, or else will rely upon regulatory standards that, by attempting 'to reflect the values and priorities of some vision of collective identity' serves only to pre-empt 'the very democratic process by which collective identity is to be determined'.[91] We could read this, in Kantian terms, as the ethical law that self-perfection is a matter reserved for the noumenal being herself;[92] she cannot make the perfection of others to be her maxim – otherwise, she would make them merely a means to an end and not treat them as an end in themselves, which is something that cannot be made universal.[93]

As we have seen, Post eschews these managerial ambitions for the conduit function in all its forms. We can, therefore, imagine him saying that if there is a function that the press *must* perform, then there must be some oversight body empowered to check on that performance such that failure to perform it is reason to intervene. This, of course, is the move he detects in the Meiklejohnian logic that, say, Sunstein and Fiss deploy. It is a move that he cannot condone for it would surely negate the rhetoric of an

[90] See, eg, *News Corp UK Ltd v HMRC* [2018] UKFTT 0129 (TC), [17].
[91] Post (n 2) 2368.
[92] I Kant, *The Metaphysics of Morals* (L Denis, ed, M Gregor, trans) (Cambridge University Press, 2017), [6:386].
[93] I Kant, *Groundwork of the Metaphysics of Morals* (M Gregor and J Timmermann, trans and eds) (Cambridge University Press, 2012), [4:429]; see discussion in ch 8.

uninhibited press that the Supreme Court championed in *New York Times v Sullivan*.[94] Hence, his concern that:

> Structures of control acquire their own life, turn, and bite the progressive hand that establishes them. If we create organizations of heteronomy, we shall all, sooner or later, be condemned to inhabit them. We shall become the subjects of a power not our own.[95]

Post's squeamishness may well be derived from the collective inexperience of regulatory oversight that the US enjoys. In mainland Europe, especially, and elsewhere, in fact, there is an established culture of regulating, if only on a voluntary basis, the conduit function of press freedom as it relates to societal interests in, say, accurate information.[96]

The position this leaves us in, as a set of moral arguments, is that the press (or, in fact, any entity) can be juridically compelled through the Hohfeldian analysis of right-duty to compensate another for the wrongs they commit, but cannot be forced to serve society (be that needs or wants) as to the provision of accurate information and diverse opinion, in service to the grand repository. Whereas the press can be chastised, ethically, for its failure to provide accurate information (eg, by adverse regulatory adjudication), it cannot be penalised (through fines, etc). This is so because societal interests in specific press outputs (satisfying the grand repository) cannot be made to meet the right-duty analysis that liberal democracy understands, ie, wrongdoing–causation–harm.

Take, for example, the problem of hate speech disseminated through the press (of which the corn-dealer example is a fledgling type). We can make strong moral claims to show that hatefulness is wrong. Likewise, we can show, evidentially, harm to individuals. Where we struggle is to make the connection between speech and harm as to amount to legal causation. If a person takes a newspaper, becomes convinced by its toxic worldview (eg, that immigrants are the cause of a depressed economy, that benefits recipients are scroungers, that single mothers are responsible for the country's moral decline, that the trans community is brainwashing children, that Islam is rampant, etc, and acts on their views (espousing racist rhetoric, etc) then they themselves are the cause of the harm, not the newspaper, for they have chosen to accept, and act upon, this toxicity. To blame the newspaper, although tempting, is to absolve the racist of her own toxic moral choices.[97]

B. Post's Uneasy Relationship with Autonomy

There is much here that, presumably, Post would agree with. Although he draws upon Habermas at various points in his work,[98] still he could not abide the extension of

[94] *New York Times v Sullivan* 376 US 254, 270 (1964).

[95] Post (n 19) 1136.

[96] See discussion in Wragg (n 69) 173–96. See further, P Wragg and A Koltay, *Global Perspectives on Press Regulation*, vols 1 and 2 (Hart, 2024).

[97] See discussion in Wragg (n 69) 83–109; 173–96.

[98] See, eg, 'Meiklejohn's Mistake' (n 19) 1115; 'Democracy and Equality' (n 1) 28; 'Participatory Democracy and Free Speech' (n 28) 483; and 'Participatory Democracy as a Theory of Free Speech: A Reply' (2011) 97 *Virginia Law Review* 617, 621.

Habermasian thought to include a sort of compelled speech, directed against journalists. As he has said only recently: 'We would not be the democratic authors of our own government if we were compelled to participate in the formation of public opinion in ways contrary to our own will.'[99] Moreover, in the same piece, he reasserts his commitment to political equality in public discourse, such that: 'every democratic citizen possesses an equal right to influence the contents of public opinion' regardless of the epistemic qualities (or deficiencies) within that contribution.[100] It is, as he has said previously, in the nature of public discourse that it is not perfect, nor perfectible, but instead a 'sea of tumult and discord'.[101] In this sense, Post's position emulates the Millian ideal of the irrationality proviso. In fact, he is explicit:

> The participatory approach does not focus on the cognitive cogency of speech, but rather on its facilitation of democratic participation. Even irrational and abusive speech serves this function, which is to say when it is deemed within public discourse, its regulation would both compromise the neutrality of the state and the autonomy of those participating within public discourse.[102]

Yet, there the comparison ends, for, as we have seen, Post has set himself firmly *against* autonomy as the ultimate expression of authentic free speech principle. In addition to arguing that the language of autonomy lacks sufficient precision to aid free speech principle,[103] he has also claimed, somewhat mysteriously, that autonomy theory fails to appreciate 'the importance of maintaining the social solidarity of community'.[104]

Nevertheless, Post's relationship with autonomy is not straightforward. Earlier on in his career, he seemed much more enamoured with it. For example, in his groundbreaking article cataloguing the major error in Meiklejohnian thought, autonomy plays a central role in articulating the priority of individuality over community. Here, Post is explicit that 'The enterprise of public discourse … rests on the value of autonomy';[105] 'so far from vestigial, then, the ideal of autonomy is instead foundational for the democratic project';[106] and, 'Autonomy, properly understood, signifies that within the sphere of public discourse and with regard to the suppression of speech the state must always regard collective identity as necessarily open-ended.'[107] Moreover, he is especially critical, in that piece, of Owen Fiss's Meiklejohnian thinking for its failure to properly recognise autonomy's role in the First Amendment concept: 'What Fiss apparently does not recognize, however, is that the value of individual autonomy is *inseparable* from the very aspiration for self-government that propels his own proposed revision of First Amendment doctrine.'[108]

[99] RC Post, 'Comment on Freedom of Expression in American Legal Education' (2023) 51 *Hofstra Law Review* 667, 671.
[100] ibid.
[101] Post (n 19) 1119.
[102] Post (n 2) 2371.
[103] Post (n 28) 480.
[104] Post (n 98) 626.
[105] Post (n 19) 1118–19.
[106] ibid, 1123.
[107] ibid, 1122.
[108] ibid, 1120.

Post's attachment to autonomy is no mere passing phase, for even in his most prolific period, he could still say that 'the Meiklejohnian theory … stresses the quality of public debate, whereas the participatory perspective emphasizes the autonomy of individual citizens'[109] and that 'American courts have consistently opted to protect individual autonomy against regulations of public discourse designed to maintain the integrity of collective thinking processes.'[110] Although, at times, conveyed by means of the Hegelian dialectic movement – 'public discourse merits unique constitutional protection because it is the process through which the democratic "self," the agent of self-government, is itself constituted through the *reconciliation* of individual and collective autonomy'[111] (emphasis added) – still the argument bears the hallmarks of Kantian thinking in its treatment of individual autonomy as the principal juridical concern: 'the ascription of autonomy is … the transcendental precondition for the possibility of democratic self-determination'.[112]

Elsewhere, in his extended review of Fiss's *Liberalism Divided*, Post maintains his criticism of Fiss's belief that 'collective self-determination is a social right theoretically distinct from and unconnected to individual rights of personal autonomy'.[113] In this piece, Post's sustained commitment to the value of autonomy is given its strongest form:

> Individual autonomy is not protected by the First Amendment because it is instrumentally necessary for better decision-making, but rather because it is intrinsically connected to democratic self-governance. Individual citizens can identify with the creation of a collective will only if they believe that collective decision-making is in some way connected to their own individual self-determination.[114]

And:

> The democratic value of collective self-determination thus entails the value of individual autonomy. In fact, in my view, '[t]he essential problematic of democracy … , lies in the reconciliation of individual and collective autonomy.' The free speech tradition views public discourse as the arena within which this reconciliation occurs. It does not follow from this that any of the actual policy prescriptions that Fiss recommends is necessarily wrong or constitutionally inadequate, but it does follow that in assessing their constitutionality one cannot rule out *a priori* the independent constitutional value of individual autonomy, which is what Fiss attempts to do throughout *Liberalism Divided*. To compromise individual autonomy is to compromise the foundation of the democratic value of collective self-determination.[115]

In this review, we are left in no doubt as to Post's commitment to the autonomy value. Democratic self-governance, as he understands it, is the 'reconciliation' of individual and collective autonomy, in which that individual autonomy is made manifest when

[109] Post (n 2) 2368.
[110] ibid, 2369.
[111] Post (n 19) 1128.
[112] ibid, 1131.
[113] R Post, 'Equality and Autonomy in First Amendment Jurisprudence' (1997) 95 *Michigan Law Review* 1517, 1520.
[114] ibid, 1524.
[115] ibid, 1525.

the individual is made to feel part of the process regardless of whether the outcome (either voting or the great debate in between) accords with her views or not. It is the *input* that counts – the *opportunity* to contribute.[116] Thus, 'Democratic values are not realized unless there is a linkage of individual and collective autonomy, even if collective decision-making is fully informed',[117] which leads to his ultimate conclusion that 'Democratic self-governance is the core of the free speech tradition'.[118]

These conflicting attitudes toward autonomy in Post might be assuaged, if not entirely resolved, by treating autonomy as a value within the participatory method. In this way, the irrationality proviso is maintained in Post but only contingently, as when the noumenal being finds herself within a 'public discourse' moment of opportunity to influence others. This approach finds expression in Post when he notes that:

> The First Amendment serves as the "guardian of our democracy" by casting speakers, *when* they participate in public discourse, in the role of autonomous sovereigns who are immunized from government control *when* they deliberate about how to direct the ship of state (emphasis added).[119]

In this way, self-government/participation is *not* an intrinsic value after all. It is conditional upon speech taking a form that is either intended to contribute to this (vaulted) public discourse or else happens to do so regardless of intentionality.

Post's distinct queasiness around the autonomy value is best explained, I think, by his distinct unease that an unvarnished version of it, as, say, Scanlon presented it originally, would represent an entirely unfettered, absolute entitlement to speak that would, amongst other things, tarnish free speech's reputation as a special event. Post reveals this anxiety in his 2011 defence of his participatory democracy theory:

> The immunity accorded to those who seek to influence the content of public opinion represents an unusual exception to this pervasive background regulation. The First Amendment privileges those who speak in public discourse from the obligations and responsibilities that the law normally imposes on citizens. But if the First Amendment were to spread this immunity too widely, the very social structure of community that sustains democracy might begin to unravel.[120]

As we have seen in earlier chapters, this angst is common in the American literature. If the speech content element of free speech is not something special, then the First Amendment loses its sense of importance and, more disastrously than that, would apply to any and all speech content.

Yet, it is interesting that Post should not deal with this anxiety by making the move that Mill does, by which the harm principle comes into play (see next chapter). After all, Post, in his commitment to the Hegelian reconciliation of individual with collective autonomy, positions himself to treat determinations on the value of speech content as matters beyond the juridical jurisdiction. They are, instead, he must surely say, matters

[116] See, further, RC Post, 'Legitimacy and Hate Speech' (2017) 32 *Constitutional Commentary* 651, 654.
[117] Post (n 113) 1526.
[118] ibid, 1540.
[119] RC Post, 'NIFLA and the Construction of Compelled Speech Doctrine' (2022) 97 *Indiana Law Journal* 1071, 1088–89.
[120] Post (n 98) 625.

for the *Sittlichkeit* itself to ponder. This is, after all, a constant refrain in Post's work. In 2000, it put it thus: 'to the extent that the state regulates public discourse so as to reflect the value and priorities of some vision of collective identity, it pre-empts the very democratic process by which collective identity is to be determined'.[121] In 2022, it had become:

> Self-government is a fundamental constitutional value … By ensuring that all can freely participate in the creation of public opinion, the First Amendment protects the constitutional value of 'democratic legitimation,' which is the public's sense that it is indeed engaged in the project of collective self-determination.[122]

From here, Post could retreat to the Holmesian position that only a 'clear and present danger' would permit the state to interfere with speech. In this way, although the spectre of the First Amendment might arise in any instance in which speech content is front and central to some juridical matter, it might be easily swatted aside by an astringent judge who sees that the liberal matrix of wrongdoing-causation-harm renders any such potential free speech claim nugatory.[123]

Yet Post instead moves to a position that seems distinctly contradictory to his underlying laissez-faire treatment of speech's value as a purely ethical matter. For he brings the content of speech back into the juridical domain by means of strict, rigid categorisations. This is most apparent, for example, in his embattled position, as against, especially, Martin Redish, that commercial speech is undeserving of full First Amendment protection because it displays qualities that render it unsuited to the underlying values of that Hegelian reconciliation of individual and collective autonomy. So it is, then, that the labels attached to speech become significant after all, for it is only once the label of public discourse has been safely attached to the disputed content that Post, emulating Voltaire, will fight to the death the right of the participant to say it. If, though, the label is commercial speech – by which he typically means advertising ('Suffice it to say that I regard communications that seek to sell toothpaste as different from communications that seek to influence the formation of democratic public opinion')[124] – then Post is happy to stand aside and let the state regulate it. This differential treatment of commercial speech is jarring on two levels: first, in its preference for form over substance (it is entirely possible, as Redish constantly maintains, that commercial speech *could* contribute to this discourse *despite* the apparent intention to do nothing more than turn a profit through clever advertising tricks);[125] but, secondly, and most significantly, in its unfortunate implication that commercial speech (regulatable, according to Post) is more pernicious than overt hate speech (unregulatable, according to Post).[126]

Post's adherence, then, to these rigid categorisations is most unfortunate in the untested generalisations that it must rely upon. We see this, for example, when Post

[121] Post (n 2) 2368.
[122] Post (n 119) 1088.
[123] This position is set out in more detail in ch 8.
[124] RC Post, 'Viewpoint Discrimination and Commercial Speech' (2007) 41 *Loyola of Los Angeles Law Review* 169, 177.
[125] See, eg, MH Redish, 'The Value of Free Speech' (1982) 130 *University of Pennsylvania Law Review* 591.
[126] Post (n 116).

claims that commercial speech cannot fulfil the function of public discourse – that is, of being communication 'deemed necessary to ensure that a democratic state remains responsive to the views of its citizens' because 'although informative, it is not seeking to engage the state in dialogue'.[127] Whereas, he says, 'to chill commercial speech is to lose information', to do the same to public discourse is to lose not only information 'but also the possibility of democratic legitimation'.[128] Accordingly, he says that state regulation of commercial speech is 'necessarily paternalistic' in its attempts to 'preser[ve] a fair bargaining process'. This, he says, is legitimate because, here, the state 'presuppose that consumers are vulnerable and dependent' yet it could not apply the same reasoning to public discourse speech because 'these assumptions [would] conflict with the autonomy that public discourse must ascribe to citizens'.[129] These empirical assertions also colour his position on hate speech. For example:

> Under conditions of intense conflict, persons who have no reason to believe that their speech can influence the shape of public opinion will have less reason to live together in a relatively peaceable manner under a common system of governance and politics.[130]

These generalisations are problematic to the extent that Post fails to recognise the capacity of commercial speech to have effects equivalent to political speech (such as the demonstrable fact that successful advertising determines how we live, what we value, and who we choose to be) and that political speech can manifest as commercial activity (as when political sponsors back candidates for high office according to the impact it will have upon their financial interests). Moreover, it fails to recognise that hate speech can take forms in which threats of violence loom large and informational content figures little.

Although Post does not go so far as to say that commercial speech should not occasionally enjoy constitutional protection,[131] still he cannot concede that Redish may be right in claiming that the impact of commercial speech upon private decision-making may be as important – perhaps more so – to ordinary people than political speech is upon their public decision-making. If he did, he would recognise that this rigid categorisation hinders the public discourse in those situations whereby advertising takes the form of important (as in, socially valuable) speech. Likewise, his position on hate speech suffers from its failure to acknowledge the importance of the harm principle as a means of tempering extremity. Instead, he is committed to a position in which hate speech, if censored, is the putative victim rather than the denigrated community that must endure it:

> [H]ate-speech regulation causes systemic damage to democratic legitimation. The impact of such regulation does not pertain to individual laws but instead to the risk that persons may come to distrust a political system that holds out the promise of self-determination but that refuses to hear what persons actually have to say.[132]

[127] R Post, 'The Constitutional Status of Commercial Speech' (2000) 48 *UCLA Law Review* 1, 4.
[128] ibid, 32.
[129] ibid, 55.
[130] ibid, 654–55.
[131] Post (n 124) 177.
[132] ibid, 657.

The only concession he is prepared to make has the ring of the harm principle, in tone, if not in spirit: 'If the ambient legal and social environment makes members of target groups feel safe and included, then allowing hate speech will not damage democratic legitimation, regardless of the existence of hate speech.'[133]

The irony is that this rigid formalisation of free speech problems, and their resolution, runs contrary to the general sentiment of his approach to public discourse matters, in which formality is anathema to the organic processes by which the identification of problems and realisation of their solutions are matters sacred to the discourse itself.

V. Conclusion

According to the dominant position in the established literature, the participation value is the only serious candidate for authenticity. Yet, despite its popularity, it is plagued with such difficulties that render it suitable only for those regimes that prefer community over individuality. This, of itself, should invalidate its candidacy. Whereas, initially, it is attractive for its apparent leaning toward the important and meaningful over the mundane and anodyne, it is ultimately dependent upon rigid categorisations that demand juridical oversight (in some form) and classification. This necessary managerialism runs contrary to the spirit of individuality that embodies the irrationality proviso.

As we have seen, both Habermas and Post seek to overcome, or otherwise ameliorate, this managerialism by restoring individual autonomy to the pantheon of free speech values. For Habermas, this is achieved by rendering the prone conduit to the demanding expectations of the animated electorate which, by means of this automaton, may be enriched by the grand repository that the conduit is expected to furnish, cultivate and curate. For Post, the contingency arises through the public discourse itself, for individuality is left to flourish in that environment in whatever form it dares, even if its flavour is so pungent as to be repulsive (hate speech). Yet Post's elevated plane of unfettered existence for that manifesting as 'public discourse' is itself dependent upon an ironclad discriminatory apparatus, by which (arbitrary) labels operate with impunity. Only that which meets the criterion of suitability for the 'public discourse' may enter. In Post's work this turn renders his complex moves to create an ornate system ultimately susceptible to the sharp criticisms that Bork endured when he claimed only the explicitly political should receive legal protection.

However, amidst all this intricate manoeuvring lies an important but obvious question. If, as the process theorists maintain, freedom of speech represents something of a Rawlsian bargain, in which individual power is ceded to the centre in return for the power to criticise (ab)uses of that power, then why – given the clear parallels that this position demonstrates – are process theorists so averse to autonomy theory as the ultimate authentic free speech value? Rawls, of course, was strongly attracted to

[133] ibid, 658.

the autonomy value in his theory of justice (albeit of the more limited Kantian variety). Post, as we have seen, has an uneasy relationship with autonomy, content, it seems, to keep it at arm's length as something evocative of the participatory value (and, therefore, relative to democratic legitimation), but not demonstrative of it. The next chapter will argue that this view of autonomy as something too capacious or capricious is unwarranted in the final analysis; that the autonomy value, at least as Mill understood it, *is* the best candidate for authenticity.

8

Irrationality

I. Introduction

The participation value, discussed in chapter seven, speaks clearly to the Lockean sentiment of rights against the state that are secured by virtue of one's humanity alone. In a political system of maximal enfranchisement, the principle of 'one person, one vote' vividly portrays equality in action. It also signals a series of basic entitlements that the citizen can demand of the state. In exchange for her parcel of coercive power, the state promises to provide security for her person and possessions. If we follow this logic, we reach the rule of law. If we track backwards, we reach the right to vote. These promises speak to an entitlement that cannot be lost.[1] Nevertheless, although she delegates power centrally to the state, she retains a certain portion of it. Over others, she retains, chiefly, the power to persuade. Over herself, she has absolute power. Central to both scenarios is the power to speak, through non-violent and non-coercive means, as C Edwin Baker saw clearly,[2] for if she cannot speak, she cannot ensure her powers are real.

All of this we find in Mill. In his concept of autonomy, individuality is central to life in a democracy and speech is central to individuality. His conception still has much to say about modern life, and our contemporaneous legal problems, despite its vintage. Yet Mill's arguments are routinely dismissed. If we are to rehabilitate Millian thought, then these criticisms must be overcome. Central to them, as we shall see, is the view that Mill's harm principle is too weak to sustain his thesis. As chapter five argued, this criticism misses the point of *On Liberty*, which centred almost exclusively on the absolute protection that self-regarding activity should be afforded. In an important sense, it was unnecessary for Mill to demonstrate how the harm principle operates in conditions of other-regarding behaviour because all he sought to signal was the invalidity of harm as a reason to interfere with the truly self-regarding.

Yet, despite its limitations, and the criticisms that can be made of it, the scheme remains viable. The object of this chapter is to show that greater schematic design is required, not abandonment of the principle itself. However, convincing the academic community of this point is no easy task given how firmly it has set itself against Millian principle. This resistance is a product of misunderstanding left too long uncorrected, such that the more vital criticisms of his position cannot be reached until these have been cleared away. As will be shown, certain stubborn ideas persist, notably the belief that the argument from autonomy in Mill's work requires absolute protection for all

[1] Although aspects of it might be suspended by reason of, say, incarceration or insanity.
[2] CE Baker, *Human Liberty and Freedom of Speech* (Oxford University Press, 1989) 47–69.

speech (or, otherwise, that the autonomy principle cannot differentiate between competing rights-based claims).

In its ambition to rehabilitate Mill's radical thought, and so demonstrate its continued vitality for the design of authentic free speech principle, section II below revisits Mill's principle so as to provide an outline of its key features (whilst also offering some defence of its position). Having reached conclusions about its weaknesses, section III seeks to overcome those difficulties by recalibrating the harm principle according to the verticality–horizontality dichotomy highlighted in previous chapters. In this way, it seeks to show how the harm principle operates according to the separate duty-holder positions the state must adopt when it is the source of autonomy interference or else is adjudicating between competing autonomy-based rights-claims. In the latter mode, the liberal pattern of wrongdoing–causation–harm captures the method by which competing rights-based claims ought to be settled. Nevertheless, its ambitions in this regard are limited. It does not seek to a comprehensive recalibration of the harm principle so much as sketch out the key features of this redesigned scheme. Given that the majority of this section is dedicated to describing the harm principle's operation in the horizontal mode by which the state adjudicates competing autonomy-based rights-claim, it anticipates the discussion in part four of this book, whereby application of the Millian scheme to the three contexts considered there will be explored in much greater detail. Finally, section IV defends this elaboration, in which the common critiques of autonomy-based schemes of free speech principle are countered.

II. Outline

Part two of this book was highly critical of the modern technique by which the nominated justificatory value is used as the principal definitional tool. As we saw in those earlier chapters, this technique is especially prevalent amongst process theorists, who tend to use the participatory value as the critical lens by which to prioritise the claims of political speech over all else. Likewise, those favouring the self-fulfilment or self-realisation theory will tend to argue for a broader range of speech accordingly, on that basis that more than political speech alone is required to realise optimal self-improvement. Mill, though, relied on no such typology. *On Liberty* contains no distinctions between content types and, in any event, reveals no 'theoretically interesting' (as Thomas Scanlon would later say) definition by which to do so.[3]

Accordingly, there is no preference for political speech over other forms of speech. This is apparent in the discussion, as Mill moves through examples that speak to contexts of religious faith and scientific discovery rather than political thought. This is not to say that Mill was uninterested in forms of speech altogether. As we know, he saw the realisation of individuality, in which the noumenal being contemplates the world around her and her place within it, in terms of two modes of conceptualising: 'thoughts' and 'opinions'. Clearly, the two are linked, so much so that they amount to the same thing in an important sense. The difference concerns their manifestation. Thought belongs

[3] T Scanlon, 'A Theory of Freedom of Expression' in RM Dworkin (ed), *The Philosophy of Law* (Oxford University Press, 1977) 153, 156.

exclusively to the noumenal realm. It is the internal manifestation of an opinion. Opinion, meanwhile, belongs exclusively to the phenomenal realm. It is the external manifestation of thought. The question, in Mill's *On Liberty*, concerns the justifiability of coercive force against thought or opinion.

In this system, no distinction is made between an opinion created by the noumenal self or that created by another but which an individual holds true. The opinion is simply a phenomenal thing that others can become aware of. Thought, therefore, is its opposite. It has no phenomenal quality and resides only within the noumenal mind. Accordingly, when we overlay our juridical scheme upon this descriptive account, we see why Mill should say that thought's protection from law is absolute whilst opinion's is qualified. Since thought remains within the noumenal mind, we need say nothing more about it. It is only when thought takes phenomenal form, as opinion, that the law has an interest (which is not to say it is entitled to regulate opinion per se).

Since the descriptor 'opinion' is all encompassing, Mill seeks to distinguish its different phenomenal form, not in terms of content, but in terms of relation. Broadly speaking, the opinion that affects only the noumenal being expressing it is entitled to absolute protection. The appropriate protection to be afforded speech affecting others depends upon what Mill calls the question of whether it affects them 'only with their free, voluntary, and undeceived consent'.[4] If it does then it is entitled to absolute protection. (If it does not, then protection is qualified and dependent upon the harm principle.) Hence, there should be 'absolute freedom of opinion and sentiment on all subjects, practical or speculative, scientific, moral, or theological'.[5]

This disinterested treatment of content types only partially answers the question of what counts as speech for coverage purposes. We should still need to understand what speech means as against 'non-speech'. In Mill's account, we are given only the term 'opinion'. However, since at least the time of Thomas Emerson, opinion (or, rather, expression) has been distinguished from action. This is said to follow from Mill's well-known statement that 'no one pretends actions should be as free as opinions'.[6] Emerson interpreted this distinction in hard terms, to signify a strict separation, such that anything qualifying as 'speech' belongs within the free speech paradigm, with 'action' excluded:[7] 'a majority of one has the right to control action, but a minority of one has the right to talk'.[8] Scanlon, of course, thought adherence to this strict dichotomy was 'a serious mistake' on the basis that some forms of behaviour would be excluded that ought to be included, and *vice versa*.[9] Likewise, C Edwin Baker expressed the same concern when he said: 'common sense operates less to divide the world of behavior objectively between expression and action than to indicate the perspective of the person doing the dividing'.[10] Moreover, in his criticisms of Mill's work, Alan Haworth is right, albeit in a trivial sense, to say that speech, itself, is a form of action.[11]

[4] JS Mill, *On Liberty* in *Collected Works of John Stuart Mill*, vol XVIII (JM Robson, ed) (University of Toronto Press, 1977) 225.
[5] ibid.
[6] Mill (n 4) 260.
[7] TI Emerson, *The System of Freedom of Expression* (Vintage Books, 1970) 8–9.
[8] ibid, 8.
[9] Scanlon (n 3) 156.
[10] CE Baker, *Human Liberty and Freedom of Speech* (Oxford University Press, 1989) 71.
[11] A Haworth, *Free Speech* (Routledge, 1998) 30.

However, these criticisms, do a disservice to the original. Emerson's fault lay more in the precision of his language than the underlying idea. The 'fundamental distinction' he draws lies 'between belief, opinion, and communication of ideas on the one hand, and different forms of conduct on the other'.[12] The terms 'expression' and 'action' are presented as 'shorthand' versions of this sentence, which can be understood to differentiate the communicative from the uncommunicative. Accordingly, Emerson is not saying that speech cannot involve action, or vice versa. The distinction is really between the realm of pure or non-communicative action as opposed to communicative action. Hand signals, flag waving, etc, would all count as forms of communication despite being achieved primarily by means of an obvious action. Mill would have no difficulty including these within the realm of opinion entitled, he would say, to absolute protection.

Yet Mill's commitment to absolute protection waivers, or seems to. For, later in *On Liberty*, he provides the well-known 'corn dealer' example by which to demonstrate that freedom of opinion is qualified in certain circumstances:

> An opinion that corn-dealers are starvers of the poor, or that private property is robbery, ought to be unmolested when simply circulated through the press, but may justly incur punishment when delivered to an excited mob assembled before the house of a corn-dealer, or when handed about among the same mob in the form of a placard.[13]

Here, then, the ability to disseminate opinion is qualified. Ostensibly, there is no self-contradiction, for although described as opinion, according to Mill, because 'even opinions lose their immunity, when [they] constitute … a positive instigation to some mischievous act'.[14]

From this arises the (equally) well-known distinction between act and opinion. Hence, Mill says:

> Acts, of whatever kind, which, without justifiable cause, do harm to others, may be, and in the more important cases absolutely require to be, controlled by the unfavourable sentiments, and, when needful, by the active interference of mankind.[15]

Thus, the 'opinion' that corn dealers are 'starvers of the poor' is no longer classifiable as mere opinion when dealer to the excitable crowd outside a corn dealer's house. Clearly, the setting is important to Mill because he tells us that the same opinion 'ought to be unmolested' if printed in a newspaper. This is an unsatisfactory distinction, as others have recognised.

For John Gray, the problem might be ameliorated, if not entirely avoided, if we conceive of the distinction between the two scenarios in terms of the feasibility of autonomous thinking produced by them:

> It is surely possible to regard [the corn dealer example] as making an appeal to the improbability of autonomous thought in 'excited mobs' rather than an appeal to the harm to the interests of corndealers caused by the utterances made in such circumstances: for, after all, corndealers might be as severely harmed by confiscatory legislation (passed as a result of

[12] Emerson (n 7) 8.
[13] Mill (n 4) 260.
[14] ibid.
[15] ibid.

> expressive acts uttered in the reasoned arguments of parliamentary debate) as by any sort of mob violence.[16]

Alternatively, we might seek to rescue the distinction, in the terms that Alan Haworth provides, as between oration as regulatable action and journalism as unregulatable opinion.[17] Whereas both of these analyses are intuitively appealing, neither is entirely satisfactory. Certainly, we can say, with Haworth, that the corn dealer example is frustrating at face value, since it says too little and so relies upon too much by way of implication.[18]

Alternatively, still, we might say that newspaper opinion is self-regarding whilst the orator's speaker is other-regarding because of the proximity between the speech and the likely descent into violence. This alternative would seem to arise from Mill's clarification that:

> The liberty of the individual [ie, the orator] must be thus far limited; he must not make himself a nuisance to other people. But if he refrains from *molesting* others in what concerns them, and merely acts according to his own inclination and judgment in things which concern himself, the same reasons which show that opinion should be free, prove also that he should be allowed, without molestation, to carry his opinions into practice at his own cost.[19]

Nevertheless, even this is problematic since it necessitates the inference of malignity on the orator's part – that he knew, or should have known, that the speech would lead to reprisals against this specific corn dealer – which, presumably, cannot be inferred on the journalist's part. However, we can still realise this distinction if we say that (even) the journalist's absolute entitlement to speak falls away when conditions of causation are met.

We can make progress with this dilemma if we recalibrate Millian principle by means of the verticality–horizontality dichotomy referenced in earlier chapters. For, it seems to me, Mill is trying to communicate the inviolability of both self-regarding and other-regarding speech when the vertical scenario is operative. Accordingly, if the state seeks to penalise speech *and* the state (including its functionaries) are the object of that speech, then absolute protection should follow. If, on the other hand, non-state others are implicated, then protection is qualified by the harm principle, which is to be understood according to the wrongdoing–causation–harm dynamic familiar within the positive law. This recalibration is clarified in the following section.

III. Recalibration

A. Absolute Protection in Vertical Scenarios

As previous chapters have outlined, the labels 'verticality' and 'horizontality' relate to the state's obligations in specific rights-claim disputes. The vertical scenario describes

[16] J Gray, *Mill On Liberty: A Defence* (Routledge, 1996) 105.
[17] n 11, 30.
[18] ibid, 29–30.
[19] Mill (n 4) 260.

the relationship between state (as duty-holder) and citizen (as rights-holder). The horizontal scenario differs to this by describing relations between citizens as private actors. In this setting, rights-claims sit in tension, in need of adjudication by the state to decide which of the competing claims is valid (and, therefore, determinative). Here, the state also appears as a duty-holder but those duties are of a different kind. We might further distinguish the vertical from horizontal setting by describing the citizen as solitary, in an important sense. This scenario is not characterised as a dispute between citizens as such, but purely in terms of a conflict between the citizen and the state.

The distinction between vertical and horizontal is highly significant. For it is *only* in the vertical setting that speech can claim absolute protection as against undue interference by the state. By protecting speech in this way, we realise that essential Lockean and Madisonian ideal of the state as but a servant to the people. In this way, we protect the people as ultimate sources of coercive power, and as co-authors (and co-authority figures) of law and policy. Moreover, we can say that this relationship between citizen and state neatly fits the Hohfeldian classification of right-duty since the rights-holder (speaker) and duty-holder (servile state) have clearly defined positions.

In the vertical scenario, then, the duty-holder is prevented from any response other than tolerance of the (disliked) speech because it is either purely self-regarding or else it is other-regarding, but the 'other' is confined to the state which, properly speaking, is not an 'other' but a protectable interest against (disliked) speech. Thus, absolute protection follows because to permit state interference would be to tolerate either paternalism (when the speech is purely self-regarding) or authoritarianism (when the speech is directed at the state and the state objects). On this basis, we should see why Mill would say that 'that men should be free to act upon their opinions … [when] it is at their own risk and peril'.[20] Moreover, we see why Mill should believe that citizens should be free to exist without paternalistic and/or authoritarian interventions by the state:

> As it is useful that while mankind are imperfect [*sic*] there should be different opinions, so is it that there should be different experiments of living; that free scope should be given to varieties of character, short of injury to others; and that the worth of different modes of life should be proved practically, when any one thinks fit to try them.[21]

Hence, his conclusion: 'It is desirable, in short, that in things which do not primarily concern others, individuality should assert itself.'[22]

Note that this approach to speech protection does not necessitate the same sort of typology that was criticised in earlier chapters (see criticisms of the Borkean position in chapter six). Instead, it requires careful examination of the reasons given by the state to justify its punishment of the speaker. Its absolute protection for *some* speech is a natural consequence of the recognition that the state cannot defend its position by claiming that its reputational interest has been 'harmed'. Accordingly, it is not *all* speech that fits the

[20] ibid.
[21] ibid.
[22] ibid.

description of, say, 'political speech' that would be protected, only that speech which is interfered with by the state for reasons that are invalid. Since invalidity is a proposition based upon the *coherence* of the state's reasons for action, something of the definitional difficulties signalled by Bork's critics can be avoided.

Moreover, this approach illustrates the fundamental point about the harm principle: that fact of 'harm' is a necessary but not sufficient reason to interfere with speech. For, in an obvious sense, criticism of government that gains popularity amongst fellow citizens *is* harmful. The more powerful the criticism, the more harmful it becomes. When speech is so powerful that the present government must resign, the harm to that government is undeniable. It is not only in politics that speech has this effect. When speech is so powerful that it causes orthodoxy to collapse and new modes of thinking to emerge, the harm to ways of life is inevitable. Thus, when Magellan circumnavigated the world, when Galileo championed heliocentrism, when Darwin promoted evolution, great dogmas of the past turned to dust.

In those political systems governed by the base unit of community, in which hegemony, heteronomy or homogeneity dominate such challenges to the settled order are intolerable. They must be punished if the ultimate authority of the state and/or church is to be preserved. Since even the holding of an unorthodox opinion (that is, a thought given phenomenal form) challenges this authority and so, if left unchecked, may corrupt the communal order of things, it must be punished also.

In a heterogeneous state, this intolerance for diversity of thought and opinion cannot be punished, for to do so would imperil autonomous living. It is not that autonomous being is valuable in consequentialist terms, although it can be in terms of the innovation and initiative by which enhanced ways of economic production emerges and optimised wealth and power, for the state, is realised. It is that the basis of centralised power is, of itself, a product of that initial autonomous decision by which (some portion of) individual power is delegated to the centre. Since this delegation is conditional upon the preservation of that individual's right to live autonomously, so the power to punish instances of autonomous diversity must be ultra vires. Thus, the concept of unorthodoxy must be realised and realisable in a heterogeneous state if it is to deserve the name (or quality). In this state, punishment for an expressed opinion must be due to its harm, but harm in terms other than its disruption to settled ways of understanding life.

Crucially, though, it is not the *presence* of the state in the dispute that signals the entitlement to absolute protection. For, quite obviously, if the mere presence of the state counted, then the distinction between vertical and horizontal would collapse. This point is highly significant. When rights-claims clash, as between two or more citizens, the state is asked to resolve the conflict through adjudication. Assuming that the reason for preferring one claim to another is not a sham, so as to protect its own interests, the *fact* of deciding against the speech claim does not render the claim to be a vertical claim. Thus, the content of that speech is irrelevant to the question of modality. The same speech could be penalised by the state by reason of, say, a fine for seditious libel and compensation for reputational damage. Whereas the first kind of penalty results from a vertical context, the second is horizontal. Hence, the penalty in the first is invalid, but the second is not if it conforms to the harm principle. The fact of the state penalising speech – even political speech – by way of financial penalty tells us nothing about the legitimacy of state action.

Since, as between the two orientations, the harm principle operates differently, its nature should be revisited. Of the vertical orientation, it may be said that the description 'vertical' applies only when two conditions are met. First, that the object of the speech is confined to state matters. This includes discussion of state functionaries, so long as that discussion is limited to her performance as a functionary. Likewise, it can include discussion of that person's ethical decision-making so long as the causal connection between that morality and office-holder performance is apparent. Secondly, that the state seeks to use its coercive power to suppress or otherwise punish that speech. Ordinarily, this speech will be critical in nature (albeit there is no reason why we should describe this as a condition – even speech that praises the state could be captured by the scenario if, for whatever reason, the state chose to punish it). The crucial point is that the harm principle can have no application in this scenario. The state cannot seek to justify its punitive response by citing 'harm' to itself.

B. Qualified Protection in 'Horizontal' Scenarios

This distinction between vertical and horizontal relies upon the authenticity of the reasons for distinguishing both positions. I am not suggesting that sham arrangements deprive political speech of constitutional protection just because the state *says* it is acting on behalf of other citizens. For, as we know, authoritarian regimes are rarely so intellectually honest as to admit their ambition to retain ultimate power at all costs. Instead, the reasons for liberty-depriving action are often cloaked in the superficial legitimacy of horizontal protection. In preserving, say, ways of life – including stability within the political order – the state can claim, with some justification, to be preserving not *its* interest in continued power but the *community's* interest in uninterrupted peace and freedom from disruption (including political disruption caused by changes of regime). Even (supposedly) mature democracies try this argument on, as when the Sunak administration rushed through legislation to heavily constrain rights to public protest. The then Home Secretary, Suella Braverman, sought to implement a power by which anti-protest measures would apply to any demonstration that caused 'more than minor' disruption.[23] As Mill recognises, this type of justification has prospective legitimacy but only in certain conditions. Since the delegation of power to the centre is conditional upon the preservation of autonomy, so the state is duty-bound to respond if individual autonomy is unduly undermined not only by it (the state) but also others.

A close reading of *On Liberty* reveals that an initial first step must relate to the effect of speech upon the 'other' in terms of its impact upon the will. If the object or recipient of speech changes her perceptions of herself, the world around her, etc, of her own volition, then the supposed 'harm' of this altered stated is neutralised as a reason to interfere. This is true even *though* the change is harmful in a tangible or meaningful sense. If, however, the object or recipient of speech is affected in ways that alter the will further analysis is required to determine if the interference is legitimate. The difference

[23] *National Council for Civil Liberties v Secretary of State for the Home Department* [2024] EWHC 1181.

between the two positions, of course, depends upon the preservation of autonomy. For the state is only justified in interfering with the actions of one if the autonomy of other *is* unduly interfered with.

The following sub-sections defend these propositions in greater detail.

i. Other-Regarding – Of their Own Volition

The fact that speech causes others to think differently suggests itself as such a (valid) reason. Yet, even here, that effect must possess qualities that go beyond the simple fact of changing a person's mind (or thinking). For if it is the mere fact of causing a difference in thought, then the state would be condemning a person for noumenal reasons which, as we have seen, is an invalid reason. Consider the example of Socrates. He was condemned to drink hemlock for corrupting Athenian youth through his encouragement that they reassess their intuitively held opinion. For the Athenian authorities, then, his words were not mere opinion but incitement of a sufficiently serious kind that they could say it was unduly harmful.

We can dismiss this example easily enough as an artefact of its time. Perhaps we might say that there is an essential incommensurability between the individuality-based and community-based system that render comparison meaningless. Nevertheless, for Mill,[24] the example of Socrates's persecution remained instructive. The lesson here is not merely in the severity of the state's response. For although Mill touches only briefly on the example of Socrates, still he would have to say that even if the state had, for example, fined Socrates, the action would be illegitimate.

Thus, we can extend Mill's thought about Socrates in ways that he (Mill) did not. Socrates's crime, such as it was, was to corrupt Athenian youth in terms that were, at times, blasphemous, by encouraging them to think for themselves and to re-evaluate their own places in the strict hierarchical patriarchy of their time. However, the state's response could not be described, in Kantian terms, of the meeting of coercion with coercion ('a *hindering* of a *hindrance to freedom*').[25] In the dialogue between Socrates and others, he relied only upon a questioning that challenged thought freely. According to the Millian scheme, he sought to persuade rather than coerce. There was no emotional blackmail or threats of violence. There was merely the encouragement of independent thought (independent, that is, from the state's directed form of thinking). Of course, we can say that for the Athenian state such autonomy would be disastrous if generally acted upon. Nevertheless, in the Millian (and Kantian) scheme, the encouragement to think for oneself (including, the encouragement to think *of* oneself as something valuable and independent from the state) is precisely the point.

ii. Other-Regarding – Against their Will

At this point, we might reflect upon the possibility of mere words alone being coercive. After all, coercion, commonly understood, connotes compulsion by force. The state's

[24] Mill (n 4) 235.

[25] I Kant, *The Metaphysics of Morals* (L Denis, ed, M Gregor, trans) (Cambridge University Press, 2017) [6:231].

coercive powers are incarceration or else financial penalty. Thus, when the state interferes with speech coercively, it does so physically or otherwise tangibly. Surely, words cannot have this effect. In defending Socrates above, I said that there was 'no emotional blackmail or threats of violence', inplying that the harm was contingent not upon the words themselves but the outcome of those words being implemented. It is not the threat inherent in the words if acted upon that communicate the sense of coercion: it is the conditionality within the words. Here we begin to see, I think, why Mill should choose to distinguish 'opinion' and 'action'.

Let us consider, again, what Mill says. Having said that 'men should be free to act upon their opinions – to carry these out in their lives, without hindrance either physical or moral, from their fellow-men, so long as it is at their own risk and peril', he provides the clarification that 'no one pretends that actions should be as free as opinions. On the contrary, even opinions lose their immunity, when the circumstances in which they are expressed are such as to constitute their expression a positive instigation to some mischievous act'.[26] If a person says 'Brexit has been a disaster and those that voted for it need shooting' the second clause is but figurative and unproblematic, unless that person is holding a gun and has before them a group of Brexiteers.

Subsequent punishment by the state is not for the holding of the opinion but the retributive act. Hence, we see why Mill's corn dealer example, in which punishment for the orator but not the journalist speaks to the distinction between figurative and literal expressions of extreme views. In that example, the state's response assumes the horizontal rather than vertical position. It must consider the prospect of interference with the will of one by the will of another. Here, I disagree with Gray. It is not the improbability of autonomous thought in the mob that we are meant to infer in Mill's description. It is in the *fact* of a mob before the corn dealer's house. The orator is not, we can also assume, some disinterested party who has happened upon the opportunity for discourse with an assembled audience and thinks that now would be an ideal time to wax lyrical about his deeply held views upon corn prices. He is, we may assume, the ring leader to whom the braying mob is beholden. Thus, the interference with autonomy is not that of the mob's but of the corn dealer's, who sits, fearful (we may assume), in his home, surrounded by an angry mob.

What counts as coercive, on the speaker's part, is a question of interpretation in which the hearer's response is significant. Although Mill uses the dichotomy of persuasion and coercion, that distinction is insufficient to the extent it implies exclusivity, as if anything that is not classifiable as 'persuasion' must be classed as coercion (and, likewise, that anything that cannot be termed 'coercive' must be classed as 'persuasion'). The speaker can if she likes play the part of 'tyrannous majority'. She can be vile and offensive. Although Mill, emulating Kant, would call this unethical, he is not suggesting that it should be unlawful. Similarly, the term 'persuasion' may seem insufficient as an antonym to 'coercion'. For the bank robber's demand to the teller – 'Give me the money or else'– is bound to be persuasive when he sticks a gun in her face. For Mill, these two descriptors signify the difference in real choice according to his autonomy-based scheme. When given reasons to act, the recipient of speech can still choose to ignore

[26] Mill (n 4) 260.

even persuasive speech if she wishes. Accordingly, persuasion here is not an outcome so much as an intention. The autonomous being can choose to ignore persuasion but cannot ignore coercion.

Words can be coercive even when the threat of violence, etc, is not immediate. In coercive relationships, for example, it is not necessarily the apprehension of violence, or other forms of action, that ensures compliance albeit that fear must have some bearing on the coerced individual's decision-making. Moreover, in common civil law disputes, for example, speech is coercive where it forces the individual either to repent her acts of individuality or else become a social pariah for the steadfast refusal to do so. Thus, for example, when newspapers defame or otherwise interfere with the private lives of others, they cause real harm. This harm is felt in the impact it has on (personal and/or business) relationships with others. The act, therefore, resides in these changed relationship statuses. In these scenarios, words may be directly or indirectly connected to the coercive harm to individuality, such that we can say the words themselves are coercive in generating action or else are preparatory to the harm arising from realised action. Accordingly, we can interpret Mill's distinction in terms of this fear, which we find when speech implies future action that would be harmful to the individual. In this sense, words manifest as the precursor to (harmful) action.

Nevertheless, further refinement is required since, as noted above, Mill seeks to address the problem of interferences with individuality through the lens of both law and ethics. Whereas speech can be coercive in a sense that merits juridical interference, it can also form what Mill calls 'moral coercion of public opinion'.[27] This moral coercion, of itself, takes at least two forms. There is the form by which the public seeks to influence government policy, and, therefore, has juridical effect when implemented by government to become law, and there is the other kind, which resides solely in moral virtue, by which society decides that certain behaviours are unseemly, and deserving of social condemnation. These distinctive kinds are apparent in the following:

> Like other tyrannies, the tyranny of the majority was at first, and is still vulgarly, held in dread, chiefly as operating through the acts of the public authorities. But reflecting persons perceived that when society is itself the tyrant … its means of tyrannising are not restricted to the act which it may do by the hands of its political functionaries.[28]

Hence, Mill's ethical and juridical aims are clearly given in his subsequent view that:

> Protection, therefore, against the tyranny of the magistrate is not enough: there needs protection also against the tyranny of the prevailing opinion and feeling; against the tendency of society to impose, by other means than civil penalties, its own ideas and practices as rules of conduct on those who dissent from them; to fetter the development, and, if possible, prevent the formation, of any individuality not in harmony with its ways, and compel all characters to fashion themselves upon the model of its own.[29]

Thus, the object of his liberty principle is to provide not only juridical reasons to protect individuality, but also good ethical reasons to resist moral interference with individuality as it resides within the more judgemental sections of society. The impact

[27] ibid, 223.
[28] ibid, 221.
[29] ibid.

of social mores upon individuality, of course, results from that sense of embarrassment, hurt, shame, anger, offence, guilt, etc, by which the hurtful words of others are received. This much is apparent in his view that 'the likings and dislikings of society, or of some powerful portion of it, are thus the main thing which has practically determined the rules laid down for general observance, under the penalties of law or opinion'.[30] Thus, the opinion of others can be harmful, in ways that are both ethically and juridically relevant, to relationships between the noumenal being and her family members, friends, colleagues, financial interests and the possibility of a fair trial. These effects may have no juridical significance, of course, or else they can give rise to rights-claims in the positive law, through actions in privacy, reputation and a fair trial.

In recognition of these distinctions, we might recast our classifications such that coercion is itself divided into two parts. There is what we might call legal coercion, in which the force of the words is phenomenal, causing external harm that takes tangible or intangible form. Through legal positivism, we can describe this as impacting rights and interests. There is also what Mill calls 'moral coercion', but what we might call ethical coercion (to avoid confusion), to signify an emotional response that is felt by the noumenal being but which we would not call harm (in positivistic terms) or else would not say undermines autonomy in a meaningful sense. This division is apparent within the terms of Mill's 'one very simple principle' when he describes the 'means' of 'compulsion and control' in terms of 'physical force in the form of legal penalties, or the moral coercion of public opinion'.[31] Whereas Mill, like Kant, was concerned to describe a system that spoke to both the ethical and the juridical, the former is of little interest to us, except as a point of distinction. When speech is ethically coercive – when it is emotionally manipulative – autonomy is still implied, but not sufficiently for the law to engage.

These distinctions may be further refined if we superimpose upon them the wrongdoing–causation–harm scheme that is familiar within the (liberal) positive law by which we identify instances of undue harm to autonomous living. Since this calculus distinguishes legal coercion from ethical coercion, primarily by means of the 'wrongdoing' component, the intended juridical effect of the harm principle may be realised. Of course, wrongdoing has special meaning in the positive law as that which the law prohibits. Since this offers only a descriptive, rather than normative, account, it is insufficient for our purposes.

In normative terms, we can describe wrongdoing as that which undermines autonomy. Although the fact of action being coercive provides a compelling account of itself, we shall fall into hopeless circularity if we say that coercion can be better understood as wrongdoing–causation–harm and that wrongdoing is coercion. Instead, let us say that wrongdoing is two-fold: that it must comprise an interference that prevents the individual doing as she would choose to do *and* that this interference is not justified by the interfering agent's entitlement to act in this way. For example, the employer that dismisses her employee acts in a manner that corresponds to the first clause in

[30] ibid, 222.
[31] ibid, 223.

circumstances when that employee does not wish to be dismissed. Nevertheless, the employer complies with the second clause when the contract allows her to dismiss in the circumstances, as when, for example, the employee commits gross misconduct. The question of entitlement here may be determined by the positive law and/or normativity, but we need not progress this distinction any further.

It follows then that, for state interference with autonomy to be justified, the actions of the one party must have caused harm to the other. The necessity for causation is a problem in the context of regulating that insidious form of hate speech that relates to an unascertained group rather than named individuals as such. Consider, for example, newspaper coverage that vilifies identifiable groups but in generic terms, eg, right-wing coverage concerning immigrants, Muslims, trans people, etc. That speech is bound to create a hostile environment for individuals who fit or otherwise identify with these labels. It creates animosity and real hardship for these groups. They experience harm in a meaningful sense.

Yet, the use of coercive power to regulate this vilification is hard to justify without a clear causal link between the speech and the eventual act. In the clinical language of law, the chain is broken if it can be said that the intermediate action is a new act. Consider the right-wing newspaper whose constant, illiberal worldview considers immigrants to be a profound threat to native interests (social harmony, economic success, personal living standards, a drain on public resources, etc) and expresses that viewpoint irrationality, through selective, sensational, emotive and hostile language. In response, an irate reader murders an immigrant, or her lawyer, or the politician that defends her. To say that the newspaper 'caused' this event is understandable. The toxicity of this sort of newspaper culture is undoubtedly a material factor in causing those racial and religious tensions that liberal democracy experiences. Nevertheless, from a strictly legal perspective, the causality seems too remote in circumstances where the speech – even if considered incitement – is not directed against a specific individual. This is not to say that causality cannot be proven but only that it is not straightforward. There should need to be a close nexus between opinion and event which, for Mill, of course, was exemplified by the corn dealer example, of hostile expression toward an angry mob (intent on revenge), in which the tripartite clauses of wrongdoing, harm, and causality are present.

Finally, it must be demonstrated that the wrongdoing has caused harm to individual. This condition speaks to those circumstances in which the interference with autonomy is trivial. In this situation, intervention by the state is unwarranted. In an important sense, this condition may speak to instances of ethical coercion in which the recipient is not entirely without choice in being affected. Emotional blackmail might fit this category, for example. Moreover, it might also speak to situations in which the recipient feels offence but not harm as a consequence of the speech, ie, that her ego is bruised but the damage is superficial so far as the law is concerned; for example, the writer who feels insulted by an overly critical review of her work or methods but who cannot claim to have been harmed in terms that the law can recognise as serious.[32]

[32] *Thornton v Telegraph Media Group Ltd* [2010] EWHC 1414 (QB).

C. No Audience Interest

As we have seen, the parameters of Mill's account are drawn solely from the speaker's interest in speech. Since the will to create is valued for its own sake, no instrumental evaluation of speech is permissible. One significant but overlooked feature of this conceptual design is the exclusion of audience interests.

This, of course, is anathema to the American perspective on free speech theory. For a long time, and at least since Scanlon's later work on free speech theory, audience interests have been treated as central to the formation of the value calculation by which juridical decisions are formulated. Scanlon even seeks to attribute this approach to Mill himself: 'As Mill rightly emphasized, there is significant benefit in being exposed to ideas and attitudes different from one's own, though this exposure may be unwelcome.'[33] From this position, Scanlon could convince himself that the audience, as a collection of noumenal beings seeking individual self-perfection, benefit from having, at their disposal, sufficient wealth of material interest that they could, should they so wish, to improve themselves. Here, then, is the ideal of the grand repository that we encountered in chapter six. Moreover, according to this view, the value of speech is to be enhanced by its discernible contribution to whatever preferred value we have in mind, be that participatory,[34] self-fulfilment,[35] or any other. This partly explains why political expression is of greater significance than all else, for the interest in democracy is universal in ways that interests in commercial speech or artistic speech are not. Thus, political speech should always benefit from the lingering 'thumb in the scales' to represent that greater, universal interest – if, that is, one subscribes to this view.

Yet, if we follow the logic of the scheme above, this concern – that the protection of political speech flounders unless given artificial weight in the balance – is misplaced. If the reason for interference is driven by verticality – that is, speech which the state wishes to suppress for no other reason than to protect its own interests – then the perceived 'harm' (to its glorification) is an invalid reason to interfere. There is no need to seek further and better reasons to protect the speech because all the work is done by the harm principle and we have our answer. If, though, the reason to interfere is driven by horizontality – that is, the rights-claim of a fellow citizen (be that reputation, privacy, the right to a fair trial or something else), then the formula of the liberal nexus does the work. The question is whether there is sufficient wrongdoing–harm–causation to justify the interference. If there is not – that the damage to reputation or privacy is phony or else that the right to a fair trial is not imperilled – then, again, the additional weight is unnecessary.

Where the additional weight would seem to be valuable, at least ostensibly, are those occasions where the mechanics of the justice system have failed (apparently) such

[33] T Scanlon, 'Freedom of Expression and Categories of Expression' (1979) 40 *University of Pittsburgh Law Review* 519, 524.

[34] See discussion of Robert Post's work in previous chapter.

[35] Redish saw audience interests as the key reason for his intellectual disagreement with Baker's model of self-realization: See MH Redish, 'Self-Realization, Democracy, and Freedom of Expression: A Reply to Professor Baker' (1982) 130 *University of Pennsylvania Law Review* 678, 679: 'Because I firmly believe that the value of self-realization, as I define it, may be fostered as much by the receipt of expression as by the act of expressing, I conclude that the source or motivation of the expression is largely irrelevant. Baker, on the other hand, believes that the source is all important.'

that speech is required to cure or otherwise correct the failing. That is, there is some corruption in the system such that criminal behaviour or civil wrong has gone unpunished by the state, necessitating (it is thought) speech to signal that failing to the public so that that wrong can be addressed. This is a complex scenario, which is explored in detail in chapter ten, but which, it shall be argued there, still conforms to the analysis in the previous paragraph – such speech is protectable *because* the countervailing claim (of some civil wrong to privacy or reputation or else the imperilment of a fair trial) is unsustainable. Even here there is no need for additional weight to be prayed in aid, for the speech claim is not otherwise defective.

Moreover, it should be recognised, more than it is, that the juridical method of weighing rights-claims by evidence is entirely unsuited to the apparent demands of the audience interest calculus that either calls for pure speculation about the supposed value of speech to a hypothetical audience, or else demands an absolutist approach for certain types of speech. Whereas we can measure the public interest in claimant and defendant rights-claims being taken seriously, because we can articulate concepts such as 'wrong', 'harm', etc, we are at a complete loss to do so when the public interest becomes more ethereal and circumspect, as audience interests are wont to do.

Although I put the point strongly here, I do so with greater clarity, or, rather, greater urgency, than Mill himself did. Nevertheless, even here, I think Mill can be so easily misunderstood, for his appeal to the societal benefits of a free speech guarantee – that both individual and societal epistemic advance would gain – is confined (or else, confinable) to the argument for recognising freedom of speech as a guarantee rather than the juridical question of how the guarantee ought to be realised. Thus, his moral argument for free speech protection is ethical rather than juridical. Such reasoning, then, applies only to the initial question of whether there *should* be a free speech guarantee and not the ongoing question of what it *means*.

IV. Defence

According to the orthodox view, autonomy-based conceptions are too amorphous to serve free speech's ends. This is because, if we follow Schauer, the autonomy argument applies to all rights-based claims against government and so cannot explain free speech as a distinctive, independent right.[36] Alternatively, if we follow Scanlon, autonomy alone cannot provide that necessary 'thumb on the scale' for political speech.[37] Or, if we follow Blasi, autonomy is an 'irreducible' and 'absolute' concept that admits of no exceptions by which to accommodate the 'legitimate regulatory interests' that necessitate speech's submission to superior claims.[38] No wonder, then, that Robert Post should dismiss the autonomy-based account so emphatically as lacking in 'resources to adjudicate the many situations in which the autonomy of speakers and the autonomy of audiences are in tension'.[39] Even Scanlon, who had originally espoused the Millian principle in

[36] F Schauer, *Free Speech: a Philosophical Enquiry* (Cambridge University Press, 1982) 70–71.

[37] Scanlon (n 3) 167–68.

[38] V Blasi, 'The Checking Value in First Amendment Theory' (1977) 2 *American Bar Foundation Research Journal* 521.

[39] R Post, 'Participatory Democracy and Free Speech' (2011) 97 *Virginia Law Review* 477, 488.

glowing terms should come to think it contained a 'basic flaw', namely that: 'There are many ways in which the appealing, but notoriously vague and slippery notion of individual autonomy can be invoked in political argument.'[40]

This pronounced negativity stems from a prevailing, general sense that the concept is too nebulous to offer meaningful solutions to free speech problems. Yet, arguably this reaction speaks either to a profound misunderstanding of Mill's specific usage of the term autonomy or else a confused (or else, confusing) misapplication of that term in which its complex psychological or ethical interpretation is applied, without adjustment, to juridical contexts. Through such strategies, commentators lose sight of Mill's simple (but not simplistic) understanding of autonomy, as the act of deciding for oneself, which, by its nature, eschews all external attempts to oversee, monitor or otherwise evaluate, the progression toward self-perfection. Confusion arises when commentators seek to add further criterion relating to, for example, rationality and (absolute) independence. Thus, autonomy, in the spirit of Gerald Dworkin,[41] is understood as informed decision-making. Or, as Joseph Raz (emulating Hegel) has it in the *Morality of Freedom*, it depends upon adequacy of choice.[42]

This infusion of rationality with autonomy is given to us by John Rawls who, in *A Theory of Justice*, describes autonomous action as acting 'from principles that we would consent to as free and equal rational beings'.[43] This, he says, is Kant's understanding of the principle.[44] Certainly, this is Kant's explication of the moral law by which the ethics of virtue (*Tugendlehre*) are constructed, in which autonomy, as freedom, is expressed as a product of reason. In the *Groundwork to the Metaphysics of Morals*, the supreme principle is given the form: 'the supreme condition of the will's conformity with universal practical reason … [is] the idea of the will of every reasonable and rational being as a will that makes universal [ethical] law'.[45] Yet Kant uses two different meanings of freedom. In his juridical scheme – the doctrine of right (*Rechtslehre*) – freedom is not constrained by reason. It is merely 'independence from being constrained by another's choice'.[46] Accordingly, within the *Rechtslehre*, 'what end anyone wants to set for his action is left to his free choice' subject to the proviso that 'the freedom of the agent could coexist with the freedom of every other in accordance with a universal law'.[47] This differs crucially from the *Tugendslehre* since:

> [T]his concept (the categorical ought) has its root in pure reason alone. Consequently, if maxims were to be adopted by on the basis of those ends (all of which are self-seeking), one could not really speak of the concept of duty. – Hence the ethics the *concept of duty* will lead to ends and will have to establish *maxims* with respect to ends we *ought* to set ourselves, grounding them in accordance with moral principles.[48]

[40] Scanlon (n 33) 533.
[41] See, eg, G Dworkin, *The Theory and Practice of Autonomy* (Cambridge University Press, 1988) ch 7.
[42] J Raz, *The Morality of Freedom* (Oxford University Press, 1986) 205–07.
[43] J Rawls, *A Theory of Justice*, rev edn (Oxford University Press, 1999) 453.
[44] ibid, 222.
[45] See J Rawls, *Lectures on the History of Moral Philosophy* (B Herman, ed (Harvard University Press, 2000) 203.
[46] Kant (n 25,) [6:238].
[47] ibid, [6:383].
[48] ibid.

Hence, to give a trivial example, we could say that the actions of a moneylender who refuses to defer repayment of a debt, despite being financially secure whilst the debtor is bereft, acts legally according to his rights but immorally according to ethics. It is for this reason that ethics operates not as autonomy as such, but as an '*autocracy* of practical reason'.[49] That is, it is constrained by rationality. The reason for this strict division is given by the *Tugendslehre*, as Kant understands it. Although, in its highest form, the ethical law attains at '*one's own perfection* and *the happiness of others*',[50] nevertheless 'Perfection and happiness cannot be interchanged here, so that *one's own happiness* and *the perfection of others* would be made ends that would be in themselves duties of the same person.'[51] To insist otherwise, says Kant, would be 'contradictory:'

> For *his own happiness* is an end that every human being has (by virtue of the impulses of his nature), but this end can never without self-contradiction be regarded as a duty. What everyone already wants unavoidably, of his own accord, does not come under the concept of *duty*, which is *constraint* to an end adopted reluctantly. Hence it is self-contradictory to say that he is *under obligation* to promote his own happiness with all his powers.
>
> So too, it is a contradiction for me to make another's *perfection* my end and consider myself under obligation to promote this. For the *perfection* of another human being, as a person, consists just in this: that he *himself* is able to set his end in accordance with his own concepts of duty; and it is self-contradictory to require that I do (make it my duty to do) something that only the other himself can do.[52]

Accordingly, the ethical duty to perfect oneself through '*cultivating* one's *faculties* (or natural predispositions), the highest of which is *understanding*… [which] includes the cultivation of one's *will* (moral cast of mind) … to raise himself from the crude state of his nature, from his animality … up to the purest virtuous disposition' is a matter for that person alone.[53] This principle, then, places firm limits on what can be demanded of each as part of the doctrine of right by which coercion is justifiable so as to secure individual freedom compatible with the freedom of all.

This crucial distinction in the uses of freedom, in which the notion of autonomy plays a critical role, is lost if rationality is set as a condition for autonomous action. Nevertheless, when we survey the landscape, we see that the distinction is less pronounced – and often omitted altogether – in the expectations of autonomy as a critical value in free speech principle. We see this, for example, in Scanlon's interpretation of Millian principle, in which he claims that 'the powers of a state are limited to those that citizens could recognize while still regarding themselves as equal, autonomous, rational agents'.[54] The inclusion of 'rational' here is erroneous, albeit explainable by that frustrating quality in *On Liberty* by which Mill fails to neatly separate the *Rechtslehre* and *Tugendslehre* with the same systematic precision that Kant did. For, in Mill, we find the two realms interweaved within the narrative which, intellectually, has been disastrous since scholars regularly conflate his moral ambition – that autonomous beings should

[49] ibid.
[50] ibid, [6:386].
[51] ibid.
[52] ibid.
[53] ibid, [6:387].
[54] Scanlon (n 3) 162.

seek maximal self-improvement – with his juridical principle – the supremacy of the harm principle and the crucial distinction between self- and other-regarding harm.

This confusion is compounded by psychological critiques creeping into legal analysis. In them, we see shades of that Hegelian concern by which autonomous agents may be blind to subtle external interferences with their ostensibly free choices, and – by extension – the Freudian complex of that constant mediation by the ego between the devious id and the virtuous super-ego. Gerald Dworkin's account of autonomy is paradigmatic, the autonomous state being achieved only in those who can free themselves from the inner turmoil of conflicted id-driven base desires and impulses and super-ego aspirations to moral goodness.[55] This conflict between what Dworkin calls first- and second-order desires (ie, the initial thought and further reflection upon it) causes him to conclude that autonomy is not merely the awareness of preferred actions but the resolution of this conflict, which includes the means to achieve it:

> The idea of autonomy is not merely an evaluative or reflective notion, but includes as well some ability both to alter one's preferences and to make them effective in one's actions and, indeed, to make them effective because one has reflected upon them and adopted them as one's own.[56]

Further, he says:

> [A]utonomy is … a second-order capacity of persons to reflect critically upon their first-order preferences, desires, wishes, and so forth and the capacity to accept or attempt to change these in light of higher-order preferences and values. By exercising such a capacity, persons define their nature, give meaning and coherence to their lives, and take responsibility for the kind of person they are.[57]

These additions serve to complicate the prerequisite state of autonomy required for juridical purposes. Speech that does not display these characteristics (especially irrational or 'irrational'[58] speech) would seem to fall outside if not coverage, certainly the realm of protection. In other words, speech that is not rational or responsible does not mesh with the justification for the free speech guarantee, if the autonomy value is selected. This critique is heightened if the guarantee is imbued with an audience interest.

It is for reasons such as this that Scanlon, foreshadowing Dworkin, should radically revise his position on free speech principle by arguing that autonomy must be 'understood as the *actual* ability to exercise independent rational judgment'.[59] Gray speaks similarly when describing the key elements of Mill's theory. In his view:

> An autonomous agent who cherishes that status is obliged to discount both the harm to himself accruing from the acquisition of false beliefs and the harm done as a result of acquiring a belief (true or false) via an expressive act as being always overridden by the harm done by any restraint of free expression to the interest he shares with others in remaining an autonomous agent.[60]

[55] Dworkin (n 41) 16–17.
[56] ibid, 17.
[57] ibid.
[58] ie, speech that is 'irrational' according to the tyrannous majority.
[59] Scanlon (n 33) 533 (emphasis added).
[60] J Gray, *Mill On Liberty: A Defence* (Routledge, 1996) 105.

As this passage suggests, Gray attributes not only rationality but also a sense of responsibility to the notion:

> While an autonomous agent may accept, accordingly, that the state has authority to subject him to various kinds of restraint, and while he may rely on the judgment of others about the rectitude of the state's imposing limits to his liberty, he cannot (without forfeiting his status as an autonomous agent) abrogate the responsibility he has to evaluate critically the state's actions and the judgments of others.[61]

And:

> Discharging the responsibility of an autonomous agent, however, presupposes that he possess all the resources of information and conflicting opinion and judgment which are indispensable conditions of rational deliberation and which can only be secured by the protection of liberal freedoms of speech.[62]

In the work of both Scanlon and Gray, then, we see autonomy given a distinctly Hegelian interpretation.

In summary, in this complex, psychological form, autonomy is given as a construct by which to evaluate the pursuit of self-perfection through critical life decision-making. This construct provides the formula whereby first-order preferences, especially those dictated by the id, are ameliorated by those second-order considerations that the super-ego demands. It may be that this iterative process can be made programmatic – perfected, manufactured and homogenised – so that it may be used as a critical lens by which to assess the constant pitiful strivings of each new entrant to the (human) race who aspires to optimal self-improvement. This mechanism, which presumably corresponds to notions of rationality and instrumentality, speaks to the notion of autonomy that animates Scanlon's and Dworkin's conceptions, and also speaks to the purposive notions of free speech encountered in previous chapters.

Yet, strictly, this complex, psychological conception of autonomy is irrelevant to the juridical setting, in which, if we follow both Mill and Kant, the triggering event for the liberty principle is firmly phenomenal (the fact of (external) state interference with the decision to speak) and not noumenal (the fact of internal tensions in decision-making preliminary to the decision to speak). The complex, internal disagreements between the id and super-ego, mediated by the ego, are of no concern to us, juridically, precisely because the irrationality proviso renders the value of speech an irrelevant consideration whilst the exclusive speaker orientation we find in Mill and Kant make audience considerations obsolete. Autonomy resides in the external conditions of a decision and not in its internal qualities. For, if we were to evaluate, through phenomenal means, the noumenal process, in which select noumenal beings (who, by their nature, can know none but themselves) claim to possess the formula by which to judge the progress of unknown and unknowable noumenal beings, we should misunderstand entirely the sentiment, discernible in Mill, that noumenal perfection is a mystery – or, as Holmes had it, an experiment, as all life is an experiment[63] – that cannot be known, perhaps not even by the noumenal being herself. In Kantian terms,

[61] ibid.
[62] ibid.
[63] *Abrams v United States* 250 US 616 (1919).

this understanding of autonomy would expect either the state or the speaker herself to be concerned with the perfection of others. Such externally derived conditions for evaluating the quality of autonomy, by reference to apparent inner turmoil, would run contrary to the essential premise of Mill, Holmes and Kant relating, as it does, to the absence from such critical external constraints.

All this is to say that the state of autonomy is achieved by nothing more than allowing the noumenal being to decide for herself even though, and especially when, there is good reason to think her views are suspect and her proposed decision is a mistake. This simple form of autonomy can manifest, of course, as a plea for help, a request for advice, etc, from others and still be properly called autonomy. Although such apparent delegations may appear to be derivations or, even, repudiations of autonomy – ie, by inviting others to make the decision for her – it is not so long as it can be said that the delegation is made by her willingly. In this way, we should see why Dworkin is right to say that joining the monastery or enlisting the army are acts compatible with autonomy (and the retention of autonomy) despite contrary appearances in which autonomy is forsaken (temporarily, at least).[64]

To underscore the point, if we follow Mill, Holmes and Kant, we arrive at the inescapable conclusion that noumenal authenticity (being true to oneself) is not rationality by another name, for the authority of rational thought is majoritarian – it is, as Kant says, an autocracy. Whereas rationality is vital to the phenomenal nature of the *Sittlichkeit*, it is not instructive to the noumenal pursuit of authentic living, which can and does manifest in ways that are *not* rational objectively. Take, for example, the successful professional who sacrifices the sure footing of a stable career for the uncertain promise of greater happiness in a riskier or a less financially rewarding career by becoming an artist or poet, a nurse or missionary, a tuktuk-wallah or Haenyeo.

This speaker-orientated, non-purposive account deals with at least some of the conceptual concerns raised by Susan Brison in her systematic critique of autonomy-based conceptions of free speech principle.[65] Certainly, it tackles her complaint that the 'circular' premise of Mill's account – of a right to be free from government constraints regarding speech – is 'strikingly uninformative as an argument'.[66] Moreover, the account provided here does at least overcome one of her central concerns that no harm-based interferences are permissible, apparently, under typical autonomy accounts. As noted above, hate speech amounting to public order offences could be interfered with without violence to free speech principle. Accordingly, her complaint against a specific aspect of Scanlon's early work does not apply in the Millian context described above. Brison presents this complaint as follows:

> [A]lthough Scanlon does not spell out this implication, on his view, even if hate speech leads to an increase in illegal conduct such as discrimination against – and violence toward – targeted groups, it must not be restricted, for to do so would violate individual autonomy.[67]

[64] Dworkin (n 41) 18.
[65] SJ Brison, 'The Autonomy Defense of Free Speech' (1998) 108 *Ethics* 312.
[66] ibid, 324.
[67] ibid, 329.

Yet, the Millian view outlined above neither supports Scanlon's analysis (as Brison understands it) nor prevents the outcomes that Brison seeks. Such protections, for the victim, could follow without undermining free speech principle, for they would represent the natural and obvious protection of the victim's right to autonomy, that is: so long as the liberal nexus of wrongdoing-harm-causation is met.

Yet Brison is most attracted to those versions of the autonomy argument that include audience (and bystander) interests, and which capture the deep psychological analyses relating to tensions within the noumenal being. The irrationality proviso fares poorly in these accounts for, on Brison's analysis, dis- and misinformation run contrary to the audience interests in 'rational self-legislation' and, thus, ought not to be protected under the free speech guarantee.[68] Instead, Brison is attracted to those consequentialist accounts in which audience preferences are driven both by the range of decision-making options available to them *and* 'the actual attainability of these options'.[69] This is because, she says, 'these beliefs are typically arrived at by receiving others' speech'.[70] Whether this is true or not (Brison provides no evidence for this empirical view), it presupposes that audiences cannot receive this information with the protection of speaker interests alone. Brison's reasoning here is opaque but seems to stem from Scanlon's (unconvincing) claim that since a person can still be autonomous *despite* being coerced, the presence of audience interests is required to bolster the argument (such that it can be said that censorship 'deprive[s] the audience of information they would otherwise have'.[71]

However, this argument is implausible, for the speaker's autonomy-based claim is not merely the right to speak but the right to speak without state punishment. Thus, imprisonment, the imposition of a fine, etc, is an interference with autonomy properly understood (as, presumably, Scanlon would agree). Hence, it cannot be that autonomy is preserved as Scanlon (and Brison) suggest. Moreover, the suggestion, in Brison, of a right to receive information is surely compromised by the logical ordering of events. If as the scenario presupposes, the speaker is a citizen rather than agent of the state, then the notion of an audience 'right' to the information runs contrary to Hohfeldian analysis. Certainly, it could only be a parasitic claim – dependent, that is, on the speaker's willingness to share the information. Since, proprietorially, the speaker owns the information, then her agency is determinative. In this way, the right to hear runs parallel to the right to speak. If the speaker sets conditions on the right to hear (ie, payment of a purchase price), then the right to hear is modified accordingly.

Yet, if the speaker has no 'right' to speak – which is surely the case if she is fined or imprisoned – then how can there be an audience 'right'? We should have to say that although the speaker herself has no right to speak, still the audience can resurrect this defeated claim if they wish to hear the speech. To say, though, that the speaker has no right to speak is to say not only that the state denies the speaker's rights-claim

[68] ibid, 330–33.
[69] ibid, 337.
[70] ibid.
[71] ibid, 333.

(by penalising the speech) but is *justified* in doing so. Yet, if the state *is* justified, then it is hard to imagine how the audience's supposed interest in receiving the information could plausibly succeed. For, if the speaker's rights-claim is denied because of qualities inherent in the speech itself (it is irrational or anathema) or because of its consequences (it is unjustifiably harmful), then those self-same reasons must apply to the audience's rights-claim. If the speech is irrational, anathema or otherwise harmful to third-party interests, and these reasons are valid in respect of the speaker, then there are solid consequentialist grounds to overcome the audience claim that they will benefit developmentally from this information. If, however, the speech is rational or otherwise justifiably harmful to third-party interests (or else not harmful at all), then the audience claim is validated – but so too is the speaker's because the reason to interfere becomes invalid. However, in that case, by reason of logical ordering, the necessity of the audience interest-claim to validate the speaker's claim is rendered nugatory.

However, the scenario arises in practice in which free speech claims, as speaker claims, are defeasible but rendered successful by the artificial device of an audience-orientated 'public interest' in the speech. As will be argued in chapter ten, the legitimacy of this device is questionable and, further, unnecessary, but I shall save until then rehearsal of those arguments. Meanwhile, it may be noted that this sort of device conceives the audience as a quasi-rights-giver, albeit it in the very limited sense that they cannot compel (presumably) the speaker to speak, for the Lockean reasons I have just given, but they *can* compel the state to provide the right in circumstances where the speaker alone cannot compel the state to exercise its duty in her favour. That this extraordinary power is considered legitimate by reason of autonomy strikes me as strange. For it would suggest that the individuals comprising the audience can compel the state to provide her with a specific item of 'option'-type information (in furtherance of her quest for self-perfection). This scenario presupposes that, in a practical context, our hypothetical litigant (judicial review) or defendant (criminal or civil trial) cannot sustain her own rights-claim; she must, instead, pray in aid of nameless third-party interests who, she is convinced, will derive some benefit from her speech (either instrumentally or intrinsically) and that this unknown and unknowable, speculative advantage is the tipping point by which her rights-claim goes from hopeless to unimpeachable.

V. Conclusion

This chapter concludes part three by, as a bookend to chapter five, demonstrating how the irrationality proviso may be realised juridically. It offers a scheme of free speech protection that takes Mill's position in *On Liberty* as its animating guide. This elaboration of Millian principle seeks to address the general concerns, apparent in the wider literature, that an autonomy-based account is inadequate as either too nebulous to offer a meaningful theory of free speech separate to any other liberty-driven rights-claim or else too absolute to afford the state with the necessary opportunities to interfere with speech that ought to be prevented or otherwise penalised. Of course, there are those in the community that have long disagreed with Schauer's view that free speech principle must be dramatically different to liberty in general, including Steven Shiffrin, who was notably dismissive: 'There is no reason to assume at the outset that speech is dramatically unique. It might be a part of a larger view of how human beings flourish or a subcategory of a larger value or set of values.'[72] Moreover, this chapter has sought to address Schauer's other criticism of autonomy – its absoluteness – apparent in his concern that it is 'premised on the ultimate sanctity of individual choice'.[73]

The framework, offered above, distinguishes verticality from horizontality in its initial attempts to differentiate the separate appeal of the autonomy claim as it relates to state 'overreach' of its inherent power (where the rights-claim verges closest to absoluteness) and those circumstances where the state must play the part of adjudicator between conflicting rights-claims in which the autonomy of two or more noumenal beings is in tension. Here, the liberal nexus of wrongdoing–harm–causation is determinative.

Yet, there remains much left unsaid by this chapter, especially on the horizontal plane, where many of the more problematic and attention-grabbing instances of rights-claims take place. With the proliferation of social media, speech, in its more enduring form, has given rise to new juridical problems, necessitating greater clarity in the meaning and nature of free speech on the horizontal plane. In part four, I seek to show how the Millian framework resolves these problems. I have chosen three specific problems. The first is the general concern that digital speech is a form of free speech phenomena in need of greater state protection. I address this in chapter nine. Chapter ten deals with problems of so-called 'public participation' in which citizens seeking to bring greater public attention to uses and abuses of power are (potentially) thwarted by uses of criminal and civil law to suppress critical speech. Finally, chapter eleven addresses problems arising in the workplace whereby employers act as censors of speech so as to suppress or otherwise control, indirectly, contributions to the public sphere.

[72] S Shiffrin, 'First Amendment and Economic Regulation: Away from a General Theory of the First Amendment' (1984) 78 *Northwestern University Law Review* 1212, 1238.

[73] F Schauer, *Free Speech: A Philosophical Enquiry* (Cambridge University Press, 1982) 68.

PART IV

Horizontality

9

Digital Speech

I. Introduction

In the Hegelian/Habermasian tradition, the Internet represents the ultimate expression of democratic legitimation by which government, utilising artificial intelligence and algorithms galore, can know with absolute certainty how a populus feels toward all contested propositions – and so, by that reasoning, must be the ultimate symbol of free speech in action. And yet, the Internet, as a tool, is the ultimate fruit of market insouciance, given to us not from compassion but for commerce, not for good but for gain. Therefore, even in its overtly expression-driven forms of social networking, the Internet is not a monument to philanthropy but to entrepreneurialism, by which innovation, enterprise and profit motivation explain its success, dictate its purpose and guide its future. The imponderable, resonating without resolve in the literature, is this: undoubtedly, it is valuable, in democratic legitimation terms, and speaks clearly to the autonomy value in an overt sense, since created and curated content knows the user better than they know themselves, but it resides within the grip of industry, not the *Sittlichkeit* or the state; it will be guided by market success not public education. The question of whether the state or civic society can inveigle its way into that dynamic, motivated, benevolently, to preserve autonomy or, malevolently, to control it, hinges entirely on whether it is right to speak of private property being beholden to the free speech demands of its users.

This dilemma illustrates something of the overarching theme within this final part of the book, in which we shall explore contemporary claims of authentic free speech problems in specific horizontal settings. The central concern, then, is to identify, with precision, the circumstances in which it may be said that private actors either owe duties to uphold, or are in some sense responsible for interferences with, the free speech rights of fellow citizens. The organising principle by which to analyse the issue will be the liberal formula of wrongdoing–harm–causation (outlined in chapter eight). This manifests, in this chapter, in the question of whether regulation of digital speech by the hosting platform is an authentic free speech problem. I ask this because, when we turn to the literature, we typically see an overwhelming presumption that such regulation *is* a free speech problem. Moreover, it is common for commentators to describe digital speech *as* free speech in action. Yet, there is confusion on this point. This confusion is vividly illustrated by the stark contrast in juridical positions taken on the subject by, on the one hand, the US Supreme Court and, on the other, the European Court of Human Rights (ECtHR), the Council of Europe's Committee of Ministers, and the

United Nations Human Rights Committee, which represent diametrically opposed viewpoints on the topic. This tension demonstrates why, on the question of horizontal free speech rights, I start with digital speech because, to my mind, the topic is emblematic of the authenticity crisis signalled in chapter one. How else are we to explain the gulf in principled position that separates the US jurisprudence from that of Strasbourg and the intellectual treatment of it by the United Nations Human Rights Committee and Council of Europe's Committee of Ministers?

As section II of this chapter makes clear, the essentiality incompatibility between these views captures the full spectrum of abstract thought concerning the possibility of a horizontal free speech right, from the initial question of why – or, rather, how – one private actor could owe (constitutional) duties to another to the issue of how the wrongdoing–harm–causation paradigm might manifest in this scenario. Essentially, my point here is to demonstrate the controversiality of a horizontal digital free speech right by reference to these fundamental differences in practical or descriptive explication. Sections III and IV conclude by exploring in more forensic detail the underlying problem in, first, identifying the nature of the relative obligation between private actors (section III) and, second, demonstrating the profound difficulty of articulating wrongdoing–harm–causation in the digital speech context. My task is to demonstrate how the autonomy argument, outlined in chapter eight, does not support the existence of a horizontal digital free speech right, but I am conscious my aim might seem to wander (for which I ask the reader to indulge me), for although I am concerned only with the fit with autonomy (for that is where I locate authenticity), it seems inevitable to me that I should conclude that the argument for a horizontal digital free speech right is hopeless on *any* analysis, be that driven by democratic participation, self-fulfilment or the marketplace of ideas.

II. The US and European Position Outlined

In the US, the judicial view, at least, of the right-duty dynamic is palpably clear. Since rights flow vertically from the state (as duty-holder) to the people (as rights-holders), the only circumstances in which a private actor could owe duties to another private actor would be in that analogous position denoted by the state-action doctrine. Only roles 'traditionally [and] exclusively reserved to the state'[1] count. However, despite its apparent significance to democratic legitimation, the provision of public discourse opportunities does *not* belong to this narrow category. In digital terms, of course, such opportunities manifest in social media membership and, in analogue form, everything from freelance journalism to rights to reply, to correspondence through the reader's letters section of a newspaper. As the Supreme Court has made plain, 'merely hosting speech by others is not a traditional, exclusive public function and does not alone transform private entities into state actors subject to First Amendment constraints'.[2] This principle was applied, straightforwardly, by the Californian appellate court in *Prager*

[1] *Jackson v Metropolitan Edison Company*, 419 US 345, 352 (1974).
[2] *Manhattan Community Access Corporation v Halleck*, 139 S Ct 1921, 1930 (2019).

University v Google Inc, where it held that Internet intermediaries, such as YouTube, 'do not perform a public function by inviting public discourse on its property'[3] in the same way that privately owned carparks 'do not become state actors' merely by being open to the public.[4]

By contrast, both the United Nations Human Rights Council and the Council of Europe are much more relaxed on the rights-duty dynamic, although the latter is the more emphatic of the two. In its Guiding Principles on Business and Human Rights, otherwise known as the Ruggie Framework, the UN recognises that although it is Member States that have the 'duty to protect' its citizens from human rights abuses, corporations have a 'responsibility to respect' human rights.[5] The distinction between duty and responsibility, in this context, seems to corresponds to that of law and morality. Certainly, we find the purported obligation imposed upon private actors expressed in the hypothetical imperative of morality, rather than the categorical imperative of law. The operative clauses in Principle 11, for example, which is the chief expression of corporate responsibility, follows this pattern: 'Business enterprises *should* respect human rights. This means that they *should* avoid infringing on the human rights of others and *should* address adverse human rights impacts with which they are involved' (emphasis added).[6] That the language of 'should' rather than 'must' is of a lesser order is confirmed, it seems, by the commentary to Principle 12: 'The responsibility of business enterprises to respect human rights is distinct from issues of legal liability and enforcement, which remain defined largely by national law provisions in relevant jurisdictions.'[7] This places the onus upon corporations themselves to embrace responsible decision-making by providing, at the very least, the commercially attractive position (presumably) of virtue signalling and, so, alert the international community to known (or knowable) human rights abuses in the locality, the sector, or even within its own enterprise. This imbues the framework with an obvious 'whistleblowing' dynamic.

Whether the mechanics of the framework are capable of approximating a horizontal rights/duty dynamic in broader terms is more doubtful. Some optimism is provided by the final provisions which describe the state's human rights duty in terms of a burden to create or otherwise facilitate adjudicative processes by which 'business-related human rights abuse' are investigated, punished and remedied, so as to 'counteract or make good any human rights harms that have occurred'.[8] In principle, this suggests that the state, not the corporation, bears the responsibility to make good human rights abuses caused by the private actor. Nevertheless, the jurisprudence so far is not entirely promising. So far as I can tell, the Guiding Principles have been cited in only one recorded decision by the UN Human Rights Committee – a dispute over land-grabbing in Israel, purported to have been conducted by a Canadian property

[3] *Prager University v Google Inc*, No 18-15712, 11 (9th Cir, 2020).

[4] ibid, referring to *Central Hardware Company v National Labor Relations Board*, 407 US 539, 547 (1972).

[5] United Nations Human Rights Office of the High Commissioner, 'Guiding Principles on Business and Human Rights: Implementing the United Nations "Protect, Respect and Remedy" Framework' (January 20120 HR/Pub/11/04, 1.

[6] ibid, 13.

[7] ibid, 14.

[8] ibid, Principle 25, 27–28.

development company – which the Committee decided lacked sufficient merit on its pleaded facts (it found the corporation had no real connection with Canada).[9]

Unlike the UN, the Council of Europe has no such qualms about recognising horizontal rights. In its various statements concerning the Internet,[10] the Council, through its Committee of Ministers, has replicated, and then enhanced, the UN's position so as to make explicit its view that the European Convention on Human Rights has 'horizontal effect'.[11] By inverting – or, perhaps, subverting – the logic of the US position, the Council of Europe has concluded that since the Internet, as both a technology and mass media tool, is pivotal to democratic legitimation, it must be the subject of a rights/duty construct *despite* being a form of private property, owned and controlled by private actors. This position is made explicit in its Guide to Human Rights for Internet Users,[12] which states of the right, 'You have the freedom to express yourself online and to access information and the opinions and expressions of others',[13] and of the duty, 'your Internet service provider and your provider of online content and services have corporate responsibilities to respect your human rights and provide mechanisms to respond to your claims'.[14] One striking feature of this duty as set out in the Guide is that regulatory action taken by the provider to enforce its content rules, such as deactivation of an account, 'could constitute an interference with he right to freedom of expression and the right to receive and impart information unless the conditions of Article 10, paragraph 2 of the ECHR as interpreted by the Court, are met'.[15] Explicit statements like this avoid the ambiguities inherent in the UN's position. This is not, as the UN's seems to be, the imposition of vicarious liabilities, upon Member States, concerning the actions of its citizenry (in corporate form). It is the creation of meaningful horizontality itself, as if private actors are duty-holders in this regard.

The justification to match the boldness of the claim that human rights have horizontal effect is not provided, directly, by the recommendation in which it appears. Aside from the bald statement, there is nothing more than the introductory remarks that say the guide is derived from the legal instruments determined by the Council of Europe and '*inspired* by the continuous interpretation of these rights and freedoms by the European Court of Human Rights'[16] (emphasis added). Lest it be thought that

[9] UN Human Rights Committee decision, Communication No 2285/2013, *Yassin v Canada*, decision adopted 26 July 2017, [3.8].

[10] See, eg, Council of Europe, Recommendation CM/Rec(2018)2 on the roles and responsibilities of internet intermediaries; CM/Rec(2016)3 on human rights and business; CM/Rec(2016)5 on internet freedom; CM/Rec(2016)1 on protecting and promoting the right to freedom of expression and the right to private life with regard to network neutrality; CM/Rec(2015)6 on the free, transboundary flow of information on the Internet; CM/Rec(2014)6 on a Guide to human rights for Internet users; CM/Rec(2012)4 on the protection of human rights with regard to social networking services; CM/Rec(2007)16 on measures to promote the public service value of the Internet.

[11] CM/Rec(2018)2, ibid, [2].

[12] Council of Europe, Recommendation CM/Rec(2014)6 and explanatory memorandum of the Committee of Ministers to member States on a Guide to human rights for Internet user, adopted 16 April 2014.

[13] ibid, [1], 3.

[14] ibid, [5], 4.

[15] ibid, [53], 17.

[16] CM/Rec(2014)6 (n 10) 3.

'inspiration' here signifies innovation or exaggeration, the guide states in the very next paragraph that it 'does *not* establish new human rights and fundamental freedoms'[17] (emphasis added). In other words, the guide reflects rights in existence, as stated by, for our purposes, the ECtHR.

Yet, when we scrutinise the Strasbourg jurisprudence, we find evasions rather than answers to the question. The justification for the imposition of a horizontal rights/duty construct is not so much explained as stated by the significance that the Internet has for democratic legitimation purposes. We see it, for example, in the following statement:

> The Internet has now become one of the principal means by which individuals exercise their right to freedom of expression and information, providing as it does essential tools for participation in activities and discussions concerning political issues and issues of general interest.[18]

As a bald fact, this is undoubtedly true – or, certainly, we should be hard pressed to doubt it. But then its implications are more sweeping than the Court recognises, or is prepared to acknowledge. For, by this logic, newspapers, prior to the Internet, performed the same role and ought to have been accessible to regular citizens in terms of dictating content, at least in terms of the directing the *object* of journalistic enquiry. Had that been true we might have seen a lot less fascination with prurient scandal and a lot more interest in political education for the masses. Nevertheless, as the US Supreme Court has long recognised:

> If the rule were otherwise, all private property owners and private lessees who open their property for speech would be subject to First Amendment constraints and would lose the ability to exercise what they deem to be appropriate editorial discretion within that open forum.[19]

Or, with greater wit, 'Benjamin Franklin did not have to operate his newspaper as a stagecoach, with seats for everyone'[20]

The question remains, then, as to why (or, perhaps, how) the right/duty construct can be foisted upon private actors without damage to the internal rationale of constitutional rights recognition or, more specifically, the sanctity of private property. In this way, the American and European jurist occupy irreconcilable positions. The Internet is not prone to horizontal effect *despite* its importance; the Internet must be prone to horizontal effect *because* of its importance.

We shall return to this issue shortly. Before then, we should be clear as possible on the nature of the horizontal right/duty construct as the European jurist sees it. Despite its ostensible intentions to provide clarity and absolute certainty on the meaning and nature of free speech rights online, the bald statements of rights that it provides contains a notable ambiguity, even within the simple confirmation that 'you have the freedom to express yourself online and to access information and the opinions

[17] ibid.

[18] *Yıldırım v Turkey* App no 3111/10, (ECtHR, 18 December 2012), para 54; *Cengiz v Turkey* App no 48226/10, (ECtHR, 1 December 2015), para 49.

[19] *Halleck* (n 2) 1930.

[20] ibid, internal quotation marks omitted.

and expressions of others'.[21] In one sense, this is entirely uncontentious if it means to signal no more than that the state cannot penalise digital expression if it would be prohibited from doing so in the analogue world. Thus, direct or indirect coercion – of the speaker or of the intermediary – would violate the fundamental freedom that Article 10 safeguards (the question of justification for the interference being a separate matter). Accordingly, measures to block access to the Internet, including restrictions on prisoners' access to certain Internet sites, ostensibly constitute a violation of Article 10.[22]

The alternative sense, in which a duty is placed horizontally upon a private actor raises perplexing problems of principle. As we have seen, one interpretation of the European (and UN) approach is its contingency upon the perceived societal importance of the activity rather than in the inherent qualities of the relationship between those actors. In this way, animated by its commitment that digital speech is a vital source of democratic legitimation for state actors, the duty is manufactured so as to satisfy the (perceived) need. As discussed previously, this strikes me as a substitution of the standard of 'want' for 'need'. Certainly, the imposition of this duty is hard to justify when, in the sense of the US state-action doctrine, that horizontal actor is not performing a public or quasi-public function.[23]

Then again, the European position, if it does impose public (constitutional) duties upon private (market-place) entities, *might* be justifiable if it can be said that a citizen (the prospective rights-holder) can petition the state (duty-holder) to defend her autonomous decision-making relations against another citizen (third-party) who seeks to deny her such. For this argument to succeed we must be able to detect sufficient latent contingency between the claimed right to act autonomously and the third-party's autonomy-denying actions. In this adjudicatory sense, the horizontal actors owe such interpersonal duties as resonate with their existence within a socialised community (or social contract) rather than as quasi-state actors. Clearly, this is a complex idea. Further discussion is deferred until the next section. Moreover, as we shall see, in chapters ten (public interest speech) and eleven (workplace speech), this adjudicatory function is highly context-specific.

Meanwhile, and prior to that discussion, we should recognise two further potential implications of the European horizontal effect. The first concerns the quality of the right itself; the second considers the nature of the duty. Allied to both is the sense that the horizontal 'right' is of an inferior quality to the vertical; that, even if one private actor owes a 'duty' to honour the 'right' of another, the sort of free speech right created is not as versatile or robust as it would be against the state in a truly vertical configuration. If the horizontal right/duty construct were identical, in form and nature,

[21] CM/Rec(2014)6 (n 10) 3.

[22] See cases cited in Council of Europe, *Factsheet – Access to Internet and freedom to receive and impart information and ideas* (September 2022).

[23] As with the US position, the English have long understood horizontal effect to be limited, more or less, to circumstances in which the private actor performs public or quasi-public services. Even then, horizontality is thought to depend upon there being suitable common law to develop, rather than being 'free-standing'. See Joint Committee on Human Rights (Seventh Report of Session 2003–04), 'The Meaning of Public Authority under the Human Rights Act,' HL (2003–04) 39, HC (2003–04) 382, [88]. This point is developed further below.

to the vertical, then the private duty-holder would have to demonstrate the same degree of tolerance, in sufferance of the same degree of offence, provocation and abuse that the state and its officials must endure. On that analysis, wild accusations that the human faces of the provider are sinners, reprobates, fraudsters, etc must be suffered with the same degree of humility and tolerance (but not boundless tolerance) as the public official must regardless of the reputational damage suffered. Moreover, it might necessitate that the vitriol and toxicity that unfettered political speech tends to breed must be suffered by other users, as if free speech adherence is but martyrdom in all but name.

An alternative implication, which manifests if not in the guide, then in the Strasbourg jurisprudence, is of a differential right that exists against horizontal actors, in which free speech exists but in lesser form. For example, the ECtHR has recognised a lesser right to free speech for civil servants[24] and in the employment context more generally[25] (as we shall see in chapter eleven). This differential treatment exists in the degree of 'duties and responsibilities' (under Article 10(2)) that the ECtHR is prepared to impose on journalists, such that audiovisual journalism may be held to higher standards than print since the former type 'often have a much more immediate and powerful effect than print media'.[26] Likewise, the ECtHR adopts a different approach to the nature of duties and responsibilities expected of Internet service providers for the dissemination of, say, hate speech, than it would apply to print journalism. This does not necessarily mean that a lesser standard is applied, but that assumptions about the degree of control over content production must be tested.[27] Accordingly, although the ECtHR is yet to decide an analogous case to *Prager University v Google Inc* (in which the central issue was whether the application of standard YouTube policy, on age restriction and 'demonetization', to videos posted by Prager University violated the First Amendment), it is entirely likely that it would decide that the Article 10 right was of a lesser, differential nature than that on the vertical plane.

This aspect of the Strasbourg jurisprudence foreshadows another significant difference between the US and European perspective. Even if it can be said of Europe that Internet intermediaries are Article 10 duty-holders, they are entitled to enforce usage rules that a state, in an analogous position, could not. Moreover, unlike in the US, Article 10 rights to free speech must co-exist on an equal footing with other rights, such as reputation and privacy; there is no presumptive priority for Article 10 over all else.[28] These features are recognised explicitly in the Council of Europe's Guide to Human Rights for Internet Users, which (surely) qualifies the purported horizontal effect of Article 10 by noting:

> You should be aware, however, that online service providers, such as social networks, may restrict certain types of content and behaviour due to their content policies. You should be informed of possible restrictions so that you are able to take an informed decision as

[24] *Melike v Turkey* App no 35786/19 (ECtHR, 15 June 2021).
[25] *Herbai v Hungary* App no 11608/15 (ECtHR, 5 November 2019).
[26] *Orlovskaya Iskra v Russia* App no 42911/08 (ECtHR, 21 February 2017), [109].
[27] See, eg, *Delfi AS v Estonia* (2016) 62 EHRR 6, [113]–[117].
[28] *Axel Springer AG v Germany* [2012] EMLR 15, [87]; See also *Campbell v MGN Ltd* (2004) 2 AC 457, [134]–[140]; *Re S (a child)* [2004] UKHL 47, [17].

> to whether to use the service or not. This includes specific information on what the online service provider considers as illegal or *inappropriate* content and behaviour when using the service and how it is dealt with by the provider.[29]

As the accompanying explanatory notes state, not only is the right to free speech balanced against competing rights, such as those relating to reputation and privacy under Article 8, but certain types of speech 'do not qualify for protection … such as hate speech'.[30] Expanding on its meaning, the guide notes:

> Although there is no universally acceptable definition of hate speech, the Council of Europe's Committee of Ministers has stated that the term … shall be understood as covering all forms of expression which spread, incite, promote or justify racial hatred, xenophobia, anti-Semitism or other forms of hatred based on intolerance, including: intolerance expressed by aggressive nationalism and ethnocentrism, discrimination and hostility against minorities, migrants and people of immigrant origin.[31]

It is further noted that:

> The corporate social responsibility of online service providers includes a commitment to combating hate speech and other content that incites violence or discrimination … [including] expressions motivated by racist, xenophobic, anti-Semitic, misogynist, sexist (including as regards Lesbian Gay Bisexual and Transgender people) or other bias.[32]

This approach is striking for its overt incompatibility with the US juridical approach. If there is one constant in the US jurisprudence, it is that state interpretations of speech – its aims, meaning and effect – are to be deeply distrusted. Hence, the US jurist consistently eschews taxonomical approaches to free speech protection.

The starkness of this contrast is illustrated by the decision in *Sanchez v France* in which a candidate for political office was convicted of 'producing' speech that incited hatred or violence on religious grounds.[33] The offending speech, written by others, appeared as comments underneath his Facebook update, in which he poked fun at the apparent technical issues his political opponent's website had encountered. In sentencing, the domestic criminal court found that the speech had the effect of victimising Muslims generally, and the applicant's political opponent and his wife specifically. It found that the applicant was responsible for these comments, as the original post-holder, and ought to have deleted or moderated them in light of the potential for incitement (of hatred and violence on religious grounds) that his political campaigning was likely to provoke. His appeal was dismissed; the court found that 'to associate the Muslim community with crime and insecurity in the town of Nîmes was likely to arouse a strong feeling of rejection or hostility towards that group'.[34] Subsequently, the applicant complained to the ECtHR that his conviction – for the speech of others – violated his Article 10 rights on several grounds: first, that since the speakers themselves had been successfully prosecuted, his conviction served no material purpose in addressing

[29] n 10, 4.
[30] ibid, [42], 14.
[31] ibid.
[32] ibid, [54], 17.
[33] *Sanchez v France* App no 45581/15 (ECtHR, 15 May 2023).
[34] ibid, [31].

the wrong to society that they had caused;[35] second, that the apparent obligation to monitor *and* identify illegality published to his Facebook 'wall' was too burdensome; and that, in any event, his prosecution for the hate speech of others did not adequately recognise the greater protection offered to political speech, especially during an election period.[36]

Surprisingly, the ECtHR found that his conviction did *not* violate Article 10. Partly, this outcome reflects inherent limitations within the Strasbourg model of adjudication – as an international body, it is a court of review rather than appeal. Thus, the ECtHR noted that 'it is not for the Court to express a view on the appropriateness of methods chosen by the legislature of a respondent State to regulate a given field' but, instead, whether the overall juridical methodology fits with the human rights principles articulated by the ECtHR.[37] Nevertheless, the decision seems odd even to Europeans; for Americans it is likely to induce apoplexy.

Perhaps it is a sign of the desperate levels to which serious political talk has descended in recent years, but, to those inured by populist agendas of US, UK and Eastern European politics, the disparaging comments made on the applicant's 'wall' will seem rather tame. After all, the applicant is a nationalist whose agenda is plainly bigoted. His initial post, to which the offending comments were attached, was innocuous, gloating, as it did, that his opponent's campaign website had failed to attract any visitors. This attracted 15 publicly visible comments, including the two offending ones by individuals known as SB and LR. The tone of the first (by SB) is set by the introductory sentence, referencing the applicant's political opponent:

> This BIGWIG has turned NIMES into ALGIERS, there's not a street without a KEBAB SHOP and MOSQUE; DRUG DEALERS AND PROSTITUTES REIGN SUPREME, NO SURPRISE HE'S CHOSEN BRUSSELS [sic] CAPITAL OF THE NEW WORLD ORDER OF SHARIA …[38]

The second, from LR, complained in a similar vein, of which the following (quoted verbatim) gives the flavour:

> Drug trafficking run by the muslims rue des lombards, it's been going on for years … even with CCTV in the street … more drug dealing in plain sight on avenue general leclerc where riffraff sell drugs all day long but police never come and even outside schools, stones get thrown at cars belonging to 'white people' route d'arles at the lights all the time …

After his opponent's wife complained to the police, the applicant, SB and LR were interviewed. Both SB and LR removed their comments whilst the applicant changed the privacy status of the post so that it was no longer publicly available. During his interview, the applicant protested that 'he had never displayed any racism or discrimination against anyone, and that he did not perceive any call to murder or violence in the impugned remarks, which in his view remained within the limits of any citizen's freedom of expression'.[39]

[35] ibid, [88].
[36] ibid, [88]–[89], [95]–[98].
[37] ibid, [128].
[38] ibid,.
[39] ibid, [23].

Despite recognising its long-established principle that 'there is little scope … [to restrict] political speech',[40] and that free speech is 'especially important for an elected representative of the people',[41] and so 'calls for an elevated level of protection',[42] it is 'not absolute in nature'.[43] Specifically, the ECtHR found, political speech could be curtailed where it undermined those critical societal values of tolerance, plurality (diversity), equality and dignity, so long as such restrictions were proportionate to the harm caused.[44] Additionally, since political figures have 'duties and responsibilities' relating to social harmony, they must 'avoid comments that might foster intolerance' and 'should also be particularly careful to defend democracy and its principles, their ultimate aim being to govern'.[45] Accordingly, since the propagation of a culture that

> foster[s] the exclusion of foreigners constitutes a fundamental attack on individual rights … everyone – politicians included – should exercise particular caution in discussing such matters. Consequently, remarks *capable of* arousing a feeling of rejection and hostility towards a community fall outside the protection guaranteed by Article 10 (emphasis added).[46]

Whereas politicians must be free to discuss 'delicate or sensitive matters', including proposals to tackle 'problems linked to immigration', they

> must avoid advocating racial discrimination and resorting to vexatious or humiliating remarks or attitudes, as such conduct might trigger reactions among the public that would be detrimental to a peaceful social climate and might undermine confidence in the democratic institutions.[47]

It added that, since politicians hold a special 'status and position in society, he or she is more likely to influence voters, or even to incite them, directly or indirectly, to adopt positions and conduct that may prove unlawful, thus explaining why he or she can be expected to be 'all the more vigilant'.[48]

Moreover, the ECtHR found that the election context, rather than necessitating greater tolerance for provocative speech, imposed the opposite approach since, during elections 'the positions of the candidates [on hard issues like immigration] will inevitably harden and slogans or catchphrases become more prominent than reasoned arguments. The impact of racist and xenophobic discourse then becomes greater and more harmful'.[49] Referring to its earlier jurisprudence, the Court noted that incitement to hatred is not restricted only to the encouragement of violence; 'attacks on persons committed by insulting, holding up to ridicule or slandering' others also count.[50] Furthermore, since the Internet allows for maximal dissemination of information, in an instantaneous, easily accessible and permanent form, the harm of hate speech is

[40] ibid, [146].
[41] ibid, [147].
[42] ibid, [148].
[43] ibid.
[44] ibid, [149].
[45] ibid, [150].
[46] ibid.
[47] ibid, [151].
[48] ibid, [187].
[49] ibid, [153] and [179]–[180].
[50] ibid, [155] and [176], referencing *Atamanchuk v Russia* App no 4493/11 (ECtHR, 11 February 2020), [52].

increased and the need to tackle it is heightened.[51] Accordingly, the Court held that 'the comments at issue clearly incited hatred and violence against a person on account of his or her religion and this cannot be disguised or minimised by the election context or by a wish to discuss local difficulties'.[52]

Sanchez v France is but one example of a wider pattern that illustrates the distinct differences between the US and European juridical positions. Examining it in this level of forensic detail permits us to see that the threshold for both the identification of, and justifiable interference with, hate speech disseminated online is fairly low, especially compared to its treatment in offline contexts. For example, press reporting of hatefulness, as it manifests, say, in the xenophobic attitudes of angry youths,[53] also condones, if not glorifies, wider adoption of racism amongst the similarly disillusioned yet, even where there is no impartial or balanced voice in the reporting, let alone open condemnation, the Court is prepared to protect such dissemination as a matter of press reporting:

> The punishment of a journalist for assisting in the dissemination of statements made by another person in an interview would seriously hamper the contribution of the press to discussion of matters of public interest and should not be envisaged unless there are particularly strong reasons for doing so.[54]

The fact that the broadcast remarks were 'more than insulting' and did not themselves enjoy Article 10 protection provided insufficient reason to penalise the press for giving oxygen to inflammatory ideas.[55]

Here, then, we see, in the European position, the Hegelian intertwining of community and individual interests to determine the meaning of rights. The stark contrast that this creates with the American position speaks to distinct but diametrically opposed political commitments to the people that, of itself, reflects the traditions, experiences and – ultimately – horrors of a shared community existence. For the Americans, this experience is dim and distant, reflecting a fear of authoritarianism that came from monarchical tyranny. Moreover, it came from abroad, rather than internally. Put bluntly, America has yet to experience the corrosive power that unfettered hate has when the conditions create a political climate so debased that overt authoritarianism becomes irresistibly alluring to the masses. Europeans have no such blind spot and although the experience is not within living memory, its shadow remains.

Through this admittedly unrefined and impressionistic observation upon the existence of, and reasons for, differential treatment of horizontality, certain distinctive features are prominent. First, and most strikingly, the US judge will not accept that the provision of technology to enable mass dissemination will, of itself, create a public function to satisfy the state action doctrine. For the European jurist, this is less problematic. As noted above, this creates a stark contrast between the US position, ie that the digital speech provider is not a public functionary *despite* the benefits to democratic legitimacy

[51] ibid, [158]–[162] and [184].
[52] ibid, [190].
[53] *Jersild v Denmark* (1995) 19 EHRR 1.
[54] ibid, [35].
[55] ibid.

that digital speech represents, and the European position that inverts this reasoning by substituting 'despite' for 'because'.

Yet, secondly, if the free speech principle *is* operative in this context, then the US jurisprudence suggests no differentiation in the quality of free speech right available. For example, as we have seen in, say, *Snyder v Phelps*,[56] the *object* of speech, its target, or its correlation to political action are not matters that would weaken or alter the nature of the free speech right. The fact that the grieving family in the *Snyder* case had no public status and the significant harm caused to them was not in any way counter-balanced by a discernible impact on political activity did not factor in the juridical reasoning process. In contrast, the European position demonstrates a discernible differential approach to the nature, or, rather, strength of the right on the horizontal plane. This will become in the discussion of public interest speech in the next chapter, in which the *contribution* to public interest debate is said to be significant.[57] In this sense, an initial taxonomical appraisal of the speech as political (or artistic or commercial) is insufficient because 'generalities' alone do not satisfy the legal test.[58] The American mindset is committed to a solitary or unitary free speech 'right' which, when operative, is uniform across the spectrum of diverse application. The European position, meanwhile, imagines a multitude of differential free speech 'rights' determined by contextuality.

This leads to a third tension. In the US, the nature of rights speaks clearly to individuality *above* community, in which we glimpse the Millian principle that

> if all mankind minus one, were of one opinion, and only one person were of the contrary opinion, mankind would be no more justified in silencing that one person, than he, if he had the power, would be justified in silencing mankind.[59]

In contrast, the European model embraces the Hegelian logic we saw in chapter five, by which rights reflect both individual *and* collective interests. This is clearly demonstrated by the prioritisation of social cohesion and diverse community that justifies zero tolerance towards hate speech. Through these stark contrasts, then, we see something of the authenticity crisis that grips the identification, and treatment, of free speech claims in modern life.

III. Right-Duty or Right-No Right?

If there is a right to free speech on the horizontal plane, then how does the duty to protect it manifest? In this section, I shall say no more than that *if* there is such a right then it must be, using classic Hohfeldian analysis, of the right-no right variety, rather than the sort of right-duty construct that the European position suggests. This is not to deny that the right-duty construct can apply to the horizontal plane – there are numerous examples in property, employment, trusts, family and professional relationships in

[56] *Snyder v Phelps* 562 US 443 (2011). See discussion in ch 2.
[57] *Axel Springer AG v Germany* (n 28) [90]–[91].
[58] See, further, D Eady, 'Injunctions and the Protection of Privacy' (2010) 29 *Civil Justice Quarterly* 411, 418.
[59] JS Mill, 'On Liberty' in *Collected Works of John Stuart Mill* (JM Robson ed) vol XVIII (University of Toronto Press, 1977),229.

which we can, and do, speak sensibly of private actors owing duties to other private actors with corresponding rights. My point, then, is no more than that the constitutional duty, incumbent upon the state, to uphold the free speech rights of citizens, cannot be transposed from the vertical to the horizontal plane. I will explore this idea through the lens of the academic literature on digital speech rights, of which Jack Balkin's work is exemplary.[60]

As explained in chapter eight, we can differentiate reasons for state action against speech in two ways. If the state penalises speech it dislikes in order to preserve its own position in power, then we can classify this as a vertically orientated reason to interfere. This is illegitimate according to the state–citizen pact by which all citizens divest individual power to the centre so that the state functions as a democracy governed, as it must be, by the limits of individual autonomy. If, however, the state penalises speech as part of an adjudicatory process, as occurs when rights-claims clash, then we can classify this as a horizontally orientated reason to interfere. This is legitimate if the reasons for interference comply with the harm principle.

Both orientations, then, speak vividly to individuality as the base unit of constitutional design. In the vertical arrangement, there is only one species of autonomy in play, and that belongs to the citizen. For it is nonsensical to speak of the state as an autonomous entity, the liberal tradition tells us, since autonomy is that state which only individuals can possess in virtue of their being, and as an expression of their being, which is independent of and separate to the state, and beyond the state's control. Hence, the state itself can possess no such thing. Instead, it (the state) is a device of convenience or prudence by which power is both invested and exercised for specific ends directed by the terms of the mandate. The state has powers and, although there may be considerable latitude in how executive power is exercised, still, that exercise is subject to an administrative review that is closely policed across the branches of government. When we examine the distinction between legitimate exercises of power and autonomous decision-making, through, for example, the ultra vires principle, we see a crucial distinction in that legitimate exercises of power are subject to reason in a manner that autonomous decision-making is not.[61] For it is the *subjectivity* that counts in determining if something is autonomous (ie, does the decision emanate from *me*?) not its objectivity (ie, is it a decision that others would make?).

As we saw above, if the US 'state action' doctrine applies, then, properly speaking, the private actor is treated, juridically, as if it were the state, in which case its autonomy is rendered nugatory. The same is true of the European approach in which, if a private actor is classified as an emanation of the state, it has no autonomy as such. This is even more apparent in the legal test for determining 'emanation of the state' status, in which

[60] Balkin has written extensively about free speech online. See, to name a few, JM Balkin, 'How Rights Change: Freedom of Speech in the Digital Era' (2004) 26 *Sydney Law Review* 5; 'The Future of Free Expression in a Digital Age' (2009) 36 *Pepperdine Law Review* 427; 'The First Amendment Is an Information Policy' (2012) 41 *Hofstra Law Review* 1;'Old-School/New-School Speech Regulation' (2014) 127 *Harvard Law Review* 2296; 'Cultural Democracy and the First Amendment' (2016) 110 *Northwestern University Law Review* 1053; 'Free Speech Is a Triangle' (2018) 118 *Columbia Law Review* 2011; 'How to Regulate (and Not Regulate) Social Media' (2021) 1 *Journal of Free Speech Law* 71.

[61] See, eg, *Associated Provincial Picture Houses Limited v Wednesbury Corporation* [1948] 1 KB 223.

it must be shown that the private actor is under state 'control'.[62] These two doctrines are connected by the *absence* (or suspension) of autonomy: the private actor *must* perform (or not perform) an action not because it *wants to* but because it *must*. Here, then, we see the Kantian ethical instruction given practical effect: this is the difference between the hypothetical and the categorical imperative: the *should* compared to the *must*.

Now, as we have seen, the US juridical view is that digital speech providers do not perform public services – or services of the type that are traditional to the state – but, instead, provide services to the public. The European juridical view, on emanations of the state, would seem to add an additional layer to this distinction in that it must be that digital services providers *are not* (descriptively) under the control of the state nor that they *should be* (normatively). We do not want the state to control the digital speech provision for the exact same reason that we do not wish the state to control any other form of media, for to do so would compromise the autonomous freedom we attribute to those entities and which separates media freedom in a healthy democracy from media 'freedom' in an autocracy (or any other authoritarian regime). In this sense, the European juridical view on the relationship between private actors in this dynamic (the digital speech provider and end users) seems more akin to the right-no right dynamic than the duty-right dynamic. Although the contra-indications are there (as we have seen) in the Strasbourg jurisprudence and Council of Europe's Committee of Ministers' reports, the European perspective could be interpreted in this way.

Whether the academic literature sees the relationship in these terms is more doubtful. The central theme, resonating throughout, is that of an immense power, possessed by successful digital speech providers, by which to control, manipulate and distort popular opinion and debate. This power is of significant concern to (not just) scholars working in this field, who argue that something should be done to regulate it. We find this theme in Balkin's work, in which it is typical for him to say:

> In the early twenty-first century, freedom of speech increasingly depends on a third group of players: a privately owned infrastructure of digital communication composed of firms that support and govern the digital public sphere that people use to communicate.[63]

Other commentators regularly say the same or similar.[64] It is generally assumed that since digital speech providers are 'powerful' actors in public debate, the presence of the free speech concept is established, meaning that the only question is which 'set of free speech values should govern the Internet and regulate online … speech?'[65]

[62] See, eg, *Foster v British Gas Plc* (C-188/89) [1991] 1 QB 405; *Foster v British Gas Plc* [1991] 2 AC 306.
[63] Balkin (n 60) 2011.
[64] See, eg, DS Ardia, 'Beyond the Marketplace of Ideas: Bridging Theory and Doctrine to Promote Self-Governance' (2022) 16 *Harvard Law & Policy Review* 101, 117, 'In our electronically mediated public sphere, these private gatekeepers have more power to manipulate public attention – and distort public discourse – than any government has ever had'; N Guggenberger, 'Moderating Monopolies' (2023) 38 *Berkeley Technology Law Journal* 119, 145–46, '[C]oncentrated private control is incompatible with democratic conceptualizations of public discourse'; G Abiri, 'Moderating from Nowhere' [2022] 47 *Brigham Young University Law Review* 757, 759, 'Digital platforms have significant control over our political and social communication'; S Ross, 'Speech Governance is an Autocracy: The Case for Democratizing Facebook' (2022) 27 *UCLA Journal of Law and Technology* i, 22, 'social media companies' power over the digital public sphere is deeply worrying'.
[65] Abiri (ibid) 759.

This sense of powerful influence over public debate is significant to Balkin's influential depiction of the relationship between the state, the end user, and the digital speech provider as triangular in nature. Locating the apex at the base, which represents the end user, he depicts the state and digital speech provider in the uppermost corners, thus describing separate relationships between provider and end-user as well as state and end-user. In this way, the digital speech provider is elevated, in status, to the same level as the state. Balkin's essential point here, I think, is that since private governance of public speech is as effective, if not more so, in regulating – even eliminating – certain types of speech from publicly available discourse, then the comparison to (what he calls) 'old-school' regulation (by means of coercive power) is apt.

Yet, Balkin's triangular representation tends to mislead in two important respects. First, given the equality of status (between provider and state), it assumes the form of an equivalent duty-right relationship between the provider and end-user as we find in the traditional vertical relationship. Certainly, this is how other commentators have interpreted Balkin.[66] Balkin does not adopt this position. In keeping with the US juridical view, he rejects the possibility; 'This is not a claim that infrastructure owners should be treated as state actors.'[67] It would be, he says, 'a bad idea to hold social media spaces to the same standards as municipal governments under the First Amendment'[68] since, to do so, 'would cripple [their] abilities to impose civility norms', which would be counter-productive ('many people will avoid them')[69] and would prevent providers from 'curat[ing] content … to provide personalized feeds'.[70]

Secondly, and perhaps most importantly, the triangular arrangement misleads on (what I take to be) Balkin's most explicit concern that the state might use (in every sense of that term) digital speech providers to regulate speech that it (the state) could not in conformity with the First Amendment (or any other form of free speech guarantee, we may assume). Balkin calls this 'new school regulation' – 'a burgeoning dialectic of governing power and public–private cooperation' in which 'private-infrastructure companies develop ever greater governing capacities. Nation-states attempt to co-opt these capacities through coercion or threats of regulation'.[71] This is not a triangular affair so much as a distortion of the duty-right relationship in which the provider is

[66] See, eg, S Smart and AC McManus, 'Closing the Gap between UNGPs and Content Regulation/Moderation Practices' (2022) 19 *Brazilian Journal of International Law* 269, 276; N Syed, 'Real Talk about Fake News: Towards a Better Theory for Platform Governance' (2017–18) 127 *Yale Law Journal Forum* 337, 356; CL Langford, 'Free Speech in Cyberspace: A Rhetorical Analysis of SOPA and PIPA Cyberprotests' (2013) 47 *First Amendment Studies* 85, 100; RJ Hamilton, 'Governing the Global Public Square' 62 *Harvard International Law* 117, 121; Guggenberger (n 64) 171; Abiri (n 64) 804–05 'By imposing these duties, companies will have to change their business models in ways that take into account the effect they have on their users'; B Sander, 'Freedom of Expression in the Age of Online Platforms: The Promise and Pitfalls of a Human Rights-Based Approach to Content Moderation' (2020) 43 *Fordham International Law Journal* 939, 1004, 'Ensuring that these platforms govern in the public interest has emerged as one of the most pressing challenges for freedom of expression in the twenty-first century'.

[67] JM Balkin, 'Free Speech in the Algorithmic Society: Big Data, Private Governance, and New School Speech Regulation' (2018) 51 *University of California Davis Law Review* 1149, 1194.

[68] Balkin, 'Free Speech is a Triangle,' n 60, 2026.

[69] ibid, 2027.

[70] ibid.

[71] ibid, 2020.

but an intermediary, or better yet, proxy, for censorious state interventions.[72] In this sense, it is very much vertical and linear, in which the provider disrupts the overt breach of duty by masking the state's involvement. As was argued in chapter eight, this is plainly in breach of the state's duty to the free speech rights-holder and, therefore, is unlawful.

Balkin's strategy, then, for tackling (purely) private governance of digital speech, is two-fold. First, it relies upon morality. Thus, providers '*should* recognize and protect free speech values as well as due process values in the resolution of complaints'[73] (emphasis added). Likewise, that since the state cannot force social media companies to be 'trustworthy intermediate institutions' in the dissemination of publicly valuable speech, it should create 'incentives' to achieve this end.[74] Others take their lead from Balkin here. Tim Wu, for example, argues that 'private platforms could – and should – be doing more to prevent speakers from harassment'.[75] Similarly, it has been said, that when providers employ policies that 'restrict the freedom of expression of users without effectively furthering a legitimate purpose, [they] should commit to revising their policies accordingly'.[76] As a strategy, of course, this reliance upon moral imperative is redolent of the UN's position, as set out above. This may be an effective strategy for realising greater pluralism in digital discourse – that, if providers cannot be encouraged to act more ethically, then they may be shamed into doing so – but it has nothing much to do with law.

Secondly, Balkin argues that the legal obligations digital speech providers owe to end-users manifest in a range of (what he calls) 'fiduciary' obligations concerning user data collection and usage, specifically: 'a duty of confidentiality, a duty of care, and a duty of loyalty'.[77] These, he says, create 'duties of trustworthiness and good faith toward their end users'.[78] This sort of obligation is familiar to European audiences inured in the language of GDPR. Ultimately, data protection, as a species of privacy-right, has little, if anything, to do with free speech theory.

Balkin is hardly alone in acknowledging the relative inadequacy of the duty-right construct to generate enhanced public discourse obligations between end-user and digital speech provider. Tim Wu, for example, is clear that although providers occupy 'an extremely important role in the construction of public discourse', the First Amendment is a 'bystander'.[79] Whereas it does not create a state-like duty, of itself, upon providers, it is 'I think … reasonable to suggest that basic protection of speakers and listeners can be understood as a constitutional duty to defend the basic values of the First Amendment … [against] harassment, fraud, deception, and related practices'.[80] In other words, the state, according to this analysis, would adjudicate between competing

[72] See Hamilton (n 66, in which instances of the state as 'a user and *abuser* of social media' (122) is discussed empirically.
[73] Balkin (2018) (n 60) 2026.
[74] This argument is set out in its fullest form in Balkin (2021) (n 60).
[75] T Wu, 'Is the First Amendment Obsolete?' (2018) 117 *Michigan Law Review* 547, 571.
[76] Sander (n 66) 988.
[77] Balkin (2018) (n 60) 2051.
[78] ibid, 2055.
[79] Wu (n 75) 555.
[80] ibid, 568–69.

private claims amounting to, in effect, a right–no right contest. Recognition of this limitation is apparent elsewhere, at least in a formal if not substantive sense. For example, Stefan Theil has argued that 'human rights law should take private platforms seriously as a source of significant threats, without abandoning the generally valuable differentiation of obligations between private actors and the state'.[81]

Nevertheless, even if there is general recognition that transposing the vertical duty-right construct to the horizontal plane is invalid (and that the 'duty' applies only in its ethical rather than juridical sense), still, the literature is not yet ready to admit defeat in the campaign to impose duties upon digital speech providers. Instead, commentators argue for an obligation that is *like* a duty but not quite (whatever that means). We see this in Theil, for example, where he argues for recognition of a 'modest horizontal effect'[82] by which the state might 'impos[e] *some* free-speech obligations on private actors'[83] (emphasis added).

Balkin also utilises this strategy – of the intermediate position between duty and no-duty – in his work. Even within 'Free Speech is a Triangle' we see him argue that digital speech providers should be governed by the *spirit* of the First Amendment, if not the actuality applied 'jot for jot'.[84] Thus, he argues that since the values inherent within the US free speech jurisprudence speak to the idea of a cultural democracy, in which all may contribute, so as to both influence and be influenced, then these values must frame the intellectual lens by which policies and regulatory approaches are analysed. In this sense, Balkin is aligned with both the dogmatic stringency of the 'state action' doctrine and the ethical strategy of the UNHRC policy. Thus, there is much in Balkin, as we have seen, that speaks to encouragement and incentivisation to create the optimal conditions (as he sees them) of a global public square.

Nevertheless, the lynchpin in Balkin's strategy, *is* a legal obligation, upon digital speech providers, to provide 'curatorial due process'. This is problematic, for it speaks to a duty-right dynamic that it is unjustified (so far as I can tell). Essentially, Balkin argues that by curating information to suit the end-user's interests and desires, the digital speech provider is a mass media operative that is both akin to, but substantially different from, the legacy press:

> Like twentieth-century mass media, digital curators have become important custodians of the public sphere and of democratic self-government. Hence, whether they like it or not, digital curators have social and moral obligations to the public – as opposed to legal obligations. With those obligations comes a corresponding duty to develop and abide by professional norms of curation and governance.[85]

Given the explicit exclusion of legal obligation, this 'corresponding duty' could be understood entirely in the Kantian sense of the term (such as a duty of faithfulness or a duty of keeping one's promises, etc). Yet, Balkin moves on to say that digital speech

[81] S Theil, 'Private censorship and structural dominance: Why social media platforms should have obligations to their users under Freedom of Expression' (2022) 81 *Cambridge Law Journal* 645, 649.

[82] ibid, 662.

[83] ibid, 669.

[84] Balkin (2018) (n 60) 2032.

[85] ibid, 2041.

providers, unlike the legacy press, *must* act justly when applying its regulatory policies. This he calls the curatorial obligation of due process:

> [D]igital media companies have curatorial obligations of due process. These obligations made little sense in a world in which very few people had access to mass media but are central in a world in which everyone is a broadcaster. For this reason, to the extent that digital curators block, censor, or take down content from their end users, they have obligations of due process toward their end users.[86]

The justification that Balkin offers for this 'curatorial obligation' is curious. It is a reference to his own work and the following passage, specifically:

> The more that end-users view businesses as governors, or as special-purpose sovereigns, the more end-users will expect -- and demand that these companies should conform to the basic obligations of governors towards those they govern … But what end-users may especially resent is that the criteria are kept hidden, that the takedowns are done summarily, that the rules are applied arbitrarily, that powerful people and organizations are given exceptions to the rules, and that end-users are booted off the platform without notice and an opportunity to defend themselves.[87]

Whereas it may be correct to assume that end-users do have such expectations of fair treatment, this translates to a legal right only to the extent of the contractual position. It may be that the arbitrary removal from a providers' site is a breach of contract, yet, even if so, juridical resolution of this breach will not result, for the reasons outlined below, in the preservation/restoration of the Habermasian conduit that campaigners seem to imagine. Suffice it to say that 'due process' in contract dispute terms requires only that the terms of the contract are compensated when breached, and those terms will be only what is agreed (by and large) and not what is most beneficial to public discourse.

As is common in this field, Balkin seems to assume that this sort of state-like obligation can be imposed, unilaterally, upon private actors because they are powerful.[88] As we have seen, the power of digital speech providers to direct, control and even manipulate popular thought and opinion is seen as equivalent to state power. This reasoning is apparent in Theil's argument, who criticises 'liberal thinkers who have followed [Mill]' for their failure to fully appreciate the impact of private power on liberty: 'The focus on state power has made many accounts of constitutional rights to free expression indifferent to the pernicious impact of private power.'[89] He goes on to say:

> The liberal preference for leaving private actors to their own devices operates poorly and materially reduces individual autonomy whenever grave imbalances in societal bargaining power persist: regardless of whether these are ultimate rooted in political, economic or social marginalisation.[90]

[86] ibid, 2044.
[87] Balkin (n 67) 1197.
[88] Balkin (2009) (n 60).
[89] ibid, 647.
[90] ibid, 657.

Yet, power is an implausible reason for imposing something like a duty upon digital speech providers. Not only is the power arrangement in citizen–state and end-users–digital speech providers relationships radically different – power is not given conditionally by citizens to private actors as it is to the state – the nature of that power is also radically different. The coercive powers of the state, relating as they do to security and protection, administrative and legal, is derived from the citizenry. It is power deferred from the masses to the central. It is, therefore, power that must respond to the will of the people. Private power is entrepreneurial. Status, influence and bargaining power developed through private enterprise is not derived from public power nor responsive to it in a dutiful sense. It is not power that belongs, in the final analysis, to the people. Private power is not state power by another name. Moreover, it is not devoid of autonomy. On the contrary, it *is* a manifestation of autonomy (both actual and potential). As such, it can be managed by the state according to the right-no right dynamic, not the duty-right construct.

Thus, it seems to me, this talk of 'horizontal effect' and of duty-like 'obligations' upon digital speech providers employs the wrong terminology. We cannot transpose the vertical duty-right dynamic to the horizontal plane. Digital speech providers are not office-holders whose powers are subject to popular will and the controlling notion of 'ultra vires'. Their power reflects, and is contingent upon, the success of their autonomous decision-making that led to market dominance. The most that the end-user can expect is that the state will intervene when the autonomous decisions of the provider unduly interfere with the autonomous decisions of the end-users. Accordingly, all the state can do, here, is adjudicate between competing autonomy-based claims. The appropriate Hohfeldian analysis here is not duty-right but right-no right. That is, the state must say either that the digital speech provider has no right to interfere with the expression of the end-user or that the end-user has no right to insist that the digital speech provider publish her speech (or preserve her membership).

This distinction – between duty-right and right-no right – is more than mere semantics. In the Hohfeldian tradition, the duty-right is a juridical relative in which the extent of the duty corresponds to the limits of the right. Right, here, is posited by campaigners as a right to demand of the duty-holder that they comply with their duties. The right-no right scenario, though, is a juridical opposite. The extent of the right corresponds to the extent of the no-right. If you have a right, in this sense, it means I have no right to prevent you. Thus, the right to defame corresponds with no reputational right to prevent or the right to publish personal information corresponds with no right to claim privacy is invaded by it.

If digital speech providers are subject to the constitutional duty to uphold free speech rights, then their autonomy is suspended to the extent it is inconsistent with that duty. This means, as Balkin argues, that the algorithmic personalisation of individual feeds would be inconsistent with the obligations of content neutrality imposed upon the state.[91] Moreover, a digital speech provider would have restricted – even, non-existent – rights to sue in defamation if end-user criticisms of it caused undue harm to its reputation. I am thinking here of the heavily restricted circumstances

[91] Balkin (2018) (n 60) 2027–28.

in which political actors, in the US,[92] and political corporations, in England[93] and Australia[94] (to name two jurisdictions), can sue in defamation when citizens criticise performance in public office. In *Derbyshire County Council v Times Newspapers Ltd*,[95] the House of Lords held that the corporate entity of a local authority had no right to sue, in defamation, newspaper reports that it had misappropriated funds regardless of the merits of its claims. Reminiscent of the reasoning in *New York Times v Sullivan*,[96] the Court said that:

> It is of the highest public importance that a democratically elected governmental body, or indeed any governmental body, should be open to uninhibited public criticism. The threat of a civil action for defamation must inevitably have an inhibiting effect on freedom of speech.[97]

Clearly, the inability to sue goes further than the limited prospects of successfully suing that the rule in *New York Times v Sullivan*. As we shall see in the next chapter, although the public interest in speech critical of abuses of power by private actors may trump rights to reputation, it does not preclude the ability to launch proceedings themselves and have them judged on their merits. Thus, to deny a digital speech provider the opportunity to protect its legitimate interests in reputation by harmful, untrue statements because of its role in facilitating the global public square would be characteristic of a duty deprived of autonomy rather than recognition of right to exist autonomously consistent with the autonomous rights of others.

Moreover, if there is no duty upon the digital speech provider to uphold the constitutional free speech right, then there can be no argument in favour of a positive duty upon it. Such positive conceptions of liberty were discussed in the previous chapter. They arise in the digital speech literature to the extent that commentators argue for, as Wu has it, an obligation to 'protect and promote a healthy political speech environment'.[98] Although Wu argues that this obligation falls upon the state, it would also fall upon the digital speech provider if it were under the same or equivalent duty to uphold the free speech right.

IV. Wrongdoing

According to the preceding discussion, then, it may be said that digital speech providers do not owe duties of free speech to end-users across the horizontal plane. Instead, the rights dispute, as such, is between private actors – the provider and the end-user – who call upon the state (the only true duty-holder) to resolve the conflict between them. In this hypothetical, the end-user claims that her right to autonomy has been interfered with unduly by the provider, who has denied her, in some material respect, the right to

[92] *New York Times v Sullivan* 376 US 254 (1964).
[93] *Derbyshire County Council v Times Newspapers Ltd* [1993] AC 534.
[94] *New South Wales Aboriginal Land Council v Jones* (1998) 43 NSWLR 300.
[95] n 93.
[96] n 92.
[97] n 93, 547.
[98] Wu (n 75) 568.

do something she feels entitled to do. Meanwhile, the provider denies that it has acted wrongfully; that if it has denied her, then it was entitled to do so as a manifestation of its own right to act autonomously, as a property owner. If it is to be true to its authentic liberal construct, outlined in the previous chapter, the state can only decide in the end-user's favour if satisfied that the provider's actions amount to wrongdoing in a manner that causes demonstrable harm to the end-user's autonomy. In other words, it must be satisfied that the end-user's autonomy has been materially interfered with in circumstances that do not amount to a legitimate use of the provider's own autonomy.

As noted above, the most obvious way in which this autonomy claim could be substantiated is if the provider acts in breach of contract. Yet, even here, campaigners are likely to be frustrated, for if the contract is performed as agreed, the end-user agreeing to comply with the provider's terms of service, which includes abiding by its community standards, then, so long as the provider adheres to its rules, there can be no accusation of wrongdoing should user breach of those standards result in the penalties specified under the contract (eg, censorship and/or exclusion). This much is recognised by the literature, including both Balkin[99] and Theil.[100]

Of course, as we have seen, Balkin's chief concern is that application of those terms lacks independent oversight such that decisions may be reached arbitrarily. Hence, he argues that those terms should be read subject to a 'due process' obligation. Even if Balkin is persuasive on this point, I am not sure it takes him to the position he wants to be in, which is, in effect, that arbitrary policy decisions could be undone when inconsistent with free speech norms. This would presuppose an entitlement to specific performance that our contract law traditions do not reflect. Whereas the law can compensate for any and all damages flowing from this breach of contract (if any), it cannot, without self-contradiction, force the parties to remain in a legal relationship in circumstances where one, or perhaps even both, have lost faith in the other,[101] especially where personal services are involved.[102] To insist upon this continuation or restoration of services – a proposition inherent in Balkin's idea of due process obligations – backed by a legal regime, of either direct access to the court or indirect enforcement by means of regulation would be to ignore the telling criticism that Melvin Eisenberg has previously made of specific performance: 'It is highly intrusive and highly coercive. It is backed by draconian penalties that are out of scale with the end to be achieved.'[103]

Allied to this is the problem that 'due process' would have to be assessed against corporate rather than municipal considerations, in which the reputational damage of continuing association with the end-user must be relevant. Thus, although commentators were (and continue to be) exercised by Twitter's (as was) and Facebook's decision to exclude Donald Trump from its platforms because he incited a lethal riot at the

[99] Balkin (2018) (n 60) 225–28.

[100] Theil (n 81) 648: 'I take it as uncontroversial that a private social media company may terminate a contract for services with users that breach its terms and conditions of use.'

[101] *Co-operative Insurance v Argyll Stores Ltd* [1997] 2 WLR 898.

[102] *De Francesco v Barnum* (1890) 45 Ch D 430, 438.

[103] MA Eisenberg, 'Actual and Virtual Specific Performance, the Theory of Efficient Breach, and the Indifference Principle in Contract Law' (2005) 93 *California Law Review* 975, 1049.

Capitol,[104] it is palpably clear that the decision to exclude was motivated by commercial considerations after advertisers expressed disquiet at Trump's continuing presence on those platforms despite his reprehensible behaviour.

Perhaps commentators might argue that free speech norms are relevant to contractual interpretation to the extent that (and degree to which) providers themselves claim to honour them (or else be bound by them). This strikes me as unpersuasive, not least for the reasons given in *Prager University v Google Inc*:

> YouTube's representation that it is committed to freedom of expression, or a single statement made by its executive before a congressional committee that she considers YouTube to be a 'neutral public fora,' cannot somehow convert private property into a public forum. Whether a property is a public forum is not a matter of election by a private entity.[105]

From the perspective of contractual analysis, such a statement might be dismissed as a 'mere puff' – a statement so insubstantial, objectively, that it does not communicate an intention to be bound.[106] Thus, for example, Twitter used to describe freedom of speech as its 'underlying philosophy'.[107] A court might well decide that such statements of 'philosophy' are sufficiently vague and imprecise as to lack sufficient intention on the provider's part to be bound by it especially since such philosophies are liable to shift with changing ownership (as happened in the rebranding of Twitter as X under Elon Musk).

Moreover, even if all of the above is rectified – perhaps by some sort of regulatory body that oversees breach of contract complaints, eg OFCOM in the UK – this does not mean that the terms of that contract must be rewritten to reflect the demands of the *Sittlichkeit* and the Habermasian conduit. In other words, digital speech providers cannot be forced by the state to realise the public discourse ideal that Balkin and others dream of, without damage to the underlying Lockean conception of property rights that the legal systems of mature liberal democracies are built upon.

Putting aside what I consider to be a fairly trivial breach of contract claim, how else might the scenario be understood in terms of generating legal obligations that meet the wrongdoing–causation–harm analysis of chapter eight? One strategy emerges when we read across the literature on digital speech in which, we might envisage, commentators would say the inherent power imbalance between providers and end-users, as well as the comparable power of those providers compared to the state, is sufficient, of itself, to show the formula is satisfied. This argument proceeds as follows. Powerful private actors control public debate by mechanisms that manipulate information and dictate the terms of contribution. Accordingly, some contributions are enhanced and others suppressed; some contributors are elevated and others removed altogether.

The digital speech provider is distinguished from other private actors in terms of obligations, campaigners would say, by reason of teleology. Balkin, for example, expresses this teleological claim thus: 'Digital curators *exist* to facilitate mass cultural participation, and their end users expect and depend on the fact that curators will

[104] See, eg, Abiri (n 64) 759.
[105] n 3, 13.
[106] *Dimmock v Hallett* (1866) LR 2 Ch App 21.
[107] See discussion in Sander (n 66) 949.

help them in this process' (emphasis added).[108] These dynamics – which may enforce liberal norms or otherwise run contrary to them[109] – are determined by the superior bargaining power of the digital speech provider itself. Hence Theil speaks for the literature when he complains that 'the liberal preference for leaving private actors to their own devices operates poorly and materially reduces individual autonomy whenever grave imbalances in societal bargaining power persist'.[110] Indeed, in Theil, we find the most explicit elucidation of this idea; that

> at least some private platforms that open themselves to the public ought to have obligations under freedom of expression towards their users … whenever they are structurally dominant, where they arbitrarily exclude users and where an exclusion significant impacts on an individual's societal participation.[111]

Thus, we are given a sense that the power – actual and potential – to distort public debate undermines individual autonomy and so amounts to wrongdoing. This might manifest in the Postian sense of individual inability to contribute to debate or the broader Habermasian sense of a material impact upon the quality of that debate and, so, the efficacy of mutual surveillance between state and citizenry through the conduit.

The literature states that this interference with autonomy also amounts to demonstrable harm. This harm might manifest through provider indifference toward or ineffectiveness in tackling mis- and disinformation.[112] It might do so through arbitrary (or even non-arbitrary) deplatforming, especially of politicians.[113] Instead, it might be abuse and harassment toward specific individuals or individuals holding specific viewpoints.[114] Such abuse manifests in terms such as 'trolling' or 'pile-ons', in which speakers are, in effect, stalked by obsessive end-users (either acting alone or as a group) and constantly denigrated for their contributions, intimidating them into silence. It might also manifest as a hostile state seeking to undermine the democratic processes of another by subverting public discourse to suit its disruptive ends.[115]

Causality, here, might manifest as act or omission. It may be that vigorous application of its content moderation policy leads to the harm complained of, as, for example, when posts are removed or membership revoked, temporarily or permanently,

[108] Balkin (2018) (n 60) 2045.

[109] See, again, discussion in Sander (n 66) 949: 'In practice, a platform's corporate philosophy is important, not only as a means to develop the platform's user base but also to satisfy the platform's founders and employees, who will typically want to ensure that the company's underlying mission and values are aligned with their own.'

[110] Theil (n 81) 657.

[111] ibid, 649.

[112] Ardia (n 64) 167 calls it 'shortsighted and naïve' to expect an 'informed and empowered electorate' to thrive without positive state engagement with this problem. See also Wu (n 75) 568–69 and CE Haupt, 'Regulating Speech Online: Free Speech Values in Constitutional Frames' (2021) 99 *Washington University Law Review* 751, 780.

[113] See, eg, C Calvert, 'First Amendment Battles over Anti-Deplatforming Statutes: Examining *Miami Herald Publishing Co v Tornillo's* Relevance for Today's Online Social Media Platform Cases' (2022) 97 *New York University Law Review Online* 1, 9; Abiri (n 64) 759: 'Banning @realdonaldtrump from Twitter following his incitement of the Capitol riot brought to the fore what has been clear for a while: digital platforms have significant control over our political and social communication.'

[114] See, eg, Wu (n 75) 570.

[115] See discussion of Russian interference in the 2016 US presidential election in Hamilton (n 66).

following breaches of community civility norms, etc. Alternatively, the failure to remove content or censor speakers can lead to problematic distortions in public discourse. America experienced something of this during the 2016 US presidential election campaign in which the stubborn falsehood circulated that Hillary Clinton was somehow involved in a paedophile ring operating from a Washington pizzeria.[116] Rebecca Hamilton highlights other similarly problematic instances in Myanmar, Sri Lank and South Sudan.[117]

Although the general tenor of these arguments is attractive, the liberal formula is not satisfied, it seems to me. Problematically, the notion of wrongdoing is not established. Instead, there is but two equally balanced autonomous wills in perfect tension – the will to speak using someone else's property against their wishes and the will to use one's property to deny that will to speak. Without something more, there is nothing here, it seems to me, that should tip the balance in the frustrated speaker's favour. To see this clearly, we must examine again the distinction between horizontal and vertical relationships through the lens of autonomy. By doing so, we see that denial of the will alone, by the digital speech provider, is not sufficient to count as wrongdoing in the liberal formula. This is perhaps the most distinctive difference between horizontal and vertical actors. For, in a vertical context, as between state and citizen, the mere fact of denial (of the will) without justification is sufficient to establish that wrongdoing has taken place. Thus, more simply, we should say that if the citizen can demonstrate that her act satisfies our understanding of an authentic free speech claim, and if the state seeks to penalise or otherwise interfere with that act, then the 'wrongdoing' criterion is satisfied unless the state can demonstrate that the interference is justified.

In this way, we see the inherent limitations within the idea of constitutional 'duty' as it relates to the state. We cannot meaningfully say that the state has a 'choice' over whether to honour the obligation to uphold the free speech claim or not. It must do so unless it can demonstrate some superior obligation. Hence, we can say that the state has responsibilities to all citizens, in which it must mediate between competing autonomy claims, but has no autonomy itself. Consider, for example, Balkin's claim:

> In democracy-based theories, one has to show that a nation's Internet regulation harms self-government within that nation-state. In a theory of cultural democracy, by contrast, one need only show that Internet regulation harms the global exchange of information, art, opinion, and ideas.[118]

Balkin's position here is sufficiently ambiguous to illustrate the point. If Balkin means only 'the state', then he is right to say we need only consider denial of the will to demonstrate the interference (by the duty-holder) with the free speech right. However, if he means to also include the digital speech provider (which his 'new-school' regulatory model captures), then he is wrong to say that, for example, arbitrary exclusion of an end-user by a digital speech provider is, of itself, a sufficient 'wrong' to underpin a rights

[116] G Aisch, J Huang and C Kang, 'Dissecting the #Pizzagate Conspiracy Theories' *New York Times* (10 December 2016).
[117] Hamilton (n 66) 159–61.
[118] Balkin (2016) (n 60) 1093–94.

claim by that user against the provider. For although it may be said that both the state and the provider have 'choices' over, for example, resource allocations, etc, in pursuance of their responsibilities (eg, the state to the people and the corporate entity to its shareholders), only the provider possesses the Millian sense of autonomy in which decision-making can be irrationality or else need not correspond to the rationality standard.

This is precisely because the digital speech provider is not in the same position as the state. Denial of the will does not of itself demand a justification *unless* the 'wronged' party can satisfy the harm principle. It is in the nature of autonomy, manifesting as a realm of autonomous beings, that the autonomous claims of one will be met by the autonomous response of the other. The question of whether that response amounts to wrongdoing must be more complex than mere denial alone. The digital speech provider has choices available to it, as a rights-holder itself (specifically, a property rights-holder), that the state does not. So, in a horizontal setting it must be that wrongdoing is an amalgam of a legitimate autonomous act that is met by an illegitimate autonomous response. In searching for a satisfactory sense of 'illegitimate', we must find something more than denial because, ostensibly, denial of a request to exercise the will is a choice available to an autonomous being (but not available to the duty-holding state).

In this sense, it seems to me, Theil is wrong to complain that 'arbitrary private power' is, of itself, problematic. Here, Theil gives arbitrariness its intuitive meaning as 'decision-making based on random choice or personal whim, rather than any reason or system'.[119] He goes on to say that 'arbitrary private power is suspect under a liberal commitment to free expression chiefly due to commitments to free and open debate within a pluralistic society'.[120] As we have seen in previous chapters, arbitrariness is a permissible (and consistent) quality within our notions of autonomy. From voting preferences to lifestyle choices, those with autonomy are not acting inconsistently with that principle when their decisions are erratic, irrational or unsystematic. Accordingly, it cannot be that the fact of arbitrariness itself is the problem. It must be that there is something in the *relationship* between the digital speech provider and end-user that renders arbitrariness problematic. Of course, if arbitrariness manifested in contractual terms – as, for example, trying to enforce contractual terms that did not exist or else constantly changing the nature of its services in breach of those terms, then we could say, with great ease, that this arbitrariness *was* problematic juridically speaking. In contrast, arbitrariness, in conformity with contractual terms, is *not* problematic.

Commentators might say that this additional quality is present in the fact of denial of the will that causes harm. For example, we might (mis)interpret Theil to be saying that, in his tripartite requirements for platform wrongdoing, the wrong is a compound act in which the provider's actions harm social participation (individually, as per Post, or collectively, as per Habermas) in terms that are arbitrary, serious and causally

[119] Theil (n 81) 666 (internal quotation marks removed).

[120] ibid. There is, of course, an additional problem with Theil's statement. The 'commitment' he refers to, here, is the state's: as the only free speech rights duty-holder, it is *only* the state that can be said to be committed to protecting free and open debate. For Theil to elide this commitment with the provider's contractual duties, then, is misleading. The provider's only commitments are those contained within its contract with end-users unless, that is, we can mobilise the harm principle to adduce additional ones.

connected. Thus, he is not saying, presumably, that (for example) the *fact* of platform exclusion constitutes wrongdoing since such will be permissible, on his own analysis, if justifiable (non-arbitrary), trivial (non-serious), or else is marginal because the platform is insignificant (a non-dominant provider).

However, this claim must also fail to the extent it treats harm-causation as if that, in itself, is the wrong. (In other words, that harm-to-autonomy is wrongdoing sufficient to justify legal intervention.) Harm-to-autonomy is an everyday occurrence that the law not only abides, but is positively uninterested in. Unrequited love, the unfaithful lover, the non-renewal of a business contract, the disappointed job-seeker, the failed property purchaser, the unlucky competition entrant, the commuter stuck in traffic: these are all examples of unfulfilled autonomy that the law demonstrates no interest in. This uninterest reflects not merely the absence of positive law; there are sound normative reasons why the law ought not to involve itself in these matters.

We see these reasons in Mill's *On Liberty*, in his much-neglected Chapter V, in which he is at pains to point out that harm is a necessary but not sufficient reason to interfere with autonomous action: 'it must by no means be supposed, because damage, or probability of damage, to the interests of others, can alone justify the interference of society, that therefore it always *does* just such interference'[121] (emphasis added). There can be, he says, no problematic interference with liberty when 'an individual, in pursuing a legitimate object, necessarily and therefore legitimately causes pain or loss to others, or intercepts a good which they had a reasonable hope of obtaining'. This he describes, in general terms, as simply healthy competition, which society has no interest in interfering with – legally or morally – unless some malpractice is at work (which he terms 'fraud or treachery, and force').[122] Thus, it seems to me, the overarching principle, derivable from Mill, is that wrongdoing must reflect a denial of autonomy that is not, of itself, a permissible act of autonomy by another. Thus, there must be both a denial of autonomy achieved through some improper act.

Neither is this standard met by saying that digital speech regulation is improper because it deprives others (individuals or society) of some public or socially valuable good inherent intrinsically (Post) or instrumentally (Habermas) in the suppressed contribution. This proposition might be inferred from, say, Wu, who, as we have seen, refers to digital speech as the 'primary public channels of speech' of such social significance that the government, he argues, is under a 'duty to protect listeners and speakers … and promote an environment conducive to public debate'.[123] Likewise, Balkin champions 'the global public good of cultural exchange through the Internet',[124] which is imperilled, in part, by 'new-school' regulation, such as censorship and exclusion. Although Theil's chief concern, like Balkin's, is with arbitrary or excessive applications of power by what Theil calls 'structurally dominant' digital speech providers, we see something of this broader concern in his observation that 'even if a private actor is not structurally dominant, something is nonetheless lost when speech expressing dissenting views is removed from a platform'.[125]

[121] Mill (n 59) 292.
[122] ibid.
[123] Wu (n 75) 571–72.
[124] Balkin (2018) (n 60) 1093–94.
[125] Theil (n 81) 666.

As a general proposition, our Lockean traditions prevent us from saying that the exercise of property rights to deny a socially valuable good is an act of wrongdoing ostensibly justifying state intervention. The entire edifice is in danger of collapse if, say, prosecutions for theft or conversion are at risk should the defendant claim to put the property to better use than its owner could. Similarly, a licence to use property in a predetermined fashion does not become more advantageous for the licensee depending upon the social good of that broader intended usage. This principle is deeply ingrained in our common law traditions, finding its greatest expression in the US Fifth Amendment. It is also vividly illustrated by the House of Lords decision in *Burmah Oil Ltd v Lord Advocate*,[126] in which the state sought to evade compensation for the wilful destruction of private property (an oil field) by a retreating army so as to prevent it falling into enemy hands. Whilst satisfied that the destruction amounted to a prerogative power in the circumstances, the Court could not agree that the Crown was entitled to avoid payment for that destruction. Speaking for the majority, Lord Pearce held that: 'A claim to take whatever it [the Crown] needs from the subject without payment in the general emergency of war is too wide to be supported by any doctrine of mere necessity alone.'[127] Instead, it seemed to him, 'justice requires that the sacrifice of one person's property for the common good be compensated by the rest'.[128]

However, allied to these concerns about the suppression of socially valuable speech (measured intrinsically or instrumentally) is the greater disquiet that the relative paucity of successful digital speech providers imbues those few with a power that, of itself, is tantamount to wrongdoing if not properly managed (by the state or some independent regulatory body). For Theil, this is especially troubling since 'private power … can impose heavy costs on individuals in a manner not dissimilar to authoritarian states'.[129] Moreover, he says, in relation to digital speech, 'private actors can hold a significant level of power: they set the terms and conditions of use unilaterally, alter them at will and enforce them however they see fit without any meaningful independent oversight'.[130] Similarly, as we have seen, Balkin admonishes practices of censorship and exclusion without any judicial oversight or other forms of due process.[131]

For both authors, it is arbitrariness that is most troubling. Here we see, most explicitly, the application of a public law concept – ultra vires – taken from the vertical relationship and inserted into the horizontal domain. Although both Theil and Balkin spend time explaining why they find arbitrary private power so abhorrent, still there is a sense that we are meant to accept the fact of arbitrariness as wrongful in a horizontal setting. This is more problematic than both authors (or, indeed, the wider literature) acknowledge. For all the reasons that Fuller gives us, King Rex cannot apply power arbitrarily,[132] but the same is not true, as a general proposition, as regards, say, the

[126] *Burmah Oil Ltd v Lord Advocate* [1965] AC 75.
[127] ibid, 145.
[128] ibid.
[129] Theil (n 81) 662.
[130] ibid, 662–63.
[131] Balkin (2018) (n 60) 2017–18.
[132] LL Fuller, *The Morality of Law*, rev edn (Yale University Press, 1963) 33–41.

shopkeeper. The shopkeeper can act arbitrarily in all manner of ways that the law would find unproblematic. She can, if she wants, constantly change her opening times. She can close early on a Tuesday one week and on Thursday the next. She can stock only goods that are blue in colour or resonant with positive energy. She can sell nothing but candles one week and nothing but tuna paste the next. She can refuse service to people born on a Wednesday or anyone over six foot tall. Whereas the positive law may place restrictions on her arbitrariness, especially as it relates to discrimination amongst protected characteristics and in respect of her hiring practices, these are not determined by the fact of arbitrariness alone.

Alternatively, we can understand, certainly, Theil's concerns about 'structural dominance' in terms of that central tenet in competition law that abhors monopolies and the absence of competition in the market. This concern is most pronounced in Nikolas Guggenberger's work in which he describes the 'dysfunction of the digital public sphere' as 'a market power problem'.[133] This leads him to say, for example, that 'concentrated private control is incompatible with democratic conceptualizations of public discourse',[134] especially as it relates to pluralism. To achieve this, he says, there must be 'decentralized gateways to the digital public sphere instead of monopolistic bottlenecks, and a variety of communicative spaces instead of algorithmic monocultures'.[135] We find the same point in Balkin: '[W]hen people expect and even demand that a multinational corporation like Facebook ban hate speech, it is important to have many Facebooks, not a single one'.[136]

This narrative raises important points that deserve our attention. Taking each in turn, and considering them through the wider lens of the commentary, we might start by asking what anti-competitive practices this success has created. Orthodoxy has it that we should call for state intervention when a chronic market failure arises.[137] The classic example, of course, is that should one entity (or only very few) dominate the market, then prices will rise exorbitantly as that firm (or firms) exploits its market share through heavy profit gains over marginal cost. Similar issues arise where the underlying commodity is scarce or the producer takes advantage of an unexpectedly cheap source of supply to obtain windfall profits. Alternatively, there may be externalities (such as environmental pollution) or information inadequacies (concerning hazardous products, such as drugs or other chemicals) that cause material harm to individuals and society at large. However, these classic reasons for interference are either not present in the digital speech context or else are, but do not relate to the free speech dilemma. For example, information inadequacies about the true cost of accessing 'free' digital speech services are reflected by and managed through, in Europe, strict data protection laws. This relationship is managed, in the UK, through the Information Commissioner's Office, which has the power to fine abuses of data usage.

[133] Guggenberger (n 64) 121.
[134] ibid, 145.
[135] ibid, 157.
[136] Balkin (2018) (n 60) 2035.
[137] See, eg, discussion in AI Ogus, *Regulation* (Oxford University Press, 1994) ch 1; R Baldwin, M Cave and M Lodge, *Understanding Regulation*, 2nd edn (Oxford University Press, 2012) ch 1.

Accordingly, whereas competition law might be valuable in restricting or otherwise diluting concentrated power in relation to services, it is not clear why it should prise the market open to allow for greater free speech rights to be realised. The fact of inequal bargaining power between provider and end-user is not enough to establish that. We should have to identify some sense of abuse or misuse (which, according to Mill, manifests as fraud, treachery and force) to satisfy this point. The general tenor of the literature suggests that this misuse/abuse manifests as the externality of 'pollution' – that the public sphere is corrupted by nefarious foreign or domestic interference with democratic participation, given to us in stubborn instances of mis- or disinformation. This claim, of course, prompts discussion about the source of interference which, if it is due to third parties, would suggest 'wrongdoing' means a failure to prevent or otherwise take action to address the problem. Eventually, this necessitates discussion of causation, along the lines discussed in chapter six concerning epistemology, for if third parties are corrupting public decision-making, such that voters cannot distinguish truth from falsehood when encountering corrupted digital speech, then the ultimate question to ask is two-fold: first, whether voter misperception (or gullibility) is not, of itself, an exercise in or manifestation of autonomy; and, secondly, whether interferences with such speech can be made without compromising autonomy.

Consider, for example, a practice on X (formerly Twitter) known as community notes, in which an unknown body of users comment on the veracity of factual claims. This may well be useful in correcting public misperception. Yet, as with the initial misperception that it hopes to address, its corrective effect relies upon either the same suspension of critical facilities that the original post does or else a deference toward the (presumably) superior knowledge possessed by this third party. In other words, if the argument is, as it seems to be, that end-users lack the time, education or resources to test propositions for themselves, then they must rely upon the judgement of others, be those motivated by malevolence or not. This, of course, is a risky strategy (and must be so, for it assumes infallibility in others) but commentators, as we saw in chapter six, seek to minimise or otherwise eliminate that by the moral strategy of displacing risk for blame. Thus, the person who trusts someone else to their disadvantage, seeks to convert their gullibility-based shame into a sort of righteous indignation that their trust was abused. As a matter of sociology, the practice is fascinating, but as a matter of law-based morality, the proposition is fraught. The idea that a person can be tricked into adopting a false political belief, for example, runs contrary to the fundamental tenets of, certainly, the US position, and quite possibly the European jurisprudence also, given the scepticism both traditions demonstrate toward regulation of political speech.

Similarly, I am not convinced we can elevate the seriousness of the provider's actions (or inactions) by, for example, demonstrating that it profits from befoulment of the public sphere and that this, of itself, represents an ill-gotten gain constituting 'wrongdoing'. Surveying the literature, we find that this sense of 'befoulment' takes two critical forms. On the one hand, the criticism addresses, as we have seen, the corruption of public discourse through mis- and disinformation. On the other, it could be understood, through the US lens, as the fear that either provider-driven or state-mandated enforcement of liberal norms compromises the content neutrality principle by which the state must hold itself. We see this, for example, in Balkin's 'new-school' regulatory model whereby 'governments attempt to coax, cajole, or coerce private-infrastructure owners to do their bidding'.[138] Thus, he criticises the German Netzwerkdurchsetzungsgesetz (known as NetzDG) for imposing an obligation upon global actors to remove hate speech within twenty-four hours of complaint.[139] This, he says, not only 'deputizes' private actors as state bureaucratic functionaries,[140] but also, most problematically for American citizens, represents 'a race to the bottom' by weakening their free speech rights online (as compared to offline, domestically).[141]

Alternatively, we see in Theil, Mill's idea of the tyrannous majority (discussed in chapter eight) used in conjunction with inequalities of power so as to adopt a position by which we might attack both hard left- and hard right-wing reactions that would silence dissent according to the tenets of those political norms. Specifically, he says:

> To put it mildly, there are powerful inequalities in modern societies that ultimately determine whose harmful speech is the subject of private sanctions and whose is tacitly tolerated, perhaps even celebrated as a 'natural reaction' to speech acts that the majority dislikes.[142]

Certainly, this would seem to take us closer to the notion of wrongdoing through its incorporation of force and censorship. Moreover, as we know, popular reactions – sometimes overreactions – to disliked speech can result in real-life consequences, such as loss of employment, income and social status, etc. (Although we are interested here only in whether the provider's sanction amounts to wrongdoing).

The distinction between Mill's ethical and juridical treatment of the 'tyrannous majority were discussed in chapter eight. For ease of reference, let us briefly revisit them again here. Since the state is beholden to the will of the people, there needs to be a bulwark against unfettered legislative demands by the people to control social mores since this would constitute tyranny, in a real sense, only one-step removed from the tyrant in office. For Mill, this bulwark resides in the inalienability of individuality, as we have seen. Hence, even the people (as ultimate power-holders) cannot compel the state to limit the autonomy of the noumenal being, except as the harm principle allows. However, Mill's arguments, as we have also seen, have an ethical dimension. Since society executes its 'own mandate' through its various social etiquettes and ethical codes of conduct, there should be, says Mill, protection against that form of 'social tyranny' which may be felt 'more formidable than many kinds of political oppression' for although not 'upheld by such extreme penalties, it leaves fewer means of escape, penetrating much more deeply into the details of life, and enslaving the soul itself'.[143] Hence we are given that famous quote, which Theil relies upon,[144] that:

> Protection … against the tyranny of the magistrate is not enough: there needs protection also against the tyranny of the prevailing opinion and feeling; against the tendency of society

[138] Balkin (2018) (n 60) 2019.
[139] ibid, 2012–13.
[140] ibid, 2029.
[141] ibid, 2031.
[142] Theil (n 81) 657.
[143] Mill (n 59) 219–20.
[144] Theil (n 81) 654.

> to impose, by other means than civil penalties, its own ideas and practices as rules of conduct on those who dissent from them.[145]

Yet Mill is also misunderstood on this point for he is not saying that the 'one very simple principle', upon which his argument rests, juridically constrains the ethical proclivities of polite society, as it does the state. He is not arguing for a sort of positive obligation upon the state to restrict society alongside its (the state) own negative obligation not to interfere with individuality. Instead, he is, through his simple proposition, presenting a normative position that captures both law *and* ethics. Thus, he is saying that an individual's absolute sovereignty over self-regarding action should be immune to both state interference (legally) and the 'moral coercion of public opinion' (ethically).[146] The principle constrains power, as exercised by the state over the people, but it also provides the ethical basis by which to resist commands by this demanding section of society when it expects conformity. These are both right and good reasons to tolerate individuality (or eccentricity) which speak to its (purported) social and individual benefits. Accordingly, *On Liberty* provides sound ethical arguments by which to deny the moral supremacy of society's sense of entitlement to denigrate individuality. Hostility toward non-conformity with moral and social norms may be an ethical wrong (or it may not); but it is nothing more than that.

V. Conclusion

The digital speech context provides some of the most explicit social agenda-setting activity in the entire free speech literature. In this way, free speech becomes the platform by which activists argue for a better society in which pluralism is taken seriously and the ideal of responsible voting realised. In this way, campaigners push the free speech agenda as if this were the principal or, perhaps, only barrier left to the democratic utopia. This campaign is aided, I think, by the capacity to cloak what is otherwise overt social engineering under the guise of dispassionate law reform. Of course, there is nothing sinister about this agenda – activists are entitled to believe that society would improve if voters took their responsibilities seriously and that we might move one step closer to the ultimate democratic utopia if they did. The problem is the inherent conflict with autonomy that this move must surely represent. Perhaps we would move a step closer to social utopia if voter responsibility were formalised, through interferences with the property rights of digital speech providers. Or perhaps we would move one step further away. For if the state can interfere with the property rights of digital entrepreneurs in the name of societal betterment, such that rights to autonomy are no barrier, what else can they do?

The resistance to this move to co-opt private actors into the democratic process paradigm centres on compatibility with autonomy. The principle must be seen as the bulwark against which all else rests. In a society underwritten by the rule of individuality

[145] Mill (n 590) 220.
[146] ibid, 223.

over community, there can be no legitimacy in laws that purport to forsake the commitment to autonomy when it suits the projects of others. As chapter five made clear, the rule of individuality is not utopian. It is a problem. Individuality conflicts with the ideal of a society in serious and pronounced ways. Nevertheless, if society is to be built in freedom's name, then these problems must be overcome by respecting individuality, not by discarding it. It is for this reason that Mill and Kant were so insistent upon undue harm as the only legitimate basis upon which society can proceed. But this step is not the pursuit of communal goals in disregard of conflicting individual projects. It is, instead, the resolution of multitudinous, complex conflicts between competing autonomy-based claims, in which the state delivers on its promise to give freedom to all so long as the pursuit of that freedom does not undermine the freedom of another.

As this chapter has shown, digital speech providers, as private actors, do not owe free speech duties to the populace at large. Likewise, digital speech users do not owe free speech duties to each other. Only the state has that (vertical) obligation, but only when it is directly interfering with free speech rights. When it adjudicates on free speech claims, it switches from vertical to horizontal mode, in which its duty is to realise freedom for all. It must then apply the harm principle to determine which autonomy-based claim is more pressing. It is possible for digital speech providers to breach the harm principle when its contract with end-users is not fulfilled. Yet the outcome of such a breach is *not* the outcome that activists seek. Juridical recognition of this unlawfulness will *not* lead to the kingdom of pluralistic ends that they seek. It will not create a paradigm of responsible voting. Accordingly, it seems to me, the campaign for greater free speech rights online is doomed to failure. There is nothing to be found in this space, except what the philanthropy of entrepreneurialism will allow.

10

Public Interest Speech

I. Introduction

Like its synonym 'political', the term 'public interest' holds an unfortunate position in the lexicon. On the one hand, as we shall see, it plays a pivotal role in determining the legal protections afforded to reputation and privacy, both nationally, especially in England and Wales, and supranationally, in the Strasbourg jurisprudence. The Court of Appeal has previously described the presence (or absence) of public interest speech as the 'decisive factor' in determining misuse of private information claims.[1] The Supreme Court, meanwhile, has said that if public interest speech is present then Article 10(2), European Convention on Human Rights, 'scarcely leaves any room for restrictions on freedom of expression'.[2]

On the other hand, as chapter seven demonstrated, the term is well known amongst commentators for both its inherent subjectivity and imprecision. Whereas there are clearly some topics or categories of speech that it can exclude, there is much that it cannot. By way of brief reminder, let us consider again the key strands of the argument. Central to those is the view, expressed by Kent Greenawalt, that: 'politics is not hermetically sealed off from other human concerns. Speech that is not explicitly political often has political implications'.[3] Or, as Michael Perry has it: 'every moral vision is ultimately and irreducibly a political vision'.[4] Therefore: 'It is simply confused to try to effect a separation between moral vision and political vision, between moral sensibilities and political sensibilities. To express a moral vision is inevitably to express a political vision'.[5] It is therefore no wonder that Edwin Baker should concede: 'once the insight that the personal is the political is fully accepted, the category of politically relevant speech could be virtually unlimited'.[6]

It is deeply unfortunate, then, that the categorisation of speech as being 'of public interest' should be so pivotal to our legal understanding of free speech rights given that we can neither define it with precision nor, in the final analysis, make it conform to the cardinal rule of content neutrality. For, ultimately, what the judiciary want to say is

[1] *ETK v News Group Newspapers Ltd* [2011] EWCA Civ 439, [23].
[2] *In Re Guardian* [2010] UKSC 1, [51].
[3] K Greenawalt, *Speech, Crime & The Uses of Language* (Oxford University Press, 1989) 45.
[4] Michael J Perry, 'Freedom of Expression: An Essay on Theory and Doctrine' (1984) 78 *Northwestern University Law Review* 1137, 1149.
[5] ibid.
[6] CE Baker, *Human Liberty and Freedom of Speech* (Oxford University Press, 1989) 26.

that public interest speech, or political speech, is *important* speech. Yet, they cannot do so without offending the rule that it is not for the state to determine what is or is not important for its citizens to know. Accordingly, we see the judiciary performing this strange dance in which judges constantly circle around the word 'important' without ever actually saying it, but quite obviously meaning it. In Strasbourg, this ritual manifests cumbersomely, such as:

> The Court has also emphasised on numerous occasions that, although the public has a right to be informed, and this is an essential right in a democratic society which, in certain special circumstances, can even extend to aspects of the private life of public figures, articles aimed solely at satisfying the curiosity of a particular readership regarding the details of a person's private life, however well-known that person might be, cannot be deemed to contribute to any debate of general interest to society … The Court reiterates in this connection that the public interest cannot be reduced to the public's thirst for information about the private life of others, or to the reader's wish for sensationalism or even voyeurism.[7]

In England and Wales, it has produced a jurisprudence known for both its generous and sceptical readings of the term, such that privacy-invading expression revealing the fact of an extra-marital affair, say, is sometimes said to be in the public interest and sometimes not despite the existence of broadly comparable fact-patterns.[8]

In this chapter, I propose a method of overcoming this problem – between profound judicial commitment to protect public interest speech and the conceptual imprecision of its definition. We can make progress with this problem, it seems to me, only if we accept that the solution is not to be found in further and better particulars of the definition but in the circumstances in which the definition is given privileged status in law. Greenawalt, Perry and Baker must be right in saying that both 'political' and 'public interest' speech captures all matters of moral concern. If we make further distinctions on what counts as 'important', 'valuable' or 'serious' speech in this context, we shall only sink further into the mire of subjectivity. What we can do, though, is reconcile the prospective, targeted criticisms of moral action by specific persons with the concept of individual autonomy discussed in chapter eight.

To aid this division, let us distinguish public interest as a description and public interest as a designation by means of the familiar Kantian dichotomy that separates the ethical from the juridical. Whereas the ethical description conveys the sense of moral or social concern that the issues speak to, the juridical designation confers special status upon that speech for the purposes of determining legal proceedings. This allows us to assert a distinction between the two, specifically that the fact of fitting the ethical description does not, of itself, warrant the legal designation. This will then allow us to postulate a difference between the two that transcends the definitional fit alone.

This distinction, I shall argue, ought to depend upon conformity with the autonomy argument set out in chapter eight. In the following I shall develop the essential idea that public interest speech can be vertically or horizontally aligned. Vertically aligned speech speaks to the state–citizen pact (also discussed in chapter eight) because it represents

[7] *Couderc v France* [2016] EMLR 19, [100]–[101].

[8] See discussion in P Wragg, 'Protecting private information of public interest: Campbell's great promise, unfulfilled' (2015) 7 *Journal of Media Law* 225; 'The benefits of privacy-invading expression' (2013) 64 *Northern Ireland Legal Quarterly* 187.

the retained interest in power carried over from each individual's delegation of power to the centre. Horizontally aligned speech bears no such alignment. Although it too may manifest as an interest in power, it is private power, and not that which is derived from the vertical arrangement. Ultimately, I shall say that vertically aligned public interest speech is an authentic free speech claim whilst horizontally aligned speech is an inauthentic free speech claim. This is so despite both forms matching the ethical description 'of public interest'. As chapter eight made clear, the right-duty construct of the vertical plane cannot be made to apply sideways.

As will be seen, and as chapter eight also made clear, horizontality has a distinct meaning. It does not mean that citizens (eg, the press) cannot discuss other citizens (eg, privately powerful 'public' figures). It does mean that the fit with the vertical axis must be demonstrated when citizens criticise each other in ways that cause harm to their rights and interests (eg, reputation and/or private life).

The distinctiveness and value of the horizontal/vertical apparatus will be illustrated through the positive law. Specifically, in section II, I shall use the procedural law of California regarding strategic lawsuits against public participation (SLAPPs). In section III, I shall examine the substantive law of England and Wales regarding defamation and the misuse of private information tort (which is broadly similar to the publication of embarrassing facts tort in the US).

My purpose in section II is simply to illustrate the conceptual distinction between vertical and horizontal speech as it manifests in this practical setting. As we shall see, the Californian jurisprudence provides persuasive (and unpersuasive) reasons to afford public interest speech (in the ethical descriptive sense) with special legal status despite its demonstrable harm to individual autonomy. This discussion is especially useful in demonstrating how private (horizontal) actors may be the subject of vertical speech, properly understood.

In section III, I pursue three interrelated arguments. First, following on from the previous discussion concerning SLAPPs, I question the coherence of describing all civil law disputes involving speech as a priori free speech matters. Instead, I argue that, certainly, the traditional defences to defamation can be understood as 'neutralisations' of the underlying complaint, without any reference to a special free speech guarantee. Secondly, I argue that the legal designation 'of public interest' should be reserved for vertically aligned speech. Only this should be recognised as an authentic free speech claim in these disputes. Finally, I differentiate the authentic from inauthentic public interest claim by isolating examples in the case law where criticisms of a person's morality has been given the legal designation. I argue that these cases are wrongly decided due to the absence of any discernible vertical alignment. In these cases, the judiciary has been seduced by the fit with the ethical description 'of public interest' without consideration of why this ethical fit should be given legal effect.

II. Procedure

The anti-SLAPP motion is a procedural feature of many North American states/provinces. These motions provide for expedited dismissal of meritless (or, in Ontario and British Columbia, insufficiently meritorious) proceedings targeting an act of public participation. Common to all jurisdictions, it seems, is the notion that the underlying proceedings amount to an abuse of the judicial process: that the instigator is concerned only with retaliation rather than the pursuit of personal vindication. Beyond that, precise description is tricky since different states and provinces have different legal tests/mechanisms by which to determine the specifics, thereby subtly affecting what each state/province understands a SLAPP to be. This picture is further complicated by international efforts to secure anti-SLAPP protections in Europe and the UK, in which, again, variations of the term are in operation. The anti-SLAPP motion originated in the US in the early 1990s following an influential article written by Penelope Canan and George Pring,[9] but quickly crossed the Northern border. The UK Government and Council of Europe have independently committed themselves to creating anti-SLAPP law, but only very recently.[10]

The success of the anti-SLAPP procedural tool depends entirely upon clear identification of the underlying mischief that it seeks to eradicate. This is mired in controversy because, when we read across the law and policy of these four jurisdictions, we see profound confusion over the meaning of 'public participation', such that we can easily speak at cross-purposes unless our precise meaning of the term is unpicked and specified. For example, we can say, with only some exaggeration, that the American thinks of it in terms of large land developers suing neighbourhood associations that object to its plans,[11] the Canadian in terms of consumer complaints and/or environmental activism,[12] whilst the British and Europeans have in mind detriments upon serious investigative journalism, but of different sorts – Europe is committed to eradicating organised crime syndicates and/or oppressive political regimes that would silence critics of corruption and manipulation through serious threats of violence and/or acts of assassination,[13] while the British are troubled, it seems, by the oddly specific fear that Russian oligarchs are bringing frivolous libel suits.[14]

In a sense, such definitional divergence is to be expected. The underlying terminology (ie, the two composite notions of 'strategic lawsuits' and 'public participation') is suitably open-textured that regional differences are inevitable. Indeed, we might say such variation is immaterial, in that we can make the term fit whatever anti-social behaviour we wish to eliminate. Nevertheless, the distinction between jurisdictions is

[9] P Canan and GW Pring, 'Strategic Lawsuits Against Public Participation', (1988) 35 *Social Problems* 506.

[10] For example, through the Economic Crime and Corporate Transparency Act 2023. See, further, P Coe, 'Strategic Lawsuits Against Public Participation (SLAPPs) and the Economic Crime and Corporate Transparency Act 2023' (2024) 29 *Communications Law* 1.

[11] eg, 'The paradigm SLAPP is a suit filed by a large land developer against environmental activists or a neighborhood association intended to chill the defendants' continued political or legal opposition to the developers' plans'. *Wilcox v Superior Court*, 27 Cal App 4th 809, 815 (Cal Ct App 1994); *Hupp v Freedom Communications*, 221 Cal App 4th 398, 402 (Cal Ct App 2013).

[12] eg, S Lott, R Warburton and B Land-Murphy, 'Corporate Retaliation Against Consumers: The Status of Strategic Lawsuits Against Public Participation (SLAPPs) in Canada' (Public Interest Advocacy Centre, 2004) 7: 'SLAPPs are lawsuits or the threat of a lawsuit, directed against consumers or individual citizens when they publicly criticize products or services or advocate for change. The lawsuit usually takes the form of an action for defamation … [The] evidence suggests that SLAPPs are very much a Canadian phenomenon and have been initiated against consumers for public criticism of products or services as well as against individuals for advocating on environmental issues.'

[13] www.coe.int/en/web/commissioner/-/time-to-take-action-against-slapps.

[14] consult.justice.gov.uk/digital-communications/strategic-lawsuits-against-public-participation/results/slapps-call-evidence-response.pdf.

important in the sense that if jurisdictions without a history of anti-SLAPP motions are to incorporate them, then the rationale for doing so must be (re-)established, especially if the meaning and nature of SLAPPs is to be modified (or otherwise assumed). In other words, we cannot borrow the term and accompanying procedural tools if we are modifying the terminology and rationale, consciously or subconsciously, in the process.

This point is significant given that all four jurisdictions consider public interest journalism to form part of the protected behaviour designated 'public participation'. As I have indicated, for the European and British, this *is* the paradigm. Yet, for the American and Canadian, it is included but at a distance from the core rationale for legislative change. However, this distance is not readily apparent when reading the underlying law. In Ontario[15] and British Columbia,[16] for example, the question of whether proceedings arise from public interest expression is *the* legal test to determine if an anti-SLAPP motion is appropriate, whereas, in California, public interest expression is only one of the categories of protected behaviour.[17] (By way of brief comparison, the Protection of Public Participation Act 2008, of the Australian Capital Territory, expressly excludes defamation, at section 8(2)(a), as a cause of action by which an anti-SLAPP motion can be brought.) This distance becomes apparent when we engage with the source text from which we derive the term, and some key cases, as the following paragraphs will demonstrate. Before doing so, it is perhaps important to clarify that I shall not say that public interest journalism is *never* suitable for anti-SLAPP protection. Instead, all I want to do is tease out the difference between public interest journalism and the core rationale for anti-SLAPP laws that we find in these materials.

We see the beginnings of these issues in Canan and Pring's original explication of the term. In their groundbreaking 1988 article, the authors sought to draw greater attention to empirical research findings they had conducted (the study of 100 legal disputes), which suggested a pattern of vindicative, intimidatory and retaliatory behaviour against civic-minded activity. Specifically, they noticed that 'every year in the United States, hundreds, perhaps thousands, of civil lawsuits are filed that are aimed at preventing citizens from exercising their political rights or punishing those who have done so'.[18] They provided statistics, generalised descriptions of typical and specific legal actions, and called for reform. The underlying components, comprising the concept of SLAPP, are expressed in fairly loose terms.

It seems clear that Canan and Pring were arguing against a specific kind of litigiousness rather than classifying all litigation arising from public participation as abominable per se. Thus, it is tolerably clear that 'strategic' (the 'S') must stand for something other than its plain meaning as 'clever', 'prudent' or 'planned' given that surely all litigation, especially that following legal advice, would satisfy that description (as opposed to 'ill-advised', 'wasteful' or 'haphazard', which are probably better descriptors in many respects). Given the language used by Canan and Pring, a more suitable 'S-word'

[15] Courts of Justice Act 1990, s 137.1(3), as amended by the Protection of Public Participation Act 2015.
[16] Protection of Public Participation Act 2019, ss 4(1)(a)–(b).
[17] California Code Civil Procedure, s 425.16(e)(3)–(4).
[18] Canan and Pring (n 9) 506.

would have been 'Specious', or perhaps 'Spiteful'. Certainly, something of that order would match the descriptors they use such as 'political retaliation',[19] 'intimidation and retaliation'[20] and 'repression'.[21] In this sense, the abuse manifests in the specious nature of (actual or threatened) proceedings: 'They cannot legally sue persons for exercising their political right to petition and participation in the political process. Instead, they recast the offending political behavior as common torts and thereby mask the original nature of the dispute.'[22]

This distinction between specious/spiteful litigation and cases which fail (ultimately) on their merits is recognised in Californian law. It is worth citing the positive law's position on this at length, since it explains both the nature and the justification for the anti-SLAPP motion's existence:

> SLAPP suits are brought to obtain an economic advantage over the defendant, not to vindicate a legally cognizable right of the plaintiff … Indeed, one of the common characteristics of a SLAPP suit is its lack of merit …
>
> But lack of merit is not of concern to the plaintiff because the plaintiff does not expect to succeed in the lawsuit, only to tie up the defendant's resources for a sufficient length of time to accomplish plaintiff's underlying objective … As long as the defendant is forced to devote its time, energy and financial resources to combating the lawsuit its ability to combat the plaintiff in the political arena is substantially diminished …
>
> Thus, while SLAPP suits 'masquerade as ordinary lawsuits' the conceptual features which reveal them as SLAPPs are that they are generally meritless suits brought by large private interests to deter common citizens from exercising their political or legal rights or to punish them for doing so …
>
> Because winning is not a SLAPP plaintiff's primary motivation, defendants' traditional safeguards against meritless actions, (suits for malicious prosecution and abuse of process, requests for sanctions) are inadequate to counter SLAPPs. Instead, the SLAPPer considers any damage or sanction award which the SLAPPee might eventually recover as merely a cost of doing business …
>
> By the time a SLAPP victim can win a 'SLAPP-back' suit years later the SLAPP plaintiff will probably already have accomplished its underlying objective. Furthermore, retaliation against the SLAPPer may be counter-productive because it ties up the SLAPPee's resources even longer than defending the SLAPP suit itself …
>
> For these reasons, courts and legislatures have looked for procedural remedies which would allow prompt exposure and dismissal of SLAPP suits.[23]

In this sense, the specious/spiteful nature of the lawsuit is a clear stimulus for legislative action.[24]

[19] ibid, 506.
[20] ibid.
[21] ibid, 507.
[22] ibid, 511.
[23] *Wilcox v Superior Court* (n 11) 816–7, affirmed in *Wilbanks v Wolk* 121 Cal App 4th 883, 890–91 (Cal Ct App 2004).
[24] See further, *Filmon.Com v DoubleVerify, Inc* 13 Cal App 5th 707, 714 (Cal Ct App 2017) which describes SLAPPs as 'nonmeritorious litigation meant to chill the valid exercise of the constitutional rights of freedom of speech and petition in connection with a public issue'.

Nevertheless, there is an important ambiguity in Canan and Pring's work. In describing the outcomes of the 100 cases they examined, they noted that:

> [C]learcut legal victors – those without concessions – for one party or the other occurred in slightly over half of the SLAPPs. At the first court appearance, targets won dismissals in about two thirds (68%) of the cases. *Final legal judgments favored targets in 83 percent of the finally disposed cases* … (emphasis added)[25]

This final sentence is revealing. If, as it suggests, 17 per cent of plaintiffs succeeded on the merits of their claim, then why should the litigation be classified as a SLAPP? If the underlying action has such merit that the instigator succeeds, then, surely, the case should be classified as a LAPP and not a SLAPP. Canan and Pring provide no additional justification to indicate why that 17 per cent should be thought problematic in societal terms, neither in this section nor in the methodology statement. It may be that the underlying behaviours were present (including that the claim was specious), but the jury (or judge) came to the 'wrong' decision and there was no prospect of appeal (or, perhaps, no further funds by which to appeal). I mention this only because it is significant to our picture of the mischief sought to be tackled by law if the 'S' component is typical but not mandatory. This possibility is one that we ought to have in mind as we progress through the discussion on the conversion of the ethical description into the legal designation. Specifically, the picture of the mischief changes from one that abuses the justice system because it is vexatious (specious/spiteful) to one in which the lawsuit has *some* merit but not enough to outweigh the greater public interest in frictionless public participation.[26] We shall return to this issue in section III when we consider the concept of balancing in public interest expression disputes.

Having sketched out something of the nature of the proceedings brought by the SLAPPs instigator (the 'Instigator') – ie, that it is a specious claim with menaces, as it were – I want to focus on the nature of public participation as Canan and Pring describe it. As will become apparent, this is significant because it provides the social or public policy justification by which we ought to treat SLAPPs differently from (and more severely than) vexatious litigation *per se*. Additionally, of course, it defines the distinction between a SLAPP and 'regular' vexatious litigation.[27] In this extended sense, the necessity or justification for legislative intervention (to tackle the problem) hinges both on its specious/spiteful nature *and* its disruption to frictionless public participation.

[25] Canan and Pring (n 9) 514.

[26] Interestingly, the Canadian legislation speaks more to this balancing approach. See, eg, in Ontario, Court of Justice Act 1990, s 137.1, as amended: '(4) A judge shall not dismiss a proceeding … if the responding party satisfies the judge that, (a) there are grounds to believe that, (i) the proceeding has substantial merit, and (ii) the moving party has no valid defence in the proceeding; and (b) the harm likely to be or have been suffered by the responding party as a result of the moving party's expression is sufficiently serious that the public interest in permitting the proceeding to continue outweighs the public interest in protecting that expression.' In British Columbia, the Protection of Public Participation Act 2019, s 4(2) uses substantially the same wording.

[27] This distinction is recognised in Californian law. The courts, there, are insistent that an anti-SLAPP motion is not 'a cheap substitute for summary judgment': *Commonwealth Energy v Investor Data Exchange*, 110 Cal App 4th 26, 32 (Cal Ct App 2003). See also *Lam v Ngo* 91 Cal App 4th 832, 851, fn 12 (Cal Ct App 2001).

A close reading of Canan and Pring's work demonstrates that it is the vertical apparatus of state bureaucracy that organises their thoughts on the meaning of the phrase 'public participation'. Specifically, it is the attempted transmogrification of a vertical reporting of a public law violation into a horizontal private law dispute that underpins the SLAPP concept. We see this idea throughout. They describe a typical SLAPP in this way: 'one party approached some government body or office about a matter that affected some other party. This other party then filed a lawsuit against the first party'.[28] Likewise: 'Initially, aggrieved citizens speak out to some branch of government or the electorate on a public issue … In speaking out, they … make enemies. [T]hese enemies initiate private, legal actions or counterclaims.'[29] They say that Instigators 'recast the offending political behaviour as common torts and thereby mask the original nature of the dispute;'[30] that they 'unilaterally transform the dispute topics … and move the forum of the dispute from the city hall to the courtroom;'[31] that 'they seek to reprivatize and contain a political conflict made public by the citizens' grievance'.[32] Accordingly, Canan and Pring explicate the social cost of SLAPPs as a serious threat to the network of 'private attorneys general' upon which the operation and enforcement of public law depends.[33]

Accordingly, we might draw some preliminary conclusions about the distinction between the ethical description and juridical designation as it applies to SLAPPs. Specifically, drawing upon Canan and Pring's work alone, we can say that the anti-SLAPP motion ought not to succeed simply because we can categorise the targeted speech as of public interest. There must be additional factors at stake that provide the normative justification to treat the interference as sufficiently serious for the law's involvement. If we follow Canan and Pring's reasoning, we might understand that interference in Millian terms as an unwarranted disruption to the state–citizen pact by which the state will hear grievances brought by the citizen, especially where that grievance concerns a violation of law. In this sense, the civic-minded citizen conducts the participatory act by:

> [C]irculating petitions, writing letters to public officials, reporting violations or making complaints to government bodies, conducting elections, filing lawsuits, testifying at public hearings … This legal protection of citizens' political involvement extends to contact with all levels and branches of government, and it covers appeals to sway voters on public issues.[34]

The Instigator violates the process when she sues, or threatens to sue, that citizen, on account of her public participation, *and* the lawsuit is so specious/spiteful as to constitute a retaliatory act.

This conditionality – of a specious/spiteful claim – is mandatory if we are to recognise the Instigator's status as an autonomous being who is herself part of the state–citizen pact by which she too is entitled to petition the state to hear her grievances.

[28] Canan and Pring (n 9) 508.
[29] ibid.
[30] ibid, 511.
[31] ibid, 515.
[32] ibid.
[33] ibid, 516, albeit the term 'private attorneys general' is not theirs.
[34] ibid, 506.

Whereas we can say, I think, that no *undue* harm is done to her autonomy (for there is undoubtedly harm to her interests in an obvious sense when the residents association are successful in scuppering her property development plans), because she has no right (of the Hohfeldian sort) to do as she wants, the situation is trickier to justify if we are in the realm of balancing societal interests or goods. Yet, as indicated above, if there *is* a colourable claim of individual autonomy, present in the merits of the lawsuit, then the fact of a transference from the political to the legal system ought to be, if not quite an irrelevance, then certainly not an impediment[35] – that is, unless we are to engage in balancing (see below).

The distinction between ethical description and juridical designation is further illustrated by the positive law, specifically in the Californian approach to determining anti-SLAPP motions.[36] Briefly, if the putative defendant's speech was not made as part of official proceedings (legislative, executive or judicial), then the motion applicant (or movant) must show that the speech/petition is both of public interest *and* on a public issue.[37] This additional element is significant given that, as we would expect, the term 'public interest' has been interpreted generously by the judiciary 'to include not only governmental matters, but also private conduct that impacts a broad segment of society and/or that affects a community in a manner similar to that of a governmental entity'.[38] This includes 'activities that involve private persons and entities, especially when a large, powerful organization may impact the lives of many individuals'.[39]

To be on a public issue, the discussion must 'go beyond the parochial particulars of the given parties'[40] and this must be shown from 'the *specific nature of the speech* rather than the generalities that might be abstracted from it'.[41] In *Commonwealth Energy v Investor Data Exchange*, the Californian Court of Appeal found the law rejects 'what might be called the synecdoche theory of public issue in the anti-SLAPP statute. The part is not synonymous with the greater whole.'[42] In other words, there 'should be some degree of closeness between the challenged statements and the asserted public interest; the assertion of a broad and amorphous public interest is not sufficient'.[43]

[35] See, eg, *Gwire v Blumberg*, No A134931 (Cal Ct App, 1 April 2005). (An Anti-SLAPP motion failed in respect of B's claim that disparaging postings on consumer website constituted protected activity. The claims that G had committed 'horrific fraud' that 'irreparably damaged every aspect of [B's] life' were statements of fact not opinion that had to be tried.)

[36] The Californian case law provides a mature and sophisticated jurisprudence on anti-SLAPP motions given that the statute was adopted in 1992. See discussion in *Consumer Justice Center v Trimedica International, Inc* 107 Cal App 4th 595, 600 (Cal Ct App 2003).

[37] *Briggs v Eden Council for Hope Opportunity*, 19 Cal 4th 1106 (Cal 1999).

[38] *Damon v Ocean Hills Journalism Club*, 85 Cal App 4th 468, 479 (Cal Ct App 2000). See also, *Rivero v American Federation of State, County and Municipal Employees, AFL-CIO*, 105 Cal App 4th 913, 924 (Cal Ct App 2003).

[39] *Kurwa v Harrington, Foxx, Dubrow & Canter, LLP*, 146 Cal App 4th 841, 846 (Cal Ct App 2007).

[40] *Commonwealth Energy v Investor Data Exchange*, 110 Cal App 4th 26, 34 (Cal Ct App 2003).

[41] ibid, emphasis in original.

[42] ibid.

[43] *Weinberg v Feisel*, 110 Cal App 4th 1122, 1132 (Cal Ct App 2003); relied on in *Dyer v Childress* 147 Cal App 4th 1273, 1281 (Cal Ct App 2007); *World Financial Group, Inc v HBW Insurance & Financial Services, Inc*, 172 Cal App 4th 1561, 1570 (Cal Ct App 2009); and *DC v RR*, 182 Cal App 4th 1190, 1216 (Cal Ct App 2010).

This additional element acts as a corrective to the drift, from the core of settled meaning to the periphery, that we see in both Californian law and Canan and Pring's original elucidation by the inclusion of free speech *generally* as an aspect of protected public participation. It seems to me that the arguments for special procedural measures become less compelling once we venture away from clear, intuitive categories of civic duty, such as testifying in proceedings, writing to an elected official, or complaining to an official body about violations of law, toward more traditional forms of public protest such as petitions, demonstrations and boycotts.[44] Even so, these examples more readily align with the vertical axis to the extent that they represent the citizen–state pact in action. Most problematic of all is public interest journalism since, conceivably, this may have no bearing on, or relationship to, state action as such.

Indeed, this possibility is apparent in Californian law by which a public issue matter is demonstrated (assuming that the discussion is of public interest) when the subject of that discussion is 'a person or entity in the public eye … [who is] nationally-known [or subject to] extensive media coverage', or has engaged in 'conduct that could directly affect a large number of people beyond the direct participants', or else the subject matter concerns 'a topic of widespread, public interest'.[45] In this sense, the corrective by which mere ethical description is insufficient to demonstrate juridical designation is tempered (and, quite possibly, undone) by the sheer breadth with which these wider categories and understandings of public interest journalism might creep into the anti-SLAPP domain and so undermine, or otherwise dilute, the seriousness of the public participation activity prompting the legislature to act in its favour. Unlike, say, testimony given in open court, the legal merit (and social worth) of public interest journalism is more contested, and contestable, in terms of its inherent entitlement to this special protection, even if the underlying action is vexatious.

My point here is not to rubbish all public interest journalism as if it were socially worthless, nor is it to say that public interest journalism is not an authentic category of free speech per se. Instead, it is to signal that the vertical axis, in which the processes of state by which the citizen pleads for state intervention (as with petitions) or else contributes materially to the justice process (as with court testimony) is less obvious – and may not be obvious at all – if the underlying dispute concerns, say, a local, unsuccessful contestant on a national reality TV show being humiliated on live radio by a presenter who lied when claiming her ex-husband had said she was a 'big skank', as it did in *Seelig v Infinity Broadcasting Inc.*[46] Even if we accept that the slur was not actionable per se, it is not immediately apparent why the putative defendant should benefit from the heightened protections of an anti-SLAPP motion as opposed to the usual mechanism of summary judgment. This mystery remains even after reading the judgment, for the court seems more interested in victim-blaming than in explicating any genuine sense of communal interest in the specific speech. Thus the court seems to say that the Instigator had brought the unpleasantness upon herself by virtue of being a reality TV contestant: 'By having chosen to participate as a contestant in the Show,

[44] See Canan and Pring (n 9) 506.

[45] These three categories were established in *Rivero* (n 38) 924; affirmed in *Filmon.Com* (n 24) 545; see also, *Han v Kylin Pictures, Inc*, No B282947 (Cal Ct App, 27 November 2018).

[46] *Seelig v Infinity Broadcasting Corporation*, 97 Cal App 4th 798, 805–06 (Cal Ct App 2002).

plaintiff voluntarily subjected herself to inevitable scrutiny and potential ridicule by the public and the media.'[47] Here we see in action the general principle that although the term 'public interest' is more than 'mere curiosity', the interest need not be 'significant' of itself: 'it is enough that it is one in which the public takes an interest'.[48]

III. Substance

A. Structure

Moving away from procedure, let us now discuss the ethical description and legal designation distinction as a matter of substantive law, as it relates, or might relate, to actions in defamation or privacy. My focus here is on concrete examples from English and Welsh law, which demonstrates the distinction I seek to make between defences which 'neutralise' the underlying claim, by demonstrating that the underlying autonomy claim is of the Hohfeldian no-right variety, and those that do not. In the latter instance, the public interest juridical designation acts as a trump, which both disrupts the equilibrium between rights in rights-based systems – such as those under the European Convention on Human Rights and the International Covenant on Civil and Political Rights – and relies upon a sort of specious balancing exercise which, in the worst cases, signal no more than the moral proclivities of the judiciary or else imitates crude utilitarianism of the worst kind. English and Welsh law is interesting since this latter type of free speech protection is a departure from the common law tradition, it seems to me, coinciding with the greater impact of Strasbourg reasoning upon domestic decision-making.

As signalled above, I am interested in patterns of speech in which verticality and horizontality are both detectable. In the following discussion, horizontality arises, first, in the *response* to the speech. It is not the state that is prosecuting the citizen speaker. It is, instead, a private actor who sues, ostensibly for the harm caused to her rights/interests by the speaker. For ease, I shall call the speaker a journalist but on the understanding that this is for convenience rather than demarcation, for the speaker could be anyone. Secondly, I shall be ambiguous about the status of the claimant. I am content to call her a 'public figure' since the term is so anomalous and ubiquitous, in both the Anglo[49] -American[50] and European jurisprudence,[51] that mere celebrity is sufficient to count. She may hold public office or she may not. We shall explore the distinction in context. Finally, and most significantly, the speech claims to be of public interest, in both an ethical (description) and juridical (designation) sense, because it has a 'vertical' colour to it.

[47] ibid, 808.

[48] *Nygard, Inc v Uusi-Kerttula*, 159 Cal App 4th 1027, 1042 (Cal Ct App 2008).

[49] See, eg, *A v B plc* [2003] QB 195 (a professional footballer).

[50] See, eg, *Hustler Magazine, Inc v Falwell* 485 US 46 (1988) (a televangelist). *Time v Hill* 385 US 374 (1967) is more problematic in its outcome that those who find themselves the object of public curiosity – here, a family subjected to a horrifying ordeal – have limited (if any) rights to object to even inaccurate stories about them in the press because they are 'newsworthy' persons.

[51] See, eg, *Axel Springer AG v Germany* [2012] EMLR 15 (an actor).

My argument, which seeks to limit the applicability of the juridical designation in this sort of horizontal context, has three parts. First, it disputes the necessity of a special defence in this scenario. Although it is common for the law to be framed in the language of free speech rights, as a battle between those who (purport to) exercise their free speech and those who would deny that exercise, much of the common law tradition can be understood simply, in terms of autonomy, without the need for a grand theory of free speech to explain away positive outcomes for the defendant. Specifically, the common law defences lend themselves to an analysis in which the reputational damage claim is extinguished, or neutralised, on its own terms: that the putative defendant's autonomy actions have *not* negated the claimant's autonomy as alleged. Examined through this lens, we can say that these traditional defences are not instances of authentic free speech in action – the semblance of a trump to outweigh the claimant's legitimate claim – but instead represent an acknowledgement that the claimant's claim is ill-founded on its own terms. In this way, those defences can be understood not as free speech but as a neutralisation of the claimant's claim. This is so, I shall argue, even though the positive law itself describes at least some of these defences in terms of free speech.

Having cleared the ground in this way, I shall argue that authentic instances of free speech are reserved for what I shall define as vertical speech (ie, speech directed at the mechanics of the state) and I shall distinguish this from horizontal speech (ie, speech directed at (the morality of) private individuals) which, I shall argue, is a phony free speech claim. In the subsection B below, therefore, I shall explain and defend this idea of vertical speech. I shall argue that this type of speech is a corollary form of the neutralisation argument in which the claimant's presence in the debate is tangential to its main object. Specifically, this is speech which signals state failure in pursuit of justice. This is an attack on the system rather than the person albeit the person is clearly significant to that discussion. This strikes me as the only authentic instance of free speech claim in the horizontal setting because it speaks clearly to the citizen–state pact. It is deserving of the juridical designation on that basis. Clearly, this is a more limited form of, say, Blasi's uses of power dynamic.[52] I shall defend this narrower designation in subsection C by seeking to distinguish speech that critiques power from that which would usurp it. This discussion leads to the subsection D, in which I shall use the English experience of privacy law to demonstrate how the fit with mere ethical description alone leads to confused and confusing understanding of public interest as a juridical designation which would elevate matters of pure ethics into matters of constitutionally protected speech in ways that are deleterious of autonomy.

B. Neutralisation

In this subsection, I argue that the traditional common law defences to defamation – justification, fair comment, absolute or qualified privilege – can be understood to

[52] V Blasi, 'The Checking Value in First Amendment Theory' (1977) *American Bar Foundation Research Journal* 521.

signify that the ostensible strength of the claimant's claim (serious harm to reputation) is neutralised by a proper analysis of the speech's effect upon reputation. This specific element of the argument is intended to say that defamation law is not a matter of free speech protection in the horizontal setting per se. This is part of the larger argument, set out in this section, that although defamation law is understood to concern free speech rights, this interpretation is not a matter of necessity. We can translate the positive defamation law into the language of autonomy without damage to its essential meaning and without reference to any grand theory of free speech, at least as it relates to these traditional common law defences.

This is so even though the legal rules underpinning these traditional defences are themselves explicated in terms of free speech by the judiciary, as we shall see. I should be clear, then, that in this subsection I am concerned with what we might call mid-level principles. In other words, I am offering no grand theory of free speech (or reputation) at its highest level of abstraction (see part three of this book) and neither am I concerned by the lowest level of abstraction in which we identify legal rules and principles through close textual analysis of decisions themselves. I seek, instead, to bridge the gap between grand theory and legal principle through this intermediate concept of neutralisation. I should also be clear that I do not say that authentic free speech claims have *no* place in defamation law. I reserve subsections B and C the arguments that I take to be most (and least) compelling in this respect.

With these preliminaries dealt with, I shall briefly explore those traditional defences to show my meaning that the sting of the defamatory claim is neutralised on its own terms when they are established (or, to say the same thing using different words, that the ostensible claim of harm to reputation is illusory once these defences are established on the facts).

The idea of neutralisation relies upon a specific understanding of the interest at stake in defamation claims. For example, in traditional justification cases, the idea of (substantial) truth 'neutralising' the claimant's claim is more than contentious; it would be said to wrong. It has long been recognised that the revelation may be sufficiently distressing and/or embarrassing that 'reputation' in its most general sense is jeopardised, such that the claimant experiences real harm, even though the claim fails.[53] Although it is not a defamation case, we see something of this in *Scott v Scott*, which arose from a marriage annulment on grounds of the husband's inability to consummate it due to his impotence.[54] We see it more explicitly in the protections afforded to rehabilitated offenders in English law, by virtue of the Rehabilitation of Offenders Act 1974, and in Europe, under Article 8, the right to respect for private and family life, whereby it is recognised that, at a certain point, 'convicted persons have an interest in no longer being confronted with their acts, with a view to their reintegration in society'.[55]

[53] See, eg, discussion in R Parkes and G Busuttil (eds), *Gatley on Libel and Slander*, 13th edn (Sweet & Maxwell, 2022) [12-001].

[54] *Scott v Scott* [1913] AC 417.

[55] *Mediengruppe Österreich GmbH v Austria*, app no 37713/18 (April 2022), [49].

Nevertheless, we can say, with Eric Descheemaeker, that English law has both a long and defensible tradition of recognising the principle that *veritas non est defamatio*.[56] Descheemaeker frames his argument through the lens of Roman law which distinguished *fama* (good name, reputation, fame, renown) from *dignitas* (dignity, worth, status, standing). Whereas, he argues, truth cannot injure *fama* – because reputation 'is an ellipsis and must immediately be specified to mean *deserved* reputation … [ie] a reputation founded in character' and, hence, 'Defamation exists to protect a person against stains imparted by others on their reputation, not to protect a stained character'[57] – the same is not true of *dignitas*.[58] For Descheemaeker, then, if defamation protects reputation, it must be deserved. Hence, there can be no wrongfulness in disclosing the truth that reveals the *undeserved* character. The truth neutralises the claim.

Of course, on the facts of *Scott v Scott*, it is the issue of *dignitas*, not *fama*, that arises. Even so, it may be said that the purported 'invasion' of privacy, as it were (embarrassment, presumably, provided the impetus for Mr Scott's litigation), is neutralised by the necessity of disclosure to protect (to the extent that it *does* protect) the other party's *fama*: 'The right of this lady to tell the truth and to furnish the best evidence of the truth in defence of her own character and reputation is inalienable, and cannot lawfully be taken away by any judge.'[59] These facts must be publicly disclosable – at least to polite society – so as to explain the fact of the annulment.

Similarly, neutralisation manifests in the defence of fair comment, at least to the extent it projects the Millian ideal which would distinguish mere opinion from all else. We can consider the significance of opinion at two levels. In one sense, it may be that pure opinion alone is sufficiently trivial that the law does not engage – because the words could not cause a right-thinking person to think less of her.[60] Here, there is no causative element present that should link the words themselves to the ill that claimant claims to have suffered. If those hearing the words consequently change their view of the putative claimant, the cause of harm is their ignorance rather than the putative defendant's actions. It is for such reasons that the European Court of Human Rights (ECtHR) distinguishes between statements of fact and value judgments.[61]

However, some 'opinions', such as calling the claimant a paedophile, are sufficiently serious as to amount to statements of fact given the '*inherent* gravity' attached to the allegation.[62] Thus, at the second level, the opinion is given legal protection only where

[56] E Descheemaeker, 'Veritas non est defamation? Truth as a defence in the law of defamation' (2011) 31 *Legal Studies* 1. Alternatively, we can frame this discussion through the development of Ecclesiastical Law in the Middle Ages, by which *scandalum magnatum* became English libel law. I am grateful to Tom Bennett for this suggestion. See further JC Lassiter, 'Defamation of Peers: The Rise and Decline of the Action for Scandalum Magnatum 1497–1773' (1978) 22 *The American Journal of Legal History* 216; VV Veeder, 'The History and Theory of the Law of Defamation' (1903) 3 *Columbia Law Review* 546.

[57] ibid, 16.

[58] ibid, 15–19.

[59] *Scott v Scott* [1913] AC 417, 448.

[60] *Thornton v Telegraph* [2010] EWHC 1414 (QB).

[61] *Milosavljević v Serbia (No 2)* App no 47274/19, 21 September 2021, [62].

[62] *Blake v Fox* [2024] EWHC 146, [66] (emphasis in original).

it *is* an opinion *and* the basis of the opinion is clear to the reader.[63] Accordingly, we can say that these two facts (being opinion and identifiable as such) neutralise the claimant's claim – the speech is not the cause of harm given that the 'right-thinking' audience member can see it is *mere* opinion and not a factual allegation. The interpretation is strengthened by developments in English law whereby the need for that speech to relate to a matter of public interest[64] has been removed by the Defamation Act 2013, section 3 (not that the threshold was especially onerous in any event).[65]

We see this sort of neutralisation in the rationale for the absolute privilege immunity (which extends beyond defamation, of course).[66] As is familiar to English defamation lawyers, this defence provides immunity from civil suit for those giving evidence in judicial proceedings[67] at each step of the process, from reporting a crime[68] and/or co-operating with insolvency proceedings,[69] to preparing witness statements[70] and appearance in court itself.[71] This sort of neutralisation differs from that which we saw in the justification and fair comment context, given that it is less a recognition that the claimant suffers no harm and more recognition that the putative defendant, and society at large, would suffer greater harm if such lawsuits were allowed. As the House of Lords observed in *Arthur JS Hall & Co v Simons*, it is

> a feature of the trial … that in the public interest all those directly taking part are given civil immunity for their participation … This is not just privilege for the purposes of the law of defamation but is a true immunity.[72]

Neutralisation, in this sense, is afforded, and informed, by this public policy decision.

Nevertheless, as with SLAPPs, this rationale is directed toward abuses of the justice system. We see this clearly in the Supreme Court's remarks: 'the object of the immunity is not to protect those whose conduct is open to criticism, but those who would be subject to unjustified and vexatious claims by disgruntled litigants'.[73] Moreover, although, the prospect of 'hardship' toward the putative claimant exists,[74] it may be no more than marginal: if the testimony is wilfully false, the criminal law can still punish it through contempt and perjury.[75] Alternatively, if it is mistaken, then the judicial proceedings themselves exist to determine the point. In other words, given that this testimony forms part of a formal proceeding that exists to determine truth in the most clinical setting imaginable, the risk to the claimant's interests is protected as much as the law can. Accordingly, even though guided by public policy interests, the protections

[63] Nevertheless, the problem of identifying speech as opinion rather than fact remains a problematic question of juridical interpretation. See further TDC Bennett, 'Interpretation *is* opinion: realigning the fact/opinion distinction in English defamation law' (2023) 15 *Journal of Media Law* 62.

[64] See discussion in *Joseph v Spiller* [2010] UKSC 53.

[65] See, eg, *London Artists Ltd v Littler* [1969] 2 QB 375.

[66] *Dawkins v Lord Rokeby* (1873) LR 8 QB 255, 263.

[67] See, eg, *Taylor v Director of the Serious Fraud Office* [1999] 2 AC 177, 214.

[68] See, eg, *Westcott v Westcott* [2009] QC 407, [34]–[36]; *Decker v Hopcraft* [2015] EWHC 1170, [63]–[68].

[69] See, eg, *Al Jaber v Mitchell* [2021] EWCA Civ 1190, [101]–[111].

[70] See, eg, *Watson v McEwan* [1905] AC 480, 486.

[71] *The King v Skinner* [1772] 98 ER 529, 530.

[72] *Arthur JS Hall & Co v Simons* [2002] 1 AC 615, 740.

[73] *Jones v Kaney* [2011] UKSC 13, [15].

[74] *Watson v McEwan* (n 69) 487.

[75] *Jones v Kaney* (n 72) [82].

afforded by absolute privilege may still be understood in terms of neutralisation if, that is, we accept that the 'harm' caused to the putative claimant's interest (through falsehood) can be (or, even, should be) corrected by the underlying proceedings themselves, and failing that by the criminal law tools of perjury/contempt.

However, the presence of these clear public policy considerations complicates the picture. As they recognise, any harm to the claimant's interests is to be excused by the greater good in, say, the unfettered performance in civic duty. We see this plainly enough in the judicial approach to qualified privilege as it relates to, say, the provision of employment references. This defence does not admit easily, or at all, of the 'neutralisation' analysis unless, that is, we can say that the presence of malice, by which the defence is defeated,[76] is sufficient. In the classic formulation, this public policy is expressed thus:

> It was in the public interest that the rules of our law relating to privileged occasions and privileged communications were introduced, because it is in the public interest that persons should be allowed to speak freely on occasions when it is their duty to speak, and to tell all they know or believe, or on occasions when it is necessary to speak in the protection of some (self or) common interest.[77]

Alternatively, as it was put by the Court of Appeal in *Clift v Slough Borough Council*, 'The private interest in one's reputation is to be preferred to the public convenience of unfettered communication [only] where there is no duty to communicate at all.'[78]

Moreover, the rationale for both absolute and qualified privilege are often described in terms of free speech. For example, in *Royal Aquarium and Summer and Winter Garden Society Ltd v Parkinson*,[79] the Court of Appeal held that absolute privilege 'has been conceded on the grounds of public policy to insure [sic] freedom of speech where it is essential that freedom of speech should exist'[80] whilst, in *Huntley v Ward*, it was said of qualified privilege:

> [N]o matter how harsh, hasty, untrue, or libellous the publication would be but for the circumstances, the law declares it privileged because the amount of public inconvenience from the restriction of freedom of speech or writing would far outbalance that arising from the infliction of a private injury.[81]

Similarly, it has been said of actors in proceedings: 'It is essential to the ends of justice that persons in such positions should enjoy freedom of speech without fear of consequences, in discharging their public duties in the course of a judicial inquiry'.[82]

Nevertheless, it is not clear that the judiciary uses the term in its rarified sense, as a constitutional right. It seems to me to be something much more prosaic: an ability to speak freely so as to pursue a specified public policy goal, such as serve the ends of justice (as in absolute privilege) or speak honestly in pursuit of a sense of duty

[76] *Toogood v Spyring* (1834) 1 CM&R 181.
[77] *Gerhold v Baker* [1918] WN 368, 369.
[78] *Clift v Slough Borough Council* [2010] EWCA Civ 1484, [31].
[79] *Royal Aquarium and Summer and Winter Garden Society Ltd v Parkinson* [1892] 1 QB 431.
[80] ibid, 451.
[81] *Huntley v Ward* (1859) 6 CB(NS) 514, 517. See also *Horrocks v Lowe* [1975] AC 135, 146.
[82] *Williamson v Umphray* (1890) 17 R 905, 911.

(as in qualified privilege). This limited sense marks the freedom *to* speak, as a duty, as something significantly different to the freedom *of* speech on matters fitting the ethical description of public interest. We can see this distinction, sharply on the facts of *Bryanston Finance Ltd v De Vries*,[83] a Court of Appeal case concerning a threat to send materials alleging misconduct in company affairs to various parties unless the accused paid compensation. On the question of whether the threat could benefit from qualified privilege, Lord Diplock observed:

> Although in the instant case there was no plea of privilege in respect of the threatened publication of the words to any of the recipients named it is nevertheless worth while considering what the position would have been if there had been such a plea and it had failed; for, with respect, I do not think that this raises any question of freedom of speech.
>
> A plea of qualified privilege in respect of threatened future publication of defamatory statements may fail upon one or other of two grounds. The first is that the occasion of the threatened publication would not be privileged. If so, freedom of speech is not endangered by restraining the defendant from repeating what he admits he cannot prove to be true upon an occasion when he has no duty to perform or interest to protect by doing so.
>
> The second ground is that although the occasion of the threatened publication would be privileged the defendant in making it would be actuated by malice, which would generally involve that he did not honestly believe the words to be true. Freedom of speech is not endangered by restraining a defendant from repeating something that he does not believe is true.[84]

This limited sense of free speech, which resonates plainly in Lord Diplock's words, is not the robust right to speak about matters of public interest; it is confined, instead, to the strict parameters of the duty underpinning either the absolute privilege – speech by a specific person in a specific place (eg, judges, counsel, witness during proceedings) or on a specific occasion (eg, an employment reference). Likewise, the sense of public interest is coloured by the instrumentalism of the underlying public value – justice needs proceedings; job markets need references. This instrumentality also distinguishes the sense of a free speech right from this prosaic sense in obvious ways. Perhaps it is for reasons like this that the House of Lords should say, in *Rondel v Worsley*, that: 'It is said that immunity from suit is based on the importance of maintaining freedom of speech but that is not the way it is formulated in the cases.'[85]

Excepting Parliamentary privilege for a moment (which is, in any event, a statutory protection afforded by the Bill of Rights 1689), the sanitised nature of speech (in which the freedom is either governed by its context, such as the rules of court), or else by the nature of the occasion (in which employment references are exchanged in private between the person with the duty and the recipient with an interest), it would stretch credulity to suggest that the freedom to speak here is that authentic free speech right we have been discussing throughout this book. This is not freedom in any meaningful sense of that word. Its heavily prescribed nature renders it unsuitable to freedom of speech in its conceptual sense.

[83] *Bryanston Finance Ltd v De Vries* [1975] QB 703.
[84] ibid, 735.
[85] *Rondel v Worsley* [1969] 1 AC 191, 217.

C. Authentic Free Speech: Vertical Public Interest Matters

Not all defences can be explained through the concept of 'neutralisation'. Some are explicitly framed in free speech terms. However, since the House of Lords decision in *Reynolds v Times Newspapers Ltd*,[86] and the advent of the section 4 public interest defence under the Defamation Act 2013, it has been possible to say, as a matter of positive law, that the civil law provides genuine free speech protections in strictly horizontal contexts. Moreover, in a privacy context, the defence to the misuse of private information tort, introduced in 2004,[87] has been framed in terms of protecting public interest speech.

These protections for free speech are defensible, normatively, through the language of authentic free speech principle only to the extent that the citizen–state pact is engaged, as set out in chapter eight. As that chapter anticipates, this conditionality is not satisfied merely by the ethically descriptive presence of some 'political' or 'public interest' dimension. Instead, it necessitates the existence of vertical apparatus by which the legitimate interests of the citizenry are present in monitoring that transference of power, from its dispersed source to the concentrated target of state machinery. Accordingly, although this definition is far from unequivocal, we see it at work clearly enough in the protections afforded to members of Parliament, by which they conduct the business of the House, and which protects them, in that place, from criminal or civil liability for their words. It is for similar reasons that the common law offences of sedition and seditious libel were (eventually) abolished in the UK.[88] Clearly, the idea of criminal or civil liability for bringing hatred or contempt upon the state is anathema to the overarching concept of the state's power being a temporary investiture that is given by the people themselves.

This idea is further expressed by the House of Lords, in the highly irregular case of *R (Rusbridger) v Attorney General*,[89] in which the editor of *The Guardian* had sought declaratory relief that he (and his journalists) would not be prosecuted under the Treason Felony Act 1848, section 3, for publishing a series of articles advocating republicanism. This fear – which their Lordships rightly dismissed as utterly fanciful – emanated from a strict reading of the provision, which suggested that even advocacy for the realisation of republicanism by peaceful and democratic means would be an offence (and punishable by life imprisonment). Although the action was dismissed, not least for wasting the court's time on a trivial matter,[90] the House used it as an opportunity to reiterate its commitment to free speech, eg:

> Freedom of political speech is a core value of our legal system. Without it the rule of law cannot be maintained. Whatever may have been the position before the Human Rights Act 1998 came into operation, it is difficult to think of any rational argument justifying the criminalisation of the conduct of citizens who wish to argue for a different form of government.[91]

[86] *Reynolds v Times Newspapers Ltd* [2001] 2 AC 127.
[87] *Campbell v MGN Ltd* [2004] UKHL 22.
[88] Coroners and Justice Act 2009, s 73.
[89] *R (Rusbridger) v Attorney General* [2003] UKHL 38.
[90] ibid, [28], per Lord Steyn.
[91] ibid, [7].

And:

> [T]he freedom of the press to express views and opinions on political and constitutional matters is a fundamental and central element in the life of a democratic society and is enshrined in Article 10 of the European Convention for the Protection of Human Rights and Fundamental Freedoms.[92]

They described section 3 as 'an historic anomaly in our political democracy'[93] and 'a relic of a bygone age [which] does not fit into the fabric of our modern legal system'.[94] Nevertheless, they thought it laughable[95] that a prosecution could be initiated in the circumstances: 'It is plain as a pikestaff to the respondents and everyone else that no one who advocates the peaceful abolition of the monarchy and its replacement by a republican form of government is at any risk of prosecution'.[96] This, they said, was because:

> [Y]ou do not have to be a very good lawyer to know that to advocate the abolition of the monarchy and its replacement by a republic by peaceful and constitutional means will lead neither to prosecution nor to conviction. All you need to be is a lawyer with common sense.[97]

This 'common sense' corresponds to the logic of the citizen–state pact. If centralised power emanates from its original dispersed form, then it must be for citizens to decide how that power is realised, according to peaceful and lawful means. Advocacy for republicanism aligns perfectly to the vertical orientation of the pact.

This is all very abstract. The distinction between verticality and horizontality is given greater specificity if we isolate the object of speech, and so separate issues from people as topics of communication. Clearly, a debate about republicanism – or any other critique of state governance – involves people but in the impersonal sense of office-holder rather than the *ad hominem*. The abolition of monarchy affects actual people – the present King and his family – but the reasons for that speak to the impersonal in terms of the problems or dangers inherent in *any* person holding that position. Whereas the foibles of a specific person might illustrate those issues, still the debate is not reliant upon that attack for its effect. The discussion, premised as it is on the structural dynamics of power, is an unassailable manifestation of authentic free speech because it speaks to the citizen–state pact in such obvious terms.

The rules surrounding the capacity to sue in private law give further effect to this principle. For example, as discussed in chapter nine, the clear rule in *New York Times v Sullivan*,[98] which is partially reflected in UK law by *Derbyshire County Council v Times Newspapers Ltd*,[99] upholds the rationale that the state should be prevented from suing

[92] ibid, [30], per Lord Hutton.
[93] ibid, [24].
[94] ibid, [39].
[95] ibid, [40]: 'no Attorney General or Director of Public Prosecutions would or could authorize a prosecution for such advocacy without becoming a laughing stock'.
[96] ibid.
[97] ibid, [43].
[98] *New York Times v Sullivan* 376 US 254 (1964).
[99] *Derbyshire County Council v Times Newspapers Ltd* [1993] AC 534.

its critics in defamation law. This is made explicit in *New York Times v Sullivan*,[100] in which the court endorsed the finding that to award damages for harsh criticism of official performance would be to uphold 'the obsolete doctrine that the governed must not criticize their governors'.[101] Although the decision is best remembered for its declaration of 'a profound national commitment to the principle that debate on public issues should be uninhibited, robust, and wide-open', it is the remainder of that sentence that deserves emphasis: 'and that it may well include vehement, caustic, and sometimes unpleasantly sharp attacks on government and public officials'.[102] For it is that 'sharp attack' upon officialdom that best illustrates the verticality with which this subsection is most concerned. It is this immunity from suit by public officials against critics of their official conduct that represents the vertical public interest speech paradigm in action.

Here, then, we see most clearly the context in which horizontality and verticality meet, for although it is the individual – the public official – who brings the action in private (rather than public) law (ie, the horizontal dispute), the presence of an authentic free speech right manifests in the nature of that dispute when, and only when, it is the (alleged) reputational damage that is said to be caused by the attack on her performance as a public official that constitutes the substance of the dispute. It is the presence of this subject matter which explains the outcome in *Reynolds v Times Newspapers Ltd*[103] (concerning, amid the resignation of the Irish Taoiseach, a serious allegation that he had deliberately and dishonestly misled the Dáil), in which the House of Lords expressed the importance of protection for the 'ample flow of information to the public concerning, and by vigorous public discussion of, matters of public interest to the community'.[104] Expanding on the point, it was said:

> By that we mean matters relating to the public life of the community and those who take part in it, including within the expression 'public life' activities such as the conduct of government and political life, elections … and public administration …[105]

We find the same rationale in the Strasbourg jurisprudence:

> The limits of acceptable criticism are accordingly wider as regards a politician as such than as regards a private individual. Unlike the latter, the former inevitably and knowingly lays himself open to close scrutiny of his every word and deed by both journalists and the public at large, and he must consequently display a greater degree of tolerance. No doubt Article 10(2) enables the reputation of others – that is to say, of all individuals – to be protected, and this protection extends to politicians too, even when they are not acting in their private capacity; but in such cases the requirements of such protection have to be weighed in relation to the interests of open discussion of political issues.[106]

Hence, we see here not only the importance of broad protection for the discussion of performance in office but also recognition of a division between the private

[100] n 97, 265.
[101] ibid, 272, citing *Sweeney v. Patterson* 76 US App DC 23, 24; 128 F.2d 457, 458 (1942).
[102] ibid, 270.
[103] *Reynolds v Times Newspapers Ltd* [2001] 2 AC 127.
[104] ibid, 176.
[105] ibid.
[106] *Lingens v Austria* (1986) 8 EHRR 407, [42].

and public life of that official. This was made explicit in the subsequent decision of *Von Hannover v Germany:*

> The Court considers that a fundamental distinction needs to be made between reporting facts – even controversial ones – capable of contributing to a debate in a democratic society relating to politicians in the exercise of their functions, for example, and reporting details of the private life of an individual who, moreover, as in this case, does not exercise official functions.
>
> While in the former case the press exercises its vital role of 'watchdog' in a democracy by contributing to 'impart[ing] information and ideas on matters of public interest' it does not do so in the latter case.[107]

This strict division between 'official functions' and all else provides even greater clarity on the meaning of public interest speech as a vertically orientated concern.

We also see this distinction in *Reynolds v Times Newspapers Ltd*, for although public interest speech is defined in terms 'more widely than' simply 'the conduct of government and political life, elections … and public administration' to include '(for instance) the governance of public bodies, institutions and companies which give rise to a public interest in their disclosure', it 'exclud[es] matters which are personal and private'.[108] This gives us an imprecise but discernible distinction between the public official, as a state functionary, and the private person, as a fallible being. If we could but separate the command or categorical imperative aspects of the public role from the moral choices of the autonomous being in her private life, we should have a clear demarcation between the vertical and horizontal by which to distinguish authentic from inauthentic instances of free speech manifesting as public interest expression.

These distinctions between criticism of performance in office and discussions of personal and private matters offer a meaningful method of defining the core of authentic free speech claims on public interest matters, from that which is outside, despite its apparent fit with the ethical description 'public interest matter'. Accordingly, we can move beyond the inefficiencies of an approach that treats the ethical description as the sum of the legal designation so as to make real distinctions between the two. Thus, we can say that the vertically orientated discussion on a public interest matter is the critical lens by which to separate ethical description from legal designation. Only that which satisfies this test ought to be treated as a valid defence in a private law dispute. Hence, criticisms of performance in public office meet that test because such speech fits the citizen–state pact neatly.

Nevertheless, we cannot say that *only* such criticisms should count. Although the core of meaning is to be found in the public office performance example, there is a penumbra of meaning that would still fit without collapsing into the ethical description. We can identify this penumbra with some precision, I think, if we make some preliminary divisions in types of speech. Retaining the sense that horizontal (private law) disputes relate to criticisms of the person rather than the impersonal (such as institutions or contexts), we can further distinguish allegations of criminality from accusations

[107] *Von Hannover v Germany* (2005) 40 EHRR 1, [63].

[108] n 102.

of immorality. At this point, we should also acknowledge the concept of the private (as in non-public) figure who holds no public office or state function.

With these further distinctions in mind, we can say that accusations of immorality might be germane to the citizen–state pact when they speak to fitness for public office. Hence, it could be said that in *AAA v Associated Newspapers Ltd*,[109] the paternity of a child was of public interest since the unnamed father was said to be a notorious politician known for 'extreme recklessness' in his personal affairs. Accordingly, the Court could endorse the journalistic view that 'It was important to show there had been recklessness, not merely philandering, adultery and betrayal of his wife by the politician. Recklessness is of importance when dealing with the character of a public figure and his fitness for office.'[110] Yet, as in *Von Hannover*, discussions of private life immaterial to public office fall outside this concept.

We shall return to the subject of immorality as a public interest matter in subsection D below. Here, I am interested in exploring further the idea of criminality amongst non-public figures as an object of authentic free speech claim. It seems to me that such discussions are authentic when the person/personal is discussed consistent with monitoring the use of state power. Accordingly, reports on the fact of criminality and progress in the administration of justice speak clearly to the state–citizen pact. We should have no difficulty in locating these reports in the core of the legal designation 'of public interest'. This is especially so when the justice process has failed, leaving the press to perform a valuable function in publicising the role of incompetence and/or corruption in that failure.

This scenario can be contrasted with that in which the speech seeks not to monitor power but to usurp it. Here, the press performs an illegitimate function by inveigling its way into the administration of justice in circumstances that imperil justice by hampering the investigation, jeopardising the fairness of the trial, or otherwise pre-empting the outcome of the process. To my mind, the usurpation of power invalidates the underlying public interest claim. In other words, it cannot be in the public interest for the press (or anyone) to usurp power from the proper authorities. Such usurpation represents an inauthentic free speech claim even though the subject matter may correspond to the ethical description 'of public interest'.

The distinction between authentic free speech claims, in which power is closely monitored, and inauthentic free speech claims, in which power is usurped, is familiar to us given the provisions within the Contempt of Court Act 1981. Hence, we understand that speech 'which creates a substantial risk that the course of justice in [active] proceedings … will be seriously impeded or prejudiced' is unlawful, regardless of intent.[111] Meanwhile, 'a fair and accurate report of legal proceedings held in public, published contemporaneously and in good faith' is protected by the Act enshrining, as it does, the principle of open justice.[112] Moreover, although public interest discussions on the subject matter of the trial are capable of protection under section 5 of the Act, they will escape liability only when that discussion can be said to be 'no more than

[109] *AAA v Associated Newspapers Ltd* [2012] EWHC 2103 (QB).
[110] ibid, [81]; see also [118]–[119].
[111] Contempt of Court Act 1981, ss 2(2)–(3).
[112] ibid, s 4.

an incidental consequence of expounding its main theme'[113] – a test that has proven extremely difficult to satisfy.[114]

The juxtaposition between monitoring and usurping has arisen most vividly in privacy contexts, in which litigants have sought to suppress their involvement in police enquiries. Given the risk that such involvement arouses public suspicion of guilt – that there is 'no smoke without fire'[115] – the courts have found that the fact of pre-charge arrest generates a reasonable expectation of privacy.[116] The question then becomes whether a public interest in publication exists that would trump the privacy claim.

Often, the courts have found against the defendant on this point. In the Supreme Court decision in *ZXC v Bloomberg LP*, this outcome was to be expected: the media outlet had obtained a confidential letter disclosing a law enforcement body's interest in the claimant in an active criminal investigation. There was no public interest in disclosing this interest – it was not as if the outlet was reporting, say, corruption, incompetence or improper political pressure tainting the effectiveness of the investigation.[117] In any event, there was a countervailing public interest in preserving the confidentiality of the letter which the defendant had obtained. Accordingly, any public interest in publication would have had to be weighed against the corresponding 'general public interest in the observance of the duties of confidence and a specific public interest in maintaining the confidence of the letter of request so as not to prejudice the criminal investigation'.[118]

The distinction between monitoring and usurping is given further effect in the judicial view that involvement with a police (or any official) investigation is private unless and until a person is charged. In *Sicri v Associated Newspapers Ltd*,[119] the High Court expressed the rationale in terms that resonate with the problem of usurpation:

> Although an arrest also involves the exercise of state power, it is an executive act of a provisional nature … Where the arrest is public, that could weaken or even destroy any reasonable expectation of privacy; but it would not supply or support a public interest or free speech argument of the kind advanced by the defendant.[120]

We see this concern in similar decisions,[121] including in *Richard v BBC*,[122] where the High Court derided the 'breathless sensationalism'[123] with which the BBC reported upon a police raid of Sir Cliff Richard's home amidst reports he was under investigation for non-recent sexual abuse of a minor. The Court found that this coverage, which involved a live feed from outside his home, including via helicopter, occurring over an intense 48-hour period, caused serious harm to Sir Cliff's private life, and

[113] *Attorney General v English* [1983] 1 AC 116, 143.
[114] See, eg, *Attorney General v Random House Group Ltd* [2009] EWHC 1727, [88]–[95].
[115] See, eg, *ZXC v Bloomberg LP* [2022] UKSC 5, [109]–[110]; *CWD v Nevitt* [2020] EWHC 1289, [68]–[69].
[116] *ZXC v Bloomberg* (ibid) [146].
[117] ibid, [28]–[32].
[118] ibid, [154].
[119] *Sicri v Associated Newspapers Ltd* [2020] EWHC 3541.
[120] ibid, 104.
[121] See, eg, *Hannon v News Group Newspapers Ltd* [2014] EWHC 1580, [99]–[101]; *ERY v Associated Newspapers Ltd* [2016] EWHC 2760, [71].
[122] *Richard v BBC* [2018] EWHC 1837.
[123] ibid, [300].

was unwarranted. Whereas the Court accepted that there is a general, genuine public interest in knowing that the police are investigating allegations of sexual abuse of children – whether conducted by those who abused their celebrity status to gain access to children, such as Jimmy Savile, or not.[124] Nevertheless, this did not justify naming the individual since this would be of interest only to 'gossip-mongers'.[125] Accordingly, there was no public interest to justify the invasion of privacy.

Richard v BBC is an interesting case by which to test the distinction between monitoring and usurping. Clearly, there is a problem of proportionality, as evidenced by the concerns about 'breathless sensationalism'. Moreover, the coverage itself occurred only because South Yorkshire Police had disclosed the information to the BBC in circumstances amounting to a breach of its own obligations to treat the investigation as private (there were no operational reasons why public disclosure was necessary). Nevertheless, regardless of its heavy-handedness, that coverage did at least demonstrate the integrity of the police operation to the extent that the public could see that the claimant's celebrity status garnered no special treatment. This, it seems to me, is a public interest consideration that the Court ought to have considered. Whereas this is unlikely to have changed the result, it would have given a greater sense of the legitimacy that the coverage provided. Recognition of such would have made it harder for the Court to find for the claimant since, as discussed below, the presence of a conceivable public interest (of the ethical descriptive kind) is usually sufficient to defeat the claim. This would have been unjust to the claimant given that, as the Court recognised, the intensity of the coverage conveyed the clear impression that he was guilty of the alleged crime, although the raid provided no such evidence and Richard was later cleared of wrongdoing.[126]

The way that the monitoring/usurping distinction is recognised in law – and to the extent that it *is* recognised – is intriguing. In an early case on the privacy rights of suspects, the High Court said:

> At times in his submissions, [Counsel for the Claimant] argued that the right people to investigate any criminal allegations were the police rather than the newspaper. Such a submission was difficult to square with the repeated recognition in decisions of the Strasbourg and domestic courts that the press has a valuable role as a public watchdog. Of course, the police have a vital role in the investigation of crime, but that is not their monopoly.[127]

Although the sentiment must be correct – that the press serves a valuable function by monitoring police investigations – the final sentence is troubling to the extent it implies that the press is entitled to conduct its own parallel investigations. The problematic element resides in the idea that the press has rights to, say, compel testimony or gather physical evidence, not least because the police present this evidence to the court so that it can make determinations, rather than to the public with pre-judgments on what the proper outcome should be. The obvious difficulties that such behaviours imply are

[124] ibid, [279]–[280].
[125] ibid, [281].
[126] ibid, [302], [345] and [352]. See further discussion in TDC Bennett and P Wragg, 'Was Richard v BBC correctly decided?' (2018) 23 *Communications Law* 151.
[127] *ERY v Associated Newspapers Ltd* (n 120) [71iv].

compounded by a further significant difference between the police and press as investigators. Whereas the police are regulated by various bodies, such as the Independent Office for Police Conduct, the press is not. Thus, mistakes made by the police in an investigation are capable of remedy, not least through judicial review in the final analysis, and funded by the public purse through legal aid. The same is not true of the press. Whereas, in principle, false allegations can be remedied through the law of defamation (and, as we have seen, through the misuse of private information tort), such actions must be privately funded.

Moreover, of course, there is a shortfall in the requisite evidential threshold. Whilst allegations of criminality must be beyond reasonable doubt to succeed in the criminal court, they need only be substantially true in the civil court, on the balance of probabilities, meaning that reputation may be tarnished irrecoverably by negative press in circumstances where the claimant has not committed the alleged crime in actuality.

D. Inauthentic Free Speech: Horizontal Public Interest Matters

The press understands the term 'public interest' to mean something broader than that discussed in the previous subsection. Specifically, power monitoring is treated as if it means surveillance of the rich and famous so that their moral choices may be evaluated against socially acceptable norms of the good life. When Mr Justice Eady in the High Court ruled that the [now defunct] *News of the World* had grossly invaded the private life of FIA Chair, Max Mosley, awarding him record damages,[128] Paul Dacre (then editor-in-chief of the *Daily Mail*) railed against the decision for its denial of the press's 'age-old freedom to expose the moral shortcomings of those in high places'.[129] Sounding distinctly like a Victorian moralist trapped in a world beyond his comprehension, he continued:

> Two years ago, [the High Court] ruled that a cuckolded husband couldn't sell his story to the press about another married man – a wealthy sporting celebrity – who had seduced his wife. The judge was worried about the effect of the revelations on the celebrity's wife. In an unashamed reversal of centuries of moral and social thinking, he placed the rights of the adulterer above society's age-old belief that adultery should be condemned.

Of the facts in *Mosley*, he decried the 'unimaginable sexual depravity' involved:

> Now most people would consider such activities to be perverted, depraved, the very abrogation of civilised behaviour of which the law is supposed to be the safeguard. Not Eady. To him such behaviour was merely 'unconventional'. Nor, in his mind, was there anything wrong in a man of such wealth using his money to exploit women in this way. But what is most worrying about Eady's decisions is that he is ruling that – when it comes to morality – the law in Britain is now in effect neutral, which is why I accuse him, in his judgments, of being 'amoral' …[130]

[128] *Mosley v News Group Newspapers Ltd* [2008] EWHC 1777.
[129] P Dacre, 'The threat to our press' *The Guardian* (10 November 2008).
[130] ibid.

Concluding, he noted: '[S]ome revile a moralising media. Others, such as myself, believe it is the duty of the media to take an ethical stand.'[131] Here, then, we have the sort of self-entitled mandate to expose moral non-conformity with a view, presumably, to its elimination. It is exactly the sort of moral intolerance that Mill argued against in *On Liberty*. As is apparent on its face, it champions the elevation of the ethical description – of public interest – to the status of legal designation.

Although Dacre's view is extreme, he is not alone. We find this same sense of public interest in the case law. In *A v B plc*,[132] an early decision in the post-Human Rights Act 1998 era, we see the Court of Appeal speak of the public interest in such broad terms that holding a role model accountable for their moral faults fits easily within:

> A public figure … must expect and accept that his actions will be more closely scrutinised by the media … The public figure may hold a position where higher standards of conduct can be rightly expected by the public. [She] may be a role model whose conduct could well be emulated by others … [T]he public have an understandable and so a legitimate interest in being told the information.[133]

This case concerned a married Premiership footballer who sought an injunction to prevent publication of his extra-marital affairs. The court dismissed his application by using this role model principle against him:

> [I]t is not self-evident that how a well known premiership football player, who has a position of responsibility within his club, chooses to spend his time off the football field does not have a modicum of public interest. Footballers are role models for young people and undesirable behaviour on their part can set an unfortunate example.[134]

This pattern of reasoning has found favour in subsequent decisions.

As in *A v B plc*, two of these subsequent cases concerned high-profile footballing figures. In *Ferdinand v Mirror Group Newspapers Ltd*,[135] it was applied to justify publishing news of an extra-marital affair concerning the then England captain, Rio Ferdinand, who had claimed, in a recent biography, to be a reformed character who did not cheat on his wife. The Court held that the claimant's role model status was a 'further factor in the public interest case'.[136] Specifically, it found that 'the Claimant voluntarily assumed the role of England captain. It was a job that carried with it an expectation of high standards.'[137] As such, the press was entitled to publicise, and criticise, the claimant's adultery because it 'call[ed] into question the Claimant's fitness to be the role model which was expected of an England captain'.[138] In the subsequent case of *McClaren v News Group Newspapers Ltd*,[139] which bore strong factual similarities to *Ferdinand*, the Court was equally impressed by the defendant's claim that its freedom of speech extended to criticisms of moral standards in professional sport.

[131] ibid.
[132] *A v B plc* (n 49).
[133] ibid, [11(xii)].
[134] ibid, [43(vi)].
[135] *Ferdinand v Mirror Group Newspapers Ltd* [2011] EWHC 2454.
[136] ibid, [87].
[137] ibid, [89].
[138] ibid, [91].
[139] *McClaren v News Group Newspapers Ltd* [2012] EWHC 2466.

Thus, the newspaper's discovery that the claimant, a former England FC manager, had been having an extra-marital affair spoke clearly to that agenda and, therefore, fit comfortably within the notion of press freedom.[140]

In two other cases, the reasoning was applied to businessmen rather than footballers. The first of these, *Hutcheson v News Group Newspapers Ltd*,[141] was set against the backdrop of a public dispute between celebrity chef Gordon Ramsay and his father-in-law, Christopher Hutcheson. Hutcheson had been chief executive of Ramsey's various businesses, but had been recently dismissed for alleged financial irregularities. Using the press as his mouthpiece, Hutcheson had levelled several accusations at Ramsay, including the estrangement of Hutcheson's daughter from her mother and father, of failing to appreciate Hutcheson's moral support when Ramsay had been accused of infidelity, and of being blamed unfairly for the company's poor financial performance in recent times. *The Sun* newspaper learnt that the real reason for Hutcheson's dismissal had allegedly been the diversion of company funds by Hutcheson to support a secret second family that had produced two children, about which his wife and four children had only recently learned (Ramsay and his wife having learnt of them a matter of weeks before). Hutcheson sought to prevent publication of this information. The High Court and Court of Appeal refused to issue the injunction on the grounds that there was no reasonable expectation of privacy in this information (for reasons that need not concern us) and that, even if there had been, it was in the public interest to publish it. The information needed to be published, it found, to avoid the 'very real risk of a distorted and partial picture being presented to the public of this dispute'.[142] There was, it said, a 'strong claim to freedom of expression in the public interest'[143] in *The Sun* 'being free to publish the fact of Mr. Hutcheson's second family to authenticate the allegation of diversion of corporate funds for private purposes'.[144]

The second case involves Fred Goodwin, known to the public for his role in leading the Royal Bank of Scotland, as its CEO, to the brink of collapse at the time of the banking crisis in 2008 (it was rescued by the public purse at vast expense). Goodwin obtained a temporary injunction preventing news of a contemporaneous extra-marital affair with a colleague from being published. Its purpose was partially frustrated when an MP announced in the House of Commons that Goodwin had obtained this injunction anonymously (albeit the MP revealed no details about the underlying facts or, importantly, the name of the colleague).[145]

In a subsequent hearing, pursued by the press, to vary the injunction so that it may name the colleague and publish the fact of the affair, the High Court dismissed the application so as to prevent the naming of the colleague. It did, though, allow for a variation such that the fact of the affair and a general description of the colleague's position in the organisation could be printed. There was no reasonable expectation of privacy in this information, the Court said, and even if there had been it was in the public

[140] See, ibid, [20], [31] and [34].
[141] *Hutcheson v News Group Newspapers Ltd* [2011] EWCA Civ 808.
[142] ibid, [45].
[143] ibid, [48].
[144] ibid, [47].
[145] See discussion in *Goodwin v News Group Newspapers Ltd* [2011] EWHC 1437, [21].

interest to know it. For whilst the Court rejected the claim that the public interest lay in suggesting this affair had 'distracted' Goodwin at a crucial time in the bank's financial turmoil (the Court found this to be pure speculation),[146] it did say it was 'in the public interest that there should be public discussion of the circumstances in which it is proper for a chief executive (or other person holding public office or exercising official functions) should be able to carry on a sexual relationship with an employee in the same organisation'.[147] Moreover, it said:

> It is in the public interest that newspapers should be able to report upon cases which raise a question as to what should or should not be a standard in public life. The law, and standards in public life, must develop to meet changing needs. The public interest cannot be confined to exposing matters which are improper only by existing standards and laws, and not by standards as they ought to be, or which people can reasonably contend that they ought to be.[148]

The reference here to 'improper only by existing standards and laws' relates to the opening sentence in the paragraph, in which the Court said: 'I do not reach this conclusion on the ground that NGN would thereby expose serious impropriety, still less crime.'[149]

We can trace this idea back to the decision in *Terry v Persons Unknown*,[150] which also concerned the infidelity of a footballer, in which Mr Justice Tugendhat rejected the submission that the 'conduct of one person in private must be unlawful, before another person should be permitted to criticise it in public. Otherwise the speech is not capable of contributing to a debate in a democratic society'.[151] Although we have no record of precisely what counsel said, we are told that this interpretation came from the decision in *Mosley v News Group Newspapers Ltd*,[152] in which Mr Justice Eady had said:

> [I]t is not for the state or for the media to expose sexual conduct which does not involve any significant breach of the criminal law. That is so whether the motive for such intrusion is merely prurience or a moral crusade. It is not for journalists to undermine human rights, or for judges to refuse to enforce them, merely on grounds of taste or moral disapproval. Everyone is naturally entitled to espouse moral or religious beliefs to the effect that certain types of sexual behaviour are wrong or demeaning to those participating. That does not mean that they are entitled to hound those who practise them or to detract from their right to live life as they choose.
>
> … Where the law is not breached, as I said earlier, the private conduct of adults is essentially no one else's business. The fact that a particular relationship happens to be adulterous, or that someone's tastes are unconventional or 'perverted', does not give the media *carte blanche*.[153]

Tugendhat J could not accept either that the law had 'reached [the] point' that claimant's counsel was suggesting or, indeed, that 'Eady J was saying that it had': 'As I read the

[146] ibid, [136]–[137].
[147] ibid, [133].
[148] ibid.
[149] ibid.
[150] *Terry v Persons Unknown* [2010] EWHC 119.
[151] ibid, [99].
[152] *Mosley* (n 127).
[153] ibid, [127]–[128].

passages Mr Spearman cited to me, Eady J was primarily directing his attention to the excesses of the defendant in that case. This appears from his use of the words "hound" and "carte blanche"."[154]

Developing, apparently, Eady J's point about the entitlement to hold opinions in a general sense, Tugendhat J set out, in a lengthy paragraph that deserves repeating in full, an interpretation of public interest that has come to be known as the 'freedom to criticise' doctrine:

> There is much public debate as to what conduct is or is not socially harmful. Not all conduct that is socially harmful is unlawful, and there is often said to be much inconsistency in the law. For example, some commentators contrast the law on consumption of alcohol with that on other intoxicating substances.
>
> The fact that conduct is private and lawful is not, of itself, conclusive of the question whether or not it is in the public interest that it be discouraged. There is no suggestion that the conduct in question in the present case ought to be unlawful, or that any editor would ever suggest that it should be.
>
> But in a plural society there will be some who would suggest that it ought to be discouraged. That is why sponsors may be sensitive to the public image of those sportspersons whom they pay to promote their products. Freedom to live as one chooses is one of the most valuable freedoms.
>
> But so is the freedom to criticise (within the limits of the law) the conduct of other members of society as being socially harmful, or wrong. Both the law, and what are, and are not, acceptable standards of lawful behaviour have changed very considerably over the years, particularly in the last half century or so.
>
> During that time these changes (or, as many people would say, this progress) have been achieved as a result of public discussion and criticism of those engaged in what were, at the time, lawful activities.
>
> The modern concept of public opinion emerged with the production of relatively cheap newspapers in the seventeenth century. Before that there was no medium through which public debate could be conducted. It is as a result of public discussion and debate, that public opinion develops.
>
> Recent examples in the financial field include insider dealing and dealing in works of art which have been acquired lawfully but in debateable circumstances (e.g. taken indiscriminately but lawfully from sites of archaeological interest). Examples in the field of personal behaviour include some of the new offences created by the Sexual Offences Act 2003, and the increased protection given to employees, both financially and in terms of privacy and harassment.
>
> Exploitation of weaker persons by those who are richer and more powerful commonly occurs in private places, including within families. Those who are exploited do not always protest, or welcome protest by outsiders. They may believe that they have more to fear than to hope from the outcome of a protest.[155]

The juxtaposition between Eady J's and Tugendhat J's positions is revealing. For Eady J, clearly something greater than the fact of criticising immorality is required to

[154] *Terry* (n 149) [100].
[155] ibid, [104].

demonstrate the existence of a public interest in revealing private information to the masses. However, for Tugendhat J, that element manifests in the apparent criticism that the claimant is doing something disreputable that the publisher believes should be publicly condemned. Clearly, for him the newspaper is the vehicle by which society's moral standards are to be debated, as a precursor to agitating for reform, either by means of law or else at a personal level of moral responsibility. It is the presence of this additional factor that means Tugendhat J's freedom to criticise doctrine survives the Supreme Court's later finding, in *PJS v News Group Newspapers Ltd*,[156] that 'criticism of conduct cannot be a pretext for invasion of privacy by disclosure of alleged sexual infidelity which is of no real public interest in a legal sense'.[157] Referring to Tugendhat J's finding in *Terry*, and the Court of Appeal decision in *Hutcheson*, the Court noted 'the media are entitled to criticise the conduct of individuals even where is nothing illegal about it. That is obviously so'.[158] Nevertheless, it said, 'there is not, *without more*, any public interest in a legal sense in the disclosure or publication of purely private sexual encounters, even though they involve adultery or more than one person at the same time' (emphasis added).[159]

Arguably, we find this additional element in *Terry*, *Ferdinand* and *McClaren*, as prominent representatives of the England football team; in *Hutcheson*, in the intertwining of business and personal events; and in *Goodwin*, in the power dynamic between CEO and junior colleague embarking upon a love affair. It may be that these additional elements elevate the criticisms above what the ECtHR calls 'making tawdry allegations about an individual's private life' to the level of 'reporting facts – even if controversial – capable of contributing to a debate in a democratic society'.[160] Nevertheless, there is a palpable conflict with autonomy, here, that needs to be addressed. Clearly, the discussion of a person's private life captures the ethical description of public interest in that these claimants are all public figures in its literal sense. They are known or knowable to the public. Through this greater public awareness of their lives, in which, as the Court of Appeal noted in *A v B plc*, impressionable minds might aspire to become them, their moral outlooks may be emulated by others. This influence can be said to be genuinely felt by others, even if it is only perceived, rather than actual.

Yet, to give this sort of speech the legal designation of public interest, and not merely the ethical descriptive, is deeply incompatible with the notion of individuality that the Millian principle articulates. It empowers the 'tyrannical majority' to determine the decisions that others make. This is especially so when press criticisms amount to a sustained campaign with a coercive end in mind. Often, the whole point of privacy invasion is to pour shame upon the individual either as retribution for the social wrongs they are said to have committed (such as the financial ruination of the Royal Bank of Scotland, as in *Goodwin*) or else other forms of punishments brought upon them (such as pressurising the FA to remove the captain's armband, as in *Terry* or *Ferdinand*). Moreover, the mere fact of public scorn – even if unaccompanied by

[156] *PJS v News Group Newspapers Ltd* [2016] UKSC 26.
[157] ibid, [21].
[158] ibid.
[159] ibid, [32].
[160] *Armonienė v Lithuania* [2009] EMLR 7, [39].

demands for reprisals – is enough to constitute the denial of autonomy, as if the agent ought not to make ethical decisions according to her own lights.

If this pattern of autonomy denial is given the legal designation 'of public interest' it further denies the individual legal redress for the privacy invasion because that designation renders it 'warranted' or 'justified' (as opposed to unwarranted or unjustified). The freedom to criticise doctrine would explicate this justification, in Millian terms, as harmful other-regarding behaviour (on the agent's part), thus rendering it susceptible to interference through the coercive means of public shame. However, this analysis misrepresents Mill's liberty principle, for Mill would say, as we have seen, that the other-regarding behaviour must be *unduly* harmful to warrant such treatment.

Does the fact of the agent's public figure status provide that missing element? Her actions are not that of a 'private citizen' but those of a role model whose moral decisions can be expected to be emulated by others, if we apply the reasoning from *A v B plc*. Nevertheless, this assumes that moral outlook is a public matter in specific circumstances, ie when the individual is well known. Yet there is a missing aspect of causality for this that requires greater reflection than it receives: unless the individual holds public office, they can only acquire the requisite level of public recognition if others have elevated them to that position. Today, in the digital speech era, the media does not hold the monopoly that it once did. Still, we might observe that this status – of fame or infamy – relies upon the public taking an active interest in that individual. If that interest derives from that person's attributes – skill, personality, attractiveness, etc – rather than their office, then we are no further forward in understanding the public interest in their life other than terms of curiosity derived from popularity. This popularity, be it artificial (ie, derived from the media providing them with intimate coverage) or organic (ie, derived from self-promotion through digital speech platforms), cannot be a legitimate basis upon which to sustain a public interest in criticising that person's moral conduct. It cannot be the additional element required by which to convert other-regarding harm into *undue* other-regarding harm by which to justify the coercive effects that the tyrannous majority creates when it condemns non-conformity in such terms that the putative claimant is denied legal redress through law (eg, the misuse of private information tort).

As argued above, for immorality to warrant legal designation, we should see sufficient vertical alignment between the autonomous agent's actions and the resultant public criticism. The allegation of criminality achieves something of this verticality, so long as it does not usurp the state's power to punish wrongdoing. Otherwise, we are left only with horizontality which, whilst it may satisfy the ethical description of public interest, ought not to be sufficient to warrant the legal designation. To let the tyrannous majority dictate the life decisions of others is to undermine the state–citizen pact by which each forsakes some of her inherent power by delegating it to the centre.

IV. Conclusion

If we are to make progress in separating the authentic from the inauthentic, then definitions matter. It matters that we can articulate the reasons why not all speech is capable of legal protection. It matters that we can explain what free speech means. The ultimate method by which orthodoxy seeks to make this distinction is by differentiating the important from the unimportant, the political from the non-political, and the serious from the trivial, by means of the term 'of public interest'. This analytical tool is blunter than we should like. Clearly, it can make some cuts, but not with any great precision. For critics, it incorporates too much. Juridically, it relies upon an inherent subjectivity in which generosity and scepticism will eventually determine its use. All of this is deeply unsatisfactory from a theorist's perspective.

In this chapter, I have sought to sketch out a means of making progress with this debate. It does not provide all the answers – in fact, it may produce more questions than solutions. Nevertheless, it offers a means of progress that is consistent with the autonomy value that, I say, should guide our definitional approach in differentiating the authentic from the inauthentic. As a method, it relies upon a series of distinctions, starting with the first general division between the ethical description 'of public interest' and the legal designation 'of public interest'. By allowing that the two can co-exist without, necessarily, referring to the same subject matter, we can, in principle, overcome the initial problem that the descriptive term 'of public interest' is just too broad to be of much definitional assistance (a point that commentators are broadly agreed upon).

This distinction sets up the next stage of analysis. Throughout this part of the book, I am thinking about the authenticity of free speech claims in horizontal contexts (ie, as between citizens). These are not claims that involve the traditional rights dynamic of the state suppressing criticisms of it. This raises the preliminary question, discussed in chapter nine, of the circumstances in which it can be said the *right* to free speech is at stake even in horizontal disputes. For some, it seems that the mere presence of the court, as the arbiter of disputes, signifies state action to suppress 'speech', and so legitimises the claim that the traditional vertical dynamic is in play in these horizontal disputes, but the discussion above has sought to challenge that view.

Yet, there is something strange about the various tacit dynamics in operation in these horizontal lawsuits. Ostensibly, these are disputes between two identifiable parties, both of which pray in aid the concept of an inalienable human or constitutional right to defend themselves from the attack that they, the parties, perceive in the actions of the other. The claimant asks the state to recognise that her right to reputation or privacy is undermined by the defendant's speech. Specifically, she wants the state to honour its commitment to protect her from undue interferences with autonomy caused by another citizen, in the same way she would if she were physically attacked. The defendant, meanwhile, disputes that her actions constitute an undue interference with autonomy either because autonomy is not imperilled (in the final analysis) or else that it is but that there is good reason to do so, and that this reason also accords with the self-same state–citizen pact claimed by the claimant.

The strangeness of this dynamic emerges with the added claim made by the defendant that she is protecting not only her own rights to autonomy but also the additional rights of unknown and unnamed individuals who, in the Hegelian tradition, we might call the *Sittlichkeit*. That these unquantified interests of unspecified parties are not only included but taken seriously by the court such that they have determinative weight in the dispute is very odd, to me. We might think of this in terms of the 'right' to 'tell the story' of what happened. Where that story involves state functionaries, the rights-claim chimes with the state–citizen pact in obvious ways (albeit state functionaries are still entitled to a private life). Where it does not – where it involves private citizens and the state is not involved (as it might be if there has been a miscarriage of justice), then the rights-claim, as it were, amounts to no more than the will to shame the claimant. This move amounts to an inveigling in which the storyteller assumes that it is for her, and the *Sittlichkeit*, to sit in moral (ethical) judgement of the claimant's life choices. To give such the imprimatur of law would be to transgress the argument from individuality set out above.

We also see in the positive law the creeping of the terminology 'of public interest' into these horizontal scenarios to give 'trump' status to privacy-invading and reputation-tarnishing speech where the state is implicated in the structural resolution of disputes (ie, as an arbitrator) but *not* in the speech itself. If definitional fit with the ethical description 'of public interest' is a necessary but not sufficient precursor to the juridical designation 'of public interest' what additional steps should be required for the public interest speech to count as a trump on countervailing rights and interests?

This division splits the horizontal from the vertical by distinguishing vertical actors (ie, those holding public office or working in the public sector) from horizontal actors (ie, private sector actors). Of course, this does not mean that only vertical actors can be the subject of authentic free speech claims. (Nor does it mean that all discussion about them, such as tawdry allegations about their private lives, must be given the juridical designation 'of public interest'.) The test, such as it is, as I tried to formulate it, is whether the subject matter of discussion aligns to the citizen–state pact outlined in chapter eight. Is there sufficient connection between the speech and the idea of delegated power that would warrant, say, privacy-invading or reputation-tarnishing expression being treated as a trump? In this way, the significance of individual autonomy manifests as a discussion on why the speech criticising the individual's actions should be protected. Why should the state protect speech that would deny the individual's capacity to choose for herself?

There are a range of responses to this hypothetical. In this chapter I have sought to isolate two such areas for discussion, namely, speech alleging criminality and speech condemning personal morality. Of the former, I have argued that we can distinguish speech that monitors state power (alerting us to miscarriages of justice) from speech that would usurp it (and so causes miscarriages of justice). We should attribute the legal designation 'of public interest' to the first but not the second. Although we give this first sort of speech different labels, such as open justice or holding power to account, we should not legitimise the second when, in effect, it would condemn the individual to the court of public opinion, not least because the proper authorities by which coercive power is applied are all, in one form or another, regulated so as to ensure, as much as the law can, that proper accountability exists when those decisions are flawed. Given that the press routinely rejects the prospect of compulsory regulation concerning press malpractice, and does so as a badge of honour, it is antithetical to justice to think it should be entitled to determine, for itself, what is a just outcome, and to use its coercive power to achieve the result.

Finally, there is speech condemning personal morality. This provides the most vivid illustration of the distinction between ethical description and legal designation: if the legal designation captures merely that which fits the ethical description then, as the English and Welsh experience demonstrates, all speech criticising the immorality of others is ripe for protection as a legal trump no matter what personal damage is suffered to private and family life or reputation. Yet, if we are to recognise the fact of individual autonomy, as the liberty principle suggests, then such speech should be protected *only* if it can demonstrate that this immorality is both other-regarding, harmful, and that this harm is undue because the state–citizen pact is implicated. Only then should it receive the juridical designation 'of public interest'.

11

Workplace Speech

I. Introduction

This chapter marks something of a departure in tone from the rest of this part of the book. Whereas previously it has been argued that horizontal relationships are ill-suited to the presence of an authentic free speech right, here it will be argued that an employment-based free speech right is justifiable on autonomy grounds. As will be shown, this conceivable right is consistent with the positive law of both England and Wales and the European Court of Human Rights (ECtHR) whereby such a right is recognised.

The following discussion is split into three. Sections II and III seek to demonstrate how an authentic free speech claim, rooted in autonomy, may arise in an employment relationship but not the digital speech context, despite the ostensible presence of contract underlying both scenarios. Briefly, the difference relates to the apparent control that the employer can and does exercise over the employee's manifestation of individuality if left unchecked by law. This semblance of control arises naturally in the employment context but not in the digital speech scenario. Accordingly, the impact upon autonomy is more keenly felt in the former and not the latter. This, of itself provides the framework by which the free speech claim can be constructed. However, the claim relies upon an inherent contingency that may not be true of all employment relationships (it follows, then, that the workplace free speech right is dependent upon these contingencies being satisfied). The essential contingency, here, is a question of subjection, specifically: subjection to command. If, as a product of employment, the employee subjects herself to the employer's command, then the opportunity exists for free speech arguments to gain purchase. Section IV articulates the nature of this free speech right, sketching out the circumstances in which the claim ought to succeed.

II. Context

In the English context, the employment relationship is characterised by a so-called 'mutuality of obligations'[1] in which each party – employee and employer – owes

[1] *Carmichael v National Power plc* [1999] ICR 1226, 1230. See, further, *R (Independent Workers' Union of Great Britain) v Secretary of State for Work and Pensions* [2021] ICR 372, [71]; *Groom v Maritime & Coastguard Agency* [2024] EAT 71, [103]–[113].

certain duties to the other, including, on the employee's part, the provision of personal service. This 'employee' status brings with it (a degree of) stability, for once the continuous service requirement is met the employee has the security of knowing that, under the Employment Rights Act 1996, section 94(1), she cannot be 'unfairly' dismissed without being entitled to compensation available, if necessary, through successful complaint to the employment tribunal. Being an employee thus affords greater protection than being an independent contractor or a worker whose rights are governed largely (though not exclusively) by the terms of the underlying contract and whose sense of security often begins and ends with the amount of notice required under that contract. In the absence of a written contract (or notice provision), security depends upon what constitutes 'reasonable' notice, which is likely to be measured in weeks, not months.[2]

This stability, inherent in the term 'employee', suggests that absent catastrophic external events, such as genuine redundancy situations, or inter-personal conflict, such as poor performance or serious misconduct, the employee will remain with the employer for the long term. Accordingly, an environment comprised of fellow employees, all enjoying such stability, arises in which a discernible culture results, either organically, from the employees themselves, or, most likely, artificially (even, cynically) from managerial edict, that the employee is expected to embrace. Adherence to the culture is both informal and formal. Informally, the recalcitrant or insouciant employee can expect a degree of social isolation as well as managerial friction. The failure to live up to these structural expectations, including the failure to embrace the *esprit de corps* can be expected to end in limited promotion opportunities and general employment dissatisfaction, leading to the eventual managerial hope that the employee will either move on or else not become a distraction/nuisance to others who hope to get on.

Formally, the culture is established through the employer's managerial policies, which give contractual expression to the company's values. These rules may create a positive sense of culture, especially when expressing schemes of reward and recognition, such as enhanced parental and care leave rights, or policies on well-being and support. In this way, such rules, despite their formality, are genuinely cultural, expressing a view of the employment relationship that is compassionate, inclusive and progressive. Typically, though, these rules are regulative, expressed in the categorical imperative of prohibitions, with accompanying penalties for non-compliance. Given that they usually seek to ensure smooth relations within the workplace, including the consumer experience, and the wider sense that others have of that workplace and its work, produce and/or brand, we might categorise them as being concerned with standards of civility and the protection of reputation. These are, of course, both legitimate interests for an employer to protect. The issue for us to consider is whether we should think of these interests as qualified or absolute. More specifically, we might ask if these interests occupy a spectrum that, at a certain point, tips over into controlling behaviours that undermine individuality and spontaneity. Certainly, that would be my view.

This threat to autonomy is nothing new. We can find numerous examples within the case law: of an audit clerk dismissed for persistently wearing a badge that said

[2] *Richardson v Koefod* [1969] 1 WLR 1812.

'Lesbians Ignite' because it might cause offence to others;[3] of a chef dismissed after his employer discovered his bisexuality because co-workers said they found his sexuality 'revolting' and could no longer 'eat food prepared by him';[4] of a maintenance worker at a children's camp dismissed for being gay for fear he posed a threat to the children;[5] of a blackjack inspector dismissed for fraternising with customers outside working hours without notifying management;[6] of a probation officer dismissed after it was discovered he performed at fetish and hedonist clubs and sold bondage and sado-masochistic products through his company;[7] and of a female area sales manager at a cosmetics company who refused to conform to the 'stereotype' in the industry of 'wearing a dress, heels, and makeup' and was consequently unlawfully harassed and discriminated against.[8] Problematically, from the employee's perspective, the employer is well positioned to resist unfair dismissal claims if it can show the offending conduct falls within the contractual definition of misconduct, and that dismissal upon those grounds falls within the statutory concept of a reasonable response, under the Employment Rights Act 1996, section 98(4) or, as the courts have interpreted it, the 'range of reasonable responses' that an employer might take.[9] Thus, it matters not that the tribunal/court might not have dismissed on these grounds, only that an employer within this band might have. This standard is notoriously generous and causes real difficulty when substantive rather than procedural fairness is the key issue at stake.[10] By setting the meaning and nature of expected conduct, the employer positions themselves favourably toward the prospective or hypothetical employment tribunal in misconduct cases. For it can show, by this policy, that it has informed the employee what was expected of them, conduct-wise, by setting the level of 'unacceptable' behaviour according to a definition and examples. Hence, the employer, with this policy in hand, can say that, for example, abusive or rude language, inappropriate comments, misjudged jokes and derogatory or degrading remarks about a person's protected characteristics are all promulgated examples.

Thus, we can say that a culture of stability, engendered by the legislative rights framework, brings with it both benefits and burdens for the employment relationship. Clearly, the benefit is the security of knowing that, absent catastrophe, employment is guaranteed in the long term. The burden is that they must conform to the employer's sense of what constitutes misconduct. This burden is more than merely hypothetical. The pressure to conform is measurable not only by the litigation risk that a prospective unfair dismissal claim may fail, should the employee be dismissed for her non-conformity, combined with the absence of legal aid funding for employment disputes, but also the pragmatic concern that dismissal jeopardises the employee's

[3] *Boychuk v HJ Symons Holdings* [1977] IRLR 395.

[4] *Bell v The Devon & Cornwall Police Authority* [1978] IRLR 283, 284.

[5] *Saunders v Scottish National Camps Association Ltd* [1980] IRLR 174. His letter of dismissal stated: 'Information was received that you indulge in homosexuality. At a camp accommodating large numbers of school children and teenagers it is totally unsuitable to employ any person with such tendencies': 175.

[6] *Hadjioannou v Coral Casinos* [1981] IRLR 352.

[7] *Pay v Lancashire Probation Service* [2004] ICR 187.

[8] *Stevenson v Avon Cosmetics* [2014] WL 8663532.

[9] *Iceland Frozen Foods Ltd v Jones* [1983] ICR 17.

[10] See further H Collins, *Justice in Dismissal* (Oxford University Press, 1992).

standing in the community, including the market of employers, whilst non-conformity, of itself, likewise jeopardises the prospect of obtaining a good reference, upon which alternative employment depends.

The pressure to conform with employer policies – even overbearing ones that seek to police employee relations with others, both within and outside the physical domain of the workplace – is not one we should ignore. For, when interpreting the burdens and benefits of the state's generous employee protections, we might say that the burden of an inability to terminate employment easily (and certainly not capriciously) is lightened if the employer can safeguard its blemish-free reputation and eliminate workplace tensions by dictating the terms of interactions. Whereas these diktats can be dressed in the edifying language of culture-framing, the reality of its encroachment upon individual autonomy can be concealed from proper juridical scrutiny by the law's inability to test its legitimacy except for the formal setting of tribunal proceedings. Even then, the prospects of escaping censure are promising if it is a policy that is properly promulgated, brought to the employee's attention, and reasonable to act upon (within, that is, the range of reasonable responses).

Moreover, the employer's interest in the employee's activities outside the workplace has greater legitimacy with the advent of social media. Whereas comments posted online have the potential for greater substantiation than the traditional verbal exchange, there is also greater potential for unfavourable association between the employee and employer when online profiles include details of work positions. Understandably, employers may be concerned that their reputation will be unduly affected when employees say or do things contrary to their brand values. That sense of outrage pervading intense, retaliatory social media campaigns – which the press has dubbed cancel culture – can result in the employee being dismissed and/or the employer losing business.[11] Justifying such dismissals are relatively uncontroversial when employees use social media to attack employers,[12] colleagues[13] and clients/customers.[14] Nevertheless, it can result in a culture of overzealous policing of the employee's moral compass and so represent a more problematic interference with individual autonomy. Thus, the demotion of a housing manager to a non-managerial position for expressing on Facebook his religious belief that gay church marriages was 'an equality too far' was found to be a breach of contract.[15] The employer's claim that this comment, which was read by fellow employees, brought it into disrepute, was not established on the facts, not least because his viewpoint was expressed only briefly and in temperate terms. It would have been different, said the court, if the employee had proselytised his views at work, or else had expressed them with greater fervour or

[11] Z Thomas, 'What is the cost of 'cancel culture'?' BBC Online (8 October 2020), www.bbc.co.uk/news/business-54374824; S Salai, 'Conservatives keep quiet out of fear at jobs, campuses' *The Washington Times* (21 March 2023); E Nierman, "Cancel Culture': How Business Leaders Can Protect Themselves From Negative Online Press' Forbes (27 February 2023).

[12] *Crisp v Apple Retail*, Case No ET/1500258/2011, November 2011, discussed in D McGoldrick, 'The Limits of Freedom of Expression on *Facebook* and Social Networking Sites: A UK Perspective' (2013) 13 *Human Rights Law Review* 125, 142.

[13] *Teggart v Teletech UK* [2004] IRLR 625.

[14] *Preece v JD Wetherspoon plc*, Case No ET/2104806/10, May 2011, discussed in McGoldrick (n 12) 139.

[15] *Smith v Trafford Housing Trust* [2012] EWHC 3221, [86].

hostility to create conditions for 'genuine offence' since either would have breached the employer's policy.[16]

The inclination to avoid reputational embarrassment and preserve workplace harmony, even at the cost of irritating employees by imposing strict (or the appearance of strict) policies is understandable but regrettable when, collectively, this burgeoning set of policies, covering every conceivable eventuality, projects a strategy of 'command and control', especially when it spills over into the employee's offsite free time. This antagonism arises specifically in the context of social media when employers feel entitled, it seems, to dictate how the employee uses it in their personal life. Indeed, looking at my own situation, the social media policy at the University of Leeds has a section entitled 'Social media in your personal life' which expressly purports to control the employee by reminding them that 'as a member of staff, you should be aware of your association with, and responsibilities to, the University when using social media.' It goes on to say that: 'Social media posts which could bring the University into disrepute or impact the safety of the University community, are not permitted.' It even anticipates the employee's defence that her profile had strict privacy settings engaged:

> Remember that anything you post can reach a wider audience than you originally intended. While it is encouraged that people keep their online profiles under strict privacy settings where appropriate, using privacy settings does not necessarily prevent your content from reaching a wider audience via screenshots, bystanders or compromised security.[17]

Anything which is captured electronically – even private communications with friends – is potentially ripe for disciplinary action, it seems, should it fall into the wrong hands. Thus, with its heady combination of categorical imperative and dark insinuation, even the most assiduous may be afraid, whilst the truculent are best advised to leave the online world altogether. Yet, given that events in the offline world may be captured electronically with great ease, uploaded quickly and gain a disapproving audience in moments, even that strategy is no guarantee.

This constant jockeying by backroom lawyers to anticipate hypothetical employee defences at tribunal, animated by the spirit of Holmes's 'bad man' theory,[18] is bound to create an atmosphere of resentment amongst employees, not least in the burgeoning quantity as well of quality of the employer's restrictive policies, that it is not entirely ameliorated by prospective managerial promises that strict readings of the term will not be applied. Nor does the law provide much comfort, for although, as was said in *Smith v Trafford Housing Trust*,[19] the term 'disrepute' cannot be read so widely as to cover every statement of purported offence to employee expression, still the safeguard that this represents, to the extent it does, exists only in the physical space of the tribunal hearing itself. If proceedings never reach that stage – if the employee is not advised (which is likely) and loses faith in her own case after a barrage of negativity from opposing lawyers that a plain reading of the terms defeat her claim to unfair dismissal – then

[16] ibid, [80]–[85]. See discussion in P Wragg, 'Free Speech Rights at Work: Resolving the Differences between Practice and Liberal Principle' (2015) 44 *Industrial Law Journal* 1, 4–5.

[17] hr.leeds.ac.uk/download/downloads/id/1063/social-media-policy.docx.

[18] O W Holmes Jr, 'The Path of the Law' (1897) 10 *Harvard Law Review* 457, 459–50.

[19] n 15, [55]–[60].

the safeguard has no purchase. Also, even if proceedings do reach the hearing stage, the tribunal may well conclude that the decision to dismiss is harsh but well within the range of reasonable responses that the law tolerates.

These policies therefore speak to a level of control that the employer exercises over the employee which extends far beyond directions over the nature and level of work undertaken in pursuance of her job role. They impact upon the employee's ability to be herself and upon her spontaneity, both within the workplace and beyond it. It is understandable, then, that the employee should resist this constant, creeping encroachment upon her sense of individuality by appealing to the language of rights. These rights-claims might manifest as a right to respect for privacy, as it did in *Pay v Lancashire Probation Service*; or freedom of religious belief, as in *Copsey v WBB Devon Clays Ltd*,[20] when an employee was dismissed for refusing to work on Sundays; or freedom of association, as in *Redfearn v Serco Ltd*,[21] which concerned the dismissal of driver who served the local Asian and British Asian community after it was discovered he was standing for election as a British National Party candidate (an organisation committed to 'reversing the tide' of non-white immigration to 'pre-1948 levels').[22] Most obviously, in a social media context, the rights-claim will manifest as freedom of speech, as in *Smith v Trafford Housing Trust* and *Pay v Lancashire Probation Service*.

Though convoluted, both the English and Strasbourg Court recognises the legitimacy of these claims, even in the horizontal context, after a fashion. For the Court of Appeal, the human rights protection afforded to the private sector employee in *X v Y*[23] is 'oblique'.[24] The reasons for this are perhaps more complicated than they need to be given the end result. Nevertheless, they may be summarised as follows: the public sector employee benefits directly from the wording of the Human Rights Act 1998, which specifies at section 6 that it is unlawful for public authorities to act incompatibly with Convention rights. Private sector employees have no such ostensible protection. Whether this makes a material difference in this context is doubtful given the obligation upon courts/tribunals under section 3 that statutes must be read compatibly with Convention rights, which would include the Employment Rights Act 1998, section 98. Moreover, developments elsewhere in the common law surely overshadow the Court's view that although the tribunal/court itself is a public authority, that fact alone could not create a 'cause of action under the [Human Rights Act 1998] against an employer which is not a public authority'.[25] Strictly, this is correct: breach of the Human Rights Act 1998 is not a cause of action for a private sector employee (or in any other horizontal context) but section 6 can be used to argue that pre-existing common law actions must be read compatibly with human rights, as occurred in the seminal case of *Campbell v MGN Ltd*,[26] from which breach of confidence, the equitable cause of action, became the misuse of private information tort.

[20] *Copsey v WBB Devon Clays Ltd* [2005] ICR 1789.
[21] *Redfearn v Serco Ltd (trading as West Yorkshire Transport Service)* [2006] ICR 1367.
[22] ibid, [1].
[23] *X v Y* [2004] EWCA Civ 662.
[24] ibid, [59].
[25] ibid, [58(3)].
[26] *Campbell v MGN Ltd* [2004] UKHL 22.

In any event, the Court of Appeal in *Pay* held that Convention rights apply in the horizontal context of unfair dismissal, but only when there is a positive obligation upon Member States to secure enjoyment of them. If there is not, then the distinction between private and public sector employer remains significant.[27] For our purposes, the distinction collapses given the confirmation by the Strasbourg Court in *Fuentes Bobo v Spain*[28] that Article 10 applies in horizontal contexts.[29] To my mind, the application of this vertical set of principles in a horizontal setting, so as to create constitutional rights against a private entity (an employer) is not inconsistent with the preceding discussion. This is not to say that the employer has free speech duties since, as we saw in chapter eight, only the state has these. Instead, it is to recognise that the state can, and should, decide in the employee's favour when the interference with autonomy, represented by dismissal on speech grounds, is unjustified. This can be done through the European Convention on Human Rights, Article 10, as a right-no right construct, for it would still be the state that would have the putative duty to uphold that right, not the employer as such. Its duty would be no more than to compensate the employee for the interference with autonomy if ordered to do so by the tribunal/court. The next section defends this apparent inconsistency, specifically as against the potential objection that if the free speech claim succeeds here, it should do as well in a digital speech context as well.

III. Differentiation

As will become apparent, free speech claims in the horizontal setting of an employee–employer dispute are authentic because of the comparative power that the employer holds over the employee's autonomy. Since this power is akin to the state's, in its effect if not in its form, then the argument for authenticity is made out, I shall argue.

Anticipating the objection that digital speech providers exercise if not an actual then an emerging power that is also analogous to the state's, the first part of this section seeks to differentiate the two by showing that the power of the digital speech provider is not inimical to individual autonomy. In doing so, it revisits some of the arguments set out in chapter nine.

The digital speech provider's power manifests in two ways. First, most obviously, since the provider controls the levers by which speech appears, and to whom, it has the power to dictate, behind the scenes, the scale and scope of an individual user's prominence in the speech market. This power is both omnipresent and latent – it may be sufficiently perceived to the user that she self-censors prior to posting (ie, it may have a chilling effect) or not. Gavin Phillipson and Robert Mark Simpson report that in a three-month period in 2023, Facebook removed 914 million pieces of content

[27] *Pay* (n 7) [64].
[28] *Fuentes Bobo v Spain* (2001) 31 EHRR 50.
[29] ibid, [38].

whilst YouTube removed 4.5 million and TikTok over 102 million.[30] Of course, for these authors, as well as Jack Balkan, it is this dedicated editorial control that creates, the second type of power, which is, for them, akin to the state in its reach and impact upon the *Sittlichkeit*. Paraphrasing Balkan,[31] the entity, or entities, that can control what users see, can control the Habermasian conduit by which central government and the populace correspond with each other. This political power can be manipulated not only by central government but external agencies too. Similarly, irrespective of whether its motives are pure, interference by the provider with the conduit is a corruption of popular opinion that undermines the conduit's essential purpose.

If we problematise these two types of power with respect to autonomy we see, as chapter nine demonstrated, that the impact is difficult to describe as an undue interference with autonomy. The second type of power – the power to control or otherwise influence the conduit – was examined previously. As we saw, this collective or centralised sense of power does not engage the concept of autonomy in a meaningful sense, at least not as it relates to the individual. It is only the first type of power, when the individual is excluded, that does. Yet, even here, the autonomy claim is difficult to establish, for we should need to say that denial of services – the ability to transmit the message as intended or else to preserve that message online in its original form – is not, as Kant would have it, a 'freedom … that can coexist with the freedom of every other in accordance with a universal law'.[32] As we have seen, this is problematic, since unless the application of policy, in respect of the offending post, is wrongful, there can be no claim of, say, breach of contract. Trying to overcome this problem by insisting that the intrinsic or instrumental value of speech necessitates a 'thumb in the scales' to overcome this deficiency is a bootstraps method of rationalising that is fatally flawed, at least according to the analysis in chapter nine. In other words, if the exercise of power is consistent with the terms of the underlying policy, then the breach of contract claim fails.

Yet, given that the same could be said of an employer acting consistently with promulgated policy, we must explore further the impact upon autonomy that censorship represents. As we saw in section II above, it is not simply the fact of consistency with policy that decides the issue. It is also in the *manner* in which authority makes itself felt. Both Mill and Kant were so focused upon the essential distinction between persuasion and coercion precisely because coercion damages the functionality of autonomy, that is: the capacity of the individual to exhibit autonomous decision-making by way of originality and eccentricity. Thus, Kant, for example, speaks of 'independence from being constrained by another's choice' whilst Mill decried the impact upon human development that conformity brings:

> [T]o be restrained in things not affecting [the good of others], by their mere displeasure, develops nothing valuable, except such force of character as may unfold itself in resisting the

[30] G Phillipson and RM Simpson, 'Tackling Extreme Speech on Social Media Platforms: a Normative Taxonomy of Regulatory Approaches' in E Heinze, N Alkiviadou, T Herrenberg, S Parmar and I Tourkochoriti (eds), *Oxford Handbook of Hate Speech* (Oxford University Press, 2024).

[31] JM Balkan, 'Free Speech is a Triangle,' (2018) 118 *Columbia Law Review* 2011.

[32] I Kant, *The Metaphysics of Morals* (L Denis, ed, M Gregor, trans) (Cambridge University Press, 2017), [6:238].

> restraint. If acquiesced in, it dulls and blunts the whole nature ... [W]hatever crushes individuality is despotism, by whatever name it may be called ...[33]

It is this proto-psychology, by which both anticipate Freud, that concerns them. The individual who is cowed by authority consequently becomes less of an individual. If we take this claim seriously, then the effect of authority is important to our analysis.

Hence, in the digital speech scenario, if we could say that the end-user's independence is imperilled by the manifestation of authority, we might make progress to establish a meaningful impact upon autonomy. The difficulty, as I see it, is that exclusion from the community, as the provider's ultimate sanction, is not deleterious of autonomous decision-making. Although we can freely acknowledge that the denial of the will is a critical event in establishing undue interference, it is not the only contingency. The ability to act independently must be genuinely imperilled by the provider's actions. Being unable to say what one wants is not enough. There must be some more serious event that achieves the necessary psychological impact in a meaningful way.

We need not stray too far into abstract psychological discussion to grasp the point. We can see, readily enough, in the employment context what sort of psychological impact would qualify. As we saw, above, with the University of Leeds example, the threat of serious disciplinary action and even dismissal is a sufficiently daunting prospect to count. This is sufficiently coercive that it both directs decision-making prior to the event, and so shapes personality, and is punitive after the event. The difference between digital and employment contexts are pronounced. When a complaint is made by one digital user against another, the affected user may (or may not) receive a notification to say that an investigation is taking place. She has little cognisance of this investigation other than a few anonymous notifications. It may have no public dimension at all other than an eventual error-type message to say the post is no longer available. At worst, there is a public notice that the post was removed for contravention of the platform's rules.

In an employment context, an investigation into an employee's behaviour is a serious matter. Typically, the employee is suspended (on full pay) whilst the investigation is conducted. Whereas the fact of suspension on full pay is intended to convey, both to the employee and the wider world, that the employer has as yet reached no conclusions about the employee's culpability, the fact of an investigation conveys the clear impression that the allegation is sufficiently serious to warrant the disruption, both to the work of the employee (and her closest colleagues) and to that of senior management, who must investigate. Since the process is comparable to a police investigation, the psychological impact can be expected to be similar too. Only the most hardened, perhaps of independent means, could fail to be intimidated by this process, especially in the eventual hearing itself which bears serious comparison to the police interview under caution, in both its intensity and its formality.

Accordingly, even if dismissal does not follow, the experience will be sufficiently scarring for the person of average sensibilities that if it does not put them off using social media ever again, it will make them overcautious and self-censorial. Similarly, for

[33] JS Mill, 'On Liberty' in *The Collected Works of John Stuart Mill*, vol XVIII (JM Robson, ed) (Toronto University Press, 1977) 266.

the person whose actions are found to warrant a warning, the blemish on their employment record will feel senseless as well as damaging. If dismissal does follow, of course, then future employment will depend upon if not the generosity of the prospective employer, then the willingness to overlook the fact of dismissal for gross misconduct. Although this detriment should not be overstated, still it serves to compromise further the employee's already unequal bargaining power that so typically characterises the job market. Even if the candidate has an enviable skill set, the employer is bound to consider the disruptive impact that this appointment may have upon its existing workforce. We should not underestimate this prospect, especially if the offending speech speaks to a bigoted worldview.

For the disciplined or dismissed employee, she may react to the process in several ways. At one extreme, she may feel ashamed, repentant and embarrassed. At the other, she may be unapologetic, emboldened and feel victimised. Equally, her community can also be expected to react in differential ways. Although we cannot predict these reactions with precision, in the abstract, we can speak of a general culture in which dismissal for gross misconduct still retains a shameful quality that must be overcome if future employment is to be secured. This stigmatic quality does not exist in the digital speech context. Exclusion from the online community, for breach of the rules, does not result in direct financial penalty. It does not jeopardise livelihood. It does not affect standing. There is no sense of shame or of being shunned in the local physical or online community. Assuming that there is any publicity given to the fact of platform moderation, and of exclusion, the local community may not have known her identity in any event, either because she writes pseudonymously or because she is simply unknown to them. In the digital context, there will be no consequences to her exclusion. It is not as if other providers take references before allowing new members to join, hence no stigma will prevent her from joining. Moreover, exclusion may be an entirely private event of which none but the user is aware.

It is this difference in effect, both upon the mind, through stigma and the fear of lost community status or standing, and upon personal circumstances, through the potentially deleterious impact upon livelihood, that illustrates the key difference between the exercises of power in the digital speech and employment contexts. Whereas the impact upon autonomy is real and significant in the employment context, it is artificial and strained in the digital speech context. For, putting aside denial of the will, what *is* the impact upon autonomy?

If we apply these two distinctions in the juridical setting, we begin to see why the presence of the free speech claim is phony in the digital speech setting but not the employment context. As chapter nine explained, the digital speech user might claim her exclusion amounts to a breach of contract. Since this claim is hopeless if the promulgated policy is properly applied, the free speech claim becomes the method of counteracting this outcome. In effect, she will argue that the policy conflicts with her right to free speech and must be disapplied. This same argument can be deployed in the employment setting. Thus, although in both settings, the provider/employer have ostensible arguments to justify the decision to permanently exclude which, according to the positive law, appear valid, the free speech argument provides the potential means by which to decide in the claimant's favour.

The difference, it seems to me, is that the employer's decision is coercive whilst the provider's is not. The decision to dismiss has consequences that impact materially upon the individual's autonomy beyond simply denial of the will. The provider's decision does not. Whereas it can be said of both scenarios that the claimant can still speak freely – just not in this setting – it cannot be said convincingly of the employee's situation if, as most must, she must earn a living in order to survive and that her options for earning that living are both limited and contingent upon a good reference (and the absence of a gross misconduct-related stigma). Of course, this is not to say that the potentiality of a free speech claim provides an absolute right. I shall explore its limitations in the final section. All I seek to highlight, at this stage, is the distinction in applicability of the free speech claim in these two scenarios.

It may be that the decision to discipline or else dismiss the employee for her speech is connected to digital speech, either because the employee has said something online or else is captured by others saying something, which is subsequently disseminated online. Whereas the impact upon autonomy may therefore be connected to her enjoyment of digital speech, this usage must be disentangled from it. For it is not the form of the speech that authenticates the free speech claim (in the employment context) but the consequences of interference by which the competing autonomy claims (the will to speak and the will to penalise the speech) must be analysed. Accordingly, whereas we might say that penalisation of the digital speech by the provider alone has ramifications that can be understood in terms of autonomy – such as upon her sense of self-worth, including her self-worth as a citizen engaging in public discourse – the interference is consistent with the provider's own sense of autonomy as a property owner entitled to determine for itself the rules by which its (private) property is used (see discussion in chapter nine).

Of course, the Habermasian–Postian tradition, explored in earlier chapters, would claim that the importance of open public discourse is, of itself, reason to elevate it to trump status over competing claims. In a digital speech context, the ideal can still manifest elsewhere even if not on the platform of choice. Since the individual is not being penalised in a coercive sense, she can still hold the idea and share it with like-minded individuals, once she has identified a suitably receptive audience (including those who disagree with her but wish to debate the merits). However, if her exclusion from the digital platform has consequences which carry into the employment environment, its political form has some significance in that, as I have said before, ideas and opinions about the world must originate somewhere and be exercised.[34] To insist, as an employer might, that these ruminations have no overlap with the working world is deeply problematic if the online world is the source of tension (especially when the post was made outside working hours).

Nevertheless, an employer might object to the Habermasian-Postian position on reasonable grounds. After all, the inflammatory nature of political debate, especially on contentious topics of religion, world conflict, immigration, minority rights, etc,

[34] Wragg (n 16) 8–10.

seriously disrupts productivity and workplace harmony such that its interests will suffer to a meaningful degree. To expect the private entity to tolerate this disruption in the name of democratic values is both unreasonable and unnecessary. This response is compelling, I think, if we return to our earlier discussions, in previous chapters, chapter eight especially, concerning state tolerance. For whereas the state is expected to tolerate criticisms of it, it is not expected to exercise tolerance over all political speech. So long as it intercedes on content neutral grounds, it can and must act when, for example, serious disharmony would otherwise occur, even if the cause of tension is political disagreement between citizens. In other words, interference is legitimate when the state's obligations switch from those in the vertical to the horizontal setting.

We can map this reasoning onto the employer context, with some adjustment, if we accept that (legitimate) whistleblowing is a criticism of the employer that must be tolerated by it (when the proper rules are followed). However, workplace disputes, including those arising from speech (even political speech), are the proper subject of disciplinary investigation. The employer is entitled to safeguard its interests, including the preservation of workplace harmony, if threatened by contentious speech.

These, then, are the essential differences by which the fact of power, and its exercise, by the digital speech provider and the employer, although superficially comparable, are radically different in effect. Whereas in the employment context autonomy is imperilled by disciplinary action, it is not in the digital speech context. Accordingly, the importation of the free speech claim to bolster the contractual claim in the digital speech context must be doomed to failure precisely because there is no loss of autonomy by which to ground it, let alone demonstrate that it must succeed in preference to the provider's autonomy claim, rooted in its free use of its property, as we saw in chapter nine. By contrast, the employee can substantiate her free speech claim in autonomy-based terms. This is not to say that the free speech claim should succeed merely because it is implicated. The final section of this chapter sets out the circumstances in which its presence should strengthen the unfair dismissal claim.

IV. Nature

The applicability of Article 10 to horizontal disputes between (private sector) employer and employee has presented no real difficulty for the ECtHR.[35] This much is apparent from its burgeoning case law in which employment-based free speech rights are readily recognised.[36] Yet, this is not the same right that exists against the state. It is tempered, amongst other things, by the presence of 'mutual trust' by which 'labour relations must be based … [if they are] to be fruitful'.[37] This includes expectations of 'loyalty, reserve and discretion'[38] that would not, and could not, be expected in citizen

[35] See, especially, *Herbai v Hungary* (2020) 70 EHRR 35, [37].

[36] See further, eg, *Fuentes Bobo v Spain* (2001) 31 EHRR 50; *Guja v Moldova* (2011) 53 EHRR 16; *Heinisch v Germany* (2014) 58 EHRR 31.

[37] *Herbai* (n 35) [38].

[38] *Heinisch* (n 36) [64].

speech about the state. In this way, 'certain manifestations of the right to freedom of expression that may be legitimate in other contexts are not legitimate in that of labour relations'.[39]

A good example of this principle in action can be seen by comparing the decision in *Sánchez v Spain*[40] with *Vereinigung Bildender Kunstler ('VBK') v Austria*.[41] Both involve caricatures depicting individuals performing sexual acts on another. In *Sánchez*, two employees were drawn giving sexual favours to the director of Human Resources. In *VBK*, an Austrian politician was depicted ejaculating on Mother Theresa. Both instances were described as grossly insulting content intended to make a satirical point. In *Sánchez*, the cartoon was prepared by trade union representatives who criticised the two employees, through vulgar language as well as the cartoons, for giving testimony in favour of the company in proceedings brought by the applicants. The cartoons and text were displayed on the company noticeboard. The applicants were subsequently dismissed for gross misconduct. Unlike in *VBK*, the ECtHR found that there had been no violation of Article 10.

If a taxonomical approach had been adopted, as the dissenting judges did in *Sánchez*,[42] then the speech might easily have been classified as political speech and the same outcome reached in cases like *VBK*,[43] that freedom of speech trumps all else. However, this outcome would have been inconsistent with autonomy, ie, that of the employer and of the other employees. In the language of Kant, it would have been achieved at the expense of the freedom of others, and hence could not equate to the freedom with which all freedoms must co-exist on the horizontal plane.[44] To uphold freedom of speech above all else would have meant that the employer was not entitled to protect the affected employees from a hostile environment, created by this ridicule,[45] nor that the employees themselves were entitled to protect their own reputation, which the first instance court had found had been sullied by the speech.[46]

That the right to free speech is equivalent to other rights, over which it holds no presumptive priority, means that the trump status which the right enjoys on the vertical plane is inapplicable on the horizontal. This is true even of whistleblowing despite its clear public interest qualities. Thus, whereas, say, the press would enjoy such protection when disseminating whistleblowing-like public interest speech to the public, even that which shocks, offends or disturbs,[47] the employee enjoys no such broad freedom, even when whistleblowing, unless she has followed strictly observed the formal procedures for reporting wrongdoing, either to the employer or the proper authorities, prior to public disclosure or else can explain why had procedure had to be circumvented.[48]

[39] *Herbai* (n 35) [38].
[40] *Sánchez v Spain* (2012) 54 EHRR 24.
[41] *Vereinigung Bildender Kunstler v Austria* (2007) ECDR 7.
[42] n 40, O-I14.
[43] n 41, [34].
[44] See, eg, Kant (n 32) [6:233].
[45] See findings of fact (n 40) [65]–[66].
[46] ibid.
[47] See, eg, *Jersild v Denmark* (1995) 19 EHRR 1.
[48] *Heinisch* (n 36) [65].

This insistence upon formality would be entirely anathema in a vertical context. The press, for example, is not expected to report allegations of criminality to the police before reporting to the public. Yet it is characteristic of the horizontal scenario, in which the Court balances the employee's right to free speech against the employer's 'right to protection of its reputation and commercial interests'.[49] The apparent concession by the Court – of an inferior free speech right in the horizontal context – would seem to suggest the existence of two types or strength of free speech 'right' in existence.[50] Certainly, to a US audience, the existence of this differential approach would resonate with the conclusion that free speech in an employment context is a phony: that whatever this rights claim might be, it is not freedom of speech (nor perhaps not even a right).

Yet, it seems to me, the exclusion of trump status and the capacity of interests to defeat the rights claim are both consistent with the concept of free speech, including as a rights-claim, and, therefore, can be labelled as authentic. As chapter eight explained, trump status applies only when the state overreaches in its powers, in defiance of the citizen–state agreement on power delegation. Thus, it is only when the speech concerns the state, and is interfered with by the state in protection of its own interests that the trump should apply. If, though, the state interferes with the speech in protection of (the autonomy of) others, and that purported reason is genuine (ie, it is not a sham), then the trump is suspended. Instead, the court must determine the proportionality of interference considering the fact-specific circumstances. Likewise, if the court is asked to adjudicate between two competing (autonomy-based) rights-claims, so too is the suspension of trump status legitimate. Moreover, both the court and employer may find itself in the position of duty-holder in which the court must decide between competing autonomy-based claims, and the employer between the purported right to free speech and the right to equality or freedom from discrimination in the workplace as well as the obligation to deal properly with grievances.[51]

The first step to resolve these competing autonomy-based claims is to determine the target of the employee's speech. Since the employer has the right to claim the employee's loyalty, manifesting as faithful service,[52] speech that attacks the employer,[53] its customers[54] or other employees[55] are matters fit for dismissal (as we have seen), such that the question of fairness becomes one of proportionality (assuming, that is, that they do not constitute whistleblowing). The right to free speech may have some relevance here but cannot be expected to do much work in the employee's favour when the speech is a conventional instance of gross misconduct. Given that the employee's claim to individual autonomy cannot be achieved at the expense of another's without justification, it should only succeed if it can be shown that the employer's claim is

[49] ibid.

[50] On the existence of different types of free speech right, see A Haworth, *Free Speech* (Routledge, 1998) 7–8 and 24.

[51] See, eg, *WA Goold (Pearmak) Ltd v McConnell* [1995] IRLR 516.

[52] See, eg, *Lacy v Osbaldiston* (1837) 8 C & P 80.

[53] *Crisp* (n 12).

[54] *Preece* (n 14).

[55] *Teggart* (n 13).

superficial – that is, the degree to which it impacted upon business interests was trivial because, say, very few, if any, heard or saw the offending speech, or would be unlikely to connect the speech with the employer, etc. These factors, which aim at minimisation of impact, speak to the quality of seriousness within the misconduct rather than whether it constitutes misconduct itself.

These scenarios can be contrasted with those where the speech has no apparent connection to work. As the *Smith v Trafford Housing Trust* scenario illustrates, this speech becomes the subject of disciplinary action only if the employer makes it her business to investigate. Here, the right to free speech must surely have greatest power. We can plot this power across a spectrum. The employee's individuality is fullest when her creativity, intelligence, or self-reflective nature animate the speech. This strength resonates with emblematic cases of free speech on the vertical plane, in which the church and state have vilified non-conformity. In the employment context, if freedom of speech is to manifest as a right, then it should protect the employee against vindictive, capricious or idiosyncratic reactions to speech. The fact of the employer's apparent disdain or disapproval of it ought not to be sufficient. Certainly, this would give meaning to the Strasbourg Court's constant refrain that freedom of speech 'constitutes one of the essential foundations of a democratic society and one of the basic conditions for its progress and for each individual's self-fulfilment' such that it applies not only to that which is 'favourably received or regarded as inoffensive or as a matter of indifference, but also to those that offend, shock or disturb'.[56] In this way, the right to free speech goes some way to equalising the employer's superior bargaining power and control over the employee's being.

Roughly speaking, then, we have two scenarios in opposition – one where the employee makes it the object of her will that the employer is implicated by her speech and the other where the employer makes the employee's speech the object of her will. In the first, the employee is the causative factor whilst, in the second, the employer is. This contrast in active/passive roles ought to help us determine liability. In the first, the onus ought to be on the employee to demonstrate her free speech right is in play and ought to trump the employer's rights. In the second, the onus ought to be reversed. In other words, these two scenarios illustrate where the autonomy interference is most obviously taking place. In the first, it is the employer's autonomy that is imperilled whereas in the second, it is the employee's.

As this implies, the second step to resolving the dispute – after we have identified the object of the speech – is to identify the relevant autonomy claims at stake. Having identified the 'whom' – employer, other employees, consumers, clients or other stakeholders – there must be a sense of 'how' autonomy is affected. The plausibility of this is determined by the question of how the employee's speech relates to others. This is essentially a question of causality. Starting with the employer, we should determine if the claim that the employee's speech has caused harm – in an ascertained or unascertained manner, actual or prospective – is plausible or not. Even if it has caused harm, we must then ask if that harm is too remote to apply to the employee's actions notwithstanding that application of a literal 'but for' test would confirm the

[56] *Bédat v Switzerland* (2016) 63 EHRR 15, [48].

employee is to blame. At this point, we should thus be mindful of the employer engaging in the scenario Mill warns of: treating the 'affairs of another [as if they] are his own affairs'.[57]

The principle at stake here may be stated in Millian and Kantian terms as the preservation of freedom (Kant) or individuality (Mill), such that it is not subject to the coercive control of another. That other, of course, may be the employer herself, her shareholders, her employees (or directors) or else the ultimate consumer of products and/or services. In an abstract sense, the identity of the complainant is irrelevant. It is the preservation of individuality that matters most, such that we might say, generally, that one person's freedom or individuality cannot be contingent upon the whims of another if the principle of autonomy is to be preserved. This does not mean that the complainant is wrong to complain; she exercises her own autonomy in doing so.[58] It is a question of whether it is legitimate for the employer to act upon that complaint as reason to discipline the individual.

Protecting the employee in these circumstances in the name of free speech may seem implausible. Why should the employer be liable to carry the cost of lost revenue, through diminished sales or disrupted productivity if the employee says something offensive that causes harm? Let us take the claim in stages. I am not saying that the employee is entitled to an absolute right. The competing claims should be decided on their facts, including the degree to which harm has been caused, and the extent to which the employee is the proper cause. For example, oversensitivity in the consumer or fellow employee reaction would count in the employee's favour. Although oversensitivity in the employer's reaction would, in any event, count in the employee's favour under unfair dismissal law, without any need for the additional supports of a human rights claim, still the protection of Article 10 might give extra support to the employee where the employer's response would otherwise satisfy the 'range of reasonable responses' test.[59] For example, in *Game Retail Ltd v Laws*,[60] the employee's dismissal for posting obscenity-laden rants on Twitter was found to be within that range despite the fact that the posts were personal in nature (and made outside working hours). Since many of his followers included colleagues and professional associates, the dismissal was justified.

Of course, this is not to say that the employer should be expected to tolerate all costs to its business through the employee's autonomous actions. Yet, what might be harder to accept, even as a matter of principle, is that it should tolerate *any*. Certainly, in the context of, say, negligent incompetence, the English tribunals have found dismissal to be fair in many circumstances.[61] Nevertheless, it has been found that negligence causing minor damage should be tolerated.[62] These are cases of capability rather than

[57] Mill (n 33) 301.

[58] On this point Mill says 'We have a right, also, in various ways, to act upon our unfavourable opinion of any one, not to the oppression of his individuality, but in the exercise of ours' (n 33), 278.

[59] *cf Turner v East Midlands Trains Ltd* [2012] EWCA Civ 1470.

[60] *Game Retail Ltd v Laws* [2014] UKEAT 0188_14_0311.

[61] See, eg, *Superlux v Plaisted* [1958] *The Times* (12 December 1958); *Lowndes v Specialist Heavy Engineering Ltd* [1977] ICR 1; *Janata Bank v Ahmed* [1981] ICR 791. *cf Chhabra v West London Mental Health Trust* [2013] UKSC 80.

[62] *Comerford v Swel Foods Ltd* [1972] IRLR 17.

conduct, which presuppose different aspects of employment response (ie, capability rather than disciplinary procedures),[63] but the two approaches bear comparison in that some degree of loss ought to be tolerated by the business (depending upon its size/turnover, of course).

The most problematic cases of this sort to have arisen in the UK in recent times has concerned dismissals implicating the employee's right to freedom from discrimination on grounds of philosophical belief under the Equality Act 2010, section 10(2): specifically, cases in which employees have been dismissed due to their views on transgenderism. In *Forstater v CGD Europe*,[64] the claimant acted as a consultant on projects involving sustainable development. Her contract was not renewed after her employer received complaints from fellow employees about comments the claimant had posted online. These comments, the Employment Appeal Tribunal (EAT) determined, fell within her entitlement to express her philosophical belief that sex is an immutable quality such that could not be changed through gender reassignment. The case, and others like it, are fairly technical relying, as they do, upon a specific reading of section 10(2) from the leading case of *Grainger plc v Nicholson*.[65] Accordingly, I intend only to gloss over what is otherwise a controversial and technical area of law.

However, it is worth commenting on one aspect of the reasoning in these decisions. In *Forstater* the EAT decided that the original tribunal had erred by deciding that Forstater's claim failed on one specific aspect of the *Grainger* test, namely that which stipulates the philosophical belief 'must be worthy of respect in a democratic society, be not incompatible with human dignity and not conflict with the fundamental rights of others'.[66] The first instance tribunal had reached its decision on the basis of the evidence by which it was said Forstater had demonstrated she would continue to misgender an individual regardless of the obvious hurt and distress it caused to others:

> Calling a trans woman a man is likely to be profoundly distressing. It may be unlawful harassment. Even paying due regard to the qualified right to freedom of expression, people cannot expect to be protected if their core belief involves violating others' dignity and/or creating an intimidating, hostile, degrading, humiliating or offensive environment for them.[67]

It went on to say:

> I conclude from this, and the totality of the evidence, that the claimant is absolutist in her view of sex and it is a core component of her belief that she will refer to a person by the sex she considered appropriate even if it violates their dignity and/or creates an intimidating, hostile, degrading, humiliating or offensive environment. The approach is not worthy of respect in a democratic society.[68]

Taking the right to freedom of speech into account, the tribunal found it disingenuous to suggest that Forstater's views were limited merely to the immutability

[63] See, eg, *Littlewoods Organisation Ltd v Egenti* [1976] ICR 516.
[64] *Forstater v CGD Europe* [2022] ICR 1.
[65] *Grainger plc v Nicholson* [2010] ICR 360.
[66] ibid, [24].
[67] At [88]. See *Forstater* (n 64) [15].
[68] At [90], ibid.

of sex: 'It is also a sleight of hand to suggest that the claimant merely does not hold the belief that trans women are women. She positively believes that they are men; and will say so whenever she wishes.'[69] Given the 'absolutism' of this view, and that it amounted to discrimination causing harm to others, the tribunal concluded that there was no violation of Forstater's right to free speech in the non-renewal of her contract.

However, the EAT reached a different outcome. Its grounds for doing so strike me as erroneous. It concluded that Forstater's beliefs were 'worthy of respect' because the view was 'widely shared' by others.[70] This claim is not substantiated, aside from a reference to the findings of the High Court in *R (Miller) v College of Policing*,[71] which, of itself, refers only to the third-party evidence provided by Kathleen Stock, a controversial figure in this arena. More specifically, the EAT decided that views 'unworthy' of respect in a democratic society were only those that would satisfy the requirements of Article 17 ECHR, which stipulates that Convention rights cannot be used in a manner that would destroy the rights of others.[72] Only extreme cases such as Nazism would satisfy this criterion, it said:[73]

> It is clear from Convention case law that that is as it should be; a person is free in a democratic society to hold any belief they wish, subject only to 'some modest, objective minimum requirements': per Lord Nicholls in *R (Williamson)*.[74] It is only in extreme cases involving the gravest violation of other Convention rights that the belief would fail to qualify for protection at all.

The error which the EAT makes here is to confuse the obligations imposed upon the state with those that ought to be imposed upon an employer. Accordingly, whereas, in *R (Williamson)* itself we are dealing with the tolerance that the state must demonstrate, vertically, to its citizens before coercive measures can be deployed, *Forstater* is a case of a horizontal nature. Therefore, it would have been consistent with that horizontal relationship for the EAT to apply a differential nature of expected tolerance in this setting, as the Tribunal did. The expression 'worthy of respect' could have been understood not as the state must understand it, but as fellow citizens might when they are expected to deploy their resources to accommodate the contentious views of an individual who has made plain that she does not care whom she upsets, offends, and distresses through her viewpoints. For them (the employer) to say, in effect, that the views were not worthy of their respect, in the terms that the first instance tribunal provided, would have been entirely consistent with the principle of autonomy articulated throughout this book. For why *should* transphobia – or any other unpleasant viewpoint – tie the hands of an employer and impair its own right to act autonomously to provide a place in which such narrowmindedness is met with zero tolerance? The fact that the state must tolerate such views is no answer because, as we know, it has no autonomy by which it could justify the interference.

[69] At [93], ibid.
[70] ibid, [113].
[71] *R (Miller) v College of Policing* [2020] 4 All ER 31, [19].
[72] See discussion in *Forstater* (n 64), [59] and [62].
[73] ibid, [70].
[74] *R (Williamson) v Secretary of State for Education and Employment* [2005] 2 AC 246.

Accordingly, it may be said that there are limits to the right to free speech in the workplace. This is not the right which manifests in the vertical context and enjoys trump status. It is that freedom which must be made compatible with the freedoms of others, so that the individuality of all is accommodated. Gender critical viewpoints can be accommodated in the workplace, but not when it leads to others feeling harassed and distressed by those who espouse it. This much at least was conceded by the EAT, albeit not in especially comforting or convincing terms.[75]

V. Conclusion

In an important sense, a workplace-based free speech claim is uncontroversial. Certainly, both the Strasbourg Court and English law have recognised it. Nevertheless, this recognition is both contextual and subject to criticism. Strasbourg's workplace-based right has tended to arise chiefly in whistleblowing-type cases. In England, it has arisen in anti-discrimination cases relating to the protection of philosophical beliefs that are, amongst other things, 'worthy' of respect. Both scenarios give the impression of a free speech right that speaks to the Habermasian–Postian dynamic of protecting 'political' or 'important' speech.

In this sense, the tone of this chapter is at odds with the (emergent) conventional view, firstly, in championing speech that is, or may appear, anodyne or trivial in terms of content, but which is significant as a matter of autonomous individuality. The content of speech ought to be irrelevant for the purposes of determining protection, as previous chapters have argued. Secondly, it is at odds in arguing *against* the (apparently) strong protection that philosophical belief attracts, especially that which, when promoted in the workplace, is bound to cause friction and no little resentment. This strong rendition of a right is wrong, it is suggested, to the extent that it denigrates the autonomy of others and inculcates a culture of intolerance and harassment toward them.

Arguably, the law is wrong here to the extent that it transposes a vertical obligation not to punish values that are deleterious of plurality, broadminded and tolerance onto the horizontal relationship. This transposition signals a serious judicial failure to recognise the radically different context. Whereas in the vertical setting, the free speech right acts as a trump precisely because the state can have no corresponding right derived from its own interests, it cannot do so in the horizontal given that the employer is *entitled* to take its own interests into account when responding to a rights-based claim. These interests include both the harmony of the workplace and the productivity of the workforce, both of which can be imperilled by inflammatory opinions, regardless of whether those viewpoints can be freely expressed in a democratic country without fear of imprisonment or financial penalty by the state.

[75] *Forstater* (n 64) [118].

PART V

Conclusion

12

A Radical Restatement

I. Introduction

Employing Wittgenstein's metaphor, the preceding discussion argues that orthodox theory fails by being mired in a world whereby the meaning of free speech is given exclusively by practice. Accordingly, theory serves only to reinforce pre-existing intuitions and expectations about it. Such ideas speak to a lived experience of liberal democracy that is rooted in a historical understanding of what *was* and not what *might be*. Our conceptualisation of the term 'free speech' is bounded by the limitations inherent within these proofs. Hence, conventional thought serves only to validate what is already believed about the concept – that free speech is an *important* right because society is inculcated to believe it is; that it means the right to say unpopular, offensive and downright ugly things because that is what people say it is about; that it is a socially valuable right because that is how it is understood; that it is mostly about the protection of political speech because that is how it has always been.

Yet, once we step outside the world, this distinctive feature of orthodoxy starts to look doubtful. Free speech is something given by the state to the people. It is a right in the tradition of *habeas corpus*, freedom from torture, the right to a fair trial, and freedom from arbitrary stop and search. It is a right that belongs alongside rights to privacy, to association, to marriage, to manifestation of religious belief. Common to these parallel rights is their foundation in autonomy – that is, the right to be recognised, by the state, as a person with rights. In a democratic society, that right manifests as the right to vote, with all such votes being treated as equal, and all being equal before the law.

Given this commonality, why, then, do we treat free speech differently, as something to be understood in terms of its benefits to society at large? We do not say, generally, that a person's rights depend upon how well they use them or how wider society will gain from their protection. The right to marry and start a family does not depend upon the societal value of the union. The right to association does not depend upon whether those associations are generally a good thing or not. These rights are not derived from the necessity of collective decision-making; on the contrary, they recognise the inherent value of peoples as entities *separate* from the collective.

This is not to deny that, conceptually, free speech has its origins in historic struggles by which the sanctity of individuality over nationhood has had to be established and re-established time and again, as nation states emerged and overreached in their indiscriminate power-grabbing. It could hardly be otherwise. There is no history of free speech as a right to commercial expression or pornography as compared to political and religious struggle. This history is undeniable, but that does not mean that free speech theory must be confined to such taxonomies.

The conventional methodology for determining free speech's parameters needs revising. Invariably, it starts from an embedded position, deep within the world, in which free speech is already firmly established, and it works backwards to establish its meaning. The question of why the state guarantees the right becomes the question of what it means. Through this process, shared history, political tradition, legal precedent and intuition serve only to confirm the bias inherent within the method.

In this way, we see it said that the state's guarantee of free speech resonates most clearly with political struggle, especially in those nations established by civil war or wars of independence. If that nation identifies as a democracy, in which centralised power is given by the populace through free elections, then free speech amongst the candidates, at least, is entirely necessary so that the people can decide which candidate is best to lead. It is no wonder, then, that, from this methodology, freedom of political speech should emerge as the leading candidate by which the concept of free speech is to be elucidated. In the West, it explains our institutions most persuasively, both by reference to historical struggles and to the intuitions of those who have lived through conflict and strife. Moreover, even in those countries without such heritage, it is proven in the negative, for those that speak out against the state shall be imprisoned, or worse, for their heresy.

However, as this book has sought to show, this method is erroneous. Process theory is a phony. When seen from the outside, its most (ostensibly) convincing aspects become doubtful. Political freedom is important, but that importance is given to us by recognising autonomy as the animating principle. Free speech is important, but no more than any other right. Moreover, as a right that is constitutionally given by the relationship between state and citizen, inherent in the principle of democratic governance, it is no more or less important than any other right. When rights-claims clash, we should look to the interference with autonomy as the means of determining which one ought to succeed. This is a complex process, demanding fact-sensitive outcomes, that does not lend itself easily to grand platitudes. Nevertheless, if we are to recognise individuality as the base unit of collective living in a democracy, then this is the way.

The methodological supremacy of this approach, it seems to me, is its progression from the world without (free speech) to the world with. The world that rejected the superiority of the state over all else, with the fall of Rome and the rise of Christianity, is the world that shunned the superiority of the collective over the individual. To be sure, this is a society in more than name, in which collective living is necessary. Nevertheless, it is the individual who has dominion over herself when her decisions affect only herself. She cannot be compelled to do what is best for the collective in her own life choices. Of course, this renders individuality to be inherently problematic in terms of collective living, and there are good ethical reasons why the needs of others should guide her reasons for action. Yet, these reasons can only transcend to juridical justification for interfering with her actions when the harm principle is satisfied – that is, when her acts and omissions would constitute an undue interference with the autonomy of another.

This is, by and large, how our positive laws are written. Compatibility with the positive law is not a justification of itself – as I have said, theory should guide positive law, rather than be led by it. If one should change to fit the other, it is the positive law that should yield. This requires something of a paradigm shift, however. We must stop seeing theory as something that primarily serves to explain practice.

Thus, the subtitle to this book – *A Radical Restatement* – has a dual meaning. On the one hand, it signifies the book's overall ambition to rehabilitate the radical thought of John Stuart Mill, whose pioneering work on the meaning and nature of free speech has fallen into general disrepute. Accordingly, the objective has been to show that Mill's thinking remains vital to free speech principle in action. The book has sought to provide clarifications that address its most striking problems but also, more importantly, to show that, in Mill's hands, free speech was never an isolated or independent right as such, but one aspect of a greater right subsisting in autonomy and the detachment of the individual from both the state and community, especially in relation to pressures to conform.

On the other hand, the subtitle alludes to the distance between contemporary thought and this previous thinking about free speech. In this sense, it is recognised that the conceptualisation offered here represents a radical shift in thinking (or, rather, a return to the English radicalism of Mill's time) for, as we have seen, contemporary definitions of the term locate its essential meaning in the language of value, such that it is held aloft as something special *and* beneficial to societal progress. The book resists this vision of free speech by relocating it from the realm of the beneficial to that of the burdensome. As a product of the language of individuality, free speech, as a right, is something that challenges, and sometimes undermines, progress, rather than being something that always supports or underpins it. Accordingly, the book rejects the optimistic view that holds free speech as something inherently or instrumentally valuable to democratic participation and epistemic advance. The meaning of the term cannot be derived from these two values; they are invalid as definitional lenses by which to identify the right in action. Instead, we must think of free speech, ultimately, not as something beneficial but something burdensome, such that questions about its parameters are not dominated by elaborate valuations of it, but are instead dominated by how harmful it can be before protection can be denied.

II. Meaning

If, as this book maintains, free speech is a right derivable from the state's limited power over individuality, then how are we to identify it in practice? For process theorists, meaning attaches to context. Since free speech is about democratic participation, then speech which contributes to that process fits the meaning much better than (in fact, to the exclusion of) speech that has no such connection. Hence, as we have seen, the justification for the free speech guarantee is the critical lens by which meaning is determined.

However, deriving free speech from autonomy is not a matter of filtering speech for its compatibility with autonomy itself. Autonomy is not a lens by which to limit protection to speech that puts autonomy in its best light. Indeed, autonomy has nothing to say about permissible types of speech. It can produce no such taxonomy; all forms of speech are equally valid. The only question that matters is whether the speech affects another and, if it does, how so. This is why the orientation of speech (vertical or horizontal) is significant. Speech directed at the state enjoys privileged status over that directed at fellow citizens (including state functionaries when the speech speaks not to their functions but to their reputation/private life as a citizen). Of course, speech directed at the state may yet affect citizens. Putting that possibility aside for the moment, we can say that speech directed against the state enjoys trump status. The state is not an autonomous being. It has no will, as such; it can only serve. The trump exists by virtue of the Hohfeldian right–duty relationship characterising free speech in this orientation. It is the state's duty to tolerate speech directed against it. As such, we, the people, can call for a republic, and an end to monarchical rule.[1] We can say 'Fuck the Draft!';[2] we can decry abuses; we can demand policy change. The state cannot restrict this speech to protect its own interests in a positive public image, etc. It has no protectable reputation.

The same is not true of speech directed against citizens, nor is it true of speech directed against the state which affects citizens unduly. Accordingly, the state cannot interfere with press speech demanding the government act on the escalating price of corn. It cannot do so even if the tone of that speech is intemperate or misleading, so long as the object of the speech is firmly within the sphere of state action. It can act on protests about the cost of corn taking place outside a corn dealer's house. It can do so because (and to the extent that) the reason for interference is not the message itself but the public safety concern that the corn dealer will suffer violence. Likewise, the state can interfere with press speech that targets specific corn dealers by, for example, providing their home addresses, especially when violence is likely to ensue.[3]

This approach puts the focus firmly upon the opponent's reasons for interference (and not the value of the speaker's speech). The juridical question, then, is not why we should value free speech, but why – or rather, whether – interference should be allowed. This modification changes the emphasis. It shifts our attention from qualities (or the absence of qualities) in the speech itself to the effect that speech has upon the autonomous decision-making of others. Although the change is subtle, it has significance to juridical decision-making concerning speech. We must think not of value, but of harm. It matters not that the speech is valueless, even on an objective basis. The only question is whether it harms others unduly. The speech can be entirely irrational in nature, and still protectable, so long as the harm principle is adhered to.

To be sure, political speech (however defined) remains important and retains the appearance of being privileged over non-political speech. The point, raised by the preceding discussion, concerns *how* that privilege arises (*if* it arises). It is not reached by a taxonomical approach nor by reason of value (as in worth), although if political speech remains privileged, then the potential for objection from process theorists is diminished (if not eradicated). The methodology offered in this book differs sharply from that apparent in orthodox theory. As part two made clear, the essential criticism concerns the self-referential quality that theory has assumed of late. The fundamental idea that free speech serves democratic participation and epistemic advance is rarely

[1] *R (Rusbridger) v Attorney General* [2003] UKHL 38.
[2] *Cohen v California* 403 US 15 (1971).
[3] See, eg, *Green Corns Ltd v Claverley Group Ltd* [2005] EWHC 958.

contested. Accordingly, commentators work within the parameters that this tenet sets. Free speech, then, is about knowledge production, either generally or specifically to that which would enable better public decision-making. Even Martin Redish's maverick agenda for greater recognition of commercial speech's place upon the pantheon fits the contours, for his argument is essentially that commercial speech benefits better private decision-making. Baker, too, can be understood in these terms, especially concerning press freedom. Granted, the Postian–Habermasian model of democratic participation as an intrinsic recognition of a voter's equality within the franchise is a development but is still constrained by the same essential problem.

The apparent correctness of this self-referential approach is reinforced by the proof offered by commentators. The positive law fits its essential parameters, as does the shared history and political traditions of liberal democracy, all of which speak to the significance of free speech to the realisation of individual rights within the framework of democratic participation. Intuition further reinforces the sentiment, for our lived experience promotes the same conclusion.

Yet these proofs are self-serving. Of course, the positive law, political tradition and shared history of liberal democracy illustrates the importance of democratically significant speech to societal progress and therefore suggests it as the exemplar of the term 'free speech'. These sources could hardly do otherwise – after all, the positive law runs parallel to politics and history. Intuition accords with these sources, though only for those with the lived experience of liberal democracy.

However, the persuasiveness of these sources is more doubtful than they appear. The right to free speech has existed in the West only in a relatively short time-frame. Leaving aside the non-starter that the term has meaning dating back to ancient times,[4] its first appearances coincide with the tyrannous reign of Henry VIII,[5] although these are more institutional than popular appeals. Really, it is only with the struggle for the realisation of liberal democracy that the term takes on its modern significance. Even then, it is not until the twentieth century that the US courts begin to grapple with its meaning. In the UK and in Europe, the term has greater heritage, of course, but even the expression 'free speech' as a constitutional right is still quite alien. It is not until its recognition in the European Convention of Human Rights alongside the contemporaneous International Covenant on Civil and Political Rights that the term comes alive in its fullest sense.

In saying this, I do not disregard the pockets of resistance and outlier constitutional protections that have occurred, in which something resembling 'free speech' is protected. The US First Amendment long pre-dates the twentieth century, of course. Likewise, the French Constitution of 1793 did at least contain the right to freedom of the press. My point is that these earlier constitutional rights as such were not popular in the sense that they are now. Although these constitutional arrangements secured essential freedoms for individuals, the depths of the term 'individuality' in that newly minted free world had yet to be plumbed. After all, 'freedom' itself had yet to be fully realised. Consider, for example, the scale of the franchise in eighteenth-century America and Britain: it remained the province of the elite. Globally, full enfranchisement did not take

[4] See ch 1.
[5] See M Tugendhat, *Liberty Intact* (Oxford University Press, 2017).

place until the twentieth century. Likewise, it was not until the Industrial Revolution and the advent of capitalism that individual freedoms over, say, choice of career began to emerge. The economy of Britain was still largely agricultural up until that point and (male) children would follow in their father's footsteps.

So it is only in the past 150 years, and especially the past 100, that we have had to grapple with the meaning of individuality in its fullest sense. Therefore, to say that individuality lacks heritage as the authentic value of free speech is to miss the point. If free speech is the product of autonomy, and autonomy the product of the democratic revolution by which liberalism, in its purest form, might prevail, then our intellectual endeavours should be committed to mapping out the possibilities of what this means. However, to keep harking back to the past is to betray this new world, because the significance of the political traditions and shared histories, and of the positive law that has tracked it, is in the intermediate stages of *securing* autonomy and not of *realising* it. If we are to live in the world of the future, then we must look forwards. We are yet to map out what individuality means and how it can be accommodated in a world of competing and conflicting 'individualities'.

Undoubtedly, this task – of fully conceptualising free speech as a product of competing claims to be autonomous – is complex. It does not lend itself easily to simple solutions. It requires us to map out, carefully, the numerous ways in which individual rights-claims clash. This is an involved and technical process that requires us to consider the elaborate ways in which autonomy manifests. Nevertheless, this is the challenge that we should embrace rather than resort to the simplistic model of trumps and platitudes.

III. Application

Looking forward, it is understandable that commentators should want to define free speech in horizontal terms. Technological developments are now such that each person holds a megaphone in the palm of their hands. Mass media opportunities that were once the preserve of the elite are now commonly available to all. We can each reach substantial audiences – not, necessarily, in mass numbers as such, but certainly our peers in our respective communities (in terms of locality, industry, etc) – and communicate with them instantly through the tap of a screen. This renders all of us powerful actor in shaping the *Sittlichkeit*.

Moreover, given the reach and significance of everyday speech to the formation of our outlooks, in terms of both public and private decision-making, as it relates to work and personal life, it is also understandable that commentators should be concerned about the latent power that the providers of these services have over our (digital) lives, as we have now constructed them. We have slept-walk ourselves into this position, in which our (apparently) ever greater reliance upon technology has rendered us dependent upon these service providers to a significant degree. Accordingly, if they control who is seen, what is seen, and who it is seen by, then they can control modern society to a frightening degree.

Thus, it is entirely understandable that commentators should want to use free speech as the bulwark against abuse of this latent power. Indeed, this use of free speech as a bulwark animates the whole of part four of this book, in respect of not only digital speech providers but also powerful private actors whose actions and behaviours are said to be of public interest as well as the power of employers to control the *Sittlichkeit* in potent ways by dismissing or otherwise disciplining employees for speech that it dislikes. Free speech as a bulwark against (abuses of) power, of course, has considerable heritage. It is at once familiar and intuitive.

This desire to render the right more powerful against private abuses of power speaks clearly to a potent fear that, in the future, it will be corporations and corporate actors that assume the mantle of tyranny by which we know the *ancien régime*. This fear is not irrational. We know that corporate power buys political influence and subverts the democratic process. We also know that wealth enables foreign actors, and foreign powers, to manipulate domestic decision-making. We need only look to the UK's disastrous experience with Brexit to see how easily that foreign influence can sowing fear and division to corrupt the vote. We see, now, how the dream that the information super-highway would liberate the people has become the nightmare of rampant mis/disinformation that serves only to subjugate. The Internet was meant to bring us together; instead, it has torn us apart.

All of this can be acknowledged without accepting the basic proposition that free speech is but resistance to power (in any form) by another name. Just as, on the vertical plane, free speech does not justify the progressive agenda for optimised plurality, informed decision-making and epistemic advance, so too, on the horizontal plane, it cannot stand as the antidote to unwitting dependence upon technology. As part four makes plain, to succeed with this claim, we need to be clearer why private actors should owe duties akin to the state's. This is something we have never been able to do with, for example, the press, despite the continuing myth that it owes the people 'duties' to act in the public interest and hold power to account.[6]

Although the state can impose obligations upon unwilling actors, under a doctrine like Parliamentary Sovereignty, that act of coercion would not, of itself, provide the moral normativity that we have been searching for in this book. Likewise, the purported benefits of imposing such an obligation would not be sufficient. To take the topics of chapters nine and eleven, digital speech providers and employers are property owners who are entitled, according to our Lockean traditions, to use that property as they please so long as the liberal formula of wrongdoing–causation–harm is respected. Putting that into the language of autonomy, we say that the state cannot interfere with the property rights of others unless that property usage would unduly interfere with the autonomy of another. Alternatively, as Hohfeld had it, the dichotomy of right/duty is invalid to describe the scenario because there are reciprocal rights and duties on both sides, relating to, say, the performance of the underlying contract. Instead, it is a matter of determining where the superior right lies, such that it is more accurately described as right/no right.

It is sometimes said that the state 'duty' arises by the mere fact of adjudication, especially when it decides against the free speech claim. This strikes me as implausible. It could be said, with equal merit, that should the state adjudicate against property rights

[6] See P Wragg, *A Free and Regulated Press: Defending Coercive Independent Press Regulation* (Hart, 2020).

(in favour of free speech), then its duty to protect property rights is also engaged. This reasoning puts the state in an impossible position. Essentially, the argument seems to rely upon the further tacit claim that, in such deadlocked scenarios as this, free speech should succeed because it has trump status and requires a 'thumb on the scale' in its favour. However, this is fallacious reasoning. It assumes either that the state cannot rule against free speech rights-claims, which is wrong, normatively, or that (supposed) audience interests in the speech should prevail.

The validity of recognising such audience interests was explored in chapter ten. If the base unit of constitutional design is the language of individuality, then communal interests in speech are meaningless to juridical reasoning. The natural consequence of this is that there can be no audience rights to hear speech. Such rights, if they could exist, would have to be inferior to the speaker's. Yet, if the speaker has the right to speak, then the right subsists with her. If, the speaker has no such right, it is because the adjudicator (ie, the state) has found that the autonomy claim of her opponent is greater. Audience rights, then, can have no bearing on this because, to use these as an additional reason to protect speech would be to rely upon an unsophisticated sense of utilitarianism. It would employ a crude numbers game that unfairly prejudices the original claim-holder's freedom. As a general claim, then, the 'audience interest' in speech can have no validity, for there is an equal and opposite civic interest in legitimate property rights being upheld.

The state does have a duty to protect speech in (truly) vertical scenarios (and no right to deny the claim). Here, speech must be afforded trump status. The state cannot do otherwise – at least, not legitimately. Yet, in a horizontal scenario, no such trump status can exist, as a general proposition, because the state must carefully evaluate the competing claims to discern which of the opposing autonomy-based claims is superior. Of course, it is possible that there is a genuine public interest in protecting speech over the competing rights-claim expressed in, say, privacy, reputation or fair trial terms. Nevertheless, it seems to me that the most pressing (and, perhaps, only) reason to do so is when the justice system has failed the victim. In those circumstances, the speaker is entitled to report the failing to citizens at large. Other than that, though, it is hard to see how the notion of an audience interest in speech is a valid reason to trump an equally matched (or superior) opposing rights-claim.

The question posed in chapter nine and further explored in chapter eleven concerned property/contract rights by which a digital speech provider and/or employer might discipline/dismiss an end-user/employee. In a digital speech context, there is mileage in the claim that non-performance of the provider's duties under the contract constitutes a breach. However, this does not take us to the position that commentators want to be in by which it can be said contractual breach constitutes a constitutional problem of free speech. The dispute, here (between end user and provider) must be framed in the language of contract rights, not constitutional ones. Such a breach is not a matter of free speech; it is a matter of non-performance, for which the remedy is damages, not vindication of (constitutional) rights to speak. We cannot make it a constitutional matter simply by identifying the purported societal benefits to democracy that would follow from proper performance of the contract. In any event, this scenario only covers those (limited) scenarios where the contract is *not* performed. When it is – when end-users are suspended or removed according to the rules – then free speech rights-claims gain no purchase. It seems to me that there is nothing in that scenario by which we can say that the autonomy of the speaker has been unduly interfered with. They wanted to use the property of another to say something that the property owner told them not to use their property to say. Where is the problem of autonomy?

We are better placed to make that claim in employment scenarios, however. For here, at least, we can identify something akin to coercion when an employee is dismissed for saying something that the employer disliked. Even contractual rules that would allow for such dismissal may be found invalid when drafted so broadly as to give the employer ostensible power over the individual's right to make choices for herself. This scenario is of a different nature to the digital speech context, if we accept that an income is a material necessity (not to mention relative job security and the prospect of a good reference) in a way that access to a specific digital speech service is not. This does not mean that all speech-based dismissals are invalid, nor that an employee's free speech right is an absolute. Instead, it recognises the possibility of meeting the liberal formula of wrongdoing–causation–harm in the workplace.

INDEX

www.ingramcontent.com/pod-product-compliance
Ingram Content Group UK Ltd.
Pitfield, Milton Keynes, MK11 3LW, UK
UKHW020905190926
475560UK00010B/280

9 781509 958283